Library of
Davidson College

China's New Development Strategy

China's New Development Strategy

Edited by

JACK GRAY
and
GORDON WHITE

*The Institute of
Development Studies,
University of Sussex,
Brighton, Sussex, UK*

1982

ACADEMIC PRESS

A Subsidiary of Harcourt Brace Jovanovich, Publishers
London   New York
Paris   San Diego   San Francisco   São Paulo
Sydney   Tokyo   Toronto

ACADEMIC PRESS INC. (LONDON) LTD.
24/28 Oval Road
London NW1

United States Edition published by
ACADEMIC PRESS INC.
111 Fifth Avenue
New York, New York 10003

Copyright © 1982 by
ACADEMIC PRESS INC. (LONDON) LTD.

All Rights Reserved
No part of this book may be reproduced in any form by photostat, microfilm, or any other means, without written permission from the publishers

British Library Cataloguing in Publication Data
China's new development strategy.
 1. China — Economic conditions — Congresses
 I. Gray, J.   II. White, G.
 330.951'05   HC427.5

ISBN 0-12-296840-9

LCCCN 81-68984

Printed in Great Britain by
St Edmundsbury Press Ltd, Bury St Edmunds, Suffolk

LIST OF CONTRIBUTORS

Marc Blecher, Department of Government, Oberlin College, Oberlin, Ohio 44074, U.S.A.
Lisa Croll, Contemporary China Centre, Queen Elizabeth House, Oxford University, U.K.
John Gardner, Department of Politics, University of Manchester, U.K.
Jack Gray, Research Fellow, The Institute of Development Studies, University of Sussex, Brighton, BN1 9RE, U.K.
Colina MacDougall, Financial Times, Bracken House, Cannon Street, London, EC4, U.K.
Neville Maxwell, Institute of Commonwealth Studies, Queen Elizabeth House, 21 St Giles, Oxford, OXL 3LA, U.K.
Mitch Meisner, James Madison College, Michigan State University, East Lansing, Michigan 48824, U.S.A.
Peter Nolan, Jesus College, Cambridge University, Cambridge, U.K.
Thierry Pairault, Centre de Recherches et de Documentation sur la Chine Contemporaine, Ecole des Hautes Etudes en Science Sociales, Paris, France.
Tony Saich, Department of Politics, University of Newcastle Upon Tyne, Newcastle, NE1 7RU, U.K.
Andrew Watson, Centre of Asian Studies, University of Adelaide, Australia.
Gordon White. Fellow, The Institute of Development Studies, University of Sussex, Brighton, BN1 9RE, U.K.
Michael Yahuda, London School of Economics, Houghton Street, London, WC2, U.K.

PREFACE

This book was conceived as an attempt to look at new directions in Chinese development strategy since the death of Mao Zedong in September 1976. Our purpose is to provide a sound basis, useful to scholars and students in many different disciplines, for understanding events which have moved very quickly.

Most of the chapters in this volume are based on papers presented at a conference on "China's New Development Strategy" held at the Institute of Development Studies at Sussex University in November 1979. They were revised in the light of the spirited discussion and debate at that conference and to take into account events in China during 1980 and early 1981. They provide detailed empirical accounts of the rapid and often puzzling changes in China from late 1976 to 1980 and, it is hoped, offer some avenues of analysis for understanding the deeper dynamics of Chinese society for specialists and non-specialists alike. Superscript numerals in the text refer to Notes which are to be found at the end of the book.

The authors would like to express their gratitude to the contributors for their willingness to cooperate with the editors and to commit their ideas to paper even though events in China often seemed to be running ahead of them. We are grateful also to those participants at the conference who contributed to the intellectual preparation of this book but are not included among its contributors. Our gratitude also goes to Penny Barraclough, Meriel Price and Fiona Pearson for helping to prepare the final manuscript.

Jack Gray
Gordon White.

Brighton, 1981.

CONTENTS

List of Contributors	v
Preface	vii
Contents	ix

1. Introduction: The new course in Chinese development strategy: context, problems and prospects
 Gordon White   1

I POLITICS AND GOVERNMENT

2. New directions in politics and government
 Tony Saich   19
3. China's foreign relations and the modernization programme
 Michael Yahuda   37
4. Administrative level and agrarian structure, 1975-80: the county (w)as focal point in Chinese rural development policy
 Mitch Meisner and Marc Blecher   55

II INDUSTRY AND TRADE

5. The management of the industrial economy: the return of the economists
 Andrew Watson   87
6. Industrial strategy (January 1975 – June 1979): in search of new policies for industrial growth
 Thierry Pairault   119
7. Policy changes in China's foreign trade since the death of Mao, 1976-1980
 Colina MacDougall   149

Contents

III RURAL DEVELOPMENT

8. The distributive implications of China's new agricultural policies Peter Nolan and Gordon White	175
9. Rural enterprise in China, 1977-79 Jack Gray	211
10. The promotion of domestic sideline production in rural China, 1978-79 Elisabeth J. Croll	235
11. The impact of China's new economic policies in the rural sector Neville Maxwell	255

IV EDUCATION

12. New directions in educational policy John Gardner	273
13. Conclusion Jack Gray	289
Notes and References	311
Index	339

1

INTRODUCTION: THE NEW COURSE IN CHINESE DEVELOPMENT STRATEGY: CONTEXT, PROBLEMS AND PROSPECTS

Gordon White

Institute of Development Studies, University of Sussex, Brighton

The basic purpose of this book is to examine and evaluate the changes in Chinese development strategy — in politics, economics and social policy — which have occurred since the death of Mao and the arrest of the leftist Shanghai group in late 1976. The papers in this volume address three sets of questions. First, what has changed? How much continuity is there between the policies of the late 1970s and those of the preceding decade? To what extent is the new Chinese development strategy consistent with the ideological and institutional legacy of Mao's era? Has there been a decisive break? Each paper attempts to interpret changes in specific areas of policy. This task is made difficult by the continuous flux in China which renders such accounts obsolete with bewildering rapidity. It is not made easier by the fact that policy strategies have changed dramatically *within* the post-Mao period, in the wake of changes in the CCP leadership. Second, why have things changed? — are the new policies a rational response to deficiencies in the Maoist experiment, or should they be explained rather in terms of political factionalism or class re-alignments? Third, how valid are the new policies as a remedy for China's developmental goals and problems? — do they give a clear blueprint for China's future? Do they express a sophisticated and pragmatic understanding of developmental problems? Or do they embody a good deal of uncertainty, conflict, ignorance and groping for *ad hoc* solutions? Fourth, what problems are likely to arise in the implementation of the new strategy? To what extent will the bold moves towards "market socialism" in 1979-80 remain mere paper policies, constrained or made ineffective by the institutional and economic realities of Chinese political economy? Indeed, *can* things be changed in a major way, or has the mould already set? To the extent that the new policies are effective, what distinctive problems will they encounter? What impact will they have on social unrest and political conflict? Is China heading for a period of rapid modernisation in conditions of stability, as the current leadership promises, or for a new stage of fluctuation and conflict characterised by problems which the present leadership can scarcely as yet foresee?

Most of the authors in this book agree that there have been sweeping changes in major areas of policy since the death of Mao. There have been two phases: first, during 1977-78, movement towards a mobilisation model reminiscent of the Great Leap Forward and then, beginning in 1978, a change in direction towards economic "readjustment" and a form of "market socialism".[1] In this introduction, I shall concentrate on the latter period, that of Dengist dominance, heralded by the Third Party Plenum in December 1978.

Several key themes run through the changes in different areas of policy: the primacy of economic goals, notably efficiency, productivity, growth and enhanced consumption; a concerted effort, at the verbal level at least, to decrease state control, to free the economy (and also politics and culture) from the trammels of bureaucracy by expanding the use of economic, as opposed to administrative, methods of economic regulation; a combined process of selective recentralisation and widespread decentralisation in the state sector (Pairault; Watson), the latter being part of a wider move towards a kind of regulated quasi-market system based on independent cellular units linked by contractual ties i.e. the enterprise in industry and the production team in agriculture; an increase of economic links with the West and Japan, both in trade and capital flows, leading to the establishment of joint ventures and special export zones (MacDougall); a relaxation of political and ideological controls to allow greater intellectual and cultural expression and more freedom for individual political dissent (Saich); and, lastly, an abandonment or downgrading of previous Maoist values, notably those of redistribution, mass mobilisation, intermediate technology, collective effort and local and national self-reliance.

Swingeing policy changes there have been, but this judgment should be qualified in several respects. First, there are important areas of policy continuity, for example, in agriculture and, as Yahuda argues in his article, in foreign policy in the realm of power politics. Second, as several contributors to this volume point out, changes in policy made in Peking are not necessarily translated into changes at intermediate and basic levels. Third, some of the "new" elements are actually resurrected from earlier periods, notably the mid-1950s and early 1960s. Fourth, the basic institutional pattern established in the 1950s and consolidated in the 1960s and early 1970s remains intact, indeed certain arms (such as the legal system, the machinery of "representative" government and the party control apparatus) have been strengthened. Bureaucratic control in the state sector and the commune system in the countryside are still the dominant forms of political economy, though both are under attack from the bolder market reformers. Though ideological control has been loosened to some degree, the principle of official orthodoxy still remains; it has been invoked to counter critical voices raised during the Democracy Movement, and to silence leftist criticism of the "four modernisations" creed. The principle and reality of Party dominance has been reaffirmed through the stress on "the four principles" and no serious political challenges are tolerated: witness the strangling of the democracy movement in Peking, the persecution of leftist and liberal heretics alike, and the unedifying show-trial of the Shanghai group in late 1980. Leninism – or rather Stalinism – is still very much alive.

Qualifications apart, however, the new course has brought changes so systematic and far-reaching that they seem to vindicate the Maoist analysis of "two-line struggle" which was previously dismissed as simplistic by many Western analysts. Reactions to the shift, both in China and abroad, have ranged widely from hearty approval, through dubious acceptance, to horrified rejection. Among Western analysts, reactions tend to vary with the ideology or the disciplinary background of the individual. Some who are in the neo-Marxist or radical traditions, and who identified strongly with the Maoist programme regard the new course as Thermidor, as a betrayal of the Chinese revolution and an abandonment of its basic principles.[2] It is fashionable now to sneer at the "starry-eyed" foreign Maoists of the late 1960s and 1970s but such attitudes are too easy in retrospect and sometimes disingenuous. True, there was a good deal of misinterpretation and wishful thinking among Western sympathisers and a marked tendency to superimpose Chinese solutions on Western problems and vice versa. But the Maoist programme did seem to represent a serious attempt to grapple with some of the major problems of societies calling themselves socialist, and to implant in the development process the authentic socialist values of equality, participation and collectivism, in a way very different from that of its Eastern European counterparts. It is not surprising that many Western radicals and socialists looked on the experiment as a source of hope and inspiration. Interest in foreign models is hardly confined to socialists – after all, the present Prime Minister of Britain finds her inspiration in Chicago. Moreover, favourable evaluation of Maoist political economy was not confined to leftists, the Maoist project was inspected approvingly by a wide range of experts from many fields and countries, and with different ideological approaches. Furthermore, Chinese realities have always proved difficult to comprehend, even for "China specialists" or "China watchers". So much more so for the admiring visitors of the early and mid-1970s, particularly since they encountered a systematic effort by the Chinese to mislead them. Tawney, writing in the 1930s, had this to say about the difficulty of understanding China:

> Political forces in China resemble Chinese rivers. The pressure on the dykes is enormous, but unseen; it is only when they burst that the strain is realised. The visitor, who sees only the externals, inevitably miscalculates the force of the current.[3]

As the 1930s, so the 1970s – most of the wisdom of "China specialists" is still retrospective. It is also obvious that some of the people who look with condescension on the "naivety" of foreign Maoist sympathisers are ready to accept the propaganda position of the present Chinese leadership and repeat it, often verbatim, in the Western media – the "naivety", if this is what it is, has merely shifted its ground.

On the other hand, the new course in China has been welcomed by many analysts, academic and otherwise, who regard it as a return to sanity and rationality. They have many telling points to make about the disorganisation, inefficiency and overpoliticisation of the Maoist period and they rightly stress the material and psychological benefits accruing to many Chinese through the new emphasis on consumption and on cultural laisser faire. But such analysts tend to define "sanity" and "rationality" in conventional Western, not to say "bourgeois" ways. In contrast to their radical predecessors who wanted us to be more like China, they want China to be more like us. They often fail to see, in allegedly "pragmatic" innovations, the problem of their relevance to and their impact on Chinese society and on the future of China's socialist modernisation. Thus, for example, the benefits of greater openness to the West and of large technology imports tend to be elevated over the potential costs. A cursory knowledge of the dependency literature would give one pause in such judgments. The alleged advantages of the market are vaunted, and its dark side — the inequalities, instabilities and insecurities we are now facing in the West — is turned to the wall. Indeed, in some cases this favourable evaluation is linked to underlying interests — the continuing lure of the China market and the competition to exploit it among individual and national capitals.

Apart from these two groups, there are many who are confused or ambiguous about the new course. Prominent among the confused are those development experts who lauded the "Chinese model" in the early and mid-1970s and tried to devise means to "transfer" parts of it to other countries, both developing and developed. But the question of its applicability to other societies was rendered absurd by the clear demonstration in the late 1970s that it was not even applicable to China, indeed that it was regarded with the utmost hostility and cynicism by the post-Mao leadership. Other analysts, including many professional students of China, are ambiguous about the new course. They see many of the problems of the Maoist model and recognise much of value in recent trends towards economic rationalisation and politico-cultural relaxation, but they are concerned lest the basic values of the Maoist programme should be forgotten, and they are worried about the social, attitudinal and political implications of the new policies for both socialism and development in China. It is hoped that the information and analysis in this volume will go some way towards dispelling this uncertainty, or will at least indicate more precisely the points at which uncertainty lies.

The Demise of Maoist Politics and the Rise of "Pragmatism"

To understand what came after the death of Mao, we must understand what came before. In terms of information, we are inevitably prisoners of factional struggle within the Chinese political élite which produces a dialectics of distortion. This, together with the pervasive secrecy of the Chinese system, makes the task of analysis most difficult. The current demonology against the "Gang of Four" is only marginally, if at all, more accurate than the anti-"revisionist" polemics of the Cultural Revolution — the Manichean manner is common to both. When we pick our way through the political thickets, however, a fairly consistent picture emerges. It is a picture of the failure of the Chinese left in its decade of opportunity.[4]

The Maoist movement suffered from severe political weaknesses. In spite of its strong emphasis on "the continuation of class struggle in socialist society" and on the identification of an incipient "new bourgeoisie" spawned by the institutions of state socialism, this position never received systematic and authoritative elaboration. Mao's own public utterances dwindled into short Delphic "directives", pregnant with ambiguity; Yao Wenyuan preferred the oblique style of literary criticism, while Zhang Chunqiao produced only one important piece of analysis (in 1975), failing to complete his intended project of writing a new class analysis of Chinese society. The political practice of leftist leaders often contradicted their theory. Their authoritarian and intolerant methods failed to square with their democratic pretensions. Most basic, the revolutionary rhetoric of the Cultural Revolution aside, they failed to make a break with the structural and normative logic of the Leninist form of state socialism; they used hierarchical means to bring equality, authoritarian means to bring democracy, the invocation of obedience to encourage initiative. The personal political skills of radical leaders were also unimpressive. They relied too heavily on Mao whose political influence waned along with his health; they contravened Mao's own common-sense principle of the united front, taking on too many opponents at once and failing to secure the middle ground, thus isolating themselves rather than the enemy. This was one expression of a sectarian or "closed doorist" approach to politics, conducted under an ill-defined banner of "class struggle". They polarised political relationships artificially. They "absolutised" issues. Consequently, not only did they fail to gain supporters among strategic élites such as scientists and technicians, economic managers, social scientists and specialised administrators, but they were unable to build a stable base among the masses. Moreover, though their policies reflected important socialist values and promised tangible benefits in many areas, radical leaders ignored or under-played issues of great importance to many Chinese, particularly in the cities: the desire for faster increases in living standards, greater political and cultural freedom, greater national strength and international status, and more social stability and harmony. The sectarian style meant that people or methods which might have contributed to a faster growth in standards and promoted greater economic efficiency *without* compromising Maoist values were dismissed as "bourgeois". To intensify the problem, their radical policies were often implemented in a non-radical environment, with the result that they were degraded at the intermediate and basic levels through unprincipled factionalism, personal hostilities or "connections", and manoeuvring for sectional advantage. The original content of policy became lost and the blatant gap between theory and reality created apathy and cynicism. The political weakness of the left was also in no small part due to the formidable nature of the opposition: majority sentiment within the most powerful segments of the state and economy seems to have been against Maoist initiatives from the start. In fact, the surprising thing is not so much the swift end of the radical challenge but the fact that it was able to get off the ground in the first place and stay in the air for a decade. Indeed, some of the instances of poor political practice listed above can be seen in retrospect as a desperate response to overwhelming opposition.

In sum, the left fell partly because it was infirm and partly because it was pushed. In the last analysis, Maoist leaders failed to mobilise broad and lasting support for their policies, notably among the urban population; they failed to convert laudable goals into real beliefs and behaviour at the grass roots; and they failed to link the ideals of participation and equality to the concrete questions of material improvement, political freedom, social security and economic efficiency. They failed at least to the extent that they could not successfully counter the allegations of failure on these counts. Yet at the same time, the Maoist left preserved and developed much that was valuable. They strengthened the commune system in the countryside. They created a popular spirit of criticism and potential defiance. They produced a general spread of egalitarian values and a strong notion of fair balance between cities and countryside. They also raised important issues crucial to the socialist programme. They did not solve them, but at least they put them on the political agenda. It is much to the detriment of the present policy line in China that it denies these achievements utterly, and paints the period from 1966 to 1976 as one of unmitigated gloom. This is more an expression of political antagonism than a considered intellectual analysis. In this respect, the present leadership are the same as their leftist opponents.

The central intellectual problem here is how to place such judgments within a systematic analytical framework which can explain the shifts in Chinese economic strategy. It is particularly important to be able to explain the dramatic nature of changes since 1976, the fact that they have not been partial or piecemeal — the fact that they form a mirror image of the preceding strategy in so many areas.

Certainly, *political* factors are a crucial determinant of change. Factional struggle in the higher reaches of the CCP has a dialectical logic which tends to polarise policy programmes into unsatisfactory alternatives, i.e. "optimal" choice of policy options is not allowed to operate, given the Scylla and Charybdis of "ultra leftism" and "revisionism". Current analyses of factional struggle differ considerably, ranging from a traditional Pekinological view of naked (or scantily-clothed) power struggle, to a Maoist view of struggle between broad ideological tendencies represented by different leaders. Emulating Jiang Qing (Chiang Ching), Western analysts have set up a veritable "hat factory" producing labels for the contestants: "radical/moderate", "revolutionary/pragmatic", "radical/conservative", "idealist/materialist", etc . . . with permutations. In analysing the new strategy, particularly between 1978 and 1980 when the policies and personnel of Deng Xiaoping emerged triumphant, there needs to be a "rectification of names". The "radical/moderate" dichotomy is unsatisfactory since it carries an implicit (anti-leftist) value-loading; it also tends to suggest that differences are based on different *approaches* to similar goals, whereas the opposing factions seem to have different sets of goals as well as different orders of priority. The term "pragmatic" is deficient for the same reasons, and also because certain aspects of the new course cannot be described as "pragmatic" even by sympathetic observers: resort to the printing press to solve economic problems, the fervour for foreign technology and consumption patterns, blinkered assumptions about the beneficial impact of foreign contacts, and a narrow economistic approach to complex socio-political problems are not indisputably pragmatic views. Terms like "pragmatic" and "moderate", moreover, tend to assume policy rationality and relevance.[5] They tend to obscure the political, ideological and material roots of conflict, as Suzanne Pepper points out when she describes the new course in educational policy as "a conservative challenge to the radical opposition, [rather] than as a pragmatic or moderate solution for China's educational problems".[6] "Conservative/radical" is also unsatisfactory since, in regard to the basic system of Stalinist political economy inherited from the 1950s, certain aspects of Maoist policy were conservative whilst on the other hand many of the proposals mooted or implemented during 1979-80 represented a fairly radical attack on the existing bureaucratic economy. Perhaps the most accurate approach would be to place the opposing strategies on the familiar political continuum of "left-right", a characterisation which allows comparison with politics generally, and socialist politics in particular, in other societies. Given the heavy imprint on each strategy by a single leader, moreover, "Maoist" and "Dengist" would also not be inappropriate. We should bear in mind, of course, that all such dichotomies are convenient oversimplifications, which do not capture the complexity of political attitudes and alignments within the Chinese state.

However, machiavellian or moralistic analysis of political factors tends to divorce politics and ideology from the policy content of everyday decision-making. *Policy analysis* is important, with particular attention to problems of policy implementation and impact. Many analyses of the new course, particularly by economists of various ideological hues both in China and abroad, adopt a kind of cost-benefit analysis of Maoist and post-Mao policies, and argue for the conspicuous rationality of the latter. Such accounts are useful in pointing to problems of poor co-ordination, waste and inefficiency during the Maoist period[7] and the results of their inquiries highlight the importance of poor policy performance in undermining the credibility of political leaders and building support for a programmatic alternative, within the State apparatus and among the population at large. However, there is a marked tendency for this type of discourse to degenerate into economistic and technocratic modes of thought, in which "rationality" and "efficiency" are undefined. This tendency is visible in the work of China's own new economists, and it tends to ignore or gloss over the political and socio-cultural factors which limit the range of choice and action. There is a danger here of converting the real world into a world of two-dimensional geometric precision, based on unrealistic assumptions, and then hoping to arrange for the real world to conform through "social technology".[8] While policy analysis veers into technocratic ideology, our search for causation is directed outwards — to a structural analysis of Chinese society and to the relationship between ideologies and existing or emerging class forces. In fact, both politico-ideological and policy analysis tend to restrict the scope of explanation to a relatively narrow, though crucially important, segment of Chinese reality, failing to place political dissension and policy alternatives in a broader social environment.

At a deeper level of analysis, therefore, one can argue for a *structural or class analysis* of strategic changes in Chinese politics and development policy, which seeks to identify social forces which set the parameters of political struggle and policy debate. This kind of analysis is already familiar to students of state socialism in Eastern Europe. Elaboration of this argument would take too long here. Suffice it to advance the hypothesis that the new course in China, notably the move towards "market socialism" during 1979 and 1980, marks the presence of important new class forces in Chinese society and represents their attempt to rearrange society according to their own vision and their own interests. Though the sponsors of the turn-about may be, as Yahuda argues, older intellectuals and cadres, their influence rests upon new forces. These are technocratic strata — professional administrators, economic managers, scientists, technicians and educators — whose power is rooted in basic-level processes of material production and social reproduction. They have risen as a product of the statist political economy established in the 1950s, in cooperation with and yet in competition with the politico-bureaucratic élite in the Party apparatus and intermediate-higher state organs. In addition to these two class aggregations — essentially two types of cadre (*ganbu*) — there are the "masses" (*qunzhong*), ordinary workers and peasants without power or position, themselves split into strata. These three basic class agglomerations have found representation in the Party, and their existence is reflected in the political struggles of the past two decades. The Party's left reached out to a motley collection of groups among the general population, notably the less favoured or more insecure segments; the Party's right, symbolised by the reform politics of 1978-80, is linked to burgeoning technocratic strata who use their crucial role in the modernisation programme to gain access to decision-makers and political organisations; between these two is the "Leninist centre", which embodies the principle of one-party dominance and the planned/administered economy, with its strength concentrated in the Party-government apparatus. The centre, for the foreseeable future, is the fulcrum of Chinese political economy — it defines the basic parameters which make or break leaders, which structure policy agendas, and which establish the limits of reform, from both left and right.[9] The trend in other state socialist societies in Eastern Europe, notably in the Soviet Union, has been towards a pattern of accommodation between sections of the Party-state élite and the new technocratic strata, marked by a series of economic reforms comparable to those being implemented in China in 1978-80. In China, this process of class accommodation and reform began in the early 1960s but was interrupted by the Cultural Revolution, and was only able to re-establish itself in full force after the removal of the Shanghai group. The "four modernisations" is the charter of this alliance and the new educational policies are the best context for viewing its class content with relative clarity. However, accommodation does not mean merger: the bases of power of the two class constellations are different, as are their methods of social reproduction. Both groups may have interests in the demobilisation and domestication of the working class, to be achieved through the familiar combination of carrot, stick, cooptative participation and ideological hegemony; but they are ready to compete for and mobilise working class support in their mutual competition — the "masses" are not, as some Maoists believe, the predominant preserve of the Left, a point proven conclusively by the mobilisation of "conservative" forces during the Cultural Revolution and by the liberal upsurge of the Democracy Movement in 1978.

The main intellectual problem is how to link together these different analytical approaches — they should not be treated on an "either-or" basis. Clearly, as one moves from the deceptive clarity of hypothetical structures to the complex and ambiguous realms of policy debate and political struggle, there is a great need for qualification, for adjustment and specification of links between levels of analysis, layers of abstraction, and realms of social action. Yet, as in the case of a *pointilliste* painter who can create a seemingly homogeneous colour from an amalgam of different colours, the links are there and, with careful research and elaboration, they can be delineated. Moreover, this holistic approach — jargon apart — is surely nearer to common sense. For instance, I would not respect an analysis of the Thatcherist swing in Britain in 1979 which confined itself merely to a discussion of competing political élites and policy programmes and changing "public opinion". There was clearly a shift in class power, which the opposing politicians represent and their policies reflect. Though the contours and dynamics of state socialist societies are less easily defined, the same type of dynamic is in operation and it needs a multi-tiered analysis to comprehend it fully.

As in the UK case, moreover, our understanding would be incomplete if we confined ourself to merely domestic factors — the many pressures of the international political economy are an important determinant of political alignments and policy options in China, as Friedman has argued forcefully.[10] Politico-military threats from both East and West, the technical advance of foreign economies and the impressive economic performance of China's Third World capitalist neighbours (the "four tigers": south Korea, Taiwan, Hongkong and Singapore) have exerted pressures on Chinese policy makers, and have clearly limited the range of independent experiment "allowed" in Chinese development strategy (for example, leftist emphasis on native and intermediate technology to the detriment of advanced, primary and secondary training at the expense of higher, etc.). From many points of view — notably military capability, economic productivity and mass consumption — there are compelling fears that China will "fall behind" the rest of the world and such arguments provide a powerful impetus for the liberalised international economic policies of the new course.

The New Course and its Impact

To specialists in Third World development, the new Chinese strategy will probably prove less interesting since it is far less distinctive and innovative than its predecessor; to this extent, there is no longer a "Chinese model". On the other hand, it may prove of instructive value — either negatively or positively — to socialist governments in the Third World which are struggling to establish efficient economic systems and beneficial relations with the global economy. On the old question of the "relevance" of Chinese experience to development in the Third World generally, one can argue that its relevance has not decreased, but is now "relevant" to different people and for different purposes. The new course provides ammunition in the development debate to more conventional, not to say conservative, analysts who can now cite China to support arguments for the advantages of free trade and unrestricted capital movements, the superior regulative role of the market *vis-à-vis* planning the weakness of collective agriculture and the priority of growth over distribution. To this extent, if there is a new "Chinese model", it can be used to buttress arguments for and tendencies towards the greater integration of Third World economies into a global political economy, dominated by and structured in the interests of the metropolitan capitalist economies, and to oppose arguments for "self-reliance", planning and co-operation, and indeed the socialist developmental alternative as a whole.

On the other hand, the new course is of considerable interest to specialists and practitioners in socialist development, given the striking similarities with other state socialist societies, notably in Eastern Europe. For students and citizens of the latter, many of China's recent innovations are *déjà vu;* for China specialists and the Chinese themselves, the experience of Eastern European and Soviet reforms over the past two decades provides valuable information for understanding the new Chinese strategy and predicting its future impact. The reforms of 1978-80 make a valuable contribution to a great number of theoretical and practical debates within the socialist world: over the nature of the basic dynamics of socialist development; the shift from a centralised Stalinist model of administrative allocation to a more responsive, flexible and decentralised economic system; the transition from extensive to intensive economy; the gradual move from an accumulation-oriented to a consumption-oriented economy; the relative importance of different forms of ownership (state, collective and private); the balance between the major economic sectors (heavy industry, light industry and agriculture); the role of market mechanisms in economics, and liberal reforms in politics, and the connection between these two spheres; and the developmental consequences of greater ties with the international economy.

In the Chinese context, the new strategy may have a beneficial impact on aggregate income levels, macro- and micro-level economic efficiency and on the range of intellectual and cultural expression — at least in the short run. These achievements, already in evidence to some degree, should be recognised and applauded. At the same time, the new course has many inherent problems, which are exacerbated by the extreme degree of the reaction against the Maoist heritage. The priority of modernisation has temporarily been allowed virtually to obliterate that of socialism. At the ideological and moral levels, the vitreolic campaign against the "ultra-leftism" of the "Gang of Four" has had a damaging impact on genuine socialist values of equality, self-sacrifice, collectivism and mass participation. Both Chinese and foreign commentators have pointed with alarm to a dramatic decline in social morality and political commitment (notwithstanding official statements to the contrary, in the everyday world the latter now tends to be dismissed as "old hat"). At the popular level, the new policies have encouraged trends towards privatisation, both in institutions and attitudes, and towards a general spread of materialistic motivation. It is an open question whether these losses are compensated by the economic, political and cultural improvements of the new course. There is certainly a case for remodelling the strategy so as to strike a better balance between old and new, and between the worthwhile content of the preceding Maoist experience and that of the present course. In arguing for greater "balance", however, we are thinking within the familiar paradigm of policy-analysis/"rational decision-making"; in view of the political and structural factors discussed earlier, such a hope might prove unrealistic.

Moreover, the distorted way in which present policies have been introduced as polar opposites to allegedly disastrous Maoist alternatives — often in the face of the facts — increases the likelihood of their creating trends which are difficult to reverse or control. For example, although the new policies to revitalise private economic initiative in the countryside and restrict the role of collectives, particularly above the production team, are supposed to operate within limits and according to regulations, they can, and indeed have (as several contributions to this volume testify) set in motion processes of decollectivisation which are difficult to restrain. Similarly, attempts to improve the flexibility and responsiveness of industry by introducing market mechanisms and increasing enterprise autonomy have already led to financial imbalances, inflation and price instability, contributing to a climate of economic uncertainty. (These trends will also be exacerbated by China's greater integration with the fluctuations of the world market, as Yahuda argues). Policies of specialisation and concentration, and a more differentiated application of the principle "distribution according to work" in wage policy, may also increase inequalities, both between and within classes, regions and economic sectors (notably rural and urban). Moreover, the greater impingement of foreign forces, from Vogue models to *The Sound of Music* to Western advertising designed to "educate" the Chinese consumer, not only accelerates the spread of "unhealthy" Western social values (of which the new leadership does not approve), but also raises consumer aspirations to unrealistically high levels which will exert tremendous pressures on the authorities in future, and have already given rise to "black" trafficking in foreign consumer goods. The uneven geographical impact of the Western presence — in the big cities, in the east and particularly in the special enterprise zones — will also exacerbate inequalities and create tensions. So will the islands of foreign or overseas Chinese affluence and privilege (the latter was an explosive issue during the Cultural Revolution) now mushrooming in the form of special housing projects initiated in 1979-80. There is a concomitant danger posed by the creation of inequalities in response to the foreign impact: either piecemeal through differential access to the tangible benefits which the foreigner brings in (notably currency or its equivalent, and commodities acquired through special shops or channels); or, more basic, by the formation of quasi- "comprador" strata whose position — whether as commercial middlemen, intellectuals or officials — depends on foreign contacts and foreign resources. Though this process is unlikely to go as far as the dire predictions of dependency theory portend, it does have a potential to create tension and hostility within Chinese society at large, particularly against a background of millennial Chinese cultural pride and the Maoist doctrine of "self-reliance".

The new course also faces an opposite problem, that of various forms of powerful *constraint* which stifle new policies in their cradle or stymie them half-way. We can identify at least three types viz. "objective" or material, politico-bureaucratic and societal or "mass" constraints. The objective material constraints have already made themselves felt and have been an important component of the rationale for the policy of "readjustment" adopted in 1978: the climatic vagaries and technical intractability of agriculture, strategic resource bottlenecks in industry, and the constriction of foreign markets. The political and bureaucratic constraints have been equally visible, arising in response to two basic challenges posed by the new course. First, the premium on modernisation as the nation's central task makes the role of politics and ideology in general, and of the Party in particular, less essential.[11] As Saich shows, the Party has been instructed to draw in its horns, to refrain from intervening in practical administration and the exercise of expert judgment, and to concentrate on its true task of overall "leadership". Second, the economic role of the state apparatus generally has come under attack as reformers have sought to substitute "economic mechanisms" for administrative regulation. These reforms look reasonable in the papers of the economists, but are political dynamite because they presume a major redistribution of power: from conscious to "unconscious" agencies and between conscious agencies. As Soviet and East European experience has shown, it is these basic political problems which have posed the most serious obstacles to the implementation of the reforms. Third, there are many "mass" constraints since the working-class may not prove as pliable as technocratic blueprints envisage and may thwart the best-laid plans of the reformers: most notably, informal networks among factory workers can blunt the impact of new incentive schemes and of new methods for improving the organisation of production. Thus reforms may be mooted and not get off the ground at all; they may only achieve partial success and lapse in consequence; or, even if they are successful, they may be undermined by the contradictory nature of a system which is half reformed and half not.

Thus the new course may founder on both success and failure. The more problems it encounters, the greater the likelihood of partial reversion, either to a renewed form of leftist Maoism or a more conservative Party-bureaucracy dominant strategy which rejects the tenets of "market socialism". The bases for such a reversion clearly exist at the levels both of leadership and of popular support. The former draws its strength from two sources: first, the continued influence of Maoist ideas and practices among Party-state cadres and Party members: witness the strength of the "whateverists" in resisting the "pragmatist" policies of Deng Xiaoping introduced at the Third Plenum in December 1978;[12] second, Maoist commitments aside, the first group would gain active or passive support from other political and bureaucratic groups which feel their position threatened by the innovations of 1979-80. To a considerable extent, these categories may overlap, particularly given the huge influx of new Party members and cadres during the

Maoist decade. They and their allies are now ensconced in the lower and intermediate levels of the State, and could only be dislodged by a wide-ranging purge which would threaten the stability of the new leadership. Repression has already been visited on an unknown number of "supporters of the Gang of Four", thus creating a new stratum of political victims eager for a "reversal of verdicts" — to enlarge their numbers at this stage would be self-defeating.

At the mass level, there are two main sources of support for a strategic shift in development policy: first, from the widespread discontent arising from long-standing social tensions which successive leaderships have been unable to solve (notably the problem of urban unemployment and the "down to the countryside" programme); second, there are those individuals and groups who may object to specific elements of the new strategy, or, more implicitly, are moved to discontent by the structural changes it brings about. Regardless of their general ideological orientation, this patchwork of discontents can be manipulated to advantage by anti-Dengist forces.

In sum, the new course may well be just another phase in the zigzag path of Chinese development strategy. Recurrent swings between policy alternatives have reflected the inability of successive leaderships to solve perennial developmental problems and mitigate social tensions. Moreover, each alternative, when put into practice, has generated its own tensions and discontents, thus paving the way for a return by its previous opponent or the rise of a new alternative. Unless Chinese politics is now firmly set in an unbreakable class mould through the alliances of the late 1970s, the same fate may await the Dengist endeavour.

I POLITICS AND GOVERNMENT

2

NEW DIRECTIONS IN POLITICS AND GOVERNMENT

Tony Saich

School of Government, Newcastle-upon-Tyne Polytechnic, Newcastle.

Although the period until 1982 has been designated as a period of "readjustment, restructuring, consolidation and improvement of the national economy"[1] major decisions about the future direction of Chinese politics have been made. These consist of a fusion of new elements and elements resurrected from the past. Both the implication of the title of this paper and the impression deliberately maintained in the People's Republic of China through the official media is that post-Mao China has made a complete break with the past. This break was symbolised by Hua Guofeng's speech to the Eleventh National Congress of the Chinese Party in 1977, when he pointed out that the eleven year Cultural Revolution had been successfully completed.[2] A new course was signalled by Hua's Report on the Work of the Government to the First Session of the Fifth National People's Congress (NPC) in February 1978.[3] China was to embark on a "New Long March" with the "Four Modernisations" as the goal to be realised by the year 2000. Implicitly, and later explicitly, socialist construction is to have "economics in command". This paper will start by considering the reassessment of the past and its implications for the future. It will then proceed to detail and assess changes in work-style and structures of politics and government in the PRC since the First Session of the Fifth NPC. I have chosen to concentrate on the style and framework of politics and government not only because democracy and socialist legality have been key themes since the congress, but also because other papers concentrate on the changes (or otherwise) in both general and specific policy areas.

The Ghosts of China's Past: Ideological Reassessment as a Guide to Action

Re-evaluation of the past, although apparent earlier, started in earnest following the Third Plenum of the Eleventh Central Committee (December 1978). On the surface, the plenum urged China to forget the past, look to the future instead and concentrate on socialist modernisation now that the campaigns against the Gang of Four had been successfully completed.[4] However, other decisions taken by and statements made at the Third Plenum had the opposite effect. Far from forgetting the past, they led to a review of the whole of the 30 years of the PRC. To quote from the communiqué:

> The session had a serious discussion on some major political events which occured during the Great Cultural Revolution and certain historical questions left over from an earlier period ... [It] examined and corrected the erroneous conclusions which had been adopted on Peng Dehuai..[5]

Mao's own role was not exempt

> [The session] emphatically points out that the great feats performed by Comrade Mao Zedong in protracted revolutionary struggle are indelible ... It would not be Marxist to demand that a revolutionary leader be free of all shortcomings and mistakes and errors. It would also not conform to Comrade Mao Zedong's consistent evaluation of himself.[6]

In other words, not only was it now permissible (within limits) to criticise Mao, but the revision of past history could go backward in time beyond the Cultural Revolution and include the Great Leap Forward.

The political response was predictable. Provincial level Party committees convened meetings to review and reassess their work during the last 20 years. At these meetings, not only were "verdicts" dating from the Cultural Revolution reversed, but it was admitted that mistakes had also been made since 1958.[7] The Jiangsu Party meeting even went so far as to say *inter alia*:

> In 1959 some people who criticised were mistaken but not all were. And

in any case all cases should be treated in a democratic way.⁸

Ye Jianying, in his speech on the 30th anniversary of the founding of the PRC, referred to the three "leftist" errors which had occurred during the late fifties: the broadening of the scope of struggle against the "rightists" in 1957: the rashness of 1958's economic programmes; and the inept conduct of inner-Party struggle in 1959.⁹

The major issue dividing the leadership since the fall of the Gang of Four, the Cultural Revolution, has been resolved. The policy initiatives associated with it have been rejected and the major figures who gained as a result of the Cultural Revolution have either been removed from power or had their power effectively curtailed. With the rehabilitation of the Cultural Revolution's main target, Liu Shaoqi,¹⁰ the view of the Cultural Revolution which remains is of a misguided leader launching a disastrous "leftist" movement which led to the emergence of the even greater excesses of the Gang of Four.

The important question of defining strategic economic plans for the future has also been resolved. The basis of the "New Long March" was to be the 1976-85 Ten Year Plan presented to the Fifth NPC. The plan set forward a series of ambitious targets and bore resemblances to Mao's twelve year plan of the mid-fifties which had preceeded the Great Leap Forward. Indeed, the initial rhetoric began to mirror that which accompanied the Leap: references were made to the general line of the Great Leap of "going all out, aiming high to achieve greater, faster, better and more economical results in building socialism". However, the ambitious targets did not accord with the pragmatic policies of economic planners such as Chen Yun. The Second Session of the Fifth NPC (June 1979) postponed the plan and substituted a three year period of "readjustment, restructuring, consolidation and improvement of the economy" for the years 1979-81. At the Third Session of the Congress, Hua Guofeng formally announced the abandonment of the Ten Year Plan and stated that preparations were in progress for a new Ten Year Plan for 1981-90. Hua stated that to "revise this outline of the (old) Ten Year Plan after more than four years would be meaningless".¹¹

The resolution of leadership differences has been accompanied by a reassessment of Mao's thought to provide an ideological justification of the policies now being pursued. A total rejection of Mao's thought is impossible because of the unique historical position which it has attained. However, certain elements of his thought have already been discarded or played down. Current accusations that the Gang of Four broke down the "inner organic connection" of Mao's thought and approached it highly selectively[12] could equally be laid against the present leadership who cast Mao in a "positivist" light. Although they need to establish their legitimacy by reference to Mao's thought, they have dismantled the cult around Mao and criticised some of his political practice. According to Hua an assessment of Mao will be made public at the Twelfth Party Congress and he anticipated some of its findings in an interview with a Yugoslav newspaper.[13] He referred to Mao as the "most outstanding figure in Chinese history" but added that he was not a God and was therefore fallible, notably after 1957. As Chairman of the Party, Mao also bore responsibility for the serious mistakes made by the Party during the Cultural Revolution (1966-76). The illness during the last years of his life is used to excuse Mao from the excesses of the period, which are attributed to the Gang of Four.

The present leadership have made it quite clear that they should have the right to revise Mao's thought in the light of new conditions arising during the march towards the four modernisations. Such flexibility is necessary because a mechanical approach to Mao's thought, regardless of time and place, limits the ability of the present leadership to introduce new policies and develop different policies to suit changing conditions. The Party's task "on the theoretical front" is seen as the integration of "the universal principles of Marxism-Leninism-Mao Zedong Thought with the concrete practice of socialist modernisation" with "new historical conditions".[14] This process has been helped and accompanied by the attack on "the cult of the individual" and the stress on collective leadership. In July 1980 an article in the *People's Daily* acknowledged that Mao had made the greatest contribution to the development of Marxism-Leninism during the Chinese revolution but stated that "Mao Zedong Thought is not a product of the wisdom of Mao Zedong alone"[15] — it was the product of "historical" and "collective wisdom". The theoretical contribution of other "early communists" is mentioned to show that the revolutionary theory encapsulated in Mao's thought was certain to have developed in the "historical course of the collective struggle irrespective of Mao".[16] Such an interpretation enables the present leadership to acknowledge the contributions made by other communists whose views may run counter to the thinking of Mao in his later years. Such views may now be put forward as a "legitimate" part of Mao Zedong Thought. Moreover, "maoist deadwood" can be cut away and the new "collective leadership" given the right to develop Mao's ideas further.

In order to negate both the 1975-76 theories of the Gang of Four and the development of Mao's ideas on the continued existence of classes and class struggle, the Thought of Mao Zedong, as far as possible, has been re-cast in its mid-fifties mode. The works of Mao most often quoted to justify present policies are those which show his more conservative side. Two articles of prime importance are "On the Ten Major Relationships" and "On the Correct Handling of Contradictions Among the People" which were published just before and after the Eighth Party Congress in 1956. Two other articles which are often now quoted are "On Practice" and Mao's "Talk at the Enlarged Work Conference" in 1962. "On Practice" can very easily lend itself to a pragmatic interpretation which fits in with the slogan of "seek truth from facts"; it often amounts to the idea that "if it works then it must be true". The 1962 talk finds Mao in retreat from his optimism of the Great Leap and, while referring to the need for discipline, he spoke at great length of the importance of promoting democracy in order to achieve centralised unification. Importantly, Mao also admits that he made mistakes during the Great Leap Forward and that he should be criticised for them. This admission helps promote the view that Mao was after all only human and therefore fallible.

The foundation-stone of this attempt to achieve ideological flexibility is the slogan "practice is the sole criterion for testing truth" ("seek truth from facts") and the corresponding policy of "correcting mistakes whenever they are discovered". To buttress the legitimacy of their own policies the new leadership have presented these ideas as a re-affirmation of Mao's thought by attempting to show that Mao always gave primacy to practice and the need to re-evaluate theory in light of practice. This is a perfectly correct assessment of Mao's position but it remains to be seen whether the re-evaluation is in line with Mao's thought as a whole, whether it represents a substantial deviation from it or whether it represents a general decline in the force of ideology as a determinant of policy outcomes. Zhang Chunqiao is now accused of putting forward the formula "theory-practice-theory" and is reported to have said that "whether one is right or wrong ideologically is determined by theory, which deals mainly with ideological problems",[17] a view which clearly runs counter to current thinking. In future, it is now claimed, struggles against erroneous tendencies will proceed from reality, will bring out the facts and reason things out to convince others, and will stress investigation and study. The new policy proposes to be "strict in ideological criticism and lenient in taking disciplinary action".[18] It is hoped that this approach, combined with the emphasis on distinguishing between "antagonistic" and "non-antagonistic" contradictions will help increase discussion and democracy both in the Party and in society at large.

An important factor promoting unity and stability is the changed attitude towards classes and class struggle in socialist society. The Third Plenum of the Eleventh Central Committee pointed out that class struggle was no longer the principal contradiction in society and that the Party's work should henceforth be concentrated on modernisation.[19] This view, which was presented by Hua Guofeng at the Second Session of the Fifth NPC, is intended to dismiss Zhang Chunqiao and Yao Wenyuan's ideas about class, as "idealist", and to ignore the development of Mao's thought during the sixties. Zhang and Yao sought to explain how classes and class struggle could exist in a socialist society after ownership of the means of production had been transformed. Although the most blatant inequalities — between capitalist and worker, landlord and peasant — had been removed, inequalities based on relative skills, strength or occupation persist. Zhang and Yao thought that these continued inequalities could give rise to privileged groups seeking to perpetuate their vested interests in the status quo, who would be reluctant to see the realisation of the principle "from each according to one's ability, to each according to one's need". They went further than Lenin (who thought that "bourgeois right" would continue to exist without the bourgeoisie) by seeking to show that the continued existence of "bourgeois right" provides the basis for the development of a new bourgeoisie.

It is now said that in the past class struggle was viewed as far graver than it was in reality, and the "mid-fifties Mao" is quoted to justify the present concentration on production rather than class struggle: "Our basic task has changed from unfettering the productive forces to protecting and expanding them in the context of the new relations of production."[20] The current approach to questions of class and class struggle is essentially similar to that for which Deng Xiaoping was criticised in 1976. He was accused of placing class struggle on a par with scientific experiment and production, rather than taking class struggle as the "key link". In fact current analysis appears to go further by making class struggle subservient to production: at all times class struggle is a means; the basic goal of revolution is to liberate and develop the social productive forces.[21] Class struggle is not written off completely, but the view taken is that of the mid-fifties: some bourgeois elements remain as do remnants of bourgeois and feudal ideology, but it is denied that socialism can contain seeds for the growth of a new bourgeoisie. Under the dictatorship of the proletariat it is felt that class enemies can no longer become a "fully developed reactionary class" and openly confront the proletariat. This view helps promote political unity and stability as it denies the necessity for "large-scale, turbulent, mass struggles". Class struggle is now perceived in terms of people's attitudes to the four modernisations:

> In future, class struggle will mainly centre around socialist modernisation and be made to serve socialist modernisation; its main manifestation will be the struggle between those defending the four modernisations and those trying to undermine the realisation of these modernisations.[22]

A further implicit criticism of Mao was Ye Jianying's acknowledgement, in October 1979, that the "good name" of the Eighth Party Congress (1956) had been restored. This congress is a symbolic occasion for the present leadership because it was convened when socialist transformation had been basically completed and when the Party was turning its attention to socialist construction. The congress decided that the system of class exploitation had been virtually eradicated and that the major task was to develop the productive forces, a view which finds its echo with the present leadership. Consequently, the basic contents of the documents adopted by the congress are still considered to be of relevance. The major contradiction identified by the congress was that between the "advanced socialist system" and the "backward productive forces". This paradigm pre-dates Mao's thinking during the Great Leap, his later views on new forms of class struggle and the ideas developed by the left during the Cultural Revolution.

This reassessment of the past has been accompanied by prescriptions for the future and, in large measure, new policies are a response to the shortcomings of political practice during recent years. The fall of the Gang of Four was followed by criticism of both their policies and their political practice. The Cultural Revolution, far from curing the problems of bureaucracy, created a far worse bureaucracy. Although it did trim numbers, it made the affairs of state and political decision-making even more remote. Radical attacks on allegedly "bourgeois" institutions of law and order meant that many Chinese citizens felt insecure and open to arbitrary arrest and detention. The root of these problems, it is now maintained, is the undermining of democracy and legality in the Party which affected society at large.

In part, the negative aspects of Party work-style have been blamed on the large influx of new members admitted during the Cultural Revolution who were "influenced by non-proletarian thought".[23]

The Gang of Four are accused of rashly admitting people into the Party and promoting new cadres at the "double-quick" in some places and units. This led to "unhealthy tendencies" which, it is claimed, even affected some veteran Party cadres. It seems unlikely that these "tendencies" can solely be put down to the new membership. They must also derive in part from the objectives, policies and the very nature of society which preceded and survived the Cultural Revolution. One major target of criticism is the catch-all of "bureaucratism". This covers a wide range of sins, from overstaffing to the work-style of cadres who "divorce themselves from the masses", set up "independent kingdoms", suppress democracy and violate the law.[24] Indeed, some cadres are said to have transformed themselves from "public servants of the people" to "masters of society", using their positions to seek privileges by accepting bribes, graft or embezzling public funds.[25] These faults are also traced to institutional origins, such as "irrational rules and regulations which provide privilege for cadres far beyond their needs and far above the average people's living standards".[26]

The other major criticism of cadre work-style identifies defects under the heading of "feudalism" or "feudal patriarchism". These are considered to be the result both of hangovers from the past, such as attitudes towards authority, and of "feudal fascism" promoted by the Gang of Four.[27] An authoritative article in *Guangming Daily* in 1979 not only concluded that the previous 12 years of Chinese history had been feudalism, not socialism, but also, by implication, included the years 1958-61.[28] These years were "feudal" because there was rule by an emperor, there were no laws or courts and there was arbitrary arrest and torture. The National People's Congress did not meet often enough and the author, Li Honglin, felt that, as a "democracy", the system did not even match up to that of capitalist democracies. One main feature criticised as "feudal" is the excessive power given to one person and the problems that such a concentration of power creates. In consequence, there has been renewed emphasis on the need for collective leadership. According to the *People's Daily,* "it is impossible for mistakes not to occur if a single individual makes all the decisions"; such "one-man tyranny" is impermissible since the "ability of any individual is limited".[29] To help avoid this problem less publicity is given to particular leaders. Chairman Hua set the example at the central work conference which preceded the Third Plenum by stating ". . . when the local authorities and various units send reports to the central committee for its views, these reports should not be addressed to Chairman Hua and the central committee . . . Do not call me the wise leader, just call me comrade".[30]

To overcome these problems, policies have been put forward with two main objectives: to promote democracy and a democratic work-style and establish socialist legality. The roots of the former are traced to the May Fourth Movement (1919), the Yanan Rectification Campaign (1942-44) and, more recently, to the officially sponsored April Fifth Movement of 1976. Socialist legality is seen as demanding a system of rules and regulations, known by and applicable to all citizens, to replace the more arbitrary and uncertain situation during the last years of Mao's life. The new State Constitution of 1978 re-affirmed the rights to freedom of speech, correspondence etc. and guaranteed citizens the "right to appeal to organs of state at any level against any infringement of their rights", with the provision that "no-one shall suppress any complaints and appeals or retaliate against persons making them".[31] We shall discuss these two areas of policy change in the following sections.

Democracy in the Party

The revival of intra-Party democracy is identified as being crucial not only to solve problems of "Party life" but also problems in society as a whole.[32] A variety of policies have been put forward to strengthen collective leadership and to revive institutions such as the commissions for inspecting discipline and the Party schools. On 9th October, 1979, the Central Party School reopened and, while priority was given to reopening those at the provincial level, it was made clear that if conditions permitted Party schools were to be set up at the county level. The Central Commission for Inspecting Discipline was set up by the Third Plenum and held plenary sessions in January 1979 and January 1980. In practice, the Central Commission and those at the lower levels have a sphere of activity much broader than a narrow definition of term "discipline" would suggest. The Central Commission has played an important part in restoring discipline and democracy by resurrecting rules and regulations flouted since the late fifties. Although it monitors minor abuses, its most important task is to "ensure that the Party's ideological and political links and organisational principles are implemented".[33] The Commission drew up the "Guiding Principles for Inner-Party Political Life" adopted by the Fifth Plenum in February 1980. This document contains twelve principles designed to restore the Party norms which operated at the time of the Eighth Party Congress before leadership consensus broke down — the implicit criticism of Mao is clear. The principle of collective leadership is stressed, combined with division of labour and a system of individual responsibility. Elsewhere it has been stressed that the correct relationship between a secretary and the committee under that person's jurisdiction is one between "the individual and the collective" and not "superior-subordinate, or head of family-dependants". Collective leadership and personal responsibility are to be "two sides of a coin. While all important matters should be discussed and decided on by the Party committee collectively, the actual work of carrying out the decisions should be the responsibility of different individuals."[34] The Guiding Principles also introduce measures to curb the role of individuals: publicity for leading members is to be factual, "no unprincipled glorification of them is to be allowed" and "no museums are to be built for living persons and not too many should be built for dead leaders".[35] The principles stress that free discussion should be safeguarded, but they also stipulate that once a decision has been made it should be firmly adhered to.[36] The Commission has also drawn up some draft supplementary educational materials for study by cadres. They contain a code of cadre behaviour to help prevent cadres from using their position to further their own ends.

Though it is difficult to assess the success of such measures, it is reasonable to assume that Party members are still reluctant to speak out, bearing in mind the fate of those who did so in the past. However, apparently there has been a revival of "Party life" and on occasion "contending ideas" have caused confusion. The situation in the Party in mid-1979 has been described as a "turning-point" and compared with passengers in a car turning a corner: they are all shouting at each other and some are falling out of the vehicle as they argue over its direction.

But such "contending" has limits; the objective is not unlimited but guided democracy. Two groups in particular have been identified who cannot enjoy the rights of democratic expression. First are those dubbed the "whateverists", ie. who believe that whatever Mao said was correct. This group was tolerated initially and people such as Wang Dongxing and Wu De kept their Party and government posts but at the Fifth Plenum their "resignations" were accepted. The second group are those in the Party who have gone beyond the permissible degree of freedom, and have been labelled "anarchists" or "bourgeois liberals". Throughout 1980 Party discipline, Party leadership and Party spirit have been stressed and people who seek to "kick aside" the Party committees to practice "democracy" have been criticised. Intra-Party democracy is still not seen as an end in itself, but as a means to achieve the Party's central task — the four modernisations.³⁷ Democracy must therefore operate within limits; the Party continues to face the classic dilemma of democratic centralism — how much democracy, how much centralism?

Democracy in Society

This dilemma is even more apparent with regard to society as a whole. The Chinese leadership has realised that a degree of democracy is both desirable to promote modernisation and inevitable given the proposed rapid transition changes in Chinese society, notably in the cities. The Party has found itself unable to impose stringent controls on the expression of opinion and has thus found itself in an ambiguous position of wishing to promote democracy yet at the same time "guide" it. The wallposters calling for "socialist democracy" sat rather uneasily within these guidelines. Some of the posters on "Democracy Wall" in Beijing went beyond criticisms of Lin Biao and the Gang of Four and criticised the current leadership. The "reversal of verdict" on the 1976 Tiananmen Incident by the Beijing Party Committee (15 November 1978) gave impetus to the Democracy Movement centred on the Wall at Xidan.³⁸ The "April Fifth Movement" was now presented as a spontaneous popular uprising and it was hardly surprising that this official recognition sparked off a similarly spontaneous reaction in late 1978 and early 1979. The leadership's attitude was always ambivalent to the Democracy movement and finally became hostile. Deng Xiaoping praised it when it first emerged but later attacked it in a report to cadres in Beijing on 15 March 1979. The opinions expressed were felt to be incompatible with the need for stability and unity and, in late March 1979, the Beijing authorities decided on new rules and regulations prohibiting posters or publications attacking communism, the thought of Mao Zedong or Party leaders.³⁹ A further clampdown followed in November 1979 and later the Wall was closed down and people were only allowed to put up posters registered with the authorities in a park on the outskirts of Beijing. Finally, in September 1980 even this right was removed when the Third Session of the Fifth National People's Congress decided to approve the proposed amendment to article 45 of the State Constitution. The "four bigs" — the right to speak out freely, air views fully, hold great debates and write big character posters — have been deleted from the article.⁴⁰

By contrast, since the summer of 1978 intellectuals within the system have had a field day of freedom unparalleled since 1949.

Haltingly at first but with an ever-gathering momentum, they have been able to read, research and write about previously taboo subjects — the "no go areas" — as well as consider the question of censorship itself.[41] Starting with the first love story to be published for over twelve years in August 1978,[42] a genuine policy of "Let a Hundred Flowers Bloom, A Hundred Schools of Thought Contend", (commonly known as the "Two Hundreds Policy") was followed to such an extent that by October 1979 it was possible for intellectuals to talk openly about "art for art's sake" and the benefits to be gained from politics-free literature.[43] Official policy at present is that writers should praise the bright aspects of society but should also expose the dark side.[44] However, again there are limits — literature can be critical but not overly so. While it is recognised that realism is the lifeblood of art, this is not taken to mean that one should write about everything in life.[45] Even so, intellectuals have benefitted from this cultural freedom and from a variety of other measures designed to improve their material conditions, boost their status and ensure their support. Perhaps most important, intellectuals are now a designated part of the "working-class". This means that on future occasions when the "re-education" of intellectuals is considered necessary, it will be dealt with as a contradiction *among the people* — a question of mild reform not radical remoulding.

One area which might represent a decrease in democracy is the new view on the question of worker's participation in the management of industrial and commercial enterprises. Chairman Hua stated in February 1978 that revolutionary committees in factories would be abolished.[46] The "broadly based composition of cadres, technicians and workers" has been replaced by a return to a system of "division of responsibilities with factory directors taking charge under the leadership of the Party committee". At the Shoudu Iron and Steel Company, for example, all decisions must be made by the Party committee before being put into practice by the factory director. However, in cases of emergency the director has the power to take "prompt action before reporting to the Party committee." Day-to-day affairs are run by a working committee comprising the director, four deputy directors and "responsible technical and administrative cadres".[47] It is felt that this committee makes the work of the former revolutionary committee redundant and, in fact, many of the revolutionary committee's members serve on the working committee. Moreover, managerial staff are no longer expected to "participate in production" as a means to help close the gap between mental and manual labour. Such a divide is now considered to be a necessary consequence of the socialist division of labour.

To counter the view that the present system represents a decrease in work-place democracy, a great deal of stress has been placed on the role of basic-level elections. It is argued that the right of workers to elect and remove leading cadres at the grass-roots level is an important guarantee of their participation in enterprise management.[48] Deng Xiaoping, at the Ninth National Trade Union Congress in October 1978, proposed that heads of workshops and shifts in factories should be elected directly by the workers. This policy has been implemented in some units: for example, the Beijing Foreign Languages Printing House Workers elected their own workshop cadres by secret ballot;[49] at the Shanghai No.1 Printing and Dyeing Mill, workers and staff dismissed a workshop director and elected a new one "in a democratic way".[50] The higher levels of factory administration are not subject to direct elections. It is felt that the administrative sections have too few people to constitute a sufficient electorate and that the workers under these sections have too little contact with the section chiefs. In this situation an opinion poll is conducted among the personnel of the administrative sections and representatives of the workers, such as the workshop heads.[51] At the Shoudu Cement Works, for example, opinion polls were conducted prior to the reappointment of chiefs to the sections of planning, production, design and finance. In total, four of the twenty-one cadres under consideration were removed from office because of their failure to secure the approval of the majority.

The main forum for participation by the workers is the workers' congress.[52] Although the workers have been removed from administrative bodies concerned with the day-to-day running of enterprises, these congresses continue to give them some say in enterprise management. However, the powers of the congress are circumscribed by the fact that the factory leadership decides when a congress should be convened and the nature of the agenda. Before the congress, the delegates canvass for suggestions from fellow-workers and these are presented to the factory leadership for consideration. The congress discusses major issues concerning the enterprise, and passes resolutions on production plans, management regulations, labour organisations, welfare and labour protection. Any proposals which the leadership considers "feasible and rational" are taken up.

The present Party leadership sees elections as playing an important part in the promotion of democracy. Measures have been introduced to ensure greater accountability from those elected. A new chapter has been added to the electoral law, for example, stating that electors, or electoral units, have the power to supervise and recall their deputies. Another new procedure seeks to ensure that elections are, within limits, competitive — in future there are to be more candidates than places. For direct elections it is suggested that candidates should exceed the total number of places by 50 to 100 per cent while for indirect elections the number of candidates should be 20 to 50 per cent higher.[53] Candidates can be nominated by the Communist Party, democratic parties, people's organisations or by any other voter or deputy as long as the application is seconded by three other people. The constituencies are divided according to work units and residential quarters. This increase in the role of the ballot will obviously serve to diminish the importance of mass electoral meetings although it is not intended to rule them out entirely.

The scope of elections is also being extended. In addition to the election of work-place cadres, the principle of direct elections for people's congresses has been extended to include the county level.[54] In the second half of 1979 experimental elections were conducted in 66 units and it is planned to complete elections in the other 2000 county-level units by Spring 1981.[55] By mid-August 1980, the direct election of county-level people's congresses was already under way in 13 provinces.[56] At present it is not considered possible to introduce direct elections throughout the whole country although the idea has been mooted in the press. For example, an article in *Red Flag* stated that direct county elections would not only contribute to the formation of country governments but would also "lay a solid and reliable foundation for direct provincial — or even national — elections".[57]

Party-State Relations

In order to prevent the overconcentration of power, the present leadership has sought to re-create the distinction between Party and state. During recent years the overlap of Party and state has meant that the Party has actually been *implementing* policy. Such a practice is normally condemned but during the Great Leap Forward and the Cultural Revolution the organs of Party and state below the Centre were virtually identical. In 1967 and 1968 following the attacks on the old Party and state organs, they were replaced by revolutionary committees, heralded as a "brand new organ of proletarian power". For a while these committees combined Party and state functions in one body. Though this total collapse of the distinction between Party and state was partly rectified with the rebuilding of the provincial Party apparatus from 1969 on, revolutionary committees and Party committees continued to share the same functional departments causing a persistent confusion over the division of responsibility between the two bodies. Despite continued official insistence that the Party should make the major decisions and the revolutionary committee should "consciously accept the Party's leadership in exercising power and carrying out its work",[58] problems over the correct division of labour continued. These problems were not eased by the fact that the leadership personnel of the two committees were often identical. Party committees in some factories were criticised for handling such trivial matters as family disputes and water temperatures in bath-houses.

To recreate a clear division of responsibility, the post-Mao leadership set about reviving elements of the pre-Cultural Revolution and pre-Great Leap Forward systems of organisation. The 1978 State Constitution referred only to the purely administrative functions of the revolutionary committees referring to them as the executive rather than the permanent organs of the people's congress at the corresponding levels. In February 1978 Chairman Hua announced the end of the ubiquity of the committees when he announced that they were to function only at levels of government above basic-level units.[59] Consequently they were abolished at the prefectural level and replaced by administrative offices established by the provincial level revolutionary committee. In factories, schools etc. they were replaced by a return to a "system of division of responsibilities . . . with factory directors, production brigade leaders, school principals, college presidents and managers taking charge under the leadership of the Party committees".[60] The Second Session of the Fifth National People's Congress went even further and abolished them altogether. Peng Zhen announced that "local revolutionary committees are to be replaced by local people's governments" and that the posts of provincial governor, mayor and chairperson would be restored.[61]

Renewed stress on the functional separation of Party and state has been accompanied by the appointment of different people to parallel Party and state posts. At the Third Session of the Fifth NPC Hua Guofeng said that "the Central Committee, learning from historical lessons, had decided that, as a rule, the first secretary of a Party committee should not concurrently be provincial governor, or chairman of an autonomous prefecture, or of a county or city".[62] Previously it was common practice for the Party first secretary to be chairperson of the revolutionary committee. During 1979 and 1980 every province and equivalent held people's congresses to elect their standing committees and to re-establish the people's governments.

In every instance someone other than the Party first secretary was elected to the post of governor, mayor etc. and in the five autonomous regions cadres from the minorities were elected to the position of chairperson. The objective of this, according to Hua, is to prevent "over-concentration of power and the holding of too many posts concurrently by one person" and is aimed at "effectively and clearly separating Party work from government work".[63] This would enable Party leaders to "concentrate their time and energy on solving the Party's major problems, while all levels of government under the State Council would have a complete and efficient administrative system from top to bottom".[64]

In the past the interlocking of Party and state personnel has been particularly noticeable at the centre. Until mid-1980 all the Vice-Premiers of the State Council were high-ranking members of the Central Committee and Politburo but in July 1980 it was announced that five of the Vice-Premiers were to resign from their posts while retaining their Party positions.[65] At the same time it was announced that the highest posts in the Party and state would again be held by different people — as had been the case up until Mao's death. Hua Guofeng, while remaining Chairman of the Party handed over his post of Premier to Zhao Ziyang. These leadership changes were endorsed by the Third Session of the Fifth NPC.[66]

Changes in the State Apparat

The Chinese press since the fall of the Gang of Four has stressed that the state apparat has been strengthened. This is an all-embracing phrase, the meaning of which varies widely from the insistence that cadres must have their authority respected to the revival of certain institutional forms, such as the people's procuratorate, discredited during the Cultural Revolution. Most notable has been the attempt to devise a form of "socialist legality" embodying a system of rules and regulations applicable to all. Following the Fifth NPC, a Commission for Legal Affairs was established and a series of laws introduced. At the Second Session of the Fifth NPC Peng Zhen introduced the drafts of seven laws, including the first criminal code and law of criminal procedure, and the organic laws for the people's courts and people's procuratorate. These laws came into effect on 1 January 1980.

The procuratorate exercises authority to ensure the observance of the Constitution and the laws of the state and to protect the rights of citizens. It decides whether to approve a request for arrest made by a public security department, and also whether the person, if arrested, should be held criminally responsible. By contrast, the 1975 Constitution had a new article which gave the Public Security Bureau the right to make arrests without authorisation from the people's court which, to an extent, enshrined the arbitrary power of the police in the Constitution. In the new system, moreover, the role of the masses has been reduced. Although the masses are still to be drawn in to discuss and give suggestions on important criminal cases[67] the phrase of the 1975 Constitution that "the mass line must be applied in procuratorial work and in trying cases" has been dropped.

The equality of all before the law has been emphasised. Peng Zhen has stated that "no-one can be accorded the privilege of disobeying the law" and that "all persons who violate the law or commit crimes, regardless of seniority, position or how great their merit, must be punished according to law".[68] As yet, however, these attacks on privilege have fallen mainly on the lower-middle ranks of the bureaucracy while those at the higher levels have remained untouched. Also the Soviet experience has shown that over time criticisms of privilege can be absorbed by the system. However, the code of criminal law and the law of criminal procedure should help to promote the policy of the equality before the law. The law forbids anyone to extract confessions by torture, to gather a crowd to beat, smash and loot and to detain illegally and prosecute on false charges. Its concern with order is further highlighted by the fact that it is an offence for anyone to disrupt order in production, teaching, scientific research and "the life of the people". It also contains the first official Chinese definition of "counterrevolutionary" behaviour, defined as "an act which attempts to overthrow the political power of the dictatorship of the proletariat and the socialist system".[69] In practice this means that it is now formally a crime to work against communism.

Conclusion

In recent years it has been dangerous to attribute too much permanance to the contemporary state of affairs in China, but it is tempting to see the present period as one of the victory of a new, or revived, political line leading to a period of relative stability. The major source of division, the events of the Cultural Revolution, has been resolved. The theories which sustained the Gang of Four have been rejected and history re-interpreted in a way such as to discredit the left since 1956. This paper suggests that the reassessment of China's past has stopped at the Eighth Party Congress and that policies now being implemented resemble those rejected after the congress and those implemented during the early sixties. However, there have also been completely new developments, such as the unprecedented degree of freedom allowed to intellectuals, new legal codes and the opening to the West. The resolution of policy debates has been accompanied by a resolution of the problem of succession. Although Deng Xiaoping and Chen Yun cannot pursue an active political life for very much longer, they have supporters in the key positions of the Party-state structure.

The last period of retrenchment and consolidation (1961-63) was the prelude to the bitter struggles of the Cultural Revolution. But it is difficult to envisage such a recurrence during the present period of retrenchment, not in the least because with the death of Mao there is no-one in the leadership capable of launching such a challenge. Is there then a potential for future conflict? The tendency is for political struggles in China to settle down into disputes between technocratic modernisers and between different apparats competing for the allocation of scarce resources. As a possible counter to this view there is still evidence of considerable opposition to the new policies at the middle and lower levels. The policies being pursued are similar to those which gave rise to the inequalities and frustrations which found an outlet during the Cultural Revolution. This, combined with the possibility that the new policies do not deliver the promised rise in people's standards of living, could give rise to a new wave of unrest. Though it is unlikely that this would result in a movement like the Cultural Revolution, it is probable that it might find a more subtle expression. One thing is certain: the political problems inherent in China's development strategy will not go away. Past experience has shown that established institutions and codes of conduct function well during periods of leadership unity. Past experience has also shown how easily these can disintegrate at times of leadership conflict. It remains to be seen whether any future differences over development strategy will be contained by the revived norms of political procedure or whether they will again be shattered.

Acknowledgement

I would like to thank David S.G. Goodman for his advice while preparing this paper.

3

CHINA'S FOREIGN RELATIONS AND THE MODERNIZATION PROGRAMME

Michael Yahuda

Department of International Relations, London School of Economics and Political Science, London

The Dimensions of Change in China's Foreign Relations

It can be argued that in contrast with domestic developments China's foreign policy has not undergone a fundamental structural change since the death of Mao. Thus the thrust of China's foreign policy can be seen as a continuation of the major realignments begun by Mao and Zhou at the beginning of the 1970s. It was they who initiated the détente with the United States, the policy of seeking an internationalist state-centred united front against Soviet social imperialism, the opening to Yugoslavia, the new relations with the small and medium Western powers including Japan. It was they too who presided over China's policies towards Chile in 1973 and Angola in 1974-75. Likewise the roots of the Sino-Vietnamese conflict may be traced to the 1971-72 realignment of China's global policy and Zhou En-Lai's openly declared opposition to the domination of Indo-China by Vietnam.[1] Whether or not Sino-Vietnamese relations would have followed the same course had Zhou not died in January 1976 is open to debate, but it is clear that the conflict cannot be seen as simply a consequence of China's new course since the death of Mao. Indeed it is hardly surprising that Soviet writers label the new course as "Maoism without Mao".[2]

However, if China's external relations are examined from a larger perspective than those of power-politics within a competitive inter-state system, a very different picture emerges. In a book written before the direction of China's new course of modernisation had become clear I had suggested that China's global posture could be characterised as a variant of "socialism in one country".[3] This referred to a position in which China's socialist domestic economic and political systems had been deliberately insulated from the outside world. Both foreign capitalist and non-capitalist influences were largely excluded. At the same time China engaged vigorously in the inter-state competitive political system to build up opposition to super-power imperialism especially of the Soviet Union. It is true that the Chinese variant of socialism in one country did not involve absolute economic autarky: it did allow for a growing volume of trade with Western countries and Japan for the purchase of certain commodities like grain and steel as well as for injections of advanced technology in the form of "turn-key" projects and chemical fertiliser factories. This was, however, limited by China's insistence on maintaining its overall trade in balance. Nevertheless even in this regard there were those in China who argued before the downfall of the "Gang of Four" that this trade should be limited much further if not actually stopped altogether.[4] Thus before the onset of the new course, China was playing an international role similar to that which, according to Mao, the Soviet Union had played in the 1930s. By concentrating on socialist construction at home and by utilising the contradictions of the imperialistic inter-state system, China would be the reliable base area for world revolution as a socialist bulwark against the main danger of social imperialism.

From this perspective it is clear that since the adoption of the new modernisation programme in 1978 China's international position has changed radically, taking China a long way from the posture of "socialism in one country". The new programme specifically calls for certain sectors of the economy to focus on producing goods for export. China's leaders have frequently suggested that China's abundant raw materials could be exchanged for advanced technology and negotiations have been conducted with multi-national companies and Western governments for them to supply and operate advanced technology for the exploration and extraction of various mineral resources. The new programme also involves various forms of direct foreign capitalist investment in China. Several zones have been opened, the first of these adjacent to Hong Kong and Macao, as a home for joint ventures in which both the capital and the management will be supplied from abroad in return for guaranteed profits. Meanwhile individual Chinese ministries and regional authorities have contracted with foreign companies involving them in short, medium and long term debts. However, the government has not drawn on many of the lines of credit established with foreign governments and international banking consortia with a combined value of several tens of billions of US dollars, preferring to wait for better terms of interest available to it as a developing country. China nevertheless has acquired a foreign debt of at least US $3.4bn.[5]

This greater association of the Chinese economy with the international economic system will be intensified by the plan to focus on the more prosperous and economically advantaged regions as high priority development areas. Typically, these regions already benefit from better infrastructural supports in terms of transport facilities, access to essential supplies, marketing systems which are more than local, a pool of relatively more skilled labour, etc. Current projections call for concentrating advanced foreign imports in these regions. Even if these regions should not be opened to foreign capital like the two small districts near Hong Kong and Macao it is clear that much of their economic operations will be guided by norms of profitability, productivity and management closer to those observed in the West than has been true of the previous 30 years of the PRC. A certain proportion of the output will be earmarked for foreign markets if only to pay for the large external debt which has already been contracted and the even greater volume of debts which have been projected. The late Professor Eckstein has already shown how the repercussions of the 1973-74 international economic crisis adversely affected China's economy as a consequence of the much more limited trade of that period.[6] Now that a much larger proportion of China's economy will be involved in external economic relations, it follows that the economy as a whole will be more greatly affected by the vagaries of the international economic system. This cannot but limit proportionately the scope of socialist planning and controls.

The deliberate opening of the Chinese economy to external influences has also been accompanied by political changes, one aim to which is to provide an orderly framework which both accommodates the new external economic relationships and provides a milieu in which they can be further extended. The most obvious of these is the re-establishment of institutional regularity along pre-1958 Great Leap Forward lines and the promulgation of a series of new laws including one specifically on joint ventures. But there is also much about the new political order as a whole which has the effect of bringing China more closely into line with the values and those principles of "rationality" which sustain the international (largely capitalist) economic system. For example, the emphasis on socio-political stability and the repeated declaration that there will be no more mass movements doubtless serve primarily domestic purposes, nevertheless they also accord with the normative preferences of the main actors within the international economic system. The same may be said of the new emphasis on professionalism and on policies which enhance the position and status of intellectual and managerial groups. The general shift towards the prime goal of modernisation has been accompanied by the explanation that any trend towards egalitarianism and more even distribution can only follow after the achievement of modernisation and a much higher level of prosperity. Whatever the merits of this in terms of Marxist theory, it is clearly a departure from the principles of Maoist economics as developed since the Great Leap Forward. But it also brings China more into line with the economic principles of the world economic system.

It may be objected that by stressing the growing congruity of the operations of the Chinese economy with those of the world economic system, insufficient attention has been paid to the autonomy of the Chinese state and its capacity to regulate the interactions of its domestic economy with the outside world. Clearly one of the major achievements since the liberation of 1949 has been the consolidation of a unitary Chinese state which, on the one hand, has effectively centralised domestic political power and economic management and, on the other hand, has established China as an independent great power in world affairs able to regulate all aspects of its interactions with the outside world. The changes in China since the death of Mao may be seen as not the product of irresistible pressures upon the state from interests in civil society, but rather as the result of the victory of one set of state leaders over another after a twenty year conflict over the question as to "Whither China". In this sense the depiction of the conflict in the Cultural Revolution as a two line ideological struggle is not without merit. Moreover implicit in the positions of both sets of protagonists was the view that it is control of state power which is decisive in bringing about the desired changes in the domestic society and economy and also in foreign alignments. To be sure neither divorced control of state power from supportive social bases. But the crucial arena for struggle was the state.

Not only has the Chinese state (or more accurately, the leaders who wield state power) initiated the new course in China's international economic relations, but these new relations are either conducted by organizations which are administratively part of the state structure itself or by enterprises whose operations are controlled by various economic and political means. Furthermore the importance for external relations of sovereignty in both legal and political terms allied to the centralisation of political power within China means that China's leaders will continue to be able to exercise strict control over the scope of China's external relations.

Clearly the significance of state power should not be underestimated and it should not be thought that China somehow already has become locked into an irreversible relationship of interdependency with the world economic system. The Chinese authorities have already demonstrated their capacity to back-track on commitments with foreign companies when they felt in danger of having been over-extended. Thus one of the immediate effects of the initial process of economic readjustment plans early in 1979 was the unexpected delay on contracts with several Japanese major companies, which led to shock waves through the Japanese economic establishment. But in due course nearly all the contracts were renewed within six months on better financial terms for the Chinese.[7] In principle the new course is reversible. Whether or not it will be reversed in fact depends on those who wield state power. Nevertheless, according to Chinese figures the total value of foreign trade in 1979 was equivalent to 18 per cent of the GNP which is a very high percentage and it suggests that the economic costs of cutting back on foreign trade could already be high.[8]

Foreign Policy and Modernisation

Since the adoption of the new programme China's leaders have frequently declared their interest in a tranquil international environment as the best setting in which the Chinese people could concentrate upon domestic economic development.[9] Indeed this parallels similar statements after the end of the Korean war in 1953 when China fully embarked on its first five year plan.[10] That was the domestic setting against which China adopted an active foreign policy of reaching accord with the non-Communist states of Asia and of taking the initiative in seeking to establish better relations with the United States. This period of China's foreign policy, usually labelled the "Bandung phase", ended in 1957-58 to a large extent because of the unrelenting hostility of the United States. But in the current period the public emphasis on the desirability of a tranquil international environment has not been accompanied by

Chinese moves to find ways of reducing the conflictual elements in China's foreign relationships. On the contrary, the modernisation programme has been accompanied by moves which have positively intensified them and which may be said to have played no small part in actually raising the level of tension in China's immediate international environment. The most notable of these is the rapid development of enmity with Vietnam which has already led to one Chinese punitive war with warnings about more to come. Meanwhile Chinese diplomacy has been actively seeking co-operative relations with Western countries not only for help in the modernisation programme but also to establish an anti-Soviet united front. There can be few developments more alarming to the Soviet leadership than the emergence of a *de facto* alliance between its principal enemies in the East and the West. This conjures up the age-old spectre of a beleaguered, encircled Russia.

This raises the issue of the compatibility of China's foreign policy with the domestic policy of economic modernisation. To be sure the issue could be formulated differently and, perhaps from a Chinese perspective, more fairly: to what extent are developments in the international environment themselves inimical to China's pursuit of domestic economic modernisation? In this view, China is confronted with a globally expansionist Soviet Union which is using Cuba as its proxy in Africa and Vietnam as its proxy in Southeast Asia. The Soviet threat is seen as a global one which requires an effective response principally from the Western powers against whom the Chinese argue the threat is primarily aimed. But where it impinges on China the Chinese perforce will not shrink from effective counter-measures. Thus the limited war against Vietnam was initially justified as a response to alleged military provocations on the border. But, as Chinese leaders both before and since the war have stated, the war was to designed to "teach Vietnam a lesson". As has been made perfectly plain by these leaders and by the Chinese side in the negotiations with Vietnam, the "lesson" is that Vietnam cannot simply invade and occupy its neighbour Kampuchea even with Soviet backing without suffering severe consequences. The Vietnamese have declared the situation in Kampuchea to be "irreversible" while China's leaders have reserved the right to teach the Vietnamese "another lesson" as long as this continues. This is not the place to analyse at length the origins and development of the Sino-Vietnamese conflict, let alone to seek to assign responsibility to one side or the other. What would seem to be more fruitful would be to discuss the policies which China has adopted to counter the alleged Soviet menace and examine their compatibility with the new domestic programme.

From its establishment in 1949 the People's Republic of China has been under threat from the overwhelmingly more powerful superpowers. The policies which were adapted from the experiences of the Chinese revolution to meet the American threat in the 1950s and in most of the 1960s have been increasingly applied to meet the Soviet challenge in the 1970s. As China's leaders have repeatedly asserted, the only way to resist an expansionist power on the global scene is by vigorous opposition. Attempts to establish co-operative relations with the expansionist power as a way of persuading it to behave differently have consistently been denounced by China's leaders. Thus at present China's leaders have stated that, while they do not oppose arms limitations agreements as such, these should not be relied upon. In their view that is the road of appeasement. In a sense it is possible to regard the Chinese limited war against Vietnam as designed to serve as an example to others of how alleged Soviet advances through proxy powers should be stopped.

This conflictual approach towards the most critical issue of the inter-state competitive system differs from that adopted by the Western powers with whom China seeks co-operation in opposing the Soviet Union and in helping China's modernisation programme. Successive American administrations have sought to establish co-operative relations with the Soviet Union within the framework of détente. Even Chairman Hua's favourite Western politician Mrs Thatcher, who yields to none in the conviction with which she argues the need for defence preparedness against the Russians, claims a desire to promote co-operative patterns of relations with the Soviet Union in the spheres of security, trade and the communication of ideas.

One of the consequences of these different approaches to the inter-state competitive system was the opposition which many Western governments registered against China's incursion into Vietnam. Indeed an American presidential representative criticised the invasion in a public speech in Peking at the time.[11] Moreover not a single Western government has evinced interest in joining with China in an international united front against the Soviet Union. It is one thing for these governments to declare their interest in the emergence of a strong and prosperous China as a factor for peace and stability and it is quite another for them to share China's views on the Soviet Union and how best to deal with its alleged expansionism. Even those in the West who have advocated "playing the China card" have not done so for the purpose of establishing an anti-Soviet alliance. Rather they have envisaged the China "card" as a kind of a trump to be played in the superpower game so as to induce more "co-operative" behaviour from the Soviet Union. In other words it was seen as a means to make détente more effective rather than to do away with it. However since China's attack on Vietnam less has been heard of the "China card". The Soviet invasion of Afghanistan in December 1979 did bring it to the fore for a while as the Carter administration agreed to supply China with "non-lethal" military equipment. But as détente seemed to founder, interest in the "China card" declined once again.

The Russian invasion of Afghanistan has put a halt to the first set of Sino-Soviet negotiations for 15 years in Moscow with the aim of improving bilateral relations at the state level. The talks which began in September 1979 were held up in any case by disagreements about procedures and agenda. The Soviet side wanted these to be confined strictly to bilateral inter-state questions, whereas the Chinese wished to raise the issue of alleged Soviet "hegemonism" as applied especially to Indo-China. Whatever prospects may have existed for these talks have been put aside by the Afghan crisis. There has long been an argument advanced in the West that, for reasons of balance of power politics arising particularly from the dynamics of the tri-lateral relationship involving the United States, it was in the joint interests of the Chinese and Russian leaders to begin a dialogue to reduce the level of hostility between them. Otherwise the United States would be left in an especially advantageous position while they would continue to be tied in inflexible positions with regard to each other. The adoption of the new course in China, it is now argued, should facilitate in the long run the opening of a Sino-Soviet dialogue. Since the ideological underpinnings to the Chinese critique of Soviet revisionism have been totally eroded, the Chinese can hardly attack the Soviet leadership for practices which they have vigorously adopted themselves. Nevertheless it is far too early to suggest that China's policy towards the Soviet Union has substantially changed, or that China's conflictual approach to what has been termed here "the inter-state competitive system" is in the process of being eroded. However, one indication that the Chinese position may be softening was the pronouncement in Peking in October 1980 that a new world war is not necessarily inevitable.[12]

It should be noted that the occasion for the new Sino-Soviet talks in 1979 arose out of the Chinese declaration, in April of that year, that they intended not to renew the 30 year old Sino-Soviet treaty of alliance and the suggestion that the two sides meet to agree a new framework for their relationship. The talks which have eventually materialised are taking place against a background of deep-seated mutual suspicion and antagonism. Paradoxically the Sino-Vietnamese conflict can be seen as a catalyst in bringing the two sides to the negotiating table. From a Chinese perspective clearly it would be advantageous to dissociate the conflict with the superpower northern neighbour from Vietnam in the south with whom one war has been fought and with whom more wars may yet be fought in the near future. The fact that the Chinese delegation in Moscow insisted on the inclusion in the agenda of alleged Soviet hegemonism in Indo-China is a pointer in this direction. From the Soviet perspective, the Chinese invasion was embarrassing as it highlighted the limited extent to which the Soviet Union was either willing or able to come to the aid of its ally. Indeed there were indications of Vietnamese dissatisfaction with the failure of the Soviet Union to administer more effective assistance.[13] The Soviet reaction at the time was initially to accuse the United States of collusion and finally to congratulate the Americans and themselves on having sucessfully resisted the alleged Chinese design of bringing about a conflict between them.[14] In other words the Soviet leadership saw the question of their involvement in the Sino-Vietnamese conflict in the context of superpower politics. Doubtless such considerations loom large in their calculations regarding the Sino-Soviet negotiations.

Another element in Chinese thinking on the negotiations with the Soviet Union may be the role which increased Sino-Soviet trade can play in China's modernisation plans. With an annual trade turnover to the value of over 530 million Roubles, the Soviet Union already ranks as China's fifth largest foreign trade partner.[15] This is a trade which could be substantially increased. Soviet technology on the whole may not be up to the most advanced levels of Japan and several Western countries, but it is more advanced than the bulk of that produced in China and, even more important, it may be more readily adapted to Chinese conditions. After all a great deal of Chinese technology is derived from Soviet technology supplied in the 1950s. Moreover much of the administration of the economy and of foreign trade in China is still patterned on the Soviet model. It can further be argued that there is potentially a greater complementarity in Sino-Soviet trade than in China's trade with the West as there is a larger market in the Soviet Union for China's light industrial products such as textiles. By contrast one of the major stumbling blocks to the rapid expansion of China's trade with the West is the small market for China's products or the quotas imposed on products such as textiles. Interestingly, the prospect of greater trade was one of the reasons given for improving Sino-Soviet relations by a Hong Kong journal said to be close to the viewpoints of Deng Xiaoping.[16]

However, even if it can be granted that the new course in China has had some influence on the conduct of foreign policy, there is still overwhelming evidence to suggest that what I have called China's conflictual approach is still the dominant one in China's foreign policy. Nowhere is this clearer than in Sino-Vietnamese relations. Arguably it was Chinese policy which drove Vietnam into a close relationship with the Soviet Union and by calling Vietnam the "Asian Cuba" the Chinese seem to have exaggerated the extent of Soviet control over Hanoi. The basis for the Sino-Vietnamese conflict was established independently of the Soviet factor, but it would appear that China's general analysis of Soviet global activities was the dominant element in Chinese thinking about the Vietnam problem. Despite an apparent agreement between China and the countries of ASEAN on the desirability of a Vietnamese military withdrawal from Kampuchea, deep disagreement in fact exists. The Chinese leaders wish to see Vietnam so battered and torn by its military occupation that it is humiliated and compelled to withdraw. The ASEAN countries in their different ways, however, seek an accommodation with Vietnam rather than its humiliation.

This paper has argued so far that a certain incongruity exists between China's declared preference for a tranquil international environment within which to pursue the four modernisations and China's actual policies within the inter-state political system. Curiously it can be argued that the two elements of the incongruity stem from the same intellectual source. One constant theme behind the modernisation drive is the nationalist one of transforming China into a strong modern country so as to avoid the kind of humiliations which it had suffered in the hundred years or so before liberation in 1949.[17] Few can mistake the nationalist emotional undertones, or indeed overtones, of China's approach to the Indo-China problems. Witness the bitter Chinese charges of betrayal of trust and of the sacrifices endured by the Chinese people on behalf of Vietnam. Note should also be taken of the inflexible and emotionally charged way in which China asserts its sovereign claims to the disputed islands and territorial waters in the South China Sea. Likewise underlying the dispute with Vietnam is China's implicit claim to have a say in the shaping of the power relations of Indo-China. This may be seen as a nationalist claim traditionally asserted by great powers towards their smaller neighbours. Similar nationalist passions can also be identified on the Vietnamese side. Interesting parallels can be drawn between the emotional reactions of both sides of the Sino-Soviet conflict and between those of China and Vietnam. But in the latter case China is cast in the role of the Soviet Union and China in the role of Vietnam. Thus it is China which complains of ingratitude and of the narrow nationalism of Vietnam which has sold out to the great enemy, while it is Vietnam which complains of attempts to control it and of a traitorous withdrawal of aid and related technicians so as to stimulate economic chaos. Finally, in this context, notice should be taken of the way in which deep ethnic animosities have been aroused by the events of the conflict; hostile traditional images have been reinforced and fears have become self-fulfilling.

There is no way in which it can be argued that China's recent policies of confrontation have been guided by the economic aims of its modernisation programme. The economic costs of the war were so high that it is rumoured that the newly re-elevated Chen Yun was moved to protest.[18] In budgetary terms alone, the need for increased spending to pay for the war and to meet the costs of strengthening border defences meant that defence allocations had to be significantly increased.[19] However, aside from the more obvious expenditure implications, the continued state of high tension requires constant military readiness in both north and south. It continually raises the issue of the need to purchase advanced weapons systems on a "quick fix" basis so as to plug the more obvious holes in China's defence capabilities. Any foreign currency spent on this is currency denied to the civil sector, any credit used for such purchases will sooner or later have to be repaid by output from the civil economy. Scientists, technologists and skilled labour deployed on military projects are precious and scarce personnel denied to the tasks of economic modernisation. While it is true that in the past year the modernisation of defence has slipped from first to last in the listing of the four modernisations and that no-one has challenged publicly the general policy that military modernisation can only follow rather than precede the modernisation of the economy, it is also true that the requirements of military preparedness in the south and in the north simultaneously impose heavy demands upon the resources available to the central government.

Relations With the West and Modernisation

If China's relations with the Soviet Union and Vietnam have been dominated by military and political conflict, relations with the

West and Japan have been more clearly related to China's modernisation programme. But it would be misleading to suggest that China's approaches to these countries have been dominated exclusively by economic or technological considerations. The "Soviet factor" has loomed large in China's policies often to the embarrassment of the Western governments concerned. This was evident during Deng Xiaoping's tour of the United States and Hua Guofeng's European tour. Although both sets of visits were officially acclaimed as great successes, the Carter administration took care not to associate itself with Deng's criticisms of Soviet hegemonism and was acutely embarrassed by Deng's interview with *Time* magazine on the eve of his visit in which he actually mentioned the possibility of a Sino-American alliance.[20] The West German government was so alarmed lest Hua Guofeng should unsettle its delicate relations with the Soviet Union that it took steps to advise Hua in advance of his visit against the wisdom of severely hostile criticisms of Russia on German soil.[21] Nevertheless there were signs that China's more open approach to the outside world and the West in particular has brought about a closer understanding of the complexities of Western politics and of Western diplomacy. Thus during his visit to the United States Deng took care not to dismiss SALT or détente out of hand. Rather he more effectively questioned the wisdom of placing reliance upon these processes. It was almost as if he appreciated that to have openly criticised the foundations of American foreign policy could have been counter-productive. Likewise Hua Guofeng in Western Europe confined himself in public speeches to statements of China's known position of "hegemonism". The Soviet Union was not once mentioned by name, nor did he comment in public on European policies and their response to Brezhnev's arms reductions proposals.

It is clear, however, that the main arena of change in China's foreign relations has concerned the Western world and Japan. Two aspects may be isolated for discussion. The first concerns trade and the second relates to the reorientation of China's domestic society to external (i.e., primarily Western) influences. Since China's foreign trade is analysed in a separate paper there is no need here to explore this in detail. But a few points are in order with regard to the way in which the newly emerging trading relations are already changing China's foreign relations and also with regard to the role of foreign trade in the modernisation programme.

Perhaps the most interesting point to be made with regard to China's growing trade relations with the advanced industrialised countries is the uneven way in which this has developed. For example, despite repeated Chinese declarations of the significance they attach to West European countries in trade as well as political/strategic matters, their trade is so heavily weighted towards West Germany that it exceeds the combined total of trade with Britain, France and Italy. Japan which has long been China's leading trade partner now accounts for a greater volume of China's trade than the combined total of the next four trading partners. Despite America's prestige in Chinese eyes as the world's power house of advanced technology and as the world's most modernised country, most of China's growing imports from the United States are agricultural products.

In view of China's current reappraisal of the import of foreign technology after what is acknowledged as a too hasty and ill-considered series of such imports in 1979-80, it is too early to identify trends in China's policy in this area. Exceptions in this regard are China's policies towards Japan and to what might be called the "Chinese family" outside China. Both Japan and the external "Chinese family" have been long regarded by Western economists as China's most natural economic associates and therefore it should not come as a surprise that, having embraced a more outgoing policy, China should establish close inter-locking relations with them.

Interestingly, China's leaders have set the pace in declaring the sorts of new relationships which they have in mind and that this has embarrassed to a certain extent the audience to whom these statements have been directed. During the course of his visit to Japan Vice-Premier Gu Mu said the following to a press conference:

> An economically developed and technologically advanced Japan and a gradually modernized China cooperating with other friendly countries in the Asia-Pacific region would in a very large measure ensure stability in the East. And this combined force would be far from insignificant in stabilizing the world situation.
>
> The overwhelming majority of the nearly 1,000 million Chinese and Japanese people who desire to live on the best of terms and cooperate closely in the fields of economy, trade, technology and culture *constitutes a mighty force, a tide which no-one can dam.*
>
> Both our countries want to develop further the friendship and co-operation between our two governments and between their economic, trade and other circles. This friendship and cooperation is to the advantage of both countries and is conducive to the course of anti-hegemonism and world peace. This is true with regard to the present reality and still more so from a long term point of view. [emphasis added]

He went on to add that the wide possibility for bilateral trade and co-operation arose out of the complementarity of their economies: Japan was "highly developed, with a sophisticated technology and a higher level of management." China, on the other hand, was "rich in minerals and other resources, with a vast territory, and it was very close to Japan."[22]

While such a relationship may be welcomed by important circles in Japan, the government was anxious lest the Southeast Asian countries might be alarmed by such a prospect. The specific issue on which such apprehensions were focused was the Chinese request for a low interest development loan from the Japanese Overseas Economic Cooperation Fund. Having initially sought a loan up to $5.5 bn. in early September, the Chinese authorities eventually settled for an application for only $2.5. But even this reduced figure was regarded by the Japanese government as excessive. It sought to limit this kind of aid to China so as that it should be seen to be proportionate with similar loans to the countries of ASEAN.[23]

Hua Guofeng's remarks at the press conference on the occasion of the establishment of diplomatic relations with the United States were directed to the political dimensions of China's relations with Chinese living overseas including those of Taiwan:

> It has been our consistent policy that all patriots belong to one big family whether they come forward early or late. We hope that our compatriots in Taiwan will join all the other Chinese people including our compatriots in Hongkong and Macao and overseas Chinese in making further contributions to the cause of reunifying China.[24]

The political approach to the overseas Chinese has been complemented by a wide variety of economic measures designed to draw on their advanced skills, economic know-how and foreign capital as an important component of the modernisation programme. In this regard the domestic and external dimensions of Chinese politics are closely interlocked. The domestic programme includes as one of its key elements a new deal not only for intellectuals but also for those with family links with overseas Chinese. The restitution of profits to the former capitalists has also had the effect of allaying residual suspicions of the Communists by overseas Chinese capitalists. In short, the new domestic united front may be seen as indissolubly linked with the unprecedented attempts to draw the overseas Chinese into China's economic and political orbit. So far this applies principally to Hongkong and Macao, but overtures have been made to overseas Chinese elsewhere in Southeast Asia. It remains yet to be seen how the host countries in the area will react to the closer relations being established between sections of their overseas Chinese communities and China. The problems of Indo-China, the Sino-Vietnamese conflict and the refugees have overshadowed this question. In particular the ASEAN countries have been preoccupied with Vietnam, with the result that China and the ASEAN countries, especially Thailand, have evolved parallel policies. Deng Xiaoping has more than once pledged Chinese assistance in the event of a Vietnamese attack on Thailand. Therefore the incipient conflict of interest between China and the Southeast Asian countries over the loyalties of the overseas Chinese is so far dormant, except with regard to Indonesia.

Perhaps the most significant development in China's new orientation towards the West is the opening of China in many ways, not all of them controlled or co-ordinated, to Western influences. The entire course followed since the Great Leap Forward more than 20 years ago through which a distinctive Chinese way of socialist construction had been evolved has now been set aside. A self-confident China, secure in its vision of socialist construction, could perhaps have carried out the maxim of using foreign influences selectively to serve the cause of socialism. But a China which is unsure of its socialist identity, with a constantly changing economic programme, with its administrative and management systems under criticism as in need of great change, is hardly in that position. China is clearly undergoing a period of great transition. Meanwhile its gates have been opened to a wide variety of Western influences which are being absorbed apparently uncritically and in a haphazard way. China's managers have been told that they must learn from the management systems of the capitalist West. China's television has been replete with images of the modernised consumer societies of America, Japan and Western Europe as pictures of a future for China in which Chinese citizens too will benefit from comparably high standards of living. Young urban Chinese who during the Cultural Revolution were inculcated in the belief that social virtue was to be found only in China, that foreign things were somehow decadent and that foreigners were people to be held at arms length have now turned full circle. Frequently disillusioned with politics, they pursue individual interests in which they have also been encouraged by the new emphasis on material incentives for individual labour and achievement and the reversion to elitist social and educational policies. Thus just as the previous pattern of excluding foreign influences may be regarded as an unhealthy and exaggerated tendency so the contemporary tendency to see value only in foreign things may similarly be seen as unhealthy and overdrawn.

The current turn around in China's attitudes to the West perhaps should be seen within the perspective of China's modern history in which there has been an underlying conflict between what may be called the nativists and the Westernisers. It has been a long drawn out conflict between those on the one side whose instinctive and intellectual tendencies have been directed to historic and cultural sources drawn deep from China's cultural traditions and those on the other side who have looked to the outside for inspiration and models for adapting China to the modern world. These conflicting tendencies have taken different forms in different periods. Since 1949 three major stages may be identified: the Soviet period of the early 1950s in which a struggle developed between those like Mao who argued that "we must not eat pre-cooked food" and those who later chided him for not "learning from" and "uniting with" countries "stronger than our own". The next stage was the nativistic one of the Cultural Revolution. Both periods built up countervailing tendencies, but they left China as a self-reliant, socialist, independent major power on the world stage. The new stage of Westernisation derives its social base and political force from a new alliance between the older intellectuals and the older cadres who as the main victims and survivors of what they see as the Cultural Revolution holocaust are committed to a vision of modernisation whose roots can be traced to Chen Duxiu's slogan of "Mr Science and Mr Democracy" of the May Fourth period. It would seem that it is within this intellectual framework that China's recent political history is being re-evaluated.

But the extent to which China has been opened up to the West should not be exaggerated. One of the important legacies left by Mao is a unified state with effective patterns of political controls. So that by March/April 1979 China's leaders were able to impose limits upon Chinese contacts with foreigners in China when it was felt that these were getting out of hand during the turbulence of that year's Spring Festival. It has been argued that the great influx of Western tourists to China, which is due to be extended by the building of large chains of luxurious hotels in China's important cities, may lead to the kinds of social problems which such developments have given rise to in other third world countries. There are already accounts by Western visitors of prostitution and other corrupt practices developing in the vicinity of big hotels. However these social problems seem to be caused more by domestic factors than simply by contact with wealthier foreigners. The problem of urban unemployed youth (or more accurately of youth awaiting job assignments) allied to that those who have illegally returned to the urban areas who accordingly lack both residence permits and ration cards and cannot apply for employment, means that there is a certain pool of people who will be drawn of necessity to the shadier aspects of the "unofficial" economy. Nevertheless the question as to whether the growing influx of tourists (as opposed to the smaller numbers of interested visitors of recent years) with their distinctive demands for leisure and entertainment will not have a profound influence on Chinese society is a serious one. Similar developments in the Soviet Union do not seem to have constituted a challenge to the social or political order. But an argument can be made that the influx of evidently more affluent Western tourists has contributed to the lack of general appeal of officially propagated values. If the analogy with the Soviet Union is valid it would appear that the Chinese authorities will also not lack the political and social controls to limit the impact of such Western influence upon Chinese society. One respect in which Chinese and Soviet conditions differ concerns the presence in China of many citizens with overseas Chinese links. This has led to the practice over the last three years of hundreds of thousands of overseas Chinese visiting people in China laden with a wide variety of highly prized Western consumer goods. Another dimension of the growing inequalities in China is between those who have access to such "goodies" and those who do not. In this sense the problem of controlling the impact of Westernisation in China is immensely complex and it may be said to arise to a large extent from the psychological and practical problems of opening to the West. Much depends on whether and how soon China's leaders, intellectuals and managers can find a "Chinese" path to modernity which will at the same time facilitate access to the advanced technologies and managerial systems of the West while evolving a distinctively Chinese approach or model.

Conclusions

This paper has argued that China's foreign policy cannot be seen as being dictated by the priorities of economic modernisation. It has further suggested that it is fruitful to distinguish between what might be called the inter-state competitive system (the realm of power politics) and the world economic or trading system. China's policies within the first system display great continuities with those established by Mao and Zhou at the beginning of the decade. The greatest changes have been registered in the second system. The two interconnect at a number of different levels, but in operational terms it is the role of the Chinese state which facilitates the linkage.

Unlike the Western countries (including Japan), to which China is orientating itself in both systems, the state predominates as both the controller and the agent for contacts at all levels. Such problems as do arise derive from inherent contradictions and incompatibilities between different Chinese goals. Thus China's behaviour in the realm of power politics is dictated by what I term a conflictual model of world politics which does not facilitate the emergence of a tranquil international environment in which to pursue the domestic course of modernisation. Another related problem is the opening out to Western influences at a time of transition in which China is groping towards a new sense of self-identity and at a time in which inequalities are bound to grow in China and in which not all expectations can be fulfilled. The opening to the West has also brought realisation of the difficulties of paying for the massive array of imports in which different Chinese authorities have expressed interest; hence the various schemes for compensation trade and joint ventures. Over and above these problems looms the security question of maintaining two ongoing conflicts on the northern and southern borders simultaneously. In a context in which China's original ideological objections to the Soviet Union have been whittled away, as China itself has adopted virtually every single aspect which it opposed so vigorously before, the road is now open to a Sino-Soviet rapprochement. Indeed it would square the two circles of China's divergent practices in the two world systems. It would substantially guarantee China with the tranquil international environment which it needs for effective modernisation and it would enable China to gain access to advanced technology from a source which would welcome China's light industrial exports.

4

ADMINISTRATIVE LEVEL AND AGRARIAN STRUCTURE, 1975-80: THE COUNTY (W) AS FOCAL POINT IN CHINESE RURAL DEVELOPMENT POLICY

Mitch Meisner

James Madison College, Michigan State University, Michigan

Marc Blecher

Department of Government, Oberlin College, Oberlin, Ohio

Introduction

In 1975 elements in the Chinese leadership attempted to establish a comprehensive policy line for rural development. Issued as a set of guidelines for setting up "Dazhai-type counties," the programme publicised most notably in a speech given by Hua Guofeng at the National Conference on Learning from Dazhai in Agriculture, seems in retrospect an attempt to reinterpret and extend on the most general level a set of policies and "experiences" that had been in evidence since the Cultural Revolution, and which grew out of earlier experiments with collective rural economic forms since the formation of people's communes. The five years since Mao's death have seen the rapid dismantling of this agrarian platform as a whole, although various individual planks remain. Reasons stem from varied sources — reanalysis and very broad-based criticism of the apparent political underpinnings of the 1975 programme, this in part allowing for a general reassessment of the rationality of much of the agricultural and rural development strategy applied since the Great Leap Forward, especially the "grain first" policy, and the various approaches to rural income formation depending on self-reliant cultivation and sale of primary agricultural commodities, especially grain.

Throughout the period of attempts to generalise a rural development policy from the strands and cross-currents of experience in the years to 1975, and then the intense period of reformulation of policy from 1976 on, a certain structural emphasis has been apparent: this concerns *the key role of the county in rural development administration and political leadership.* The 1975 policy was based on attempts to extend what were considered the key general lessons of the Xiyang County experience in reproducing the apparently phenomenal success of Dazhai Brigade since the late 1940s. Since 1978, press criticism indicating both national and local attacks on the Xiyang county leadership, including its famous political leader (later to become Politbureau member and Deputy Prime Minister) Chen Yonggui (Ch'en Yung-kuei), began to appear. By the summer of 1980, major criticism of Xiyang County's post-Cultural Revolutionary leadership, all colleagues and allies of Chen Yonggui, began, while Chen's political fortunes in Beijing also waned. Critics focused especially on the 1973-76 years, but also excoriated the way the Cultural Revolution power-seizure of 1967 had been handled in the first place, and by implication, many of the policy assumptions underlying apparent post-1967 economic successes. For a variety of reasons, the larger historical lessons of the Dazhai and Xiyang experiences — the transformation of a poor, mountainous area "through hard struggle" — are still not under attack.[1] But as of this writing (mid-1980) we see more of the "facade" being chipped away, and in recent months perhaps the beginning of a frontal assault. Earlier criticisms of egalitarianism in the Dazhai payment system and of its strong emphasis on collective rather than individual forms of remuneration[2] have now been supplemented with allegations that certain data were falsified, that excessive amounts of state funds were made available to Xiyang County, and that these and other funds were spent in a profligate, wasteful manner on ill-planned or unnecessary large-scale projects (such as a large water control project) or inefficient enterprises (such as Xiyang's famed hand tractor factory). Continuing attacks on the political leadership of Xiyang County and Jinzhong Prefecture, to some extent mirroring in a reverse fashion some of the factional disputes of the Cultural Revolution, now presaged the retirement from high national office of Chen Yonggui. Recent attacks have linked Xiyang with the ultra-left, a new development.

One thing this latest round of criticisms indicates, perhaps, is the *political salience of the county*. A focal point of the attempted general policy formulation of the mid-1970s, the county is still a powerful institution in rural China, and in rural development policy implementation more particularly. This may be based on its structural characteristics. But, in what way are its structural characteristics linked with the twists and turns of substantive economic, political, and social policy shifts, which in relation to rural policy in the last decades have been quite dramatic? This discussion is intended to take up the questions surrounding the key role the county has played in Chinese rural development strategy, look at possible structural factors, at the different kinds of substantive emphases involving the county, including possible implications for social relations and societal conflict in rural China, and the implications for continuity and change in current agricultural development policies and practices insofar as they affect the county's role. We will find that insofar as direct strength and responsibility of political leadership for guiding action by lower-level units within the collective agrarian sector is concerned, especially in relation to overt redistribution goals within the peoples communes, the weight of the county appears to have been diminished.

Whether or not decreased weight for political action by the county Party Committee and possible collective sector allies (especially brigade party branch committees, we suggest) in turn implies a reversal in rural "class relations" in development as might be suggested by analogies with earlier periods is an interesting question, but one that turns out to be rather ambiguous and difficult to answer. In fact, the relatively explicit attempt by the 1975 programme of establishing Dazhai-type counties to work on the basis of a fairly strong class line tied to other redistributive elements may have been one of the problematical elements in the policy in the minds of at least some in power today, tying it fatally to the past.

Few scholars have examined closely the relationship between forms of state/collective management of local, especially rural, economy and class relations in post-1949 China. The problem of management of a developing economy, much of it rooted in the daily and seasonal work of agrarian settlements, rapidly responding to modern initiatives of industrialisation and other processes, and doing so within a conflictual socialist framework, is a considerable one. There is no simple solution, especially none which is simply given by historic formulae or straddling easily considerations of economic efficiency, social equality and popular power. In relation to such analysis, the work of Mark Selden[3] on the "mass line" in the administration of border region government and economy in the Yan'an period, and especially the pathbreaking political analysis by Franz Schurmann[4] of the social implications of inner-party conflict in the 1950s and 1960s, come to mind. In particular, Schurmann's work on alternative forms of decentralisation of political and economic administration hotly debated by Chinese leaders in the late 1950s may shed light on the social implications of current shifts. The major outlines of Schurmann's analysis, ascribing class implications to the decentralisation debates of 1957, will be considered in more detail in the concluding section of this analysis. But although suggestive, similar distinctions in terms of the old lines of class analysis may not be so easily drawn for changes originating in today's political and economic system. In the following sections on the structural significance of the county in local development administration and on interpreting the content and implications of the faded Xiyang-Dazhai-type county development schema, we shall argue that the 1975 programme, at least in its ideal design, pushed quite far certain issues identified as having a class character, particularly those involving inequality of collective units and the loci of political power, quite far. It may turn out that such attempts in the China of the 1970s and 1980s as changes in policy regarding rural development and the use of political power to intervene in such development for specified ends were not highly practicable and perhaps rested on partly or wholly unworkable conceptions of class relations and class conflict derived from earlier periods.

The County as a Historical Entity

Several major questions followed when the Chinese revolution achieved state power. Among other things, fundamental problems of social relations and economic development posed questions for the form of organisation and character of action of the nascent Communist governmental and administrative system. More deeply, the nature of the state and its involvement in social-economic management and development issues of urban-rural and industrial-agricultural institutions, including the degree and speed with which collective forms would take precedence over private ownership, were intertwined with and had obvious implications for changing social relations. For the matter of class in the new society there were, *inter alia,* issues of relations among old and new rural strata (and also among the latter themselves) that emerged from land reform, rural-urban stratification, and eventually, divisions among richer and poorer collective communities.

In the summer of 1955, Mao Zedong successfully pushed through a policy on full-scale agricultural collectivisation that to a significant degree decided the issue of private versus collective in favour of a rapid movement to the latter. But given the speedy pace of change, inherent tensions remained, having to do with size and management of the collective unit, production relations within the collective economy, and the relation of the collectives to surviving private endeavours. These fundamental tensions in development policy and socio-economic structure continue to pose problems for evolving units of state administration. In the remainder of this section we shall describe the historical and structural position of the county in China.

Historical background

The county has been an important unit of basic territorial government since Imperial times, and throughout the Nationalist and Communist periods. This prolonged existence of the county suggests familiarity as its greatest attribute. But in its incarnation in the 1970s as an attempted focal point of development efforts, the county acquired new functions and a renewed significance.[5]

County government may be considered to be a structured meeting between state and society. In the Imperial period, the county was the lowest level of direct government and the primary point of contact with rural society. The county magistrate supervised the collection of taxes, adjudicated local civil and criminal cases, and maintained public order and welfare. Effectiveness of county administration, however, did not rest simply on its own operations. The powers of the magistrate, a civil official assigned from outside, were reinforced by a system of local social and economic power in which local land-holding gentry sought to secure their interests.

The orbit of the gentry reached to the county capital, but tended in the main to connect through a series of social pathways that ran to the basic "standard marketing towns" (later urban centres of the enlarged townships or *da xiang* in the 1950s).[6] The local market towns were common crossroads for members of all rural strata and special meeting places for the gentry.[7] The gentry helped to arrange large-scale water control projects, public (and private) defence and relief, and local elites generally held the reins (with regional variations) of clan-based social networks that cut vertically through class divisions. By these civic and social webs of affiliation and control, the labour and loyalty of ordinary peasant producers were harnessed by rural elites.

Peasant village communities were not highly autonomous, nor were poor peasants easily unified. There were no significant common village land-holdings or other public goods for example, and as private small-holders or tenants, peasants could not easily affiliate on a class basis. To be successful, then, peasant movements needed the adherence of portions of the local gentry and other mobile or lumpen classes, the suspension of local authority structures, or the protection of an outside armed force. It was the structural position of the peasantry in rural society which Mao[8] was trying to describe when, on the basis of his investigations in Hunan province in 1926-27, he wrote:

> A man in China is usually subjected to the domination of three systems of authority: (1) the state system (political authority), ranging from the national, provincial and county government down to that of the township; (2) the clan system (clan authority), ranging from the central ancestral temple and its branch temples down to the head of the household; and (3) the supernatural system (religious authority), ranging from the King of Hell down to the town and village gods belonging to the nether world, and from the Emperor of Heaven down to all the various gods and spirits belonging to the celestial world. As for women, in addition to being dominated by these three systems of authority, they are also dominated by the men (the authority of the husband). These four authorities — political, clan, religious and masculine — are the embodiment of the whole feudal-patriarchal system and ideology, and are the four thick ropes binding the Chinese people, particularly the peasants.

Attacking these hegemonic networks during long years of the protracted rural revolutionary struggle, the Communist Party managed to replace customary rural authorities at the county level and below with its own offices and armed power. This provided the basis for fundamental restructuring of rural society and economy, the destruction of the landed gentry as a class and a political power, and their replacement by a more egalitarian division of landed property and other agricultural assets as well as a structure of class-based peasant power. After land reform, a series of collectivisation measures led within a decade to the formation of a large, integrating unit of rural collective economy and government, the people's commune.

The county after collectivisation

During the Chinese Revolution, both before and after 1949, the county continued to be a major unit of political and administrative control in Chinese rural society. The Communist Party supervised land reform from the county and its subunits. County government became thoroughly bound up in rapid successions of economic development strategies linked to societal transformation. The relation of specific institutional arrangements and development programme has been a subject of great interest.[9]

After much cogitation and experimentation with the scope and composition of units of rural government and collective ownership,[10] the people's commune settled down by 1961 to around the size of the former enlarged township,[11] the county remaining entirely a unit of the State. The commune, which incorporated the former township government, remains *partly* a unit of state administration. Its highest ranking (i.e., commune-*level*) officials are civil servants appointed, ranked, and paid by the *state*. But the commune-level administration is at the same time the highest of a three-tiered system of *collective* rural ownership. Thus, though commune-level administration carries out many normal governmental functions such as financial administration, local marketing, management of schools and medical facilities, and local militia defence, its economic base is juridically and practically rooted in local society. The brigades and teams which comprise the commune as a whole are hamlet- or village-level collectives, and even industrial and sideline enterprises operated by the commune-level are treated as collective rather than state-run units in terms of management and finance (although, for reasons which remain mysterious to us, for *statistical* purposes they are grouped with state-run enterprises of all types at the county level and above). In the socialist vocabulary, the persistence of the commune system signifies the continued existence of collective ownership rather than, as in the case of industry, a higher stage in the march toward communist society of "ownership by the whole people." Thus, the great bulk of the rural economy is organised within tiered units of collective ownership, whose workers — the Chinese peasants — are, significantly, called "members" (*sheyuan*) in ordinary language as well as official usage, and are, especially at the team level, more like coequal shareholders than employees. The "wage" (i.e., the work-day value) of the members of a rural collective, unlike that of workers in state enterprises owned by the "whole people," varies much more directly with the rise or fall of collective profits.

If the commune, despite its partial state character and many governmental functions (taken over from the former township), is in economic terms essentially an aggregation of local village collectives, the county, though small enough to have regular, immediate communications with basic levels, is entirely a unit of the state. The county contains both government and Party offices, but these have been for practical purposes combined under the principle of "unified leadership by the Communist Party," (though this may become subject to change now). This means that the Party organisation has been dominant in all decision-making at county level.

Because the county leadership is expected by higher level policy-makers to show results in programme implementation that depend on its direct leadership within the local arena, the county has the burden of establishing an effective connection between itself and the collective institutions rooted in society. Higher-level bodies like the province and its intermediary co-ordinating level of leadership, the prefecture, do not have to make such a connection. Thus, as with the county of Imperial China, the contemporary problem for the county's role in development administration is set by its location at the most sharply defined structural meeting point between institutions of state and society. (We are aware that there is always some ambiguity to this formulation because of the mixed character of the people's commune as well as the significant institution of Communist Party [hence, "state"] power at the brigade level. This paper does not explore the commune as such, but evidence suggests that though the commune may at times play the role of purely implementing state-sponsored programmes to lower levels of local society, its collective economic character imparts a strong societal component as well and subjects it to strong influences from basic-level interests.[1,2]

The county is the major political centre at the basic levels of rural society. As the heart of the Communist Party organisation in the countryside, the county has been responsible for leading special movements toward far-reaching reforms, for medium-scale planning and project management, and for supervising routine agricultural activities carried out by the collectives. The county Party committee is in charge of overseeing the careers, education and activities of Party members and cadres at the Grassroots who, though locally rooted farmers, villagers and neighbours, are linked through Party membership to observe central discipline and view the revolution as a whole. The pre-eminence of the Party in all spheres of rural government and of the county within the rural local Party organisation, has seemed to distinguish the county as the most prominent locus of political power or authority in the countryside. This has made it a particular object of dismay of some analysts (including, it would appear, many in China) who regard a superordinate political orientation as an irrational displacement of what would be a more useful emphasis on purely administrative or technical matters and market forces.[13]

The county as a unit of state government has a series of administrative technical bureaux (*jü*) and sub-bureaux (*Ke*, or "sections") for dealing with subject matter ranging from agrarian science and technology to finance and trade, and important technical staff offices within the county executive itself. The counties are in charge of making available to lower-level economic producing units resources allocated from the greater economy.[14]

Students of Chinese development administration have wondered about the degree to which the county enjoys autonomy within its sphere of operations. Of course county cadres are subject to supervision from higher authorities both in policy matters and in career terms. Top county officials are apparently ranked in the State civil service according to the size and economic strength of the county.[15] Falkenheim tends to argue that province-level authorities make decisions and county leaders carry them out. The county cannot on the whole be understood as a unit expressing local (in our terms, societal) interest.[16] The degree of autonomy of the county may depend on the issue. Major campaigns based on central policy decisions or special economic efforts such as agricultural mechanisation depend considerably on orders and inputs from above.[17] For example, according to one former county official:

> In 1971 [our] county set up electrical industries, producing motors and transformers, as well as radio components. The county didn't really push this, but the province had called on every county to get into production of electrical items, so we did a little. So no, it wasn't the county's idea to go into production of electrical items; but given that the province called on them to do so, it was their idea to produce the transformers of which we couldn't get enough through unified distribution.[18]

In this case the county followed a production decision order from above, at the same time serving its own need for materials that could not be acquired from outside.

The activities of the county in the local development arena indeed reflect the degree to which county leaders act as down-the-line administrators of central policies to the broad society. In his very useful treatment of pre-Cultural Revolution politics, Ahn discusses Chinese criticism of the county for functioning mainly as a "conveying centre" of tasks set at higher levels to the collective sector. In turn, the county leaders spent much time reporting to provincial/prefectural supervisors on the implementation of their orders. According to one report, leading cadres of YingKou County in Liaoning Province spent two-thirds of their time conferring at the provincial or prefectural levels.

One particularly explicit self-criticism published in the *People's Daily* in 1965 states:

> The [county] committee also discussed the problems of what were called "hard" and "soft" tasks. A "hard" task refers to a task which is required to attain certain targets as set by the leading organ at a higher level, while a "soft" task refers to the task originating from the demand of the peasant masses . . . Formerly, two different attitudes were adopted toward these two tasks. The "hard" task was firmly fulfilled, while the "soft" task might be fulfilled or left unfulfilled.[20]

In contrast, the strongest case made for county autonomy, rooted in what she sees as a growing material base of near autarky, was made by Audrey Donnithorne, describing the possibility of a "cellular economy" at county level.[21]

There is no question but that the weight and complexity of county government, the size of the rural economy partly under its purview by virtue of the dramatic growth of rural industry, and the possible lines of intervention in the collective sector available to it all give the county a continuing, if not increased position in Chinese rural development today. Yet, even this statement must be qualified in light of current adjustments. For example, one may point to the overall growth of both state owned industry located or directly managed at the county, as well as commune and brigade-run industry within the collective sector, and under the supervision of a branch of the county government (the county Second Light Industry Bureau in one county we have studied in depth),[22] as evidence of the growing weight of a diversified county-level economic establishment. But recent changes in state policy also suggest that from the county's point of view some of the more autonomous aspects of such development of industry at and below the county level may be disappearing. For example, in Hebei Province's Shulu County, various forms of collective or "county-run collective enterprises" (not speaking of those strictly within the people's commune sector) had at least until 1979 contributed some of their profits to the use of vertically organised bureaus (such as the Second Light Industry Bureau) or to an "extra-budgetary fund" outside the purview of the higher-level state fiscal and planning authorities. Such income had been used primarily upon the decision of county government authorities to invest in industry or agricultural support projects. A major water-control project affecting the land of ten communes was thus undertaken in 1977-78 using several million yuan from an "extra-budgetary fund". Such unattached monies had been important because many counties (apparently at least the better-off ones) tend to contribute a larger sum in industrial and other income from taxes and profits transferred to provincial and higher authorities than they get back as funds designated for expenditures by the county government in the comprehensive state budgetary process. But in interviews in 1979, Shijiazhuang prefecture officials outlined new reforms which would have the effect of bringing these untied monies under prefectural control. In reference to this point, we note that although there is also a broad tendency under way to try to leave more profits as retained income in the hands of local level enterprises, this decentralising move may also take away from the power of county officials. This shift, started experimentally in Sichuan under now Prime Minister Zhao Ziyang, is now being generalised. But in this change, though enterprise autonomy in the locality may benefit considerably, the powers granted to factories are essentially opposed to those that might otherwise be enjoyed by local *state* authorities at county level. So, the shift of control over some sources of productive income may be up to higher levels or down to the enterprise, the latter a structural move resembling what Schurmann called Decentralisation I.

Also, current attempts within the industrial sector to rationalise and standardise production of machinery, including in particular agricultural machines, suggest that production initiatives undertaken at county level in a blaze of publicity in the 1970s may shift to more centralised operations. The recent attack on Xiyang County for the economic failure and continuing "cover-up" of the true facts in relation to its hand tractor factory may in part be related to political attacks against the post-Cultural Revolution leadership of the model county and Jinzhong prefecture. But we found examples of similar critiques and moves toward specialisation, rationalisation and centralisation in farm machinery manufacture in both Hebei and Hiangsu provinces.[23] In some cases, commune and brigade enterprises were being integrated into county machinery enterprises as parts subcontractors; in others, independent manufacturing efforts (of tractors, for example) were being closed down or closely supervised for specifications, and plants integrated as subsidiary specialised manufacturing sites for centralised enterprises which design and supply farm machinery (more cheaply and efficiently it is stated) to a wider region.

Moreover, in terms of budgetary and other financial relations with the province and the centre, the county is scarcely autonomous. Here we see a process in which the county government collects revenues according to quotas set by the higher levels of the state and makes expenditures only in categories and amounts fixed and allocated by those same higher levels. It undercollects or overspends only at the peril of incurring financial penalties.[24] As mentioned above, untied sources of funds seem to be disappearing under current policies. In addition, though the industrial base at the county level has grown considerably, the profits on the whole have flowed upward into higher level state coffers. (The most recent third session of the Fifth National People's Congress has announced its intention, unclear in precise form as yet, to reform this system by requiring state-run enterprises to remit only taxes, but not profits, to the higher levels of the state.) The quality of county administration may be important in helping along an ever more important county and commune industrial base, but such responsibility does not necessarily constitute a case for growing autonomy; as we have suggested, the apparent direction at present seems to be toward enveloping the county in an increasingly interdependent set of relationships rooted in a more complex, widely integrated structure of industrial planning and production.

The County as Focal Point of Development

All issues surrounding the relation of county to society and to upper levels of the State appeared weightier in the fall of 1975 when a month-long conference convened first in Xiyang County, Shanxi Province and then in Beijing attempted to focus future Chinese agricultural development around a specific county model. The major thrust of this conference was to focus the endeavours of lower-level collective units in an increasingly county-centred development effort linked with a comprehensive national effort to increase levels of rural mechanisation. The movement to build so-called "Dazhai-type counties," based on the phenomenal growth of Xiyang county, the home of the national model Dazhai brigade and the first county dubbed "Dazhai-type," dated on a national level from the North China Agricultural Conference of 1970. But never before had it been so highly elaborated and specific criteria grouped together and made so explicit.

It should be noted that Chairman Hua Guofeng's speech at the 1975 conference placed a concurrent emphasis on the "great task of mechanising agriculture" to be accomplished in the main under the impetus of national (and provincial) authorities. But, agricultural mechanisation was to be related to the further stimulation of local industrialisation and the growth of brigade and commune-run enterprises, while also being furthered by increased investments from within the collectives of labour and other resources in farmland capital construction and infrastructural development.[25]

In his address, Hua projected that by 1980, at least one-third of all counties in China should be "Dazhai-type." What was a Dazhai-type county? Hua listed six criteria:

1) A county Party committee leadership core that firmly grasps the Party's line and policy and is united in struggle.
2) Established the dominant class power of the poor and lower middle class peasants, able to struggle resolutely against bourgeois activities and to exercise effective supervision and reform measures over class enemies.
3) Cadres at the three levels of county commune, and brigade who like Xiyang cadres persevere in participating in collective production labour.
4) Rapid development and sizeable results in basic farm field construction, agricultural mechanisation, and scientific cultivation.
5) Collective economies expanding uninterruptedly, and in which production and income of poor communes and brigades attain or surpass those of middle-level communes and brigades in the locality.
6) An all-around development of agriculture, forestry, animal husbandry, sideline industries, and fisheries, a great increase in productive output insuring a big contribution to the State and, for commune members, a step-by-step improvement in standard of living.

Xiyang County, in Shanxi Province's mountainous Taihang region, suffered from a short growing season, water conservancy problems and a shortage of arable land. From the fall of 1970, the Xiyang success story was promoted in China as an inspiration to rural development in all areas in the country, rich or poor. The message appears in another wave of media publicity in Spring 1973, and there is reason to believe that the elements identified with the Dazhai-Xiyang experience, especially since 1967, were given very high priority in development policy throughout these years, in central pronouncements at least, and in varying degrees in various localities.[26]

Of Hua's six criteria, two concern the role of leadership, perhaps as a way of emulating Dazhai Brigade's own experience of a long-tenured, vigorous leadership "core" (i.e., Party branch committee) dedicated to unity and continuity.[27] In a late 1973 report to a meeting held jointly by the Ministry of Agriculture and Forestry and the CCP Beijing Municipal Committee, Chen Yonggui stressed the importance of local leadership most strongly, arguing that there is a link between active leadership and maintaining the "relative stability of the work force" — the latter a key substantive goal of the 1975 programme.[28]

Though in 1980 the Dazhai-Xiyang programme begins to be linked with "ultra-left" political and economic policies identified with the Cultural Revolution, the actual criteria enunciated by Hua and other leaders suggest a critique or at least a modification of some significant such elements. For example, emphasis on the unity of the county Party committee leadership core (i.e., its standing committee) suggests the need to promote strong political direction while guarding against factionalism, a negative legacy of Cultural Revolution politics. In addition, the growing scope of county functions, in particular responsibility for rural industrialisation, also suggests this concern for insuring effective executive power in the county.[29]

A second leadership criterion (actually third on Hua's list) calling for heavy participation in collective productive labour by county, commune and brigade cadres seemed to strike at bureaucratic elitism and the separation of the local cadres from the everyday toil of the peasants. The model Xiyang leadership had in 1967 established guidelines for such participation: 100 days per year for county cadres, 200 for commune cadres, and 300 for brigade cadres.[30] As Hua emphasised, the experience might help county leaders to deal with their inadequacies. Some county Party committee leaderships suffer from "softness," "lack of concentration," and "laziness" ("*ruan*," "*san*," and "*lan*"), said Hua. In his address Hua also stated that new blood should be recruited into county Party leaderships from among basic-level activists distinguished in the movement to learn from Dazhai. These would most likely be brigade cadres — who head the most dynamic unit within the commune structure. For example, Li Xishen, the county vice-secretary and *de facto* leader of Xiyang County until his dismissal in 1980, was recruited from a local brigade (Wujiaping); and Li Suoshou, the first secretary of neighbouring Pingding County, was formerly Party branch secretary of Nannao Brigade in Dazhai Commune. In general, however, other evidence, both from interviews with emigres and with Chinese officials in 1979, do not suggest widespread existence of this recruitment/promotion pattern in the years following. It is now regarded, in fact, as a version of the Cultural Revolution practice of officials rising too precipitously, in a Chinese analogy, like helicopters.[31]

Hua's second criterion argues for the "dominant class power of the poor and lower middle class peasants, able to struggle resolutely against bourgeois activities and to exercise effective supervision over class enemies." This appears to point to insuring support for the growth of collective economic institutions and adherence to them as a main source of accumulation and income distribution. With an economy that still relies on manual labour, and major investments to be made in land improvement and water conservancy (to provide a field for efficient introduction of machinery and modern inputs), the most crucial of all goals was to maintain full commitment by a stable, collectively-organised agricultural work force. Hua stated:

> For example, we must pull back labour power which has left the area to engage in individual endeavours, organise dispersed individual craft workers, return to the collective wasteland or private plots cultivated in excess of amounts stipulated by government policy, and straighten out tendencies to neglect accumulation by distributing all and consuming all.

But why the strong *class*-oriented guideline? Here the programme veers to the left and raises, as we shall see, the terms of a very questionable analysis.

The recall or control of labour outflow is obviously not a cure-all in every type of rural environment in China, although it is held to have been crucial in the experiences of Dazhai and Xiyang themselves.[32] For example, it was argued by one former county-level official interviewed in Hong Kong that in parts of Guangdong which had better conditions and/or higher labour density, recalling labour from extra-agricultural pursuits really did not bring much improvement in agriculture — in fact, it could lead to serious losses in both private *and* collective income. Nonetheless, in those areas recall of labour power was strongly emphasized by county leadership, apparently in an over rigid way. Particularly in areas where peasant culture remains strongly wedded to private as opposed to collective sources of income, an unbending insistence on carrying out such restrictive measures could have a negative effect.

Hua also stressed the need for major improvements in the productive base and the means for exploiting it, to provide a material basis for social/political goals expressed in the model. Obviously material and technical capacity and not just inspired leadership were needed.[33] He specifically called for diversification in agricultural production and enterprises, and linked this with both public accumulation and improvement in the standard of living for individual peasants, points strongly emphasised in present policies as well. It is notable that this document does not, at least on its face, signify a "grain-first" policy now so vigorously criticised. Improvements in the agrarian base, technology, and diversity of production should be associated with increasing economic equality among lower-level collective units. This may appear to be a leftist goal; but as Nicholas Lardy[34] has recently suggested, the present policies encouraging specialisation, so closely associated with a more "moderate" leadership programme also embody an economic logic and perhaps a felt commitment to increased equality among units, localities or regions, as places which suffered economic losses over many years due to policies emphasising grain production can now realise greater prosperity through production of higher-priced commodities to which their natural and human conditions are more suited.

Farmland capital construction and water conservancy projects are immense enterprises in China. They are seen as bases for securing stable yields and for making it possible to apply mechanical means to agricultural production efficiently to gain output justifying their use. Farm capital construction, costly as it is to collective budgets and the private endeavours or leisure-time of peasants, can be a long-term endeavour at any level of collective organisation. Its most successful development seems to come when county leaderships can on the one hand mobilise the basic-level units to contribute labour to individual projects, and on the other, organise special county-sponsored teams and equipment to implement major projects. Depending on how they are financed, such county-centred capital construction projects may have a redistributive effect among as well as within the local collective units — both because the benefits of county sponsored projects may go to poorer units or because the county may hire extra workers from poorer units at higher return to their home collective to take part in large-scale projects. Certainly the optimal effort in long-term capital improvement to the agrarian economy is a major part of present agricultural development programmes, and no unit below (or above) the county level really has equivalent ability of the county's to mobilise, direct, and guarantee support, including financial, for such work.[35]

The criterion that calls for equalisation of poor collectives within the county in both production and income points to an enormous problem and helps to understand better the strategic emphasis placed on the county in 1975 (as well as some of the great difficulties in this strategy). It has been frequently noted that even if collectivisation enables China to narrow individual income gaps within collectives, there is no guarantee against polarisation among collective units. The persistence or increase of inequality among collectives militates against enlargement of the collective unit and may be a source of discontent and setbacks to socialist goals. Why was the county chosen to solve the problem of inequality among collective units?

First, the county is a source of funds and material inputs that can be used to help promote equality among units. This is not so much in terms of direct subsidy but in terms of promoting a capacity for growth in selected units. Pairault[36] points to evidence of significant use of county funds to improve the productive capabilities of poorer units in Xiyang County. In Xiyang 80 per cent of the county budget was allocated to agricultural investment in 1976, and the county secured some 17 per cent of the total cost of basic farmland construction and water conservancy from the state.[32] The example of a large water conservancy project in Shulu County has already been mentioned. Communes do use funds accumulated at the commune level, especially from commune enterprises, for internal redistribution in the form of projects or assistance designed to strengthen the economic performance of poorer brigades and teams.[37] But without strong county leadership they are not likely to contribute in any way outside their own jurisdictions.

Second, as Communist Party centre, the county is best able to translate into practice overall policy intended to transform socio-economic relations. At the basic levels the brigade Party branch is an equivalently strong Party organisation, and it is arguable that dynamic brigade party leadership in conjunction with the county Party committee are most likely to implement equalisation programmes.[38] The brigade is most suited to organise its economic and human resources to make maximum use of new opportunities presented, and the county is best able to maximise and direct new resources to where they can be best used.

Here the commune is in a more difficult position than the county: because it is rooted partly in local society, and because it is a collective unit responsible solely for its own affairs rather than a unit of the state, it is more subject to conservative or cautious local impulses in the face of risky programme — yet it lacks the direct economic power and opportunities for long-term, face-to-face, neighbour or near-neighbour relations with the peasants and their grassroots leaders in the production teams that brigade leaders can have. At the same time, insofar as trust and identification with lower levels is concerned, the commune is "tainted" with the identity of the State for members of rural society suspicious of statist designs, yet it lacks the concentrated political organisation and awesomeness of the county not to mention its access to valuable material and technical resources.[39]

The County in Development — Strategic Factors and Implicit Political Programme

In summary, we would like to specify three important factors in the heretofore prominent role of the county in Chinese rural development programmes. The first is the structural characteristics of the county located just above the junction of State and society. An entirely state unit, the county can be knowledgeable about and in direct contact with daily affairs at the production levels of society. Cadres' participation in labour and supervision of all Party members in rural society provide avenues of contact. Low enough to have direct contact with leading grassroots cadres of local communities, county officials at the same time have bureaucratic ties and obligations to higher levels of the state, and there the factor of direct, face-to-face contact exists as well. Commune cadres do not have those contacts, whereas leading county cadres frequently attend enlarged national-level Party/government meetings.

A second major factor is that counties have increasingly become industrial entrepreneurs or managers. Industry is both intended as a direct producer for agricultural needs and a consumer of agricultural raw materials. At the same time, it produces county revenue and employs peasants. Aside from making the county government larger and more complex and bringing the county into closer relation with the urban/industrial sector, the development of rural small-scale industry gives the county increased resources with which to affect the economic lives of rural residents-*cum*-members of the people's communes. The development of rural small-scale industry increases the ability of the county to play a redistributive role in relation to the production and incomes of lower-level collective units. It is likely that more balanced demand for the products of county industry increase the ability to plan for more uniform production and distribution of certain products.

Along with rural industrialisation at the county level, major aspects of farmland capital construction, water conservancy, and other infrastructural developments as well as scientific and technological research and extension can only be carried out with county leadership and sponsorship. The enlargement and *planned* development of these programmes which, with agricultural mechanisation, will provide the effective material basis of rural modernisation, should make possible much more balanced and efficient application of labour in the rural sector. Making best use of labour in the rural setting, co-ordinating labour-saving improvements and seasonal labour surpluses with new labour-utilising projects will be of major value in Chinese economic development.[40]

The position of the county in a state-society nexus, and the increasing resources and complexity of the county economy due to rural industrialisation and other large-scale projects are linked to a final factor: the quality and political character of leadership capacities vested at the county level. County leadership is placed and equipped to promote far-reaching, collectively-based, and redistributive economic development projects. Pairault notes that the movement to learn from Dazhai (the "self-reliant" brigade) became in the Dazhai-type county movement in actuality an "interventionist politics" designed to offer active assistance to backward units.[41] The characterisation is apt, but as Pairault himself suggests, it would not be a politics of charity, but a programme intended to supply aid that will be of utmost utility precisely because it goes to those who by receiving it are most able to help themselves. The possibility of such a process demonstrated in Xiyang County generated maximum effort from its constituent collective units by making strategic investments of both its leadership resources and growing stock of material goods and money. Whether or not this was possible partly because of large outside investments of state aid in the 1970s, as is now alleged by Xiyang's critics in China and out, remains to be investigated further. But it does appear that county leadership was especially valuable in carrying out massive land reconstruction and water conservancy projects, but it also intervened at times to provide material back-up support simply to get communities through hard times and bolster *collective* morale. Such policies in turn made it more possible to carry out the overall goal of stabilising the collective agricultural work force at the highest possible level.[42]

The promise of a county-focused development plan was to make it possible to link, by active, co-ordinative leadership, all collective units with potential energy and initiative to supplies of local or external resources that could boost them to a level where collective efforts begin to pay off. On a broad and flexible scale within a county, especially in line with a growing county industrial system, such a strategy would be likely to pay off in balanced and resilient patterns of growth. Some coaches like a "deep bench."

We believe that what the Dazhai-type county development programme involved most clearly was the extension of political and material incentives to local cadres, especially those at the brigade level, to assess local problems and potentials and formulate plans by which to achieve significant growth, given the back-up and support, both in planning and material terms, that can be offered by the county. In essence, the Dazhai-type county programme called for entrepreneurial linkages between the collectives, that is, the communes and brigades, and the primary agent of the state (county), oriented toward both growth and redistribution of development capabilities. In this programme, both county and collectives commit themselves to a collectivist pattern of development that relies on activist political leadership within given institutional forms to provide the major dynamic force for incorporating increasingly available material inputs in a successful pattern of economic growth.

As Marianne Bastid has written:

> Since the Cultural Revolution, the authority and responsibilities of the county level are going through a revival which reminds one of the administrative pattern in imperial times, though its basis is different.[43]

The net effect of the approach to rural development enunciated in the 1975 National Conference on Learning from Dazhai in Agriculture was to place a very great stress on the political factor. This was because of the redistributive character of the overall criteria for economic success and because of the relative inclination toward self-reliance as the basis for receiving further outside aid. Given the continuous growth of a diversified local rural economy, especially its industrial sector, it is hard to imagine any Chinese rural development policy that would not give a place of some importance to the role of functional leadership by county agencies. But a redistributive growth policy based on integrated planning for the county as a whole and requiring mutual, perhaps sacrificing contributions by collective units requires a high degree of political and ideological commitment, especially if grandiose, labour-intensive projects are tried, if the starting point of the various collectives is relatively unequal, and if the level of outside aid available (and of farm commodity prices) is not high. All the political tension inherent here would be intensified to the extent that recognition as being a successful unit eligible for aid is subject to political wheeling and dealing, exercise of favouritism, factionalism, etc. Undoubtedly, the policy strengthened an emphasis on the role of political authorities and factors — on the county Party committee, its allies within the collective leaderships and supporters at prefecture and province, and the fighting slogans associated with class struggle that gave such leadership its putative legitimacy. Their powers would be particularly strong because of the structure of the Chinese state at the time, the unified leadership exercised by the Party over government affairs and the personal weight of Party bureaucrats in relation to the individual lives and careers of Party members at the grass roots. We believe that it is partly this highly demanding, if not loaded political requirement for the Dazhai-type county programme, as well as possible economic insufficiencies it entailed, that contributed to its dismantling at the end of the decade.

Recent Policy Shifts: Implications for the County Role

The passage from Bastid, recalling the role of the county in imperial administration, suggests that this is where we came in and it is time to go. But Chinese politics in recent years has refused to allow research to end where it is meant to and scholarly pronouncements to be finished. For some time after the replacement of leadership following the death of Mao Zedung, it appeared that agrarian policies associated with CCP head Hua Guofeng's 1975 Dazhai Conference address would remain effective. But at the turn of the 1980s, a series of growing shifts in rural policies suggest that the quantity of minor changes are turning into a qualitative shift of major dimensions. Another type of strategy may be seen in the process of adoption (or revival, under changed conditions). Hence, we may now perceive and contrast within the past few years two types of directions available for rural development.

As has been evident in increasingly blatant self-critical statements by Chinese leaders (though usually even more critical of their predecessors), growth in Chinese agriculture, for as long as several decades, is seen to have been seriously deficient. In line with such massive criticism, a series of policy changes have been announced. Most dramatically from our point of view, the salience of political leadership and overt political desiderata in rural economy has been diminished in relation to the role of economic forces worked out through attention to market relations and strengthening of the economic institutions that make such relations possible.[44] The rehabilitation of long-silenced "revisionist" economist Sun Yefang and publication of his economic writings as well as the prominent role of Xue Muquiao is a very important indication of this change. The basic tenor of present policy critiques is to insist that the best indication of good leadership is the extent to which leaders are able to grasp and follow "economic laws"; this is the philosophical core of contemporary Chinese pragmatism. Severe criticism has been levelled at all practices that smack of using administrative methods ("handing down orders") to substitute for indigenous motivation calculated according to economic advantage. In institutional terms, the autonomy of the team has guaranteed protection as never before — this, obviously, in contradistinction to the ambitions of brigade leaders to "level-up". The team is to have maximum control of its production plan without interference from upper levels, and it is to have the right to increase attempts to gain income from a variety of sources. Overemphasising grain production as a key to capital accumulation in collectives is warned against. In some instances, perhaps even in terms of broad regional specialisation, cash-crop production, fruits and nuts, timber, animal husbandry, and sideline industry may legitimately serve as the principal sources of collective income. Teams *and* individual households are encouraged, simply put, to get rich. Editorials characterise earlier programmes as having started from the premise that to be poor is good. A variety of privately-oriented practices such as household sidelines, private plot production, and petty-trading on rural free markets are at a minimum to be protected, and in effect encouraged. So long as economic management does not devolve entirely to the household level, authority in teams may be allocated to smaller work groups. Finally, several recent articles indicating direct criticisms of Xiyang county "ultra-left practices," their leadership and institutions, add to the urgency and political weight of the policy shifts.[45]

A major shift is to make clearcut planning distinctions between policies for different areas. Some will be handled as "commodity grain bases" or "industrial crop bases." The actual administrative content of this programme remains elusive even in discussions with Chinese planners,[46] and the policy itself may be formative, subject to change, or even fleeting in existence. It appears that these base areas will receive special allocations of modern producer inputs. While it is generally felt among Western observers that such regions will be selected on the basis of an established record of high production and prosperity, Nicholas Lardy[34] reminds us that some of these grain base regions "lack adequate water resources and consequently now achieve relatively low per unit grain yields." Be that as it may, a recent editorial states explicitly that the benefits of agricultural mechanisation cannot, as was suggested in the 1975 programme, be achieved for all units across the board. Certain regions, localities and units will be targeted for maximum available supplies of agricultural machinery or subsidised investments for their production, while in others semi-mechanisation or manual labour will continue to be the main basis for agricultural production for some time to come. And these areas may have to depend for their advancement on a much more completely self-reliant policy in capital accumulation.[47]

Related to this, it is likely that in poor areas in general there will be less emphasis on farm capital construction and grain production and more on the development of subsidary sidelines, special industries, and other income producing measures. There may even be an increasing willingness to tolerate the outflow of labour as an income maintenance measure for poorer households or units.[48] Criticism of past policy as being directed against the economic demands and motives of the peasantry, as being overly redistributive in nature, and ignoring the necessity of "economic laws," suggests that market relations organised on a freer basis will become much more important in rural economy. Obviously, the Chinese leadership at present argues that despite some success stories of full-blown collective commitment to "common prosperity" (rising together), by and large peasants have been demoralised by overemphasis on collective accumulation and need to be released to follow their economic noses. This will be in harmony with a policy that no longer stresses self-sufficiency in grain production, that allows for local and regional specialisation from the point of view, presumably, of comparative advantage, and by implication, calls for an expansion of exchange among areas to make up for local deficiencies.[49]

What will happen to the county as focal point for development? All evidence points to a lowering of its sights and a reduction of its power, especially to combine economic growth policies with specific socio-economic and political goals. The stress on free play of economic forces as opposed to political leadership in development is a key indication of this. The criticism of redistributive measures as dangerously blunting the "socialist enthusiasm" of the peasants is likely to see a weakened significance for the critical relationship in the Xiyang strategy between county political centres and activist commune and brigade leaderships, especially the latter. In all likelihood, state functional bureaucracies and planning agencies on the one hand and individual households on the other will also become more prominent in economic decision-making, and in general quite busy with the continued elaboration of technical innovation, greater flexibility in cropping, and changes wrought by the third session of the Fifth NPC in fiscal and financial powers of local producers and government agencies. For example, in a 1978 comment on the relation between present agricultural development plans and the

1975 Dazhai-type county "package of policies", Dernberger and Fasenfest argue that while political-institutional elements of the programme, such as emphasis on brigade decision-making in collective activities and associated "more radical aspects" of the campaign were removed, rural material investment aspects of the programme were not. They mention specifically farmland capital construction, water conservancy, changes in cropping patterns, rural small-scale industries, increasing application of technical innovations, and various forms of agricultural mechanisation including wider electrification which are all to remain.[50] It would seem that given the dimensions of these projects and the already significant accumulation of industrial investment at county levels, a major role for county government will remain in any event.

Of all questions raised by the appearance in rapid succession of two contrasting rural development strategies in the past five years, the most provocative may concern *the interests of the societal groups potentially served by each.* Since this question, and the framework of our study and of this volume, suggest consideration of the interrelationship of societal interests and state structures, we turn for inspiration to Franz Schurmann's perceptive work on the Chinese policy debates of the 1956-57 period over alternative plans for decentralisation. In his analysis, Schurmann explicitly connected arguments about political and administrative organisation *vis-à-vis* state leadership of economic activity and the impact of alternative policy outcomes on differentiated societal interests and resulting conflict.

In that debate, Schurmann argued, two identifiable sets of advocates within the Communist Party promoted two varying strategies for decentralisation of economic leadership. Schurmann tied "Decentralisation I" to Chen Yun, a long-time Communist Party leader active in economic policy-making and considered to be "conservative" in his advocacy of less mobilisation and more reliance on market forces and material incentives, smaller collectives, and less emphasis on massive heavy industry. "Decentralisation I" called for a maximum degree of decision-making power to be vested in the hands of producing units. Schurmann argued (p.198) that "Putting decision-making power into the hands of producing units also meant creating external conditions for the autonomous exercise of such power, namely some form of market conditions." The emphasis on markets and more direct material incentives is, in Schurmann's view (p. 198), associated with a more liberal class policy and "the growth of free-market tendencies [which] would have reduced the powers of regional administration to direct the economy in the area of their jurisdiction."

The alternative, "Decentralisation II," and the form adopted at the end of the debate, Schurmann associates (p. 196) with Mao, Liu and Deng. This called for placing of greater power in the "hands of lower-echelon administrative units," i.e., the provinces, prefectures, and counties. Decentralisation II is based on the principle of social mobilisation, co-ordinative rather than vertical forms of administration and control (emphasising strongly the role of the Communist Party organisation at the several regional jurisdictional levels), and in general, we would add, the prominence of political leadership and class-oriented collective institutions over market arrangements. In a brief observation which has enormous relevance to the present policy shifts, Schurmann notes (p. 199) that one reason behind the preference of the majority at that time for the second model of decentralisation was,

> ... the fact that the Agricultural Producers Cooperatives in 1957 were apparently again coming under the control of what was euphemistically called "prosperous middle peasants." Tolerance toward "prosperous" peasants in Communist China has generally gone together with economic relaxation and permissiveness toward the market. Since the "prosperous" peasants were less amenable to Party control, greater freedom for them inevitably meant less control by Party-dominated regional government over the peasantry. Social mobilisation, of course was intended to have the opposite effect. Thus both the *economic* consequences of decentralisation I and the *social* consequences of cooperatives dominated by "prosperous" peasants would have had significant *political* consequences.

Looking at the tentative outcome of major policy shifts more than two decades later, there appears at first glance a suggestion of parallel occurrences and parallel implications. The present policy that looks very much like a victory (finally!) for Decentralisation I may have been achieved by the shift or absorption of the advocacy of Deng Xiaoping and like-minded colleagues from the decentralised compromise of the centralists (i.e., Decentralisation II) with its heavy statist component to what for convenience sake may be called the Chen Yun or "economists" position.[51] Preliminary reports of the deliberations of the August-September 1980 National People's Congress evidence decentralisation both of central to local public authorities, but mainly and overwhelmingly, the placing of much more authority (and autonomous control of vital funds) in the hands of the managers of economic producing units.

Given this ultimate shift, should one carry over to today Schurmann's suggestion that the policy of Decentralisation I applied (in 1957) in the rural areas would have amounted to a change in relative class positions, favouring former advantaged rural classes or individual class members who survived land reform and early collectivisation? Would, in other words, there be implications of major proportions for the class structure of rural society during the present period of development? To the extent that Decentralisation I depends on a freeing up of private economic activities and market-oriented production planning, even today it may be argued that the prestige and relative importance of former middle-class peasants, prosperous "new" middle-class peasants who emerged right after land reform, and rich peasants and their children and allies in the villages (including some cadres) would be enhanced. Although individuals from all rural strata have in the past taken part in activities that in radical phases are labelled "spontaneous capitalist tendencies," the organisers and expeditors of such activities have tended in the early 1960s and, evidence suggests, is some places even by the mid-1970s to come from among the formerly more economically advanced or entrepreneurial strata or rural society.[52] The group that might lose out from this new policy mix will be those commune members whose income potential for one reason or another had been lower and had benefitted from county-localised redistributive growth, and, similarly, poorer units, or even counties or regions, who are not likely to have the same range of material goods and capital investment funds extended to them under the new policy as had been or would have been in the past by the Dazhai-type county approach. Whether or not greater opportunity and leverage given these people and units to participate in self-enriching sideline activities and specialised agricultural production will make up the difference is an open question.

In addition, the recent alteration of the class line in the countryside, and in most cases the dissolution of land reform-era categories in application to the present speaks to an even stronger analogy between Schurmann's interpretation of the class implications of Decentralisation I (and by implication Decentralisation II), and our view of the possible social significance of the eclipse of the county-centred, class-conflict oriented programme of the Dazhai-type county strategy. In a momentous historical judgement, the Communist Party decided in early 1979 to lift the last sanctions against former landlords and rich peasants who have since land reform been stigmatised as class enemies, been targets of frequent political campaigns in the countryside, and been subject to economic discrimination as well as limitations on their civil and political rights. The new policy has stated that the children of such people are to be treated from the outset as ordinary peasants and not saddled with their parents' labels.

However, such a carryover in implications for present class relations may be more apparent than real, or appropriate only in a partial or marginal way. In 1957, Deng Xiaoping endorsed Decentralisation II and the policies of rapid mobilisation and large collectives which were later embodied in the Great Leap Forward. His transparent invocation of the analogy of conflict of cats and rats to depict solutions to economic problems hitherto understood as embodying class struggles among human animals signified a strenuous renunciation of the earlier policy and a beginning of the abandonment by some veteran revolutionaries of the use of class labels from the 1940s to analyse contemporary economic relationships. It is true that in the present day we do see, even in economic terms, significant unevenness in the distribution of income and opportunity. But these seem related more fundamentally to differences among localities in the level of development of the productive and material base and of the specific branch of the economy than to class status as fixed in the land reform.

While some descendants of former elite classes may still be potentially the most powerful and energetic actors in service of individual advancement given the freedom and institutional channels to do so, as Schurmann argued about in the pre-Great-Leap debates,[53] there are manifold other sources of differentiation emerging with the growth of a modern Chinese economy: differences between urban and rural residence, industrial and agricultural employment, official or non-official position, household size and "hand-mouth ratio", as well as the significant differences among collective units, areas, and even whole regions in terms of material endowment. Of these, that involving the original type of class differentiation in the old rural society may be the least important. Thus, the recent decision to remove class discrimination against the remnants of old village elites may be more a recognition of reality and the need for ending an atavistic form of discrimination than a pandering to the interests of a group ready to seize the reins of economic ambition and leadership once markets and self-seeking may be loose once again in the Chinese countryside. It may also be an attempt to harness the economic skills and energies of some of the old economic elites and their children within a basically collective economic framework.

In this regard, we may now make several points in relation to the analytical basis of the Dazhai-Xiyang county emulation programme for rural development. First of all, the programme attempted to overcome inequalities arising from the new collective institutions and productive relations in socialist China. The most important and original part of the programme would seem to be that involving the desire to find ways of resolving inequalities among communes and units within them and, by means of the political and economic leadership of county authorities, making maximum use of local resources and competing with other counties for additional financial aid from higher levels of the state. At the same time, however, the political analysis and basis of legitimation of political power used to undergird this objective was that invoking the old language of rural class and class conflict, "poor and lower-middle-class peasants", etc., and their intended organisational surrogate in political terms, the county and collective Party committees. Although the 1975 programme was *not,* we believe, a creature of what has now become known as the ultra-left of the 1970s, its incidence as a policy and ideological statement to be used by a variety of political leaderships at the sub-provincial and county level may well have tended in the direction of implementing radical policies on a wholesale and militantly politicised basis as is now charged. Given the complexity of sources of inequality of economic position and power (in localities) in contemporary China, especially the very difficult ones of inter-unit and inter-regional inequality within the form of socialist collective ownership, the basing of a comprehensive programme on a class analysis that harks back to the old days of the Civil War and Land Reform may well, as Mao once warned, have been a basis for confusing enemies and friends.

What we may see, in this light, in the flight from "politics" to "pragmatism" is the continuing inability to find a socio-economic or class analysis appropriate to the Chinese situation at this historical juncture while at the same time adequate to orient both dynamic economic development programme and clearly socialist political leadership. In so far as the question of redistribution is concerned, the goal has arguably not been abandoned;[34] in light of the reorientation of policy toward local politics and the decentralisation of leadership, it has been reoriented in a very important structural way.

To illustrate this point by comparison, the kind of redistribution envisaged, apparently, in the "Dazhai-type county" strategy called for a high degree of redistributive growth within the local county milieu, based in the first instance of maximum generation of local resources based on the mobilisation of labour power and other capacities, supplemented by external funding to activist county leaderships and their subordinate units.[32] Today we see *another type* of redistributive policy being attempted, one more macro-economic in scope and dealing with different societal inequalities. Current criticisms, including those of the degree of state aid given to Xiyang County itself, suggest that self-reliance by the poor and continued growth by the better-off as parallel means toward growth with increased equality may both be illusory strategies in present-day China. Instead, policy makers are pursuing a programme that involves — at least for the immediate years — a large-scale redistribution of income mainly between urban and rural society and between industry and agriculture via across-the-board, massive rises in prices for agricultural commodities, especially for above-quota sales. This would certainly benefit all agricultural producers, but because of the 50 per cent bonus for above-quota sales of grain, the very biggest and most efficient producers would do the best. The poorer and less well endowed units or areas, therefore, would be left with the other branch of the policy: the ability to engage in specialised production of cash-crops or sidelines, go on the market individually or collectively, and the like. This set of approaches would seem to portend a reduced role for the county in economic redistribution.

Despite the present view that political leadership, collective incentives, and redistributive policies have acted as brakes on peasant enthusiasm, and therefore hindered, especially since 1958, the growth of productive forces and output in rural China, it may turn out that the rural population, and crucial members of rural society such as many brigade cadres, for example, are divided on this point. It could be that we are in for a period of conflict or compromise and even combination of elements from the two approaches. But it is possible also that relative movement from one to another will engender a new round of political conflict, with a different set of aggrieved rural actors. Whether county "leading cores" will slip back into a more relaxed administrative posture and tend to their tractor factories or take a more activist and "radical" (if the word still means anything) posture may depend both on the strength of inheritance of their "Dazhai spirit" and the relative economic capacities of their unit. Because of the scope and size of the economic base and functions of the county in 1979 as compared to 1956 or 1957, it may be less easy — or even less intended — than it would have been in 1956 to diminish the political weight of the county government had "Decentralisation I" been implemented at that time. If the present policies suggest that "Decentralisation I" is in the works today, it will run up at least against the accumulated economic endowments and increased functional responsibility of county government.

One point remains to be made. The extreme and sustained upheavals of the Cultural Revolution, continuing factional conflicts in Party and non-Party units, and uncertainties, setbacks, or uneven successes in economic development have led apparently to some degree of crisis of political legitimacy of the Chinese revolutionary state. Many of the steps taken by Chinese leaders since 1976 seem designed to deal with this crisis — tightening Party organisation, placing impediments in the path of more unregulated forms of dissent (such as the "four big freedoms") and seeking ways to involve members of the public and of various institutions of the social economy in regular, orderly procedures of representation, participation, and conflict resolution. Hence, for example, we may understand attempts to explore patterns of political participation by workers and staff members in industrial units as part of the search for an orderly democratic element in Chinese institutional practice. Similarly, despite the apparent downgrading of the political preeminence of county Party leaderships in overall economic decision-making, we note with interest the initiation of constitutional changes that call for direct elections to county legislative bodies.[54] Such activity may well have the cumulative effect of restoring and strengthening the popular legitimacy of county leadership institutions and therefore make it easier for the county to resume a more extensive role in integrating rural economic and social development policies should the intention arise; the structural preconditions are already in place.

II INDUSTRY AND TRADE

5

THE MANAGEMENT OF THE INDUSTRIAL ECONOMY: THE RETURN OF THE ECONOMISTS

Andrew Watson

Centre of Asian Studies, University of Adelaide, Australia

The profound re-examination of all aspects of economic policy that has taken place in China since the death of Mao Zedong has provided some fundamentally new perspectives on China's path of economic development. The emphasis on such issues as changing systems of ownership and distribution, revolutionary mobilisation, self-reliance and mass participation in economic decision-making, all of which became the hallmarks of China's developmental strategy during the Cultural Revolution, has disappeared. In its place, arguments have been advanced and evidence amassed to show either that the strategy was not working and counter-productive or that it was not being implemented in the way claimed. Whatever the merits of those arguments, the speed and extent of changes in economic policy since 1976 have clearly shown that, in as far as the previous strategy was implemented, it rested on very fragile foundations.

Discussion of economic policy in the post-Mao period has, by contrast, given primacy to questions of technological change, profitability of investment, productivity, the rate of growth of output, the role of economic incentives, and the use of "managed" market forces. Such considerations have not only led to the rejection of many of the policies of the 1960s and 1970s but also to a re-evaluation of the whole process of development in China since 1949.

Questions of principle related to such things as socialist planning, ownership and methods of economic administration that have remained relatively settled since the 1950s have come under close scrutiny. The result has been that some of the fundamental problems of development in China are no longer discussed solely within the framework of the centrally-planned Soviet model of the first five-year plan or the decentralised, mobilisation model of the Great Leap Forward and the Cultural Revolution. The way has been opened for wide-ranging discussion and experiment which is eclectic in nature and profoundly pragmatic in orientation.

Once the basic system of ownership is changed, so the argument runs, the true measure of correct policy is whether or not it raises output and living standards, realises the law of value (defined to mean that commodity values are determined according to the socially necessary labour-time required to produce them, including both living labour and "dead" labour or capital), increases profitability per unit of labour or per unit of capital, and leads to technological modernisation. Development thus becomes essentially a question of the technical efficiency of policies according to such criteria. Other social and political issues are defined as dependent upon or subordinate to the realisation of these goals.

Against such a background, China's economy has entered a period of experiment and change. There is considerable flexibility in adjusting and re-adjusting economic policy at the centre and wide variations in practice at the lower levels. At the same time, as many reports in the Chinese media indicate, there is considerable inertia at all levels of economic management. Reforms aimed at reducing bureaucratic complexity are not always accepted, and lower level cadres have been reluctant to implement changes which could make them vulnerable to criticism should central policy be revised again. As a result, in some areas new policy is quickly adopted and sometimes overstepped, while in other areas it is only being introduced slowly. Furthermore, in most instances where such things as new forms of management or new methods of distributing investment are introduced, it is stressed that these are experimental. The draft "Decision on Several Questions Concerning the Acceleration of Industrial Development" put forward in July 1978 with the aim of final modification by the end of the year have not, at the time of writing, been officially revised and published.[1] Indeed, the evidence shows that many of the recommendations of that draft have been rapidly overtaken by later developments. It is therefore not yet possible to be definitive about many of the features of current policy. While the overall thrust towards a form of market socialism and a mixed economy appears set, the ultimate balance between the plan and the market, the appropriate forms for economic administration, and the precise methods for managing the economy through "objective economic laws" remain undecided.

In what follows, I shall look at the various ways in which this re-examination of economic policy has affected Chinese industry. First, I shall examine the evolution of policy over the period 1976 to 1980. I shall then proceed to examine some of the specific issues in industrial policy concentrating particularly on the role of the market, the mixed economy, decentralisation of controls and the banking system, and enterprise self-management.

The Evolution of Policy 1976 to 1980.

The background

As I have elaborated elsewhere,[2] the framework for discussion of economic policy in China both before and after the death of Mao has been that provided by the Marxist analysis of the relationship between the forces of production and the relations of production. During the Cultural Revolution, the overwhelming emphasis on the problems of class struggle in Chinese society and on the call to carry out revolution in the social superstructure placed the issue of the transformation of the relations of production at the forefront of discussion of industrial policy. The main targets for criticism were the policies labelled "profit in command", "production first", "experts running factories", "technique first", "controlling, restricting and suppressing the workers", and "material incentives".[3] The large, integrated corporations introduced in the early 1960s which operated as independent economic units able to expand their activities according to the needs of production and profitability were denounced as capitalist "trusts" and disbanded. At a theoretical level, economists like Sun Yefang were condemned for downgrading class struggle and replacing it by the struggle to raise productivity and to implement "objective economic laws".[4] The attempts at reform that ensued from these criticisms therefore mainly centred in the area of the relations of production and concerned such things as methods of industrial organisation and management, forms of work incentives, and worker participation in technical and economic decision-making.

During 1975 and 1976, when the struggle between Deng Xiaoping and his supporters and the "Gang of Four" dealt with economic questions, articles supporting the Gang's position underlined the belief that the industrial policies denounced during the Cultural Revolution had "hindered the development of the forces of production in industry" and that only when the "capitalist things in the superstructure and in the relations of production" had been swept aside could the socialist base be consolidated.[5] Although, as Brugger points out,[6] the written evidence suggests that the Gang was always careful to present an integrated view of the relationship between the two aspects rather than one entirely divorced from the forces of production, and although arguments such as that put forward by Zhang Chunqiao in his article, "On Exercising All-Round Dictatorship Over the Bourgeoisie",[7] stressed that it would take a long time to transform fully the relations of production, nevertheless the main thrust of the Gang's position was that it was necessary to pay attention to:

> the reaction exerted on the system of ownership by the two other aspects of the relations of production — the relations between men and the form of distribution — and to the reaction exerted on the economic base by the superstructure; these two aspects and the superstructure may play a decisive role under given conditions.[8]

Indeed, as many articles of the period stressed, it was seen as necessary to "bring into full play the dynamic role of the socialist superstructure in consolidating and developing the economic base".[9]

In contrast to this position, the arguments mounted by Deng Xiaoping during 1975 gave primary to the "major determining role of the productive forces, practice, and the economic base in general historical development".[10] In Deng's view, though the relationship between the relations of production and the forces of production was complex, the main goal was to serve the development of the economic base. The only way to test the correctness of a political line was whether or not it promoted the development of the forces of production. Deng expanded this view by arguing that the greater the development of industry and technology the more rigid the demands they placed on society, be it communist or capitalist, and he found support for his case in Engel's "On Authority".[11] Deng believed that the experiments of the Cultural Revolution had stood in the way of the development of the forces of production and should be swept aside.[12] The key to this position lay in the arguments that, once the system of ownership in China had been transformed, the attainment of socialism was ensured and that science and technology and the managerial systems they embodied were neutral in class terms.[13]

After the death of Mao and the arrest of the Gang of Four, this analysis, which had been so roundly denounced during the previous two years, rapidly returned to the fore. Even before Deng was officially rehabilitated, the press was giving full support to his position and Engel's "On Authority", for example, appeared on the front pages of the Renmin Ribao.[14] At the same time, the blame for a declining rate of economic development and for lost production due to factional struggles and neglect of economic policy was laid at the door of the Gang of Four.[15] On the basis of these arguments, therefore, the way was open for the new leadership to concentrate on undoing the experiments of the Cultural Revolution, on reviving the economic experiments of the early 1960s, and on introducing policies aimed at achieving technological modernisation and an acceleration in the rate of growth of output, policies which differed markedly from those predominating in the 1960s and 1970s. Symbolic of this change was the return to positions of influence of economists such as Sun Yefang and Xue Muqiao, and the revival of the economic analyses advanced during the early 1960s in the pages of journals like *Jingji Yanjiu (Economic Research)* and *Jingji Guanli (Economic Management)*.[16] This tranformation was not, however, realised quickly. After 1976, economic policy passed through several distinct phases each involving an intensification of the process of change.

1976 to 1978

The first phase lasted from October 1976 until the Fifth National People's Congress in February 1978. During that time the framework for industrial policy was that provided by the call to realise the four modernisations and by Mao's "On the Ten Major Relationships", officially published for the first time in December 1976.[17] In practical terms, the process of introducing the industrial policies outlined by Deng in his speech of September 1975 was begun.[18] These included such things as strengthening management and managerial rules, restoring the status of engineers and technicians, providing clear directives for realising the eight planning targets (output volume, product type, quality, consumption of materials and fuel, labour productivity, costs, profits and use of liquid capital), greater regional co-ordination leading to greater specialisation by production units, firmer central planning and tighter control of investment policy, and increased import of foreign technology. The emphasis on improving productivity and quality was backed by a call for greater use of material incentives. Throughout 1977, policy statements and conferences on economic issues concentrated on criticising the

Gang of Four and establishing procedures to implement these policies.[19] While much of the rhetoric of the discussion still retained references to "taking class struggle as the key link" and defences against the kind of criticisms made during 1975 and 1976, the overall thrust insisted that "increasing or decreasing production is an important criterion in judging whether a revolution is successful or not".[20]

Although these developments represented a distinct break with the innovations of the Cultural Revolution, innovations which in any case had been unevenly implemented and continuously subject to modification,[21] they still retained many of the basic features of the Chinese economy that had been present since the 1950s. They relied on the concept of decentralised planning with state control of the major targets and the key items of accumulation and distribution. Upward reported figures remained the basis of planning which, as always, required negotiations between different administrative levels, and local conferences to balance supply and demand between consuming units. Indeed, as subsequent reports have indicated, the influence of Soviet practices in terms of vertical controls was still strong in the state-owned, centrally-planned sector despite the various experiments in regional decentralisation that had taken place in the 1950s and 1960s.[22] What is more, the concomitant problem of factory managers attempting to overcome constraints and meet their targets through "supply agents" and various forms of "*blat*" or "going by the back door" was also a familiar part of the scene.[23] The reforms proposed by Deng did not directly address these issues, and the form of decentralisation remained that of decentralisation to local levels of administration and not to units of production.

As expressed in their most ambitious form by Hua Guofeng at the Fifth National People's Congress in February 1978, the drive for the four modernisations revived much of the spirit of the period immediately before the Great Leap Forward.[24] Although the basic role of agriculture was affirmed, the prevailing emphasis was on a period of rapid industrial development between 1978 and 1985. A group of 120 key large-scale projects were central to the plan which aimed at lifting the rate of growth of the value of industrial output to 10 per cent a year and at large increases in the areas of power, fuels, raw materials, and transport and communications, including doubling the output of steel. Hua insisted that the completion of the large projects should be guaranteed. Although the ambitious scale of this plan was recognised before the end of the year and policies of readjustment were already being discussed, subsequent reports have shown that the effect of the four modernisations drive during 1977 and 1978 resulted in a jump in the rate of accumulation and investment. By late 1979, articles in the press were critical of "blindly seeking high targets" and of the fact that heavy industry had consistently received the highest proportion of investment and consumed the greatest amount of raw materials and power.[25] It was pointed out that the rate of accumulation which had already been running at an average of 33 per cent for most of the seventies had increased to 36 per cent in 1978.[26] Since this was now considered both excessive and, by depressing consumption, counter-productive, appeals were made to cut back on the capital construction programme. This theme, which became dominant in 1979 and 1980, underlined the extent to which the four modernisation campaign of 1977 and 1978 had re-awakened the heavy industry aspirations of the mid-1950s.

1978

Almost as soon as Hua's speech at the Fifth National People's Congress was made, however, discussion of economic theory and economic policy among the economists of the newly founded Chinese Academy of Social Sciences and among theoreticians in the Party began to point the way towards an entirely different approach to economic development in China. In some respects, the direction this might take was already signalled by Hua Guofeng when he referred to the need to apply the law of value to state planning and to make greater use of financial and monetary methods of managing the economy.[27] While these remarks were not prominent in Hua's speech, it was concern with issues of this kind during 1978 and 1979 that led to the readjustment in economic policies that took place after the Third Plenum of the Eleventh Central Committee in December 1978 and to the shift towards forms of market socialism that subsequently ensued.

These developments entailed substantial and far-reaching adjustments to the policies of the four modernisations which had so recently been acclaimed. They also involved considerable re-thinking of the arguments put forward by Deng Xiaoping in 1975 and consideration of issues which Deng had not even addressed. More fundamentally, they implied a complete re-evaluation of the economic policies associated with Mao Zedong. In reviving and extending the experiments of the early 1960s, it was not only the Gang of Four and the Cultural Revolution that was being undermined. The Great Leap Forward and the framework for development associated with Mao was also being directly challenged, as well as the material balance planning of the 1950s. Inevitably such questions required considerable political debate and preparation. They required "emancipation" from the view that the major aspects of China's developmental strategy had been laid down by Mao Zedong.

At a theoretical level this was begun by the campaign launched in the *Guangming Ribao* on 11 May 1978 to establish that "Practice is the sole criterion for verifying truth". The succession of articles and speeches dealing with this theme all implied that Mao's thought was not absolute. It could be modified by practice and in the light of new conditions. Once this argument became established, the way was open to relegate Mao's policies to their historical context and to take entirely new initiatives. In political terms, this also required the removal from positions of influence at the central level of any remaining adherents to Mao's views. The result was the debate between the "practice" faction and the "whateverist" faction during 1978.[28] The "whateverist" faction, which was alleged to adhere to "whatever Mao Zedong thought or did", was eventually forced to give way at the Third Plenum in December by agreeing to the appointment to prominent positions of people like Chen Yun and Hu Yaobang who were closely associated with the new political and economic trends.[29] Eventually the key members of the "whateverist" faction such as Wang Dongxing and Chen Xilian "resigned" and were removed from their Party and state posts at the Fifth Plenum of the Eleventh Central Committee in February 1980.[30]

Against this political background, the second phase in the evolution of economic policy thus lasted throughout 1978. During this year there was an intense re-examination of the four modernisation programme and the theoretical basis of economic policy in the pages of journals like *Jingji Yanjiu* and *Guangming Ribao*. Economists argued the case for making greater use of the law of value, for greater attention to economic results measured in terms of profitability of investment and productivity of labour, and for the use of material incentives as reflected in the principle of "payment according to work done". The economic experiments of the early 1960s, including the various decisions of the period on industrial policy and on the formation of large integrated corporations or "trusts", were held up as positive models. In essence, the arguments came to be summed up by the call to obey "objective economic laws" and to manage the economy by economic rather than administrative methods. A number of major developments in July 1978 set the seal on this trend which culminated in the decisions to readjust economic policy at the Third Plenum in December.

The development of July 1978 most directly relating to industrial matters was the announcement of the Central Committee's draft

"Decision on Several Questions Concerning the Acceleration of Industrial Development", also known as the "thirty points".[31] In general this document reiterated the major points made by Deng Xiaoping in 1975 with additions and alterations to reflect the changes that had occurred in the intervening years. The various rules for enterprise management and post responsibility within industry were outlined, with considerable emphasis on bringing into full play the professional skills of managers and engineers. The state plan was to be fulfilled on the basis of the "five fixes" (fixed nature and scale of production, fixed personnel and organisation, fixed consumption and supply quotas, fixed capital allocation, and fixed relations of co-operation with other enterprises). Within this framework, once the eight plan targets were met, the enterprise could retain some profits for bonuses, welfare or new investment. The way was also opened for the formation of integrated corporations or networks of enterprises where specialisation of production could take place on the basis of contractual linkages. The aim was to overcome the tendency for enterprises to attempt to internalise all aspects of the production of their end products, a tendency which was seen to be wasteful of capital investment and forced on managers by fears that the unreliability of supply of materials or semi-finished products through the planning system would jeopardise their chances of meeting their targets.

Other aspects dealt with by the draft decision included such things as a clear demarcation of responsibilities between the localities and the centre, greater freedom for consuming units to influence product type and quality, and considerable emphasis on the import of modern technology and the growth of foreign trade. Although these proposals did allow for greater freedoms at the enterprise level and also reflected the concern with issues of profitability of investment and economic results, they were all still within the overall framework of target planning and administrative control of the economy and did not represent a fundamental shift to the new perspective. Nevertheless, to the extent that they were directly related to the "Seventy-point decision on industry" of 1961[32] and to efforts to undo the policies associated with the Cultural Revolution, they did mark the beginnings of the transition to the policies of market socialism.

A second important development in July 1978 was the holding of the National Finance and Trade Conference on Learning from Daqing and Dazhai held 20 June to 9 July 1978.[33] Despite the reference to the two great models of the Cultural Revolution period and Hua Guofeng's call to sweep away the aspects of the superstructure and the relations of production that "shackle the productive forces and hinder their development",[34] the focus of the conference was not the types of reform advocated during the Cultural Revolution but changes in China's economic administration that would bring the law of value to which Hua had referred in his February speech into effect. The conference called for greater use of pricing policy, taxation methods and credit policy in order to stimulate and control the economy. The commercial and banking departments were seen as having a major role in regulating economic activity. The use of economic levers in these areas was seen as reflecting the "objective economic laws" and as means of "turning the law of value to good account".[35] As stated by Li Xiannian, the aim was to "get maximum results at minimum costs and meet the needs of consumers while ensuring reasonable profits".[36]

Implicit in these arguments is the assumption that profitability per unit of capital investment should be the major measure of enterprise performance and the basis on which further capital investment could be obtained as interest-bearing loans from the banks. Furthermore, the discussion of the use of pricing policy and greater sensitivity to the needs of consumers also meant greater reliance on market forces to guide the process of distribution. Apart from its impact on the status of financial and commercial departments, making them equal to producers and assigning them a key role in the articulation of the economy, the conference provided a major stimulus to the moves towards market socialism. Subsequent discussion of the pitfalls of administratively decided prices, targets and distribution all underlined that the framework of economic discussion in China was no longer simply that of undoing the perceived damage caused by the factional struggles of the Cultural Revolution but also a re-evaluation of all policies implemented since 1949.[37] The Gang of Four ceased to be the only culprits and were now seen as obstacles to the reform of deep-seated problems.

The last and by far the most important development of the middle of 1978 was a speech by a leading Party theoretician, Hu Qiaomu, on "Observe Economic Laws, Speed up the Four Modernisations".[38] The speech remained unpublicised until October and, given the political context of the economic debate, its publication may be seen as a sign of the decline in the position of the "whateverists". Hu argued that economic laws were like natural laws which applied regardless of the form of society in which they operated. The change to forms of socialist ownership changed the ways in which the laws operated but did not change the laws themselves. It was necessary, therefore, to abandon administrative ways of running the economy in favour of compliance with these objective laws. It was also possible for China to learn from many aspects of capitalist economic planning and managerial techniques. Planning should accord with the law of value so that success should be measured by lowering the unit cost of production, and raising labour productivity and the rate of profit of the funds invested. In effect, profit should now be measured in relation to invested capital rather than in relation to costs, leading to the end of the practice of free supply of capital for industrial enterprises from the state budget. Furthermore, the income of employees and their bonuses should be directly related to the rate of profit measured in this way.

Although Hu stressed the importance of planning, he underlined that, as practised in China, it had created problems of waste and corruption, and there was no procedure for measuring efficient use of capital. He therefore called for reforms to ensure stricter cost accounting, price setting according to the law of value (taken to mean that the price of a commodity should be determined according to the cost of labour, materials and capital used in production plus a reasonable profit), and decentralisation of controls to enterprise level. Enterprises should have greater say over their use of capital and profit. Regulation of their activities according to the various state targets should be realised through contractual relations between the state and the enterprise, and between enterprises. Commercial and banking departments should also play a major role in structuring the economy.

In making his case, Hu referred directly to Hua's call at the recent Finance and Trade Conference for China to observe "objective economic laws". He underlined the "key significance" of that call.[39] Indeed, its significance can scarcely be underrated. Once the objectivity of economic laws was combined with Deng's earlier stress on the objectivity of technological imperatives, the way was open for a complete transformation of economic policy. The criteria for judging the correctness of policy could now be found in these new "objective" yardsticks. Furthermore, there was little requirement to justify policy in terms of political effect since political success could be assumed on the basis of the changes in the system of ownership of the 1950s. According to Li Xiannian, China's previous failure to recognise the importance of these laws could be traced to the persistence of "bureaucratic" and "self-sufficient" tendencies inherited from the "small producer mentality" of pre-1949 China.[40] It was argued that these tendencies had been reinforced by the influence and defects of Soviet-style planning during the 1950s.[41] Significantly, Hu pointed out that even the recently publicised draft on industrial development did not accord with the demands of the "objective laws" and needed reconsideration.[42] The direction in which discussion of economic policy was heading was thus already far beyond the guidelines put forward by Deng in 1975.

1979 to 1980

The decisions of the Third Plenum in December 1978 set the seal of Party approval on these arguments. Although the major concern of that Plenum was agricultural policy,[43] the corresponding need to scale down the ambitious plans of the four modernisations programme was recognised, and moves to change the structure of the industrial economy were begun. The third phase in the evolution of economic policy thus lasted throughout 1979 and 1980. During that time there were numerous local experiments with ways of implementing the new policies. Sichuan, in particular, emerged as a pathbreaker under the guidance of Zhao Ziyang, whose prominence in reformist policies contributed to his elevation to the state premiership in September 1980.[44] Overall there was a consistent trend throughout the period towards a form of market socialism in which considerable independence would be granted to individual industrial enterprises and the state would regulate market relations through the banking system and control of key prices and targets. The emergence of a mixed economy also received official sanction.

As early as January and February 1979, the main features of the emerging policies were already very clear. Deng Xiaoping's famous pragmatic saying that the colour of a cat did not matter so long as it caught mice (i.e. that it is economic results that matter) was revived.[45] The growth of a mixed economy with complementarity between the plan and market competition was promoted as a way of overcoming bureaucratic practices and co-ordinating the activities of China's 380,000 industrial enterprises, as well as the multitude of other economic units.[46] The possibility that the introduction of the market mechanism might create problems through uneconomic competition and greater inequalities was recognised, but this was seen as a reason for caution rather than for not going ahead with the reforms.[47]

The role of the banking system in regulating investment, credit and interest rates was further explored at a conference in February.[48] Meanwhile there was widespread discussion of strengthening enterprise independence by giving factory managers the freedom to control surplus funds, negotiate contracts for production, and engage directly in marketing their products at state controlled prices. Warnings were issued that enterprises that were not making a profit had to become profitable as soon as possible or face the prospect of closing down.[49] It was also announced that a decision by the Ministry of Finance in late 1979 had already authorised enterprises which met their planning targets to establish special funds at a rate of 5 per cent of total wage bill from which individual and collective material incentives could be funded.[50]

Apart from theoretical considerations, the readjustment of the four modernisation plans between March and June 1979 was also based on an analysis which argued that the capital construction front was over-extended. Too much capital was directed towards projects with a long gestation period or with limited profitability. Heavy industry was receiving too much investment at the expense of the development of light industry and agriculture; and problems with the supply of fuel, power and transport were preventing the effective use of the capital construction that was completed. In addition, it was necessary to devote more attention to raising individual consumption levels and increasing the supply of consumer goods.[51] All of these points were incorporated in the decisions on policy changes outlined by Hua Guofeng and Yu Qiuli at the Second Session of the Fifth National People's Congress in June.[52]

Alongside these adjustments, concern was also expressed at the foreign exchange problems China was facing as a result of the large increase in imports. Yu stressed that the development of exports needed special attention and that, where domestic substitutes could be found, imports should be cut back.[53] Nevertheless, as Gu Mu, a member of the State Planning Commission, pointed out, this was not intended to imply any reversal in the overall policy of expanding foreign trade and importing modern technology.[54] In fact the enactment by the Congress of the Law on Joint Ventures governing the conditions for foreign investment in China underlined that this was not the case. Furthermore, the drive to study and introduce foreign management methods was also enthusiastically maintained. The feature page devoted to industrial management in the *Guangming Ribao* had carried regular articles describing practice in Japan, the United States and elsewhere,[55] and this was continued in each issue of the new journal, *Jingji Guanli*, which began publication in January 1979. The Chinese Business Management Association established in March 1979 saw one of its prime functions as the study and introduction of managerial techniques from abroad.[56] Indeed, as a prominent member of the Association informed me during an interview in November 1979, he believed that management methods in China were in general very weak and it was necessary to learn from foreign countries.⁵⁷

Throughout the remainder of 1979 and 1980, there was continuous analysis of the advantages and problems associated with greater enterprise independence and market operations. Although towards the end of 1979 analysis of the purpose of socialist production suggested that there was still some resistance to the growing dominance of market relations and the production of consumer goods,⁵⁸ the apparent resolution of that discussion in favour of the argument that the goal of socialist production was to raise the living standards of the people and to meet their material needs, i.e. production for consumption rather than production for production's sake, resulted in further stress on the virtues of market competition. It also led to increasing acceptance of the emergence of a mixed economy with strong private and collective sectors existing under the dominance of state-controlled economic activity. The need to provide a new framework for economic activity was recognised by renewed interest in the formulation of laws of contract, of employment, of environmental protection and so forth, and by the re-establishment of the Chinese People's Insurance Company.⁵⁹ In addition the problem of circulating market information was met by a growth in advertising, symbolized by the launching in October 1979 of the fortnightly newspaper, *Shichang (The Market)*.

Despite the optimism throughout 1980 that the managed market and the mixed economy were essential for China's economic development, there was also evidence that their introduction was generating a new range of problems. During 1979, the increase in the state purchasing prices for agricultural commodities and the increasing freedom for industrial enterprises and service units to adjust their own selling prices led to a steady rise in wholesale and retail prices.⁶⁰ By January 1980 it was found necessary to hold a national conference to discuss ways of stabilising prices and reducing the growing "anarchy" in price fixing.⁶¹ Nevertheless, the situation did not improve and in March 1980 a national forum of directors of commercial bureaus had to issue an eight-point guideline aimed at bringing prices under control, reducing excessive profit-making, and ensuring value for money.⁶² Eventually these calls had to be backed by a joint circular from the State Council and the Central Committee calling for observance of price controls and a stop to arbitrary price increases.⁶³ Evidently the pressures on factory managers to generate profits and the link between profits and bonuses were being reflected in an increasing tendency to exploit the market as a means of raising enterprise revenue.

A similar problem of control also existed in the area of capital investment. Editorials in the *Renmin Ribao* in November 1979 indicated that, despite the adjustments in policy earlier in the year, the capital construction programme had still not been sufficiently scaled down.[64] A major problem, as pointed out by Zhao Ziyang at a Party conference in Sichuan in March 1980,[65] was that considerable amounts of capital were now accumulating at enterprise level outside of the direct control of the state. Enterprises needed more "guidance" in the best use of those funds. As a result, although it was possible by the time of the Third Session of the Fifth National People's Congress in August 1980 to claim that there had been some reduction in state budgetary outlays on capital construction and a speeding up in the rate of completion of new projects,[66] the emphasis laid on continuing to cut back on this expenditure indicated that the problem had far from disappeared. Wang Bingqian, the Minister of Finance, pointed out that although budgetary expenditure had been reduced, extra-budgetary outlays by localities and enterprises using the funds now under their own control had increased.[67] The total investment in capital construction had not, therefore, changed much over the previous year. There was a growing need to exercise control over all the funds involved, including credit and foreign funds. Wang argued for still stricter rules for capital investment with careful measurement of the profitability of investment, closer scrutiny of the use of foreign funds, and punishments for those responsible for inefficient use or misuse of funds.[68] The fact that the state budget had run into deficit, due in part to the loss of control over prices and incomes, also contributed to the sharp reduction in projected budgetary outlays on capital construction for 1980/81. Subsequently new regulations governing state controls over the use of foreign funds were issued giving the banks greater authority in checking loans and setting interest rates.[69]

Despite these efforts, however, there was considerable evidence by late 1980 that the problem was far from being resolved. On 2 December the *Renmin Ribao* carried an editorial which stated that capital construction expenditure was still far too high. The budget deficit had not yet been cut back and a further round of adjustment to the four modernisation programme was required. Once again expenditure on imports had to be curtailed. A report from Sichuan indicated that the major problem was still the extra-budgetary funds, which accounted for more than half of all capital investment. The growing diversity in sources of accumulation and level of control over this capital was making the task of limiting its use more and more complex.[70] In an interview in late November Wang Bingqian indicated that in 1981 further attempts to control the situation would be made.[7][1]

In many ways the difficulties in controlling prices, bonuses and the use of capital at lower levels were the inevitable outcome of the transfer of power to the units of production and the growing freedom for production and service units to exploit the market. Factory managers, who were under strong pressure from outside to increase profitability per unit of capital and from inside to generate higher profits in order to pay more bonuses, could be expected to raise prices as high as possible, to keep as much of their production as they could outside of state controls, and to embark on investment programmes best suited to the immediate needs of their enterprise rather than to the local or central plan. Having granted enterprises and localities much greater economic autonomy, the state was now in the position of trying to find new ways to influence the outcome. The move from "administrative" to "economic" controls was thus proving far from easy. Nevertheless these difficulties were not yet seen as insuperable and, while the tone of discussion of economic issues in late 1980 indicated greater caution and less optimism about how quickly the goals of the four modernisation programme might be reached, there was no indication that the underlying strategy of developing a mixed economy based on market relations would be abandoned. The problem remained that of finding a workable balance between state regulation and economic independence for units of production.

The above chronological account of the evolution of economic policy from the death of Mao until late 1980 has demonstrated that policy formation passed through three distinct stages. The *first* lasted from late 1976 until the end of 1977. During that time the ambitious programme for the four modernisations was formulated, and changes in the structure of the industrial economy were inspired by the analysis presented by Deng Xiaoping in September 1975. Although these developments negated many of the innovations attempted as a result of the Cultural Revolution, they still fell within the framework of decentralised planning and state control of the key features of the economy. As such, the publication of Mao's "On the Ten Major Relationships" was a fitting reflection of the direction policy had taken.

The *second* stage lasted throughout 1978. Despite the fact that the four modernisation programme received its most forcible expression at the National People's Congress at the beginning of the year, discussion of economic policy among the newly rehabilitated economists and prominent Party leaders and theoreticians argued strongly against administrative planning in favour of the use of "economic" levers to manage the economy. Ultimately these arguments saw the root of China's economic problems not only in the factional struggles and experiments of the Cultural Revolution but also in the whole structure of material balance planning as inherited from the Soviet Union during the 1950s. The case was therefore mounted for introducing a form of market socialism. To do this, however, it was necessary to downgrade many of the key political and economic policies associated with Mao Zedong and to change many of the assumptions on which the four modernisation policy was based. Even the analysis put forward by Deng Xiaoping in 1975 required reconsideration. The fact that the four modernisation programme itself was already running into some practical difficulties contributed to this process of re-evaluation.

The *third* stage of policy evolution was begun in early 1979 and has lasted up until the time of writing. Successive adjustments were made to the targets and policies of the four modernisations programme, and various experiments to find ways of realising the new approach to development were carried out and generalised. Throughout the period there was a strengthening of arguments in favour of the spread of market relations between producers and consumers and in favour of a mixed economy. Although by late 1980 there were many indications that these experiments were generating a number of difficult problems, there was as yet no sign that the overall direction of change would be reversed. In sum, therefore, over the whole period from 1976 to 1980 there was a consistent trend away from the developmental strategy associated with Mao towards a form of market socialism. Nevertheless, this process was not a smooth one and, as I have indicated, involved considerable political debate. It was also related to changes in policy over a wide range of social and cultural issues. In what follows I shall examine the impact of this process on some of the key areas of industrial operation. For ease of analysis I have attempted to divide my discussion into a number of discrete topics but it should be borne in mind that they are all closely related. The decentralisation of economic authority to units of production implies reliance on the use of "economic" levers to control the economy. This in turn leads to growing importance for the use of market forces and the toleration of a mixed economy. All of these developments force reconsideration of such things as the role of the banking system, the structure of industrial organisation and the methods of enterprise management.

The Reform of Economic Administration and the Role of the Market

Following Hu Qiaomus's call for the observance of "economic laws" in July 1978, a large number of articles began to appear in economic journals analysing the history of economic planning in China and suggesting ways of reforming economic administration.[72] Essentially these articles argued that although the command planning system copied from the Soviet Union had played a positive role at the time, it had left a legacy of problems. Consumption was determined by production and there was no direct link between producers and consumers which could act as a way of disciplining producers to improve quality and meet standards. Production was only concerned with value and volume of output, there was no attempt to improve profitability or seek quick returns. In general the emphasis was on large-scale and long-term heavy industrial development with all enterprises striving to become completely self-sufficient. Apart from the inherent difficulties of attempting to run an economy the size of China's in a totally planned way, the system created pressures on factory managers to strive for excessive allowances of investment and raw materials and to "go by the back door", making informal contacts with other enterprises and material suppliers in order to meet their targets.

The way to escape all these drawbacks was to change the planning system radically. The various forms of administratively decided targets should be abandoned, enterprises should have greater autonomy and their success should be measured principally according to the profit rate of capital calculated using production prices.[73] Enterprises should become individually responsible for their own profits and losses. They should have control over their own funds so that the material rewards to employees became related directly to profitability, and they could invest and expand according to the needs of production. Consumer preference should act as an important stimulus to improve profitability and quality, and to encourage enterprises to expand production in ways required by the economy.[74] The role of the state should become that of determining the general speed of development and the key proportional relationships. It should do this through pricing policy, taxation (to adjust externalities which distort enterprise profitability and produce windfall profits), credit availability, duties and licences, currency controls, interest rates, depreciation allowances and so forth. To ensure that these methods worked, it was still necessary for the state to retain controls over the banking system, transport and utilities and the supply of some vital, strategic materials. Such controls, however, should be restricted to the minimum.

The profound impact of all this on China's economic structure was clearly recognised, and most of the economists making these arguments suggested that a number of small-scale experiments were required first. Nevertheless, it was already recognised that the market would have to become a major force in the distribution of capital, labour and commodities,[75] and it was this aspect which received increasing attention in theoretical discussion during 1979 and 1980.[76] China's previous neglect of the market mechanism, it was argued, was the result of confusing a market economy with a capitalist economy and a planned economy with a "natural" or self-sufficient economy.[77] The consequences were that production was divorced from the needs of consumers, that prices were not related to value and hence output value, profit rate and enterprise targets were all measured in terms of administratively determined prices and did not reflect actual enterprise performance, that capital was made available on "free supply" and was not used efficiently, and that enterprises and localities strove to become fully self-sufficient. Instead it should be recognised that there was an interrelationship between the existence of commodity production, the use of the law of value (exchange value determining prices), and the market mechanism.

Some economists believed that this situation was "external" to the socialist economy in that the existence of state-owned, collective, and small-scale private sectors combined with the prevailing low level of development of the forces of production placed limits on planning and required commodity production and exchange through the market. Most, however, argued that, on the contrary, commodity production and the market mechanism were inherent in socialist society (not to be confused with full communism) because the basis of social relations was work done. Differentials between the quality and amount of work done by individuals or enterprises would be reflected in differences in their income through the process of exchange at equal value through the market.[78] As a result socialist society required both the plan and the market. The plan was the way of recognising the fundamental identity of people's interests while the market was a means of recognising the differences between enterprises and individuals in production.

Having established this theoretical justification, economists proceeded to argue that market forces should operate in the distribution of commodities, capital and labour.[79] The sale of commodities in the market, including the sale of raw materials and producer goods, should determine levels of output and the development of products. Both fixed and circulating capital should be provided through the banking system in the form of interest-bearing loans with the banks using the profit rate of capital as a measure for determining which enterprises should obtain loans. Labour should be allocated more flexibly with enterprises given more choice over whom they employed and freedom to request that unwanted labour should be reassigned. Individuals should also be allowed to have more scope to choose their own employment. Although a free labour market was not seen as desirable, some relaxation was required and those unemployed and looking for work could be paid a subsistence income from a "social insurance fund".[80]

Inevitably these proposals rested on the assumption of granting considerable enterprise autonomy. They also accepted that fluctuations and changes in prices would have to be allowed in order to reflect changing market relations. In that respect it was pointed out that the existence of stable prices disguised changes in relative productivity between sectors and enterprises, and led to rationing, which did not stimulate increases in the production of urgently needed goods. Price flexibility also entailed competition. Such competition would become a way of relating supply and demand.[81] Moreover, since enterprise profit and employee income were now related, competition would also have implications for managers' and workers' material interests. Unlike the socialist emulation previously practised in China, therefore, socialist competition would act as a spur to enterprises to become efficient and profitable.[82]

It was recognised that the establishment of these market relations was a reflection of the adoption of the "economic" methods of managing the economy so widely discussed during 1978. Nevertheless, it was also argued that while the market mechanism might balance the needs of the millions of consumers and many hundreds of thousands of producers in a way that a plan could not, the market was not always the most rational way of allocating labour, materials and resources in society's best interest. This was especially true in China since there was the possibility of conflict between individual consumer needs and the overall need to achieve rapid industrialisation. It was also not possible to rely on the market to make allowances for rent differentials between producers. The role of the plan, therefore, was to set longer-term aims and provide the guidance needed to achieve them.[83] This should include such things as setting the major proportional relations between accumulation and consumption, between and within different economic sectors, and between purchasing power and commodity supply. Such plans should not, however, operate through commands but through guidance, reacting to the demands coming from below. Planning methods should rely on the law of value as realised through the market and contractual relations. The state should give guidance by adjusting credit, prices, taxation, control of foreign funds, and the rules for such things as depreciation rates, wages and profit distribution. In addition some strategic investment and distribution of raw materials could be directly controlled. The state should only intervene administratively to ensure the production of some things or stop the production of others when such intervention was felt to be absolutely necessary.

Although all of these issues had been widely discussed by the middle of 1979, efforts to put them into practice only came gradually. Experiments with issuing funds for capital construction in the form of loans rather than as appropriations began late in 1979 in light industry and tourism in Beijing, Shanghai and Guangdong.[84] Contractual relations between enterprises and the supply of products relatively freely through the market rather than through state determined allocation were introduced during 1979, but it was not until 1980 that producer goods became more widely advertised and marketed. A producer goods trade market for the east China region was held in Shanghai in March 1980, and it was suggested that this might grow into a national market with regional trade markets opening up in other places.[85] In April 1980, the State Bureau of Supplies announced some tentative reform proposals whereby it would reclassify materials for distribution into three categories, those mainly under the state plan, those to be sold by designated supply enterprises, and those to be sold by the production enterprises themselves. Some of the production in the first two categories might also be sold by the producing enterprise.[86] Attempts to develop a labour market, however, were slower to emerge. Given the problems of urban unemployment and rural underemployment, this was probably a rather more difficult issue to decide. Nevertheless the encouragement given to the urban unemployed during late 1979 and 1980 to set up collectives and service units indicated a growing flexibility in labour planning which was further strengthened by the sanction given to small-scale private undertakings in urban areas (discussed below). Eventually by August 1980, a national conference on labour and employment was called by the Central Committee[87] which endorsed "a system under which the labour departments recommend people for employment, people voluntarily organise businesses for self-employment and individuals find jobs themselves under the guidance of unified state planning".[88] Employment agencies could be established by the state or collectives, and enterprises could shed surplus labour. It was hoped that the "iron rice bowl" system whereby a job assignment provided security for life at the cost of denying opportunities for transfers and dulling an individual's desire or need constantly to improve work performance would in these ways be curtailed.

All these experiments and decisions indicated that the theoretical arguments put forward by the various economists during 1979 had been approved and were being put into action. Nevertheless, it was still accepted during 1980 that the most appropriate methods for relating the plan and the market had not yet been devised, and that there were many shortcomings in the current situation. It was argued that the recent problems with prices and inflation in China came not as a result of the introduction of the market but from a lack of effective planning in keeping accumulation and consumption within the limits of the national income.[89] Meanwhile it was still necessary to reduce command planning, to loosen controls over the distribution of capital goods, and to adjust prices.[90] A similar view was that inflation was being caused by financial deficits and excess money supply.[91] Furthermore, as Zhao Ziyang revealed in March, the reforms themselves had created new problems.[92] Some enterprises were using their new freedom to speculate and make large profits. Others were investing funds indiscriminately and with no consideration of the overall situation. The uneven pricing situation with a mixture of market and fixed prices was enabling some enterprises to become very prosperous while others had many problems. In addition differentials in profitability due to advantages of equipment, resources and location were not being adequately handled. The role of the banking system and market regulation also needed strengthening. Bonuses were being issued regardless of the rules, and prices were being adjusted in an arbitrary manner. Overall, it was difficult to ensure that enterprises stuck to the rules. No wonder, then, that Zhao recommended "There should be no large-scale reforms yet this year and next. In these two years the present method of limited reforms should remain the basic rule."[93] Seen from outside, these problems seem the inevitable consequences of the development of market forces. The dilemma was thus one of either fully acknowledging the diminished powers of the state and allowing the market to become more deeply entrenched, or reasserting state controls over enterprises and restricting the role of the market. To do the former meant accepting the consequences, including greater inequalities of income, unemployment and bankruptcy while the economy adjusted, and less state influence on investment. To do the latter meant reintroducing some of the "administrative" ways of running the economy which had been consistently criticised for the previous two years. Certainly the prospects for expecting market forces to be responsive to state guidance remained very uncertain.

The Mixed Economy

Support for the growth of a mixed economy followed closely on the development of the market mechanism. Although during 1978 and 1979 most interest centred on the role of the collective sector and its relationship to the public sector, by the middle of 1980 the existence of a private sector was officially sanctioned and the Central Committee's conference on labour and employment held in August approved the guidelines for the development of the "individual economy".[94] In many ways, this approval was simply an acknowledgement of an established fact. According to one report, individually operated productive and commercial establishments had developed after the Fifth National People's Congress approved their existence in the state constitution of March 1978.[95] Even before that time small traders were operating in Chinese cities and, for example, I was able to buy unofficial publications of the texts for local operas on the streets of Guangzhou in December 1977. Nevertheless, official sanction was also accompanied by the argument that the private economy had a positive role to play and should receive support.

Articles published in late 1979 and early 1980 analysing the nature and role of collective enterprises were uniformly positive in their assessment.[96] Apart from the fact that the bulk of agriculture was collectively owned, it was pointed out that in 1977, in urban areas, these enterprises accounted for 20 per cent of the total output value of industry; they employed one-third of all industrial employees and made up three quarters of all enterprises.[97] Their virtues included the following: they required low investment but made high profits; they reacted to the market situation quickly and produced a vast number of daily necessities; many of their products, especially the high quality handicrafts, were exported and earned foreign exchange at a lower cost than other exports (the average exchange cost of US $1.00 in Beijing was Y3.00 but for some handicrafts it was as low as Y1.20); and they offered many opportunities to expand employment and utilise local resources.[98] It was also argued that collectives were socialist in character and not to be looked down upon as less socialist than the public sector.[99]

Nevertheless, it was conceded that there were differences between the collective and public sectors. As summed up by Hong Yuanpeng and Weng Qiquan[100] these were: collective assets were owned by the collective and could not be allocated and transferred by the state in the way that the assets of public enterprises could; state enterprises were strictly controlled by the state plan whereas collective enterprises were only guided and could react to the market; collectives were responsible for their own profits and losses and this was reflected in their employees' incomes, but state enterprises had to hand over profits to the state, and their losses were subsidised while their wages were guaranteed; and finally the cadres and workers in state enterprises were assigned but those in collectives were employed according to need. It was in some ways ironic that Hong and Weng's analysis assigned to the collectives the very virtues which were said by many economists to be absent from the state sector and which the reforms to industrial organisation were aimed at realising. The implication appeared to be that in some ways collective ownership was superior to public ownership. Certainly it was agreed that in many parts of the Chinese economy the collective form of ownership was more appropriate to the level of development of the forces of production than any other.[101]

An interesting aspect of this discussion of the role of collectives was the conscious comparison with the structure of industry in Japan where the "clustering" effect of small-scale industries around larger and more modern enterprises is an established phenomenon. One article referred to Japan's example using the analogy of a pyramid with the collectives at the bottom and a modern industry at the top.[102] Clearly an integrated relationship of this kind between state and collective enterprises lay behind the Changzhou model which was publicised during 1978.

The Changzhou model was one of a number of methods for developing urban collective undertakings that were given prominence during 1978 and 1979.[103] Cited in the "thirty points" of July 1978, the Changzhou "dragon" was popularised as an example of high-speed industrial development in a small-to-medium sized city. Each dragon consisted of a grouping of state-owned and collective enterprises according to various contractual and subordinating links around one or two major products. The model had developed during the 1960s and was seen as promoting specialisation and efficiency. It was argued that it enabled the collectives to raise their technical level quickly and incorporated the flexibility of collectives into the planning system.

A further experiment was the development of collectives by the urban unemployed, young people generally known as "those awaiting work assignment". This had begun in March 1979 in Beijing and had then spread to many other cities.[104] The youths were able to set up services such as foodstalls, clothing repairs and barbers shops and also, where conditions existed, formed contracts with industry to do process work or supply parts.

Some of the arguments supporting these developments were extremely pragmatic. According to Hong and Weng:

> In judging whether or not a system of ownership is progressive, we should not look at its level of public ownership but at whether it corresponds to the nature of the forces of production. Everything which can suit the needs of the development of the forces of production and promotes the rapid development of the forces of production is superior. If it does the opposite then no matter what the level of public ownership, it can't be called superior.[105]

Although the advantages to China of the development of such collectives are shown by the empirical evidence quoted and by the experience of subsidiary enterprises in the countryside over the past twenty years, this is clearly not an argument with which all Marxists would agree. Subsequently almost the same formulation was used by a prominent reform economist, Yu Guangyuan, in the *Renmin Ribao* to argue in support of the individual economy.[106] Yu stated that:

> the co-existence of the three kinds of economy – the socialist state-owned economy, the socialist economy based on collective ownership by the working masses and the socialist subsidiary economy is possibly the type of production relations most conducive to the development of productive forces at the present historical period in China.[107]

By the "socialist subsidiary economy", Yu meant individually owned and operated undertakings.

Shortly after Yu's article, the *Renmin Ribao* carried a report by Jiang Yingguang which further explored the case in support of the private sector.[108] Jiang reported that after December 1978 there was steady development of the urban individual economy and by May 1980 some 50,000 urban households were involved of which around 10,000 were in Shanghai and 10,000 in Liaoning. Jiang saw their role as providing supplementary services such as clothing repairs, knife sharpening, and hair cutting in the home for the aged and infirm. He stressed that they were available at many odd hours, provided new employment outlets and ensured good service. As with collectives, it was necessary to overcome any remaining "left" suspicion of this sector and to stop social discrimination against people engaged in it. Jiang argued that the nature of this sector was "subordinate to the socialist public sector and part of the entire socialist economy".

Eventually official Party backing for the private economy was given at the labour and employment conference in August 1980.[109] It was seen as contributing to the liveliness of the market, supplementing the state and collective sectors and giving them a competitive foil, providing more employment, and helping restore special handicrafts and food products. Significantly, the guidelines for operation allowed individuals or families to set up businesses, and "apprentices" could be employed. If necessary, individuals could raise the capital required, or they could form partnerships. Banks might even make loans. Although it was argued that this "individual economy" was different from a "capitalist economy" because it was not based on hired labour and China "prohibited" the exploitation of hired labour, the fact that apprentices could be employed indicated that some fine lines were being drawn. The guidelines also argued that "where conditions are ready, individual industrialists and businessmen should be allowed to organise such mass organisations as trade associations, and set up Party and communist youth league membership". Thus the rehabilitation of the national capitalists was complete, and businessmen were given a further form of social status.

At the time of writing, the ultimate impact on the economy as a whole of this support for the private sector appeared to be growing. Although most official arguments assigned it a subordinate role,[110] its contribution to the market situation and to employment opportunities was clearly seen to be important. Given the increasing role of the market mechanism, the potential for the rapid growth of the private sector was very great. In some respects, therefore, these proposals went far beyond the main stream of what is usually taken to be market socialism, and were more reminiscent of the situation in the very early days of the People's Republic.

The Role of the Banking System

Discussion of the question of the decentralisation of economic control in China has, at various times, involved two very different issues.[111] On the one hand, it has referred to decentralisation from the central government to the provincial and regional units of government. On the other, it has involved decentralisation to the units of production. As I have emphasised above, it is the latter form of decentralisation which has been at the heart of economic policy since 1976. Nevertheless, over the same period there has also been considerable decentralisation to provincial governments. Both forms of decentralisation place demands on the banking system as an integrating force.

The relationship between the centre and the provinces has always been a problem in the government of China. The various experiments in centralisation and decentralisation since 1949 have shown that it has been difficult to achieve a satisfactory balance. According to a survey carried out by Audrey Donnithorne,[112] in 1980 there was a high degree of decentralisation of financial controls to provincial levels. Donnithorne found that there were at least five methods used for allocating revenue and expenditure between the centre and different provinces and that almost all of them involved the bulk of revenue and expenditure accruing to the provincial level. In terms of the banking system this decentralisation meant that the head office of the People's Bank no longer imposed strict controls and quotas over loanable funds by category or regulated the relationship between deposits and loans. The provincial levels had gained considerable autonomy in these respects. Nevertheless, Donnithorne reported that the situation was still very fluid. In May 1980 provincial levels had the right to use for loans all deposits they received above the deposit target level set by the centre. By July this had been reduced to 30 per cent. The change obviously indicated the growing concern during 1980 for more controls over the rate of capital construction.

While issues of the above kind have always been a subject of debate in China since 1949, the decentralisation of economic power to the unit of production that has taken place since 1976 has resulted in a greatly extended discussion of the role of the banks in managing the economy.[113] Consideration of this question arose soon after Hu Qiaomu's speech in July 1978, and by early 1979 the framework for the subsequent changes in the work of the banks was already clear.

Much of the ideological justification for the new role of the banks was found in the writings of Lenin.[114] It was argued that Lenin had required the banks to manage and stabilise the currency, to help control prices, to keep the public accounts, to help supervise economic activity, and to play an important role in relating the socialist economy to the capitalist world. Banks in China should therefore be concerned with such things as money supply and credit, and they should be the medium for directing capital investment. The system of state allocation of fixed assets had been inherited from Stalin and it had outlived its usefulness. Reform, however, had been hindered by the Gang of Four who saw the system of currency exchange as the "soil from which capitalism grew" and they had attempted to limit the economic activities of the bank.[115]

Since banks now had to play a more positive role in directing the economy through the use of "economic levers" and in helping control enterprises, six major reforms had to take place.[116] First, all liquid capital should be issued to enterprises in the form of loans. This would ensure greater responsibility in the use of cash and prevent irrational distribution of funds as experienced through the allocation system. Second, funds for capital construction should also be issued as interest-bearing loans. This would force efficient use of capital since enterprises would have to pay interest and would therefore only request funds that were necessary. The banks should decide the allocation of these loans according to the merits of each enterprise's proposals and its profitability. The key measure would be the profit rate of capital as measured in production prices. Only a small proportion of funds should still be allocated by the state on the basis of overall social requirements rather than according to profitability.

The third reform involved greater flexibility in setting interest rates and in changing them to match the evolving situation. Differential rates could be used to direct investment in specific directions and, while low interest rates were in general desirable, they should not be so low that the borrowing enterprises could discount them and pay less attention to the strictness of their economic accounting. Fourth, the banks should play a central role in regulating contracts between units, ensuring that the conditions were met and payments were made. Fifth, the banks should help direct foreign trade and investment. The use of foreign funds and loans should be controlled through the banks which should restrict unnecessary foreign expenditure. Finally, the banks should become a major arm in the state's guidance of the economy. All the basic information on the use of capital and the functioning of the economy could be obtained from the banking system. Problems could be identified and dealt with early, and information could be given to the leadership as required. As might be expected, reforms of this nature involved consideration of a large number of technical issues. Depreciation rates, methods for measuring the profit rate of capital, methods for fixing interest rates and so forth, all have an important bearing on how the bank's use of economic levers would ultimately be realised and were widely discussed.

During 1979 and 1980 many changes in bank administration were carried out in line with the above reforms. A Construction Bank for controlling capital investment was organised in the middle of 1979 and trial regulations for the granting of capital construction loans were drawn up for implementation in 1980.[117] Regulations on foreign exchange were published and further refined.[118] In many ways these changes have begun to transform the Chinese banking system into one with functions similar to those of banks in western capitalist countries. Nevertheless, the problems with control of capital construction that arose during 1980 indicated that it was not yet able to exert strict controls over enterprises. A report on experiments in Sichuan during 1980 suggested that, at a basic level, banks had still not come to terms with the nature of enterprise autonomy and established the mechanisms for fulfilling their new role.[119]

Industrial Reorganisation and Enterprise Self-Management

The reorganisation of industry has involved a large range of issues. Arguments in favour of encouraging individual enterprises to specialise and develop contractual relations with each other have led to the rehabilitation of the large co-operations of "trusts" of the early 1960s.[120] They have also resulted in the popularisation of the Changzhou "dragon" described above, and formed part of the justification for the growth of the mixed economy so that the interstices in the planning system could be filled in a flexible way by collective or individual efforts. Many experiments have taken place in the transfer of enterprises between systems and between levels of administrative control.[121] The most fundamental aspect of all these changes, however, has been the reforms aimed at establishing enterprise autonomy.

In the early period after Mao's death, proposals for the relaxation of some controls over enterprises were still very limited in their scope. Deng's formulation in 1975 and the "thirty points" of 1978 envisaged the continuation of the eight major targets laid down by the state with the parameters for enterprise operation, the "five fixes", clearly defined. Satisfactory completion of allocated tasks would enable enterprises to retain a small proportion of their profits to use for material rewards, welfare and investment at their own discretion. By and large, however, Deng wanted more co-ordination of industrial activity at provincial level, and more central control over capital investment.

Before the end of 1978, these proposals had been extended to include the idea of permitting contractual relationships between enterprises.[122] Once an enterprise had met its obligations to the state, it should be able to use its surplus capacity freely and to form contracts with other enterprises for the purchase or supply of goods. As soon as this possibility was mooted, however, it opened the way to the proposal that the plan as a whole might be realised through contractual relations between the state and the enterprise. Controls over many other aspects of enterprise activity could thereby be handed over to the enterprise itself. The "five fixes" system came under attack[123] and discussion in the media outlined the various ways in which enterprises should become independent.[124] The discussion centred around six main rights to be granted to enterprises: the right to draw up production plans and to realise them through contracts; the right to determine the sale of goods other than those governed by contract; the right to use capital at the enterprise's own discretion provided taxes, expenses and interest on loans were met; the right to employ labour as required and to adjust wages and bonuses according to conditions; the right to fix product prices within the guidelines established by the state; and the right to refuse any burdens or levies on resources imposed from above.[125]

Many of these proposals were embodied in documents on enterprise self-management issued by the State Council in July 1979 which allowed for greater financial independence by enterprises.[126] They were also tried out in the experiments carried out in places like Sichuan during 1979. Various decisions towards the end of that year indicated that these experiments would be expanded and generalised.[127] The final extension of these arguments came with the proposal that enterprises should become entirely responsible for their own profits and losses.[128] Apart from the payment of taxes and interest on capital to the state, all other income should be retained within the enterprise, which should stand or fall according to its efficiency and profitability. State-owned enterprises would in this way become almost fully independent and in much the same position as collectives and individual enterprises. In August 1980, a State Economic Commission circular called for each province to select some enterprises to test this system. It stated that this reform should strengthen enterprise independence, but that it also required a change of the method of taxation with the use of value-added tax as the major levy on the enterprises concerned.[129]

Needless to say, if this reform were eventually widely implemented, it would ensure that the market would become the major feature of the industrial economy. In a situation where producer goods, consumer goods, capital and labour are distributed through market forces, where competition between sectors and between enterprises is encouraged, and where individual enterprises are legal entities whose major link with the state is through contracts and the tax system, the nature of planning becomes essentially a matter of governmental regulation of interest rates and taxes, and the balancing of the governmental budget.

Conclusion

The analysis presented above has concentrated on the macro level of China's industrial economy. It has demonstrated that fundamental changes are taking place in the management of China's industry which are transforming the nature of that economy from a state-owned, planned economy run according to state determined targets into a mixed economy relying on the operation of market forces. Although many of these changes are still tentative and the current situation is one of market socialism in which the state still tries to regulate the largest proportion of economic activity, the consistent trend of developments over the period 1976 to 1980 has headed towards ever-increasing reliance on market forces. If some of the experiments now being considered are fully implemented, the transformation will be complete.

Inevitably, transformation on this scale has innumerable implications for the micro management of each enterprise. Commensurate changes have taken place in the areas of managerial methods, labour organisation, worker participation in management, incentives and bonuses, trade union activity and so forth. Each of these deserve studies in their own right and could not possibly be dealt with in the space available here. I have chosen to restrict this study to the more general areas of policy because of their fundamental importance and wide implications.

As I stressed at the outset, a profound pragmatism has guided the evolution of industrial policy since the death of Mao. As expressed by Yu Guangyuan this pragmatism concludes:

> In a socialist country, at different historical periods the relations of production which promote the development of the forces of production the most are the best relations of production for that period.[130]

Once it is assumed that China is socialist because of changes in the system of ownership, virtually any form of economic administration can be justified. It is no surprise, therefore, that the current proposals for dealing with the many problems facing the Chinese economy are so radically different from those put forward in the

1950s and 1960s.

There can be no doubt that the extent of change in China's industrial economy has for the moment at least, undone virtually all the industrial policies associated with Mao Zedong since 1949. Nevertheless, at the most general level, much of what is being done can be understood within the framework of the "New Democracy" Mao envisaged in the 1940s. The ideas of a united front between different classes and social groups, and of a mixed economy under state guidance were both part of that concept. In 1949 Mao had envisaged that the New Democratic state of development would be a long one.[131] Subsequently the process of "socialist construction and socialist transformation" swept this possibility aside. In many ways, the current leadership in China appears to be arguing that many of the developments since 1949 have been premature and the New Democratic stage has yet to be completed.

6

INDUSTRIAL STRATEGY (JANUARY 1975 - JUNE 1979): IN SEARCH OF NEW POLICIES FOR INDUSTRIAL GROWTH

Thierry Pairault

Centre for Research and Documentation of Contemporary China, Paris, France.

Introduction

This paper examines the changes in Chinese industrial strategy in the years immediately before and after the removal of the Gang of Four, ending with a study of the partial "readjustment" of 1979.

The growth of Chinese industrial production between 1974 and 1976 was zero or around zero, slight in 1975 and a little higher in 1977 and 1978; for 1979 the Plan envisaged an average growth of 8 per cent and actually achieved 8.5 per cent (see Table 1). The poor performance in 1974 can be linked to social unrest, especially among workers, arising from the movement to criticise Lin Biao and Confucius. The Central Committee circular of 1 July 1974[1] revealed the existence of serious backwardness in production in many sectors, including iron and steel, the chemical industry, cement, etc. This decline in production was due not only to poor coal production and bottle-necks in the transport of iron and steel, but also to factional struggles within production units. The circular launched an appeal for calm and order, aimed at the workers, who were asked to stop criticising the government's economic policy, stop

Table 1 Industrial Production

	1973	1974	1975	1976	1977	1978	1979
Annual rate of growth (percentage)	-	0.3	5.1	0	14.3	13.5	8.5
Production (millions of yuan)	309	310	326	326	372.7	423.1	459.1

Sources: 1977 and 1978, figures given in the Report of the National Bureau of Statistics, 27 June 1979 (*PD*, 28 June 1979, p.2)
1979, figures given in the Report of the National Bureau of Statistics (*PD*, 2 May 1980, pp.1-2)
1973, 1974, 1975 and 1976, figures given in a *dazibao* in Shanghai in November 1976, summarising a speech given by Gu Mu to the Planning Commission in November 1976. Gu Mu gave percentages of growth, and from data supplied in 1979 it is possible to deduce the value of industrial production in 1973, 1974, 1975 and 1976.

making wage claims and concentrate on production and on criticism of Lin Biao and Confucius. The Marxist theory of "going against the tide" was not to be interpreted as an invitation to rebel against factory cadres and stop work, but as an invitation to "make revolution and carry out one's work". The situation was serious enough for Mao Zedong to meet Wuhan cadres in the autumn of 1974[2] and although calm appeared to be gradually re-established towards the end of the year, order was not restored (for example in Hangzhou, capital of Zhejiang) until the summer of 1975, as a result of purging leading cadres and sending in troops.[3] It was in this general state of political and social instability that Mao issued three directives in autumn 1974: first, an appeal for calm and unity within the Army and the Party; second, a request to "study theory and oppose revisionism"; and third, encouragement of economic development. This last appeal was reinforced by Zhou Enlai's report to the Fourth National People's Congress (NPC) on 13 January 1975, in which he urged China to realise the "four modernisations", embodied in a "10-year plan" drawn up during the summer of 1975.

However, good intentions for the long term were not enough to distract attention from immediate problems, notably the approaching power vacuum threatened by the deteriorating health of Zhou Enlai and Mao Zedong. The death of the premier (8 January 1976), followed by the dismissal of Deng Xiaoping, increased confusion among the masses, expressed more or less spontaneously in the Tian'anmen incident (5 April 1976). The subsequent death of the Great Helmsman (9 September 1976) and the arrest of the Gang of Four (6 October 1976) combined to foster a state of instability in

1976 which hit the economy hard.

This was the political and economic background against which the movement for the "four modernisations" by the year 2000 was launched. In the first stage, to be achieved according to Zhou Enlai by 1980[4] China had to establish "an independent and relatively complete industrial economic system". The fulfilment of this objective would have demanded great acceleration in industrial development, originally encompassed in a 10-year plan, the realisation of which was compromised by political instability. So it was a revised plan which Hua Guofeng put before the deputies on 26 January 1978 at the Fifth National People's Congress, postponing until 1985 the fulfilment of the first stage of the four modernisations. It is probable that some targets were scaled down at the same time. Whether or not this is so, production of steel, fundamental to the industrial development anticipated in the plan, was supposed to reach 60 million tonnes in 1985, representing a growth of 12 per cent a year from 1978 to 1985, much higher than the 4.5 per cent a year achieved between 1970 and 1977.

Speeding up industrial growth required reorganisation of the industrial sector, as specified first in Deng Xiaoping's "20 Points", then in the later "30 Points" for industry. However, these documents still did not seem adequate to many Chinese economists who, having first imposed a policy of readjustment, were advocating reforms which went far beyond those proposed by Deng Xiaoping.

From the "20 Points" to the "30 Points"

During 1975, Deng Xiaoping drafted a paper entitled "Some Problems concerning the Acceleration of Industrial Development"[5] called the "20 Points", putting forward the measures he considered necessary to fulfil the 10-year plan for industry. Violently criticised by the radicals in 1976, this paper was rehabilitated in July 1978 with the promulgation of the "Decision on Some Problems concerning the Acceleration of Industrial Development", called the "30 Points for Industry".[6]

To justify the legitimacy of these two documents, *People's Daily* on 1 July 1978 printed an unpublished speech by Mao Zedong, made on 30 January 1962 during a Central Committee work conference. In this speech, Mao Zedong gave his approval to the "70 Points for Industry" put forward by Deng Xiaoping at a conference of Party secretaries in the industrial sector in December 1961.[7] A few days later, on 4 July, *People's Daily* announced the promulgation of the "30 Points", pointing out that they were the successors to the "70 Points" (criticised during the Cultural Revolution), the "10 Points" (the "Circular on the Implementation of Industrial Planning to Improve Economic Growth" drawn up in 1972, probably on the initiative of Zhou Enlai) and the "20 Points" of 1975.

These two documents, the "20 Points" and the "30 Points", provide the authority for the new industrial strategy, and comparison between them illustrates the evolution and the direction of actual industrial policy.[8]

General orientation

The short-term aim of industrialisation envisaged by these two documents was to allow the establishment of "industrial systems" (*gongye tixi*) each having its special characteristics and different levels within the framework of six regions of co-operation: South-West, Central-South, East, North, North-East, North-West".[9] According to the "20 Points", Point 2 (hereafter 20/2 etc.) each region was to achieve basic autonomy in steel, fuel, energy, light industrial products and light military equipment. Though the "30 Points" is less precise on the definition of industrialisation, it does give target dates in its introduction (hereafter 30/intro etc.): a relatively complete and independent industrial system before 1980; 14 important industrial bases and the establishment of the six regions before 1985; catch up with the advanced countries before 2000.

The principle of intra-regional co-operation implies a reorganisation of production units in the direction of greater specialisation, and hence the end of "large and complete" (*da er quan*) and "small and complete" (*xiao er quan*) enterprises, which were responsible for excessive waste of resources. Specialisation (*zhuanyehua*) means "standardisation" (*biaozhunhua*), "serialisation" (*xiliehua*) and "inter-changeabilisation" (*tongyonghua*): these are the "three -ations" (*san hua*). Such specialisation, which contributes to quality and speed of production, demands the renunciation of local bureaucratic self-interest. It would be replaced by a "communist style" (*gongchanzhuyi fengge*), induced by creative self-denial expressed in a "co-operative division of labour" (*fengong xiezuo*) linked by a system of contracts (20/; 30/10). Note that the radical wing of the Party appears to have shown no marked opposition on this point, although it involves the disappearance of "complete" enterprises, a "Maoist" concept.[10]

Priorities

Although the "20 Points" reaffirmed the necessity of giving a certain priority to agriculture (20/3), they did not formally restore the sectoral order of priorities: agriculture, light industry, heavy industry.[11] In fact, the "20 Points" defined the priorities in the following order: (a) steel (from extraction to processing) (b) coal, petroleum, electricity (c) petrochemicals (d) machine-tools industries (e) light and textile industries (f) transport and communications. In other words, heavy industry — especially steel — had precedence over light industry (20/2; 20/4).

The "30 Points" were much less normative. After re-affirming that industry must serve the development of agriculture (30/14), they established sectoral priorities as follows: (a) extractive industries (b) transport and communications (c) light industry, especially petro-chemicals (d) handicrafts and consumer goods industries (30/15), and a special paragraph was devoted to the development of energy sources (30/16). In summary, it would seem that here steel has to some extent lost its role as "marshal" (*yuanshuai*) of industrial development, a principle re-affirmed even in the 1977 article of the State Planning Commission.[12]

Management of the national economy

After re-affirming on the one hand the validity and success of decentralisation, implemented since 1970, and, on the other hand, the necessity of central control of key national enterprises, the "20 Points" state that, in the framework of the regions of co-operation, greater central control is indispensable over the "general direction" and "specific policies" of enterprises of national importance under the joint management of local and central authorities.

This relatively moderate statement was immediately criticised by the radicals as "dictatorship of branch (organisation)" (*tiaotiao zhuanzheng*).[13] This fear of seeing lateral Party controls reduced in favour of vertical control by central government agencies seems a little exaggerated in the context of the "20 Points", which affirm explicitly that planning must respect the rule "from the bottom to the top, with co-operation between the two; priority for horizontal structures (i.e. Party leadership) and co-operation between horizontal and vertical structures (i.e. between Party and governmental agencies) (*zi xia er shang, shang xia jiehe: kuaikuai wei zhu, tiao kuai jiehe*) (20/13, 20/14).

The fall of the Gang of Four allowed the demand for central

control by the government expressed in the "30 Points" to be affirmed without ambiguity. This Decision distinguished between different categories of enterprises and different degrees of centralisation:

1) key enterprises in the national economy directly under the Centre
2) a few key enterprises under joint control, local responsibility being limited to ideological work within these enterprises and distribution of products allowed by the State plan in local instances
3) large and medium enterprises under joint or provincial control; such enterprises could not be further decentralised and the provinces were responsible for their administration within the framework of the central plan
4) industry operated by communes, brigades and street committees, their activities being planned by county-level organs

Under this re-organisation, central plans were to be more stringent (*yansu*). Once transmitted down to the local authorities and to the enterprises, the latter had to go all out to implement them under the supervision of local bureaux of planning, economic affairs, capital construction and scientific/technical affairs (30/11, 30/12, 30/13).

Investment policy

Measures advocated by the "20 Points" and the "30 Points" in this field were more or less identical. First was the question of modernising out-of-date equipment to get maximum return from minimum investment. The "30 Points" specified that this modernisation had to aim not only at increasing the production of out-of-date units, but also at economising in energy and raw materials to protect the environment (20/5, 30/17, 30/18). Second, over-extended, costly and often irrational net formation of fixed capital was to be subject to detailed planning (including both state-financed and locally-financed projects). There were to be no projects outside the plan and no change in planned projects. It was also forbidden to divert investment funds allocated for other uses (20/9, 30/31).

Management of enterprises

Though the two documents agreed on their diagnosis of problems in industrial management — high costs, low labour productivity, waste of raw materials (20/7, 30/12) — the political context in 1975 did not allow the authors of the "20 Points" to be as explicit as those of the "30 Points". The first document devoted only a single paragraph (point 12) to this problem, while the second document began with this aspect and devoted eight articles to it (points 2-9).

In spite of their caution, the proposals of the "20 Points" concerning enterprise management were strongly criticised by the radical wing of the Party. According to the radicals, management has a class character and to deny this is to favour the restoration of a form of capitalist management. In order to maintain the socialist character of Chinese enterprise management, it was necessary to strengthen Party control over production units so as to appeal to the political consciousness of the workers.[14]

The "30 Points" posed three questions in dealing with this problem:

(a) What are the tasks of enterprises? "The normal task of an enterprise is to produce in order to reach or surpass State plan quotas, under the command of politics . . . politics being the concentrated expression of economics, politics must reflect economic requirements. Within an enterprise, political work must therefore serve production." The Party is not excluded from enterprises, but its role is reduced to that of guarantor for the fulfilment of their production tasks.

(b) How should an enterprise be managed? An enterprise should be run by dual management: a Party secretary and a manager. Both should be technically competent and faithful to the Party. The role of the Party secretary, assisted by a Party committee, is to check that technical decisions are in accordance with government policy, to organise the workers with the help of the union and the Communist Youth League, and to develop the political consciousness and professional ability of the workers by praising the merits of old workers. The manager is responsible for production and must ensure that the enterprise is well run in all respects (production, personnel, finance, etc.) giving everyone responsibility for a definite task.

(c) What should enterprise management be based on? The authorities guarantee to enterprises participation in "five fixes" (*wu ding*). Authorisation to establish a new production unit depends on obtaining these *wu ding*. These five norms are as follows: fixed production plans and scale; fixed number of personnel and organisations; fixed supply sources and consumption quotas for principal raw and other materials, fuel, power and tools; fixed set assets and circulating funds; fixed co-ordination and co-operation. Production units must also respect eight norms of good management: output, product variety (20/6; 30/19), quality, consumption, labour productivity, costs, profits, appropriations of circulating funds.

Hu Qiaomu later observed that the latter failed to include a norm for amortisation of capital expenditure.[15] This is one of the problems we will deal with later.

Employment policy

The two documents make no radically different proposals here[16] and they differ only in the rhetorical exhortation of the "20 Points". Thus, in dealing with the problem of the technical training of the workers, the "30 Points" did not scruple to entitle the article devoted to that subject "Red and Expert".[17]

Three themes are raised:

(a) Professional training. This is defined as an urgent matter with three aspects. First, it is necessary to master modern techniques, including the need to send leading cadres of technical ministries or key enterprises abroad for training, and to invite foreign experts to China. Second, it is necessary to speed up the training of technicians, particularly specialists in management. Third, basic technical training must be provided for workers, partly through training classes and partly by the reconstruction of a corps of master workers.

(b) Remuneration. The basic principle is to pay everyone according to his work (*an lao fenpei*) i.e. the re-adjustment of workers' wages according to their qualifications and contributions and the supplementary use of productivity bonuses. Bonuses are recommended both to combat "egalitarianism" and to avoid too great variations between highest and lowest salaries. However, it is stressed that workers must understand that the level of development in China does not allow a very high standard of living.

(c) Working conditions. Generally speaking, it is desirable to promote health, social and cultural work to enhance the well-being of workers. However, enterprises should as far as possible entrust these tasks to the municipal authorities who must appropriate more funds for the purpose.

Use of foreign technology

The "20 Points" develop this topic at length, devoting two articles to it (20/10-11). Chinese economic growth requires the introduction of advanced modern technology, and China must study what is good in foreign methods and acquire these techniques in a planned and systematic way for her own use. This does not mean renunciation of territorial sovereignty, nor should it reflect a blind cult of the foreign. The introduction of foreign technology is linked to the development of exports and the demands of international markets. Coal and oil are sectors which show the urgency of modernisation while offering the possibility of commercial exchange. China must cede part of her production of coal and oil to pay for modern equipment.

The reaction of the radical wing to this programme was more than lively. Deng Xiaoping was accused of having forgotten Chinese achievements and the unhappy experience of Sino-Soviet economic relations. Such a policy, the radicals maintained, would open China to a new plundering of her riches in exchange for out-of-date plant.[18]

The "30 Points", contrary to what we have noted in other respects, adopt in this case a much more cautious attitude by comparison. No article is devoted to this subject and it is only dealt with obliquely in a paragraph demanding the strengthening of scientific and technical research which includes the need to study foreign experience (30/22). However, the article recommending an energy-saving policy states that oil and coal should continue to be the spearhead of export policy (30/16).

Hu Qiaomu's Critique

No sooner had the "30 Points" been made public than it was subjected to a basic critique by the president of the Academy of Social Sciences Hu Qiaomu. His views were formulated during a meeting of the State Council in July 1978, but were not made public until three months later.[19] This delay was aimed at disarming the growing opposition to the "30 Points" just at the time when they were being communicated to the population. Hu's remarks fall into two categories, the first perhaps addressed more to the "radical" wing, the second to the "realist" wing.

Economic laws

The "30 Points" were issued in the context of a "new flying leap" (*xin fei yue*), officially launched in 1977, which was designed to fulfil the 10-year Plan.[20] Hu questioned this approach, attacking those who "believe that economic laws grow out of social determination and the will of leading government officials, and that these laws can be modified to meet political aspirations". Hu quoted Stalin (*Problems of the Socialist Economy in the USSR*) to support his argument: "We must not confuse our annual and quinquennial plans with the objective economic laws which direct the harmonious and ordered development of the economy of a nation." Hu argued that the socialist system did not, of itself, guarantee rapid and orderly economic development, and automatic respect for objective economic laws. He also argued that China was right to adopt advanced technology from capitalist countries, *but* must do so "thoughtfully and selectively". Here Hu was condemning the irrational fever of equipment imports which was sweeping China. In summary, he disapproved of solutions which led to extreme methods (a strategy of "leap forward; blind, massive imports, etc.) which were the result more of political whim than careful economic thought.

Bureaucracy and initiative

Hu deplored the fact that the whole discussion of the system of management of the national economy always revolved round a debate on the degree and method of centralisation and decentralisation of economic decisions (vertical or horizontal distribution of power among administrative departments or even between the Centre and local authorities) and, as a result, always failed to encourage practical measures to mobilise the initiative of those actually responsible for production.

Hu then put forward four proposals for reform. One, already hinted at in the "20 Points" then further developed in the "30 Points", envisaged the setting up of industrial combines. The other three were innovations: the re-introduction of an inter-enterprise contract system which would partly free enterprise managers from bureaucratic tutelage; reform of the banking system which would give more power of control to banks while guaranteeing more freedom and therefore more responsibility to enterprise managers; economic and commercial legislation which would define the legal framework — as opposed to the actual bureaucratic framework — in which enterprise managers would carry out their responsibilities.

Through these proposals, Hu Qiaomu criticised the very heart of the policy of economic management as defined in the "20 Points" and in the "30 Points". To sum up, whereas the latter documents proposed an economic system based on planning by command and enforced by administrative decrees, Hu proposed an economic system based on more flexible planning enforced by means of contracts (inter-enterprise contracts, credit contracts between banks and enterprises, and even work contracts) which would give more power and responsibility to enterprise managers. These ideas were taken up again and developed after the Third Plenum of the Central

Committee in December 1978, especially by economists at the Academy of Social Sciences writing mainly in the journal *Jingji Yanjiu (Economic Research)* and to a lesser extent in *People's Daily*.

Readjustment and Reform

The idea of the urgent need for *readjustment (tiaozheng)* in the Chinese economy, born without doubt during the Third Plenum in December 1978, did not appear overnight as if by magic. On the contrary, its appearance was preceded by psychological preparation which took the form, first, of drawing an analogy between recent errors and those of the Great Leap Forward (1958-61) and of condemning the latter;[21] and, second, of suggesting that a policy of readjustment was essential, just as it was after the Great Leap.

The authority invoked to justify the need for readjustment was Zhou Enlai, whose speech of 19 June 1961 to a meeting of literary and art personnel was published in *People's Daily* of 4 February 1979. In this speech, the former prime minister noted that intellectual production, like material production, followed objective laws which had been ignored during the preceding years (the Great Leap Forward), and that it was necessary to follow a policy of readjustment, just as in the economic field. If we change the application of Zhou's admonition, it is easy to apply the contents of each section of his speech to the economy:

Section I: overly high targets leading to scattered efforts and waste.
Section II: the need for a return to stability and sobriety.
Section III: too much importance given to capital construction.
Section IV: respect for objective laws, problems of quantity and quality, the relation between heavy and light industry, etc.
Section V: criticism of a policy of blind imports.
Section VI: reform of management methods.
Section VII: training of technicians.

A new stage was reached with a *People's Daily* editorial, dated 25 March 1979, entitled "Readjust while going forward, go forward while readjusting", calling for the revision of investment policy. Finally, during April 1979, a series of articles appeared justifying a policy of readjustment in all sectors and re-instating the work initiated by Chen Yun in the early sixties.[22] These articles heralded the establishment of the new State Commission for Economic and Financial Affairs which was set up in late March or early April and received legal sanction at the meeting of the 2nd session of the National People's Congress in June 1979. Chen Yun was president of this new Commission.

A new era, a new slogan. The slogan of this new period of readjustment, which was to last two to three years — 1979-81 — was "readjust, reform, reorganise, elevate" (*tiaozheng, gaige, zhengdun, tigao*). In the early sixties it had been "readjust, consolidate, strengthen, elevate" (*tiaozheng, gonggu, chongshi, tigao*). The differences in emphasis are relevant to a difference in atmosphere. In the early sixties, it was officially a matter of readjusting to consolidate the accomplishments of the Great Leap Forward, since at that time it was impossible to criticise openly the excesses of the Leap. Today, readjustment, to the extent that it implies reform, is a more direct condemnation of previous practices and might therefore be more effective.

General direction

Proposals for reform of the economic system do not re-open the issue of the general direction as defined by the "four modernisations" programme, but they reject the idea of autonomous regional development and of setting up complete and independent local industrial systems. These ideas had already been criticised by Hu Qiaomu. Likewise, in an article entitled "Manage local industrialisation according to actual conditions"[23] Li Shuodong did a swift economic calculation to show the waste created by the existence of iron-making centres in provinces poor in iron and coal, waste which prejudiced the exploitation of the real wealth of these provinces. The author argued that basing industrial development on the actual conditions of each province was not in opposition to the general direction of industrialisation policy.

> Everyone knows that when we speak of creating a complete and independent industrial system, we are speaking of the whole country . . . If, by neglecting the whole concrete question of raw materials, technique, etc . . . we insist absolutely that each large region or even each administrative region and each district develops its industry as a complete and independent industrial system, we will induce in the entire Chinese economy unbalanced development and enormous waste.

To attack the policy of autonomous local development was also to attack, to some extent, the priority given to steel production. Further, Li Shuodong envisaged an international division of labour based on an exchange of Chinese minerals (tin, antimony, zinc, lead) for foreign steel. However, such criticism did not yet amount to a demand for the renunciation at a national level of "taking steel as the key link" (*yi gang wei gang*).

Priorities

At the beginning of the Cultural Revolution, an article by the State Planning Commission reaffirmed that the general principle governing industrial policy was to take "steel as the key link".[24] Till recently, this way of thinking does not seem to have undergone the slightest change, and Hua Guofeng, in his report to the 1st session of the Fifth NPC in 1978, still affirmed this principle. On the other hand, supporters of economic readjustment proposed to renounce this principle because it was not obvious to them that progress in steel production is the *sine qua non* of general industrial and economic development in China.

Since the establishment of planning, Chinese practice has been to fix steel production first and then deduce other targets from this. Economists note that if economic development effectively depends on steel production, the converse is equally true: the possible growth of steel production depends on the development of other sectors. The target for steel production must therefore be fixed according to the actual situation and possibilities in other sectors. The economists conclude that targets in the middle term for steel production (60 million tonnes in 1985) must be cut (to 45 million tonnes according to some sources) in order to conform with actual circumstances (calculated by certain experts).[25]

This reconsideration of priority for steel and heavy industry was accompanied by a re-affirmation of the following order of priorities: agriculture, light industry, heavy industry. The plan must first fix the targets in the agricultural sector and, on the basis of these, determine tasks in light and then heavy industry. The latter, reduced to a suitable size, would receive only the funds necessary for its adaptation to the needs of the other sectors.

Conditions in agriculture and light industry are not entirely comparable. Certainly, neither sector has benefitted much from State appropriations, especially light industry: agriculture needs massive investment to *modernise,* while light industry needs it *to make a start.* Light industry is the weakest link in the Chinese economy: without light industry, agriculture cannot modernise: without light industry, heavy industry cannot find markets.[26]

In the past, the order of priority was: heavy industry, agriculture, light industry, with very low rates of investment in light industry[27]:

First Five Year Plan 5.9 per cent (46.5 per cent in heavy industry); Second Five Year Plan 3.9 per cent; Third Five Year Plan 4 per cent; Fourth Five Year Plan 5.4 per cent (deflated rate: 2.1 per cent).

The figure for the Fourth Five Year Plan is not entirely comparable with those of the preceding Plans. Before (1970) light industry could be defined as a processing industry manufacturing consumer goods. After (1970) light industry also came to include a transformation industry processing raw materials — intermediate consumption — like textile fibres, for example, serving a traditional light industry in its aim but sometimes modernised in its techniques. Also, the rate of investment for 1971-75 (Fourth Five Year Plan) must be reduced from 5.4 per cent to 2.1 per cent to make the figures comparable, and so the downward trend is more striking. At first sight, this analysis may seem rather specious if we do not point out that the definition of light industry had undergone some change. During the First and Second Five Year Plans, the distinction between heavy industry and light industry was economic (i.e., between producer and consumer goods): during the Third and Fourth Five Year Plans, the distinction became more political (strategic and non-strategic goods, centrally managed and locally managed units). Therefore the deflated rate of investment during the Fourth Five Year Plan is comparable with those of the First and Second Five Year Plans, whereas the gross rate of investment during the Fourth Five Year Plan is only comparable with that of the Third Five Year Plan.

The lack of support for light industry constituted a strong check to Chinese economic development. At the present time, 30 per cent of China's disposable accumulation comes from light industry, despite the weakness of this sector. In other words, in view of the financial profitability of this sector, active support for its development would create an important source of accumulation leading to a process of rapid general growth in the medium term, for it takes, on average, only five years to recover investment in this sector (two years to build a new production unit plus three years in production).[28]

The argument that weak domestic markets would limit investment opportunities does not hold. In 20 years (1957-77), we are told,[29] Chinese purchasing power trebled, while in the same period the quantity of textiles available on ration coupons (*bu piao*) stayed the same. In an article in *Economic Research,* Liu Guoguang goes even further.[30] Not only does a domestic market for industrial consumer goods exist, but it is even able to support a policy of growth by inflation: light industry would be able to finance its development thanks to a rise in the price of its products. According to the author, such a policy is a corollary of the introduction of a "market economy" limited to certain sectors.

The argument of the weakness of the domestic market is less valid insofar as light industry is the major export industry; the contempt in which this sector has been held prevents the full expansion of its advantages in this field. *People's Daily* of 1 June 1979 quoted the example of the silk industry at Suzhou, 60 per cent of whose production is exported. In Suzhou one of the silk-spinning mills has been idle, as of mid-1979, for three months due to lack of raw materials and energy. One of the biggest mills in the city had to stop a hundred machines for the same reasons. Huang Jichang, the author of the article, pointed out that the Suzhou mills were competing for raw materials and energy with:

(a) heavy industry: in 1978, the Zhenya mill, one of the most important, had to cease production 80 times due to lack of electricity which, in the context of a general shortage of energy, was reserved for heavy industry. The loss of production amounted to a million metres of silk.

(b) rural workshops: the communes which raise silk-worms keep the best of their crop for their own handicraft mills. The result is that on the one hand, rural workshops spoil good silk thread due to lack of adequate equipment and so produce inferior silk goods, while on the other hand, the modern silk mills in Suzhou are reduced to making only mediocre-quality silks with the poor thread sold to them by the communes. The author concluded that the readjustment policy must stress support for light industry, and called on the State Commission for Economic Affairs and local authorities to protect the sources of supply for this sector, even at the expense of other sectors.[31]

Management of the national economy

National economic management is characterised both by a multiplicity of administrative centres and by centralisation of the powers of decision. Each administrative centre seeks, in conditions of severe competition, to appropriate the largest allocations of raw materials, investment funds, foreign exchange, etc., regardless of actual requirements or overall balance. Then, in order to fulfil the frequently unrealistic norms of an authoritatively imposed plan, each administrative centre is concerned only with producing as much as possible, regardless of the quality of its products, which are stockpiled in commercial warehouses which never know what to do with them. It would be pointless to expect them to act otherwise, for their actions are the result of a centralism which binds them hand and foot by refusing them any responsibility in the administration of the economy.[32]

Nevertheless, this centralism co-exists with a *de facto* decentralisation which results, on the one hand, in anarchical anti-centralism inherited from the Cultural Revolution, and, on the other hand, parallel circuits ("going through the back door", say the Chinese) created by these administrative centres in an attempt to mitigate the costs of centralism.[33]

According to Xue Muqiao, the ideal would be a delicate balance between centralisation and decentralisation according to the strategic character of the activity of enterprises. He proposed the following plan:[34]

1) banks, telecommunications, rail, air and long-distance sea transport should be the responsibility of unified national administration, but it is possible to consider setting up regional accounting agencies.
2) inter-continental transport and communications, the electricity distribution network, a few enterprises of national scope in the iron, oil and coal sectors should be put under direct State control; this should not exclude their participation in cartels (horizontal integration) or in combines (vertical integration).
3) the majority of enterprises should be under local authorities and should be able to take part in cartels or combines in order to undertake activities beyond the scope of their speciality or their province.
4) consumer goods industries should be under locally decentralised administration and their products should be marketable both by State commercial services and by non-governmental organs of distribution (the author assumes a combine).
5) local workshops should be managed by districts, communes, small towns or street committees in cities; the juridical form of these workshops should be that of a co-operative responsible for its losses and profits; distribution could take place through State commercial circuits as well as through supply and marketing co-operatives and in a free market, particularly for that part of production locally consumed.

This conception of centralism led to a new conception of the role of planning: imperative planning (*zhilingxing de jihua*) should become indicative (*zhidaoxing*)[35] or the Plan should even become an instrument of reference (*cankaoxing*),[36] at least as far as goods of non-strategic importance from an economic and military point of view are concerned and for economic transactions which do not risk putting fundamental choices in question. Moreover, the plan must be worked out from the bottom upwards (transmission to the central authorities of contracts made among enterprises, etc.) in the case of daily production (simple reproduction), but from the top downwards when investment is involved (extended reproduction).[37]

Investment policy

Investment policy is a direct result of the actual form of administration of the economy which encourages a waste of State funds and, to quote again from *People's Daily*, "there is always enough money to buy a coffin but never enough for medicine".[38] There are short-term plans guaranteeing construction and providing for the establishment of new production units, but there is no long-term plan justifying their economic usefulness. Moreover, many production units lack necessary technical improvements and/or indispensable investment upstream and downstream and respond badly to the hopes vested in them.[39]

To remedy production weakness in a sector in relation to the needs of the economy, the solution adopted by the Chinese authorities has often been to increase the number of production units in the weak sectors by establishing new units — "the coffins" — which, in the absence of investment — "the medicine" — further constrict the bottle-necks already in existence and have greatly reduced economic efficiency, even more so than the old units.

According to the pro-Peking journal *Zhengming*, published in Hong Kong, it is this policy which was at the root of the Wuhan and Baoshan scandals.[40] The Wuhan Iron and Steel Company had placed an order with the Federal Republic of Germany for rolling-mill equipment with an annual production capacity of four million tonnes. In making their order, the responsible Chinese had taken account only of China's steel requirements and had simply forgotten to take into account electricity supply in the city. The strategically important Wuhan Iron and Steel Company did not feel the effects of the actual scarcity of energy for, in order to guarantee its electricity supply, other industries were forced to close down. But if the complex bought from the Germans was to be put into operation, the total electricity supply in the province of Hubei would not be enough. More than that, the supply of steel for rolling remains hypothetical, for the city of Wuhan is incapable of providing enough steel to keep its rolling mills in full production.

The Baoshan Steel Works in Shanghai is a complex of six million tonnes capacity, ordered from Japan. To begin with, the project only involved the construction of an ironworks, but some high officials responsible for the project decided to change it into a six million tonne steel works. Leaving aside the economic profitability of the operation, it seems clear that it was initiated more on a nod of the head than after detailed study. The site chosen presented the problem of extensive shifting sands and, in spite of the injection of 10 thousand tonnes of reinforced concrete, it was impossible to ensure stable foundations for the future steel works.[41] Moreover, it was expected that this steel works would import ore for processing (mainly from Australia), but the draught of modern ore-ships requires a deep-water port which the neighbouring city of Wusong, at the mouth of the Wusongjiang (Suzhouhe), cannot offer. Therefore these vessels would have to unload their cargoes at Zhapu. Baoshan is in the northern part of Shanghai municipality, while Zhapu, to the south of Shanghai, is in the province of Zhejiang. What's more, the city of Zhapu is far enough from the Hangzhou-Shanghai railway to make the project unrealistic. In February 1979, the Chinese government informed its Japanese partners that the Baoshan contract was provisionally suspended.

Such inefficiency provides one explanation for the sharp curb put on the import of turnkey factories. It is pointless to increase the production capacity of a certain product when, first, the production units already in existence have neither the outlets nor the supplies to guarantee the full use of their production capacities and, second, the new production units offer no means of solving these problems, even if they do not actually increase them.

Besides, the Chinese authorities suffer from the constraints of a limited budget. The financial burden represented by too many projects undertaken at the same time entails an allocation of so little credit to each project that completion takes much too long. This delay in the completion of new production units results in the mobilisation of capital without benefit. The State, lacking the power to recover its funds quickly, sees its available funds still more limited. This provides a second explanation for the brake applied to the import of factories.

Moreover, the demand for raw materials for the construction of these projects aggravates the bottle-necks already existing, and therefore further blocks the development of other sectors of the economy.

Investment policy is not limited simply to the net formation of capital but concerns equally the replacement of used capital.

Management and depreciation of existing capital are two aspects too often neglected by the Chinese authorities, as Hu Qiaomu commented with reference to the "30 Points". The distinguished economist Sun Yefang returned to this problem in an article in *Red Flag*, June 1979:

> We live with a system of management of equipment dating back to the Russians at the time of the 1st Five Year Plan. Even then many people found it inadequate. This system is irrational in the first instance because it anticipates too long a period of depreciation. Our period of depreciation stretches from 25 to over 30 years (e.g., the rate of depreciation in the Anshan Steelworks is 2.92 per cent, a depreciation period of over 30 years). This regulation holds that our technical equipment acquires nil value only after a life of 20 or 30 years; in other words, this system is concerned only with what political economy calls material depreciation and neglects obsolescence.[42]

The system is also irrational in its method of regulating the maintenance of equipment and therefore in its battle against obsolescence. An enterprise allocates funds for maintenance and distributes them in three categories: daily maintenance, major repairs and modernisation. The funds assigned to the first two categories remain at the disposal of the enterprises; funds assigned to the third category, the most important, are handed over to the Treasury. However, government policy often consists of utilising these funds for new investment instead of for modernising, as intended, out-of-date production units needing renewal of their equipment.[43]

Sun Yefang therefore proposed: (a) increasing the rate, and so shortening the period, of depreciation; (b) applying a system of diminishing depreciation so that the cost price does not increase with the age of the equipment; (c) modernising production units already in existence in preference to building new ones, and thus (d) entrusting the enterprises themselves with the management of their depreciation funds.

Such a reform, if it were applied, would have two results: first, real decentralisation of some decisions concerning investment which, to be effective, would have to be accompanied by a reform of enterprise management; and, second, a decrease, mainly in the short and middle term, in State revenue: a direct decrease because certain funds would no longer be handed over to the State, and an indirect decrease because, with the increase in the rate of depreciation, the profits returned to the State would be reduced by the supplementary depreciation funds.

Sun Yefang goes still further, calling for a true re-evaluation of balance-sheets with a view to accounting for equipment at its real value (depreciation and obsolescence included). Such an operation would result in reducing the base of State resources and therefore in limiting even further its financial revenue, but this operation would prevent the authorities from continuing to squander existing capital (*chi "lao ben"*) in order to acquire new production units.

Sun's conclusion is that too often the concepts of "simple reproduction" and "extended reproduction" have been so misunderstood that they have been confused. In consequence, the second is financed with funds intended for the first, resulting in the reduction of the possibilities for "extended reproduction".

Enterprise management

The participants at a round table organised by the Economic Research Institute of the Academy of Social Sciences and the journal *Economic Research* noted that Chinese enterprises lose themselves in a labyrinth of norms:

> The economic targets of enterprises are transmitted to them individually by the administrative departments; the quantitative production norms are defined by the administrative industrial departments; the qualitative production norms are defined by the planning departments; financial production norms (cost price, profit) are defined by the finance departments. Those responsible for setting the quantitative norms have no interest in qualitative norms; those responsible for setting qualitative norms have no interest in financial norms.[44]

To keep pace with their planned production targets, enterprises tend to build up excessive stocks of raw materials in order to absorb the shocks in supply resulting from deficiences in the marketing and communications networks. In this way, parallel circuits of supply are formed ("going through the back door"). The enterprises also build up secret stocks of finished products, as much to participate in the game of selling "by the back door" as to respond immediately to political campaigns, in the course of which an enterprise must prove the effectiveness of its campaign leadership by an increase in production. Moreover, to fulfil their production targets, enterprises make use of a large labour force drawn illegally from the countryside by the attraction of good pay.

Excessive stocks of raw materials and finished products and surplus labour force combine to increase the financial costs of enterprises. It is clear that the allocation of circulating funds assigned by the State does not allow them to meet all their requirements (in

China, enterprises have no funds of their own — at least legally — authorising them to conduct autonomous management or to be self-financing). Enterprises cannot therefore respond to the demands of the financial plan (planned transfer of the profits of their undertakings). The number of burdens, including social security, sanitation, social and even cultural activities, weigh on enterprises and lead to an artificial inflation of their cost prices and to "black treasuries" allowing them to pay illegal labour, finance their stocks and even to be self-financing. These various practices are denounced as "diversion, monopolisation, retention" (*nuoyong, jizhan, liuyong*).[45]

This situation results from the lack of decision-making power of enterprise managers. He Jianzhang made the following analysis:[46]

(a) Enterprises have no power to plan or to market their production. The plan imposed on enterprises reaches them after transmission by stages from the centre to the local authorities, passing through various administrative levels. This plan, which is annual, is deduced from the planned rate of growth of the National Product. As a logical consequence, the criteria of good management formulated in the "30 Points"[47] endeavour to evaluate the efforts of enterprises in contributing to an increase in the National Product, and so to measure the growth in their production value. Enterprises have to attend only to increasing their production, and it makes no difference to them whether their profits are high or low; nor do they have to concern themselves about the marketing of their products since State agencies are in charge of distribution. "Production determines consumption" (*chan ding xiao*), but nothing guarantees that supply can satisfy demand: neither over-production nor under-production is precluded.

(b) Enterprises have no financial power. Here, the author distinguishes between the problem of management of depreciation allowances and the problem of management of profits. We have already dealt with the first in our analysis of Sun Yefang's article.[48] As for the second, it concerns "the superiority of the system of whole-people ownership", which is "eating from the common pot" (*chi da guo fan*); in other words, profits and losses are passed on to the "higher levels" in such a way that the revenue of enterprises is independent of the quality of management. This system discourages all management incentive in as much as the financial regulations which are imposed on the enterprises are such that "what is rational is illegal" and "what is legal is irrational".

Stating that "the socialist economy is only a particular form of commercial economy", the author proposes a new charter for enterprises according to which they would be given the following powers: to plan their activities in accordance with the needs of the State and of the market; to market their products provided they fulfil their contracts; to decide on utilisation of their funds after meeting State quotas; to manage their staff; to fix, according to the market, the selling price of their products (at least for the part subject neither to taxation nor to contract); and to refuse all arbitrary administrative deduction.

This charter assumes the establishment of an economic sector governed by the laws of a "market economy" co-existing with a planned sector. To justify such a proposal, a series of articles was published in *Economic Research* under the joint title "On market production and the law of value in a socialist regime".[49]

The autonomy and thus the responsibility which enterprise managers would acquire would justify the call for effective and rational management, judged not so much by the market value of production as by the added value of this production. In other words, those responsible for the national economy would no longer have to define economic objectives in terms of growth of the National Product, but in terms of growth of the added value of the National Product.[50]

This increasing autonomy would necessitate, within the framework of such a "market economy", the establishment of new relations among enterprises, and even between the State and the enterprises. What was proposed by Hu Qiaomu, and others after him, was in fact the legalisation and side application of commercial practices considered even today illegal ("going through the back door") by the reintroduction of a contract system and the drawing-up of a commercial code. These contracts would have a three-fold advantage: they would partially suppress the elaboration of a plan of allocation with its huge and rigid bureaucratic machinery; they would facilitate planning, since knowledge of the contract would allow the State to follow production exchange and development; and they would make enterprise managers responsible for their production.

This autonomy would at the same time necessitate a reform of the banking system. The simple cash-desk banks through which funds allocated by the State are distributed would become active agents in economic development. Enterprises would no longer receive a planned allocation of working capital, but would justify their needs to the banks which would grant loans with interest varying according to time, risk, etc. — the same would apply to investments.[51]

These reforms, to be viable, need some decentralisation of economic decisions and, as a result, only seem applicable to non-strategic industries. Likewise, these reforms assume that the guiding role of the Party at the level of local administration and production units should be considerably curtailed in favour of managers.

Employment policy

Peking Daily published on 18 July 1979 an interview with Xue Muqiao, in which the director of the Economic Research Institute of the State Planning Commission gave his opinions on employment policy, which are summarised here.

The Chinese government is finding it impossible to guarantee a secure job (*tie fan wan* or "iron rice-bowl") for every young unemployed person. At the same time, it is not prepared to authorise the development of free enterprise — collective or individual — and so the number of unemployed continues to grow. The towns are finding that they cannot support their total population; the countryside has its own difficulties and its capacity to assimilate the urban surplus population is very limited. Moreover, if labour rationalisation measures aimed at increasing labour productivity are taken in industry and in administration, the number of State workers and employees will fall. In the same way, mechanisation of agriculture would free surplus manual labour. The solution of employment problems lies therefore in the reform of labour management.

Xue Muqiao spoke of three major faults in the actual organisation of labour allocation: (a) its rigidity: once a person has a secure job it is practically impossible to dismiss him, and if an enterprise for reasons of profitability places a worker at the disposal of the labour allocation office, the enterprise is then forced to employ a child of that worker. Moreover, under the pretext of combatting "capitalist infiltration" (*ziben zhuyi loudong*), numerous essential activities are prohibited; (b) its authoritarianism: Xue compares the actual system of unified distribution of labour to a "marriage arranged by the parents and a go-between": workers do not get the desired posting and try to escape from it and enterprises find themselves saddled with workers whose qualifications do not meet their requirements. Xue declares himself in favour of "love marriages", ie., work contracts freely negotiated; (c) its monopoly: the introduction of work contract does not re-open to any great extent the issue of the monopoly situation in which the labour allocation bureaux find themselves. It would only reduce the powers of these bureaux by changing them into employment agencies. Xue goes further, stating that the establishment of a system of unified distribution, followed by the authoritarian suppression of joint or co-operative enterprises in 1958, entailed the disappearance without compensation of many essential activities (service trades, workshops, etc.) and a corresponding increase in unemployment for want of sufficient opportunities in State enterprises. He also proposes a return to free enterprise, either by individuals or co-operatives responsible for their profits and losses, employing youths freely associated. This would have the advantage, in addition to reducing unemployment, of improving the welfare of the citizens through the development of certain sectors such as traditional crafts, catering, building, transport, repairs, etc.

Use of foreign technology

Those who propose radical reforms in the Chinese economic system seldom raise this subject except to warn, in passing, against any policy of uncontrolled imports.

Taken together, these proposals for reform and their justification constitute a devastating criticism of the Chinese economic system. On reading these authors, it becomes clear that a policy of readjustment alone will be unable to solve the problems facing China, not only since the Cultural Revolution but even since the late 1950s.

There is a shady zone in their statements: what will the function of the Party be in a China reformed according to the views of the economists? "Enough empty talk, the people want tangible improvements", said Hu Qiaomu, quoting a lucid Mao Zedong.[52] These words show that in the eyes of the experts of the Academy of Social Sciences, the Party today is incapable of serving the best interests of the Chinese people and, in this case, what task should be assigned to it? Does not a refusal to discuss this respect already condemn any attempt at reform?

Readjustment and the Economic Plan for 1979

The economic readjustment policy and the objectives for 1979 were put forward on 21 June 1979 at the second session of the Fifth NPC by Yu Qiuli in his report on the national economic plan for 1979 and by Finance Minister Zhang Jingfu in his report on the implementation of the State budget for 1978 and the draft budget for 1979.[53]

The plan submitted by Yu Qiuli was one revised to take into account the necessity of readjustment. The revisions, regarded as essential in early 1979, were not officially presented until late June;

in other words, the industrial sector operated for 6 months on the basis of the former version of the directives (priority for steel and heavy industry, etc.), and the effects of readjustment in 1979 were very much reduced. Moreover, the real, authorised attempt at readjustment remained very limited (cf., for example, investment policy) and the reforms necessary for healthy and effective administration of the economy could not, on the admission even of the Minister of Finance, be put into operation for a long time.

Also the 1979 readjustment policy seems to be more a matter of politics — expressing certainly the growing influence of the economists — than a precise economic reality. Only a renewal of political elites would allow a new (revived) reforming will to affirm itself in concrete economic acts.[54]

The general situation at the end of 1978

The Chinese economy at the end of 1978 had the following problems, according to Yu Qiuli and Zhang Jingfu: scarcity of energy and raw materials; production norms often not achieved, particularly those for product quality and the amount of intermediate consumption; over-high investment in capital construction; excessive stocks due to bad distribution; poor organisation of international trade; and an absence of global economic equilibrium ascribed to inadequate economic management.

Priorities

Priorities were defined as follows: first, priority to agriculture; second, greater emphasis on light industry by giving it priority for energy, raw materials and transport, to the disadvantage of heavy industry. The latter aims to improve standards of living and develop export capacity. Heavy industry was to be oriented towards better use of its excess production capacity as well as towards diversification and improved product quality. Third, measures to solve the energy shortage. Besides efforts towards short and long-term increase in supplies, it was expected (a) to ensure priority in energy supply for economically profitable enterprises, closing down those making losses; (b) to control strictly the use of energy; (c) to transform oil-consuming industries into coal-consumers; (d) to put the supply of electricity under unified State control; and (e) to draw up an energy law.

Administration of the national economy

Zhang Jingfu pointed out the need for reform in national economic administration. However, such reform required preliminary studies as well as experimental trials, the absence of which prevented the complementary reform of financial administration, the domain of Zhang Jingfu. Also, it was in the framework of the current financial administrative system that a rearrangement of relations between State and local administrations was being attempted. Zhang stated that, in the near future a new step would be taken by tying local expenditure to local revenue. The aim of these arrangements was to bring about some redistribution of powers of decision to remedy a situation "where what should be centralised is not; where what should be decentralised is not".

Investment policy

There were two major concerns in investment policy. First, it was thought necessary to readjust the relationship between accumulation and consumption in order to increase the standard of living. Hence a fall in the absolute value of investment was anticipated in the 1979 budget, compared with 1978. Second, it was also thought important to readjust the distribution of investment among the three sectors, according to the order of priority, producing an extra effort in favour of agriculture.

Industrial investment policy was characterised by a fall in total investment (-24.4 per cent compared with 1978) and a slight fall in the value of investment in light industry, which seems rather contradictory at a time when the stress is on developing this long-neglected sector. There was also a great fall in the value of investment in heavy industry. The actual priority which heavy industry continued to enjoy (investment 8 times higher than in light industry, as originally laid down in the Ten Year Plan; 3½ times higher than in agriculture) was partly the result of the energy shortage. On the other hand, it was clear that steel had lost, at least for some time, its role of "marshal".

The plan was marked by an apparent absence of any arrangements for capital depreciation.

In spite of these reductions, 52.6 per cent of investment was still appropriated for industry, which showed that the building of China was first and foremost a project of industrialisation. The Chinese regime is thus comparable in the respect to other Communist regimes in the world.[55]

Management of enterprises

This subject, discussed by Yu Qiuli and Zhang Jingfu, was the subject of a national conference held at Chengdu (Sichuan) in July 1979, under the chairmanship of Kang Shien, Vice-Premier and President of the State Commission for Economic Affairs.[56] During this conference, the results of trials conducted in 400 enterprises spread over six municipalities and provinces — Peking, Tianjin, Shanghai, Jiangsu, Liaoning and Sichuan — were reported. All these are advanced regions, and are given priority industrially: in the case of Sichuan, it seems that the enterprises concerned were situated mainly in the industrial centres of Chengdu and Zhongqing.

The operation conducted in Sichuan was reported very explicitly. From October 1978, a first series of experiments was conducted in 6 enterprises before being extended, early in 1979, to a number of enterprises under provincial, municipal or local control, representing 11 different sectors. It was a question, essentially, of increasing the autonomy of the enterprises by a number of measures which included:

1) increased autonomy of production management, at least for that part over the quotas, and therefore for the supply of raw materials and the marketing pertaining to them; whence the development of a contract system.
2) greater autonomy in financial management, particularly by an increase in the share of the appropriation for depreciation left to the enterprises, as well as by the method of calculation of circulating funds formerly evaluated according to needs and financed by bank credits at a variable rate of interest.
3) increased autonomy in personnel management.
4) increased autonomy in external trade: the enterprises could sign export contracts and participate in all negotiations concerning them.

Moreover, the promulgation of five decisions to be applied on a trial basis in some selected state-owned enterprises was announced at this conference, namely:

1) regulations to increase the power of state-owned industrial enterprises over their own management.
2) a regulation on retention of profits by state-owned enterprises.
3) a trial regulation to increase the rate of depreciation of fixed assets of state-owned enterprises and to improve the use of depreciation funds.

4) a trial regulation on the taxation of the fixed assets of state-owned enterprises.
5) trial regulations for the financing by credit of the whole amount of circulating funds of state-owned enterprises.

All these measures were in the direction advocated by the reforming economists, yet however wide-ranging they might be, to be fully effective they had to be accompanied by an even more fundamental reform: the introduction of a "market economy" as demanded by the economists.

Employment policy

A major feature of the reports was the official recognition of significant unemployment, especially among the young.[57] The government succeeded in providing in 1978 3,870,000 jobs in the cities (the number of wage-earners in the cities at the end of 1978 was 94,990,000). 7,500,000 new jobs were to be created in 1979 either directly — extra employees, the creation of collective enterprises in the trade and service sectors[58] — or indirectly — lowering the retirement age of women and of some categories of workers accompanied by priority in employment for one of the children of the retired[59] and voluntary early retirement accompanied by the same job priority.[60] These last two methods, however, have the disadvantage of replacing skilled workers with inexperienced workers; the result is that the retired workers are re-employed by other production units to gain from their experience.

Use of foreign technology

The attitude towards this was rather ambiguous. On the one hand, some writings favoured a development policy "a la chinoise", underlining the dangers of opening up to the West as much by recalling the experience of China in the nineteenth century[61] as by timely publication of some of Mao Zedong's remarks on music, folklore and cooking.[62] On the other hand, the government seemed to be prepared to accept a planned deficit in the balance of trade, increasing by 182 per cent a year. In her entire foreign trade, China registered in 1978 a deficit of nearly Y2,000 million, or slightly more than 5.5 per cent of the global volume of her trade. The plan put forward by Yu Qiuli anticipated that this deficit would in 1979 reach the sum of Y5,600 million, 60 per cent of which would be accounted for by the increase — rash in the view of some — in the import of turnkey factories already in hand and the relevant technology.[63]

Table 2 Chinese Foreign Trade (in thousand millions yuan)

	1977	1978	1979
Total trade	27.25	35.50	44.00
increase		+30.3%	+23.9%
Imports	13.30	18.74	24.80
increase		+41.1%	+32.4%
Exports	13.95	16.76	19.20
increase		+20.0%	+14.7%
Surplus	0.65	-	-
Deficit	-	1.98	5.60
increase			+182.00%

Source: Report of the National Bureau of Statistics; reports of Yu Qiuli and Zhang Jingfu.

It is difficult, in the course of a year, to make radical changes in objectives planned well in advance; it is impossible to impose abruptly even urgent reforms. However, the attempt at readjustment could have been clearer and more precise. The economic plan for 1979 certainly could not be considered as a readjustment plan but, at best, as a transitional plan until such time as an economic policy of readjustment could be defined.

Table 3 Investment in 1978 & 1979 (in thousand millions yuan)

	1978	1979	increase
Budgetary expenditure	111.093	112.000	
Total investment	45.192	39.000	-3.7%
proportion of total investment in the budget	40.7%	34.8%	
Investment in agriculture	4.83	5.46	+13%
proportion of total investment	10.7%	14.0%	
Investment in industry	27.16	20.51	-24.4%
proportion of total investment	60.1%	56.2%	
Investment in light industry	2.44	2.26	-7.4%
proportion of total investment	5.4%	5.8%	
Investment in heavy industry	24.72	18.15	-26.1%
proportion of total investment	54.7%	46.8%	

Source: The reports of Yu Qiuli and Zhang Jingfu.

Obviously, sudden changes are not very desirable. "To achieve the socialist modernisation of our economy, we must first of all re-balance and re-arrange it in order to guarantee a solid base for the four modernisations. Then we must reform the system of economic management and manage our economy according to objective economic laws in order to endure good conditions for the four modernisations . . . . To readjust and to reform are contradictory, for to readjust involves a temporary strengthening of economic management unified by the Centre, while to reform assumes a decentralisation of powers. To resolve this contradiction, it is necessary first to readjust and then to reform . . . . '' This is the aim of Xue Muqiao.[64] If there could be an end to political dissension, it might be achieved.

7

POLICY CHANGES IN CHINA'S FOREIGN TRADE SINCE THE DEATH OF MAO, 1976-80

Colina MacDougall

Financial Times, London

Introduction: The Political, Economic and Historical Background

The fall of the Gang of Four, and the accession to power of a new, development-minded leadership after Mao's death in 1976, meant the growth of a new outward-looking attitude in Peking. In the years 1976-80, China plunged into a new round of trade activities, seeking to import technology, borrow money, request aid, attract investment and adopt fresh methods of earning foreign exchange. The narrow "self-reliance" of the Gang — the relegation of imports and exports to a purely marginal role in the economy — was abandoned. After a heady period of extravagant buying in 1977-78, in the next two years the leadership embraced every possible device to bring in foreign technology and capital with minimum expenditure. At the end of 1980, the worsening state of the economy forced more import cuts, but Peking continued to pursue co-operation with foreigners. All these shifts in policy can be charted in accordance with the major changes in leadership during those years.

As long ago as 1959, the collapse of the Great Leap Forward, Mao's disastrous mass mobilisation scheme to galvanise production, polarised China's leaders into "radical" and "moderate". From then to the time of his death, leadership policies in the economy and trade swung between the two, according to whether or not Mao was in the ascendant. During the 1970s, Mao and the Gang of Four — his wife and her three Shanghai colleagues — promoted increasingly radical economic ideas. These included egalitarianism, moral incentives, a prominent role for ideology, disregard of the facts of economic life such as the need to avoid waste, and stress on China's "self-reliance". Taken to extremes, as these attitudes were by the Gang, they meant little trade, no incoming aid or credits, little foreign technology and certainly no kowtowing by making products deliberately to attract foreigners.

This tendency to self-reliance was inspired in many Chinese by resentment at China's "semi-colonial" status in the first half of this century and the corruption in the 1940s under the Guomindang, caused in part by US aid. It was aggravated, particularly in Mao himself, by the quarrel in 1960 with the Soviets which caused the suspension of vital industrial projects which Moscow was supplying.

While analysing the Chinese leadership is always speculative, the immediate 1976 post-Gang leadership appears to have been made up of three loose groupings. On the left were the "radicals", who had been close to the Gang, such as Wang Dongxing, once Mao's bodyguard. Associated with them were a group of Cultural Revolution beneficiaries like the peasant leader, Chen Yongguei, of little real power. More to the right, in Chinese terms, was a group of conventional bureaucrats and senior military men of "moderate" views, such as Vice-Premier Li Xiannian, who had 25 years of governmental economic experience, and Party and Military Commission Vice-Chairman Ye Jianying (who as chairman of the National People's Congress Standing Committee was also nominal head of state).

Among this last group, whose views were more flexible than those of the radicals but probably went no further than seeking to restore the successful economic practices of the 1950s, were the supporters of the twice-disgraced Vice-Premier, Deng Xiaoping, dismissed from the leadership in April 1976. They were able to ensure his restoration to power in mid-1977 and to support him in bringing back other economic figures at or soon after the major watershed of the December 1978 Central Committee Third Plenum. These figures included former party Vice-Chairman Chen Yun and former Vice-Premier Bo Yibo, both pragmatic leaders of the 1950s and 1960s. They were shortly followed into power by bolder economic thinkers like the innovative Zhao Ziyang, party First

Secretary of Sichuan who replaced Hua Guofeng as Premier in September 1980.

Initially Chairman Hua uneasily straddled the three groups. He was, like the first two, a beneficiary of the Cultural Revolution and yet, like the bureaucrats, a man of much administrative experience. But after the Third Plenum a cleavage in the leadership became increasingly obvious, isolating the radicals and the Cultural Revolution beneficiaries, as the new economically-oriented leaders were able to implement their ideas. The conventional bureaucrats appear to have given them their support. But during 1980 Hua was gradually eased out of the leadership, resigning the premiership in September and losing the chairmanship in all but name during the trial of the Gang of Four in December.

However, even to the immediately post-Gang leadership it was obvious that the Chinese economy needed a fresh approach. Since the Leap, there had been little consistent effort to control population growth, which had expanded alarmingly. After the Cultural Revolution, grain production had risen, but not enough to improve the standard of living. Other food production had been neglected. Investment in industry had been misguided, being too much channelled into steel and machine-building, with resulting overproduction. The post-Cultural Revolution leadership had naively assumed that higher production meant greater wealth without realising the waste of resources in producing unusable goods. The disgrace of the academic economists during the Cultural Revolution and the danger of discussing alternative ideas meant there was no airing of these problems.

By 1976 many people had been demoralised by the overt political infighting. The stagnation, if not decline, in living standards had had a depressing effect. The numbers of college students and standards throughout education had fallen drastically. The influence of qualified academic and technical people had been destroyed by the Cultural Revolution teaching that knowledge and efficiency were bourgeois. Disguised unemployment was rampant.

The immediately post-Gang leadership recognised the dangers of rising population and falling productivity, and it was clearly determined from the start to bring in new technology. But it was too inexperienced, and too many of its members were too ideologically committed, to identify all its economic problems. The "moderate" leaders of that time were in any case mainly looking to the ideas of the 1950s, which would have included a massive injection of foreign technology. Despite the radical tendencies, trade, aid and credits had always been customary in post-1949 China, particularly in the

1950s. Most of China's technical progress had come through imports, financed in some cases by credits, aid, or even by Overseas Chinese investment in China. In the 1950s the Soviet bloc was the main source of equipment. Much of it was delivered as part of an aid programme and China's first Five Year Plan (1953-57) was based almost entirely on imported industrial goods.

During those years the Soviet Union supplied $1.35 billion worth of equipment to China.[1] This was all paid for with agricultural products, minerals and light manufactures, but not immediately — payments ran on until 1965, constituting what was in fact medium term credit. From 1951 until the start of the Cultural Revolution, China encouraged the inflow of investment by overseas Chinese, via organisations in Guangdong, Fujian, Tianjin and Shanghai, which were the forerunners of the investment corporations set up in the provinces in 1979.

In 1961 China took on its first credit arrangement with the west, payment for Australian and Canadian wheat. This was a sensitive issue, not so much because of the credit as for the admission that China could not feed itself after the Leap. In that year, the Chinese, in desperate straits because of food shortages, bought their first consignment of western grain. This soon became a regular arrangement even when the emergency was over because of the convenience of shipping it by sea instead of from inland China to the east coast cities. Grain imports from western countries have continued ever since, involving short-term credit over 12 months, 18 months or two years, with a down payment on purchase.

In the middle 1960s, cut off from the Soviet bloc but still anxious to improve its technology by imports, China embarked on a programme of cautious capital equipment purchase from the west. From 1963 to 1966 contracts were signed with Europe and Japan for more than 50 plants, worth more than $200 million. Some were financed under medium term credit and included the services of western technicians.

This process was halted by the 1966-69 Cultural Revolution. However, again in the early 1970s, after the death of Mao's heir Lin Biao in 1971 and before the rise of the Gang in 1974, China bought $2.1 billion worth of complete plant from Japan, Europe and even the US.[2] During this period, the Bank of China was expanding overseas contacts and even at that time was unofficially making enquiries about syndicated loans and bond issues.

But in the 1974-76 period the most extreme radical policies appeared, for instance the seemingly deliberate delays to shipping at Shanghai in 1974 which were caused by troubles fanned among dockworkers.[3] During those years western traders were very conscious of Chinese officials' reluctance to take decisions on imports or on improving export services such as packaging. There was always a suspicion that the inordinate fuss the Chinese made at that time over shipments of US wheat affected by a harmless fungus was motivated by hostility to trade with Washington. In 1976 owing to the Gang's opposition to exporting raw materials, the Japanese had particular difficulty over importing silk and oil. In the months soon after their fall, charges against the Gang referred frequently to their opposition to using trade as a means of development. Total Chinese trade fell heavily in 1976 (see Table 1), though this can be partially attributed to the dislocations surrounding the succession to Mao and the effects of the disastrous earthquake at the north China industrial centre of Tangshan.

Table 1 China's Foreign Trade ($ million)

Year	Total	Exports	Imports
1975	14,575	7,180	7,395
1976	13,275	7,205	6,010
1977	15,055	7,955	7,100
1978	21,100	10,000	11,100
1979	30,300	14,100	16,200
1980	36,400	17,933	18,466

Sources: 1975-78 *China: A Statistical Compendium,* National Foreign Assessment Centre, Washington. These are rounded to the nearest $5 million, with the exception of the 1978 figures which are preliminary and rounded to the nearest $100 million. Exports are f.o.b., imports are c.i.f.
1979, 1980: 1979 – *Xinhua* 30 April 1980; 1980 – *Xinhua* 12 July 1980. (Converted at $1 = Y1.5)

With the death of Mao and the arrest of the Gang, this period came to an abrupt end. In succeeding months, all the trade practices of the 1950s and 1960s were reintroduced. But by 1979 a greatly changed leadership was ready to implement daring new ideas. Practices barely considered in post-1949 China were swiftly introduced, such as processing and assembly for foreign firms and joint equity ventures which were previously thought of as "semi-colonial" and capitalist. The export of Chinese labour, started in 1979-80, to earn foreign exchange, recalled the days of emigration to the railways of Canada or the tin mines of Malaya. The uses of market research and consultancy implied an acknowledgement of foreign taste and expertise whcih earlier radicalism would have rejected. These sweeping changes were brought in along with drastic alteration in the domestic economy, embracing the introduction of material incentives, the profit motive, independence for individual factories and provinces and stress on an improved standard of living.

Policy generally, and trade policy in particular, since Mao's death, falls naturally into three stages which coincide roughly with the calendar years. These are the end-76-end-77 period of reconstruction and planning, the "great leap" of industry and trade of 1978, and the "readjustment", caution and innovations in trade and the economy of 1979-80. In this paper these will be linked with, in the first stage, the desire to rehabilitate the economy while maintaining some compromise with the radicals: in the second, with an alliance between Hua and the 1950s-oriented bureaucrats, who favoured massive imports along the lines of the Soviet aid of the 1950s while adopting a Mao-style all-out onslaught on Chinese problems; in the third, with the rehabilitation of long-absent economists and the appearance of new figures who wanted a mixed economy, freer competition, decentralisation and a switch of investment from heavy industry to light industry and agriculture. These new leaders threw open the doors to trade, aid and numerous commercial innovations.

The First Phase: Reconstruction and Planning

The end of 1976 to the end of 1977 period was a time of reconstruction and preparation. The top leadership still contained a strong radical element that would have opposed economic innovations, as would much of the population at large who by that time had had ten years of Cultural Revolution-type ideology pressed upon them. Deng Xiaoping, whose rehabilitation was widely expected in April 1977, was not restored to his old positions till July that year, a sign of the continuing strength of the opposition to him.

Nevertheless during this period, planning work, which under the Gang had been virtually abandoned as bourgeois, was resumed. Although economists in the bureaucracy, such as Yu Qiuli and Gu Mu, Ministers in charge of the State Planning Commission and State Capital Construction Commission respectively, were presumably drawing up the plans, the Maoist influence was still evident. Hua himself gave the strong impression of adhering to the Maoist ideas of the value of mass mobilisation and "great leap"-type policies. Even Yu and Gu, though often thought of by foreigners as "pragmatists", were accustomed to working within a Maoist framework (Yu, protected by Premier Zhou Enlai, kept his job throughout the Cultural Revolution). They were not among China's economic *avant-garde*.

This mixture in the leadership, plus the lack of proper planning tools such as accurate statistics (the statistical reporting system was destroyed in the Cultural Revolution) probably accounted for the rash economic development plans announced in 1978. Like Mao in the 1950s, the leadership of the time was planning to rely heavily on imported technology. It also favoured a typically Maoist all-out attack on economic problems, later condemned as over-hasty.

A sign of the new trends was revealed at once. At the opening of the Canton Fair on 15 October, just a few days after the arrest of the Gang, the Fair officials quoted Mao to the effect that China wished to "resume and expand" international trade.[4] While the Fair opened in some disarray, overcrowded with foreign businessmen and short of goods to sell, by the end it was clear that it had been the most successful ever. It was swiftly followed by a *People's Daily* article in November by the Ministry of Light Industry mass criticism group which said "Economic and technical exchanges between countries with different social systems are completely normal activities if they help supply each other's needs . . . this has nothing in common with the importing of foreign capital, still less becoming a dumping ground for foreign goods".[5] Other pieces in the same vein filled the press.

This was given the stamp of dogma by the publication of Mao's "Ten Great Relations" speech on 26 December, 20 years after its original delivery in April 1956. The relevant paragraphs read as follows:

> In the natural sciences we are rather backward, and here we should make a special effort to learn from foreign countries. And yet we should learn critically, not blindly. In technology I think at first we have to follow others in most cases, and it is better for us to do so, since at present we are lacking in technology and know little about it. However, in those cases where we already have clear knowledge, we must not follow others in every detail. We must firmly reject and criticise all the decadent bourgeois systems, ideologies, and ways of life of foreign countries. But this should in no way prevent us from learning the advanced sciences and technologies of capitalist countries and whatever is scientific in the management of their enterprises. In the industrially developed countries they run their enterprises with fewer people and greater efficiency and they know how to do business. All this should be learned in accordance with our own principles so that our work can be improved.[6]

The Chinese at once showed their new approach by in January opening negotiations with the Japanese on a long term trade agreement and with the EEC on a trade framework pact. But Peking was still affirming the ideological view: on 1 April, at a meeting with the Japanese, the Chinese side were recorded as saying that they planned to observe the following three principles:

1) China would not accept assistance from other countries;
2) China would not accept investment from other countries; and
3) China would not accept loans from other countries.[7]

However this attitude must have been under attack within the leadership. As the year passed, plans were being drawn up for the first stage of modernisation (1978-85). It looked as if the role for foreign technology was to grow larger and larger. The leadership summoned a national meeting on industry (the "Learn from Daqing" conference) in May 1977 at which grand plans for economic development were vaguely outlined. Afterwards the Xinhua news agency published an article which said significantly "We should import all good things that should be imported and learn from foreign countries that which deserves learning".[8]

There must have been growing recognition that this foreign know-how would somehow have to be financed, as it was in the 1950s, by foreigners. Hence in June a high-level delegation from the Bank of China toured Switzerland, West Germany, Belgium and Britain. This was a purely fact-finding mission; the Chinese themselves depicted it as a courtesy visit, reciprocating the many trips made to Peking by western bankers. Nevertheless they were familiarising themselves with what finance might be available should they wish to call on it.

In August 1977 the Party held its Eleventh Congress, the first since the death of Mao. It revealed the continuing prevalence in the Party of radical ideas. Hua in his political report said that Revolutions like the Cultural Revolution would take place many times in the future, and stressed speed in development and all-out campaigns. However, the more economically oriented figures were gaining power. Yu Qiuli was elected to the politbureau, and significantly Zhao Ziyang became a politbureau alternate member. Zhao's economic ideas owed little to Mao; as events later were to show, he favoured a mixed economy, decentralisation and an important role for competition and profit.

In September, a key economic policy statement by the State Planning Commission was published. This said that advanced foreign technology was needed to develop the economy and achieve modernisation. Still based solidly on quotations from Mao, the article argued "We must learn hard from the good experience of other countries... We learn from other countries and introduce their advanced technology, not to hinder but promote our own creativeness".[9]

The tempo began to speed up. In October the West German foreign minister Hans-Dietrich Genscher was told in Peking that China was prepared to accept a special type of bank deposit — "performance guarantees" — equal to a high proportion of the equipment it proposed to buy. This was in effect a form of loan. In November Vice-Premier Wang Zhen announced to a group of visiting British businessmen that China wanted to buy the Harrier jump-jet fighter. The Chinese foreign trade minister, Li Jiang, went to Britain and France to view steel, rail, coal and aircraft technology. Plans were under discussion for senior Chinese like Vice-Premier Gu Mu to visit Europe the following year.

However, in October the state of the economy was already giving cause for new concern. Yu Qiuli said in a speech (to the fourth session of the Standing Committee of the National People's Congress) that a new leap forward was taking shape, but that power and raw materials were short and management was poor.[10] Anxiety among the more experienced and cautious leaders was emerging in public. Vice-Premier Li Xiannian told a group of visiting Australian editors that China would not borrow money to finance the development of its economy, and that the Chinese people would have to eat less if saving was necessary to promote exports and reduce imports.[11]

The Second Phase: The New Great Leap of 1978

Despite these anxieties, the hasty and less than thorough preparations of 1977 led to the formation and announcement of a grand economic development plan to run to 1985. In February 1978, at the National People's Congress, Hua set out the broad guidelines of China's economic development over the following eight years. This was clearly going to depend on foreign trade, aid, credit and even the presence of foreign experts in China, but still contained no innovations that would have been startling in the Chinese context.

The plan was to include raising steel production to 60 million tons and grain production to 400 million. A total of 120 projects was to be built, including 10 iron and steel complexes, 10 oil and gas fields, nine non-ferrous metal complexes, eight coal mines, 30 power stations, six trunk railways, and five harbours. Some were to be totally new, others were to involve the expansion of existing plant. The value of agricultural production was to rise 4-5 per cent annually, and industrial production by over 10 per cent.

As the year wore on it became increasingly clear that the leadership had in mind the purchase of large quantities of foreign equipment as the very backbone of the plan. A rapidly-growing number of senior delegations visited Europe and Japan to look at steel plant, coal mining machinery, power generating equipment, railway technology and port modernisation. The Chinese began discussing oil and non-ferrous metals extraction with foreign companies. These were all the major items mentioned in the plan.

The degree to which the plan depended on imports can be reconstructed. Hua said that China was to produce 60 million tons of steel by 1985, double the amount produced in 1978 (30 million tons, according to Yu).[12] In mid-1978 the Chinese were seriously thinking of immediately building another complex at Anshan with Japanese help (to be of 6 million tons annual capacity). In addition they contemplated setting up a new works at Jidong in Hebei province (initially to be of 6 million tons capacity, rising to 10 million), probably with West German help. They had already begun site formation and equipment purchase negotiations with the Japanese for a plant at Baoshan near Shanghai, destined to produce 6 million tons annually. The British were asked to do a preliminary study for modernisation of the Shoudu works outside Peking, currently of 1.3 million tons capacity. This would have given them getting on for two-thirds of the new capacity planned for 1985.

Similarly, of the five harbours Hua mentioned, two (Tianjin and Shanghai) figured in discussions on containerisation with a major Danish firm, two (a deepwater channel for Baoshan and modernisation at Lienyungang) were the subject of negotiation with Dutch interests, and work at Canton was agreed with a British company. The nine non-ferrous complexes were to come in part from a deal with a large Frankfurt concern which had signed an initial protocol for the supply of 22 non-ferrous plants. Copper and aluminium works were being discussed with US and Japanese firms, while a major Swiss company was preparing a feasibility study for an aluminium refinery.

In fuel and power the Chinese opened negotiations in the summer of 1978 with US, British and French oil companies on geophysical surveys as a preliminary to offshore exploration. They bought substantial quantities of coal mining equipment from Britain and West Germany and embarked on discussions with a British coal-mining advisory group on the development of two mines at Datong. Talks began with British, French and Japanese companies on power stations.

During the summer Hua visited Rumania, Yugoslavia and Iran. What he saw during this his first trip outside China (apart from a visit to North Korea) appeared to encourage him to press for even greater speed in development. At the National Day eve reception (30 September) Hua referred again to a "new Leap Forward" in China's economy, while the *Red Flag*, the party theoretical journal, published an article in its 1 October issue noting that some second-world countries had achieved modernisation in only ten years by utilising foreign expertise.[13] Delegations, enquiries and projected deals escalated still further. The *China Business Review* estimated in its September-October 1978 issue that China at that time had $40 billion worth of equipment under discussion. Besides the steel, coal, non-ferrous, port and power station work mentioned above, the Chinese were also talking about iron ore mines (with the US), petro-chemical plant (UK and Japan), truck plant (Japan), agricultural machinery plant (Italy) and numerous smaller items such as hotels and a possible trade centre building in Peking.

As a sign of its long term commitment to trade, in the spring China had signed both the proposed trade pact with the EEC and the long-term trade agreement with Japan. The first was mainly a framework agreement expressing good intentions. It had political as much as economic value since it brought Europe and China together, but it meant little for individual countries or companies since no values or commodities were specified and businessmen were left to make their own deals. The Japanese one was different. The period of the agreement was to cover 1978-85, exchanges were to reach $10 billion each way, and in the first five years the Chinese agreed to buy $7 billion to $8 billion worth of technology and plant. The Chinese agreed to sell crude oil, in quantities rising from 7 million tons in 1978 to 15 million by 1982, and coal from a minimum of 300,000 tons in 1978 to 3.7 million in 1982. Chinese exports for the final years were to be discussed during 1981.

This was an important milestone in Chinese trading policy because it committed Peking to the export of coal and oil in specified amounts over a period of time, marking an unmistakable break with the Gang's alleged objections to the sale of China's raw materials. It also committed Peking to buying on credit — the principle of deferred payments was written into the agreement.

Peking then turned its attention to the US. In the course of 1978 the US had become a major grain supplier for the first time since the wheat-smut-affected shipments of 1974, selling about 3 million tons of wheat and 1.2 million tons of corn. The numbers of American businessmen flocking to Peking increased by leaps and bounds. There were still no deals for industrial equipment owing to the lack of full diplomatic relations and accompanying trade concessions, but both sides were clearly eager. There were two important autumn governmental visits to China, one by Energy Secretary, James Schlesinger, and the other Agriculture Secretary, Robert Bergland.

This helped on the normalisation of relations agreement, which was finally signed in December, after the personal intervention of Deng who swept aside all the Chinese difficulties. At that point it was understood that the last barrier to trade, the unresolved claims/assets question, would be settled the following year, and a trade agreement paving the way for most-favoured-nation treatment and Eximbank credits would be concluded. MFN was anxiously awaited by the Chinese who wanted to sell more in the US market, while Eximbank financing — government-subsidised credits — would enable them to import US technology more cheaply. (The claims/assets question related to the $197 million worth of property seized from US citizens after October 1949 and the $76.5 million worth of assets belonging to Chinese frozen in the US at the time of the Korean War.)

As China's trade discussions picked up speed in mid-1978, officials began to speak more openly about their plans for payment. China's post-Soviet split resistance to credits was beginning to soften, though some leaders remained cautious. Vice-premier Li Xiannian told a group of visiting Japanese that China's foreign exchange reserves stood at $3 billion, which was clearly not going to be enough to pay cash for the items under discussion. He apparently showed "a positive attitude" towards "deposits" from western countries in Chinese banks, but he made no reference to loans.[14] The British writer, Lord Chalfont, visiting Peking, was told by Li that China "might" accept a British bank loan, though he added "We don't want too much . . . we don't want to borrow more than we can pay back".[15]

In August the British Trade Secretary, Edmund Dell, led a mission to Peking during which the Export Credit Guarantee Department (ECGD), the government trade financing department, negotiated a deal with the Bank of China under which British banks would make deposits with the Bank of China under terms guaranteed by the ECGD. At the same time the Chinese told the mission they were now prepared to accept full buyer's credit (as opposed to supplier's credit, which they had previously used as it savoured less of a direct loan). In buyer's credit the purchaser arranges the financing, which is both cheaper and simpler but involves more complex documentation and negotiation over actual borrowing. During this period joint production, buyback arrangements and even joint equity ventures were mentioned privately but did not apparently have yet the full backing value of their oil resources (the cost of their oil to the Japanese rose from $13.20 a barrel at the end of 1978 to an expected $34.625 in mid-1980) and were determined to exploit it in the only way they could — with foreign help — since they lacked the necessary technology themselves. China's own domestic oil needs were increasing, and as its biggest single export it was required to earn foreign exchange. It was determined not to be exploited by foreign companies, however, and the terms on which it allowed participation were tough.

From buying technical expertise it was only a small step to buying advice on marketing and market research. A delegation from the Foreign Trade Ministry came to London at the end of 1979 to seek advice on marketing, and were expected to expand their commercial representation abroad substantially. In July 1980 the Foreign Trade Ministry made its first agreement ever with a foreign market research company to exchange market information on China for research on markets overseas.

Despite — indeed, partly because of — the new policies, China's economy faced fresh difficulties at the end of 1980. Peking was having severe problems in controlling expenditure in the provinces. Excessive capital investment was causing inflation. Heavy industry had not been sufficiently cut back as prescribed in the original "readjustment" policy. Local spending had been increased by decentralisation, which gave provinces new planning and construction rights.

To overcome the problems Peking ordered new reductions, not just domestic building programmes but in imported plant. It first postponed, and then cancelled, the second stage of the Baoshan steel project. It dropped other Japanese plants which had already been contracted for, cut a number of US projects and delayed others. As it wrestled with unfamiliar difficulties, further cancellations seemed possible.

Conclusion

The post-Third Plenum leadership brought a completely new look to China's trading policy. This leadership was disillusioned by the failure of pre-1976 Mao-style socialism to improve the lot of the Chinese. It seemingly believed that not even the more flexible practices of the 1950s, as revived in 1977-78, would be enough to solve these serious problems of stagnation and fast-growing population. Hence it introduced bold new policies in the domestic economy to stimulate competition, harder work and independence of the leadership.

During the autumn and increasingly towards the end of the year there was growing concern among westerners that the Chinese were taking on more purchasing than they could actually afford. Although in December the Chinese signed an agreement with 10 British banks on $1.2 billion worth of ECGD-backed credit, and with the French government for FF30 billion backed by COFACE (the French equivalent of ECGD), which could finance such deals, anxieties were not allayed.

Two factors then brought China to a turning point. One, the growing influence of Deng Xiaoping, was inspiring an increasing number of rehabilitations of figures condemned in the Cultural Revolution. These included, besides political and cultural figures, important economic ones such as Bo Yibo who had helped to salvage China's economy in the early 1960s after the end of the Leap. A number of influential scholars reappeared in mid-1978 and the Academy of Social Sciences, later credited with being the source of new ideas, became much more active.

The second was the growing strain in the Chinese economy. Since the Cultural Revolution the leadership, which had had no real understanding of economic forces, had been over-investing in heavy industry at the expense of agriculture, light industry and transport. In addition, the concern with results that would look good on paper — the outcome of desire to please superiors and of little grasp of how an economy really works — had brought a situation where numerous factories were producing items for which there was little demand, thus devouring power, raw materials and transport to little purpose. This was particularly true of the steel industry, where the Chinese produced far more crude steel than they could turn into finished goods. By the end of 1978 there were bottlenecks in transport, shortages of power and raw materials and every sign that precious investment was being wasted on badly run enterprises or those that were simply building up high stocks of products instead of going to alleviate growing poverty.

The Third Phase: Readjustment

In December 1978 the Central Committee held its Third Plenum, under pressure, no doubt, from Deng and his supporters who wanted to break away not just from "radical" policies but from the limited flexibility of the 1950s to innovative practices such as competition between enterprises and the use of market forces. The obvious strains in the economy were an added pressure. While the plenum, held against a backdrop of excited free expression of views at Peking's democracy wall", dealt mainly with politics, the economic situation must have been discussed.

The appointment at the plenum of Chen Yun, an elderly but capable economic administrator who had differed from Mao even in the 1950s, to the key post of party Vice-Chairman, heralded a new economic, and hence trade, policy. In June 1979, Chen Yun and Bo Yibo were appointed Vice-Premiers, and at the Fourth Plenum in September Zhao Ziyang was elected to full politbureau membership. Thus throughout 1979 the innovative element in the top leadership was steadily strengthened.

In January 1979, presumably under the influence of the newly-appointed Chen Yun, the leadership began to reorganise its priorities. As Hua later made clear in his report to the June National People's Congress, the full enormity of the task of modernising the economy was becoming apparent. Hua's sober appraisal revealed a serious decline in efficiency and productivity, a lack of balance in the economy and frightful loss in state-run enterprises. Under these circumstances it was hardly surprising that the leadership recognised the impossibility of absorbing large quantities of foreign equipment when there was already large spare capacity, lack of technical and managerial skills and inadequate infrastructure. Investment was diverted from heavy industry to light industry and agriculture. The new leadership put the stress on using foreign equipment only to supplement what China had and on a step by step approach as opposed to a leap. All large-scale import plans were temporarily suspended. There was some irony in the fact that it was these economic innovators who for purely practical purposes adopted self-reliance, the old slogan of the Gang, in contrast to the wholesale import policy of the previous year apparently favoured by Hua and the conventional bureaucrats.

To help solve the shortage of foreign exchange and modern technology the reconstituted leadership began to move more quickly towards the new ways of bringing in foreign expertise and capital. New emphasis was put on developing raw materials for export. Compensation trade, processing and assembly replaced straight trade as the basis for discussions. The joint equity venture, for which formal legislation was passed at the June 1979 NPC, became a matter for serious negotiation, of all the innovations perhaps the most startling since the investment of western capital in China had been unheard-of since 1949.

Early in 1979, however, the outlook for any sort of exchange with China seemed bleak. The speed of developments at the end of

1978 had caught the Bank of China without the cash at hand for the downpayments on the many contracts that were on the point of signature. The new thinking in Peking, with its emphasis on saving foreign exchange, began to seep through to the outside world in February. West German and British firms were shocked to be told that China proposed to pay for mining equipment not with money but with coal. This trend towards non-monetary exchanges was swiftly borne out by the disappointing visit by British Industry Secretary Eric Varley, which, though it produced a trade framework pact, resulted in no concrete deals.

Almost simultaneously the *People's Daily* announced the new economic policy in an important editorial. Investment was to be reoriented away from steel and heavy industry into agriculture and light industry, and carefully-selected areas of heavy industry such as mining and energy.[16]

On 28 February Peking dropped a new bombshell, informing Japanese firms that it was suspending some 22 or more contracts for equipment, including that for the huge Baoshan steel plant near Shanghai, together worth $2.6 billion. The reason given to the Japanese was the lack of foreign exchange, though it was clear that the problems in the domestic economy were also a factor. However, the leadership confirmed its long-term interest in trade when it pressed for an extension of its eight-year pact with Japan. This was signed in April, and increased the overall value of the pact to $60 billion.

In accordance with the new cautious policy, Peking turned away from importing technology to setting up credit arrangements and the mechanisms necessary to increase foreign exchange earnings. The exception was the revalidation of all but one of the Japanese contracts, completed by the end of the summer, underpinned by the loan arrangements the Bank of China had by then been able to make. The Baoshan plant was switched from cash to deferred payment terms (10 per cent down and the rest over five years) but other contracts remained on a cash basis. However, there was one important change; the plants were put within the long term trade agreement, thus reducing China's obligation to buy more equipment. Under the agreement, China was committed to purchasing $8 billion worth of technology up to 1985. Long delays settled over the plant westerners were earlier discussing, and not till the end of the year was there further movement. By mid-1980, many western projects — British power-stations and Dutch port renovation, for instance — had, however, been completely dropped.

The strength of the Deng group after the Third Plenum overcame any residual objections to borrowing. Following the December 1978 deal with British banks, the Bank of China swiftly signed up in the spring and summer for about $26 billion worth of credit from western governments and banks (see Table 2). US Eximbank financing was still awaiting final decisions but was expected to amount to about $2 billion in the 1980-85 period.

Table 2   World Extension of Credit to China: 1978-1979

Country	Date	Amount (US $ million)
Exim Bank Credits and Government-Guaranteed Loans		
UK	12/78	1,200
Australia	4/79	56
France	5/79	7,140 a
Italy	5/79	1,000
Japan	5/79 - 12/79	3,625 b
Sweden	5/79	350 a
Canada	8/79	1,720 a
West Germany	10/79	1,100 a
Belgium	11/79	173 a
Subtotal		16,364
Commercial Bank Credits to China		
UK	3/79 - 4/79	675
France	4/79	500
Canada	4/79	100
Luxemburg	4/79	50
Chile	4/79	10
US	6/79 - 10/79	28
Japan	8/79	8,004.6
West Germany	10/79	450
Subtotal		9,817.6
Total		26,181.6

Source: China Business Review, Jan-Feb. 1980

Note: The above Exim Bank credits carry an interest rate of 7.25 per cent annually for loans under 5 years and 7.5 per cent for credit of 5 years or more. The only credit not to conform with these OECD guidelines is Japan's $1,900 million loan in May 1979, which carries an interest of 6.25-6.5 per cent.

Interest rates on the above commercial bank loans vary according to the length of maturity; however, the interest rate on the loans of 1-5 years duration is 0.5 per cent annually above LIBOR, the London Interbank Offer Rate. LIBOR stood at 14.25 per cent for 6-month Eurocurrency credit as of Feb. 1, 1980.
a) Loans are denominated in local currency, hence their dollar value may change.
b) Includes a 10-year Exim Bank credit for Y420 billion ($1,900 million) and a 30-year Overseas Economic Cooperation Fund credit for Y50 billion ($225 million) in fiscal 1979, and an additional $1.5 billion to be disbursed during fiscal years 1980-86.

However, the Chinese were slow to use the credit, partly because they were not ready to absorb more technology, partly because interest rates were high. Some of the Japanese financing was used for the downpayments on the revalidated contracts, while in October/November some of the British loans were partially drawn down. The British ECGD deposit facility was used retrospectively to finance contracts made in 1978. But there was certainly no rush to buy even much-needed equipment with this borrowed money.

Radical objections to aid were also abandoned in the wake of the Third Plenum. Aid loans, with minimal interest, were much more attractive than commercial ones. In February 1979 Deng hinted that Peking would like to join the International Monetary Fund and the Asian Development Bank provided the Taiwan membership issue could be solved. In September it accepted $15 million from the UN and finally in spring 1980 it joined the IMF and the World Bank.

In December 1979 after months of negotiation Peking secured an aid loan from Japan, expected to amount to $1.5 billion over several years for six major infra-structure projects (coal wharves and terminals, railways, hydropower plant). Interest was to be at 3 per cent, and no repayments were due for seven or eight years. In the same week China obtained a $10 million interest-free loan from the Belgian government with no repayments due for the first decade, as part of a deal for power station equipment.

Deng's post-Third Plenum strength also meant that Chinese organisations could cultivate a much more commercial outlook. The Bank of China took on a much more entrepreneurial role. In the spring for the first time ever the Bank of China in Hongkong joined the Bank of Montreal, the Bank of Tokyo and others in a syndicated $42 million loan to build an office block. In November it became one of the lead managers in a $100 million loan to a Hongkong cement company for a new plant. In December the London branch of the Bank for the first time became a lead manager in a floating rate note issue put out by the Midland Bank.

The Bank opened a new branch in Luxemburg in June to deal on the Eurocurrency market, and was planning further branches in New York and Tokyo, with a representative office in Paris. Its retail banking business was expanding, with a branch to serve the Chinese community which opened in 1978 in London in the Soho area, and another in Manchester in 1979. In Hongkong it widened its financing facilities by in April setting up the China Development Finance Co. whose functions were to include financing projects within China by investors in the British territory.

From early 1979 the Chinese pressed the compensation trade or "payback" idea that suppliers should be paid back in the products of their own equipment, or at least with something that fell within the purview of the ministry that was negotiating for the plant. In the case of the British Steel corporation, the British side agreed reluctantly that they might help market Chinese products in the third world (though the deal fell through because of the Chinese steel cutback). It was an important element in a deal with an American company over exploiting China's copper.

Compensation trade was in fact more suitable for smaller plants, an idea the Chinese had initiated in 1978. Foreign businessmen were much more receptive to this idea. A typical case was a plant for making plastic wallpaper, sold at the spring 1979 Canton Fair by a West German supplier for installation in Shenyang. All the product was to be marketed abroad, a proportion going to the supplier in payment. However, even by mid-1980 most compensation deals were between Chinese businessmen in Hongkong and the Chinese. Westerners were still cautious about getting involved in the unfamiliar world across the Chinese border.

Simpler than compensation trade was the processing and assembly scheme, under which foreign partners provided raw materials, parts and sometimes even equipment, and the Chinese factory reciprocated with the finished product. The Chinese side received a processing fee, out of which it paid in instalments for the equipment, so that by the end of a period the plant belonged to the Chinese. This system came into operation at the end of 1978 and by the end of 1979 seemed to be the most thriving form of co-operative venture.

Partly through a desire to isolate foreign-run enterprises and partly to simplify administration, in a move unprecedented since 1949, two special areas for such ventures were designated in 1978. One was at Shenzen adjoining Hongkong and the other at Zhuhai near Macao. Here foreigners (mostly Overseas Chinese) embarked on the establishment of small factories under assembly or compensation trade arrangements. An exception was the notable contract with Harpers International of Hongkong to assemble buses at Shenzen. In the course of 1979 another one, at Shekou north-west of Hongkong, was also designated for foreign manufactures. This had the particular advantage that the China Merchants Steam Navigation Co. in Hongkong was to act as agent to save foreigners the time and effort required in negotiating with the many different branches of the Chinese bureaucracy. Two further zones further north, at Swatow and Amoy, were also scheduled for development.

Joint equity ventures, the biggest break with China's post-1949 ideology, were provided with a formal framework at the NPC in

June.[17] This legislation was too brief to enable western investors to go ahead on many deals with China. However, it did satisfy on some points. It laid down that foreign investment should in general be not less than 25 per cent, and specified no upper limit. It briefly mentioned the shareout of profits, insurance, the remittance of funds abroad, bankruptcy procedures, settlement of disputes and taxation. Most important, the document announced the creation of a new foreign investment commission which would approve or reject proposals for joint ventures. Soon after the Congress, in an even more dramatic break with the immediate past, Deng told the Japanese Justice Minister, Yoshimi Furui, on a visit to China, that Peking would permit foreign interests under certain conditions to set up wholly-owned subsidiaries in China.[18]

An alternative scheme to attract western capital was the establishment of the China Investment Trust and Investment Corporation (CITIC) which was set up formally in October 1979 with a capital of Yuan 200 million under the chairmanship of a rehabilitated Shanghai capitalist, Rong Yiren. Almost at once the First National Bank of Chicago signed an agreement with it to help channel investment into the Chinese economy and a Californian investment company, the Eaton-Shen Pacific Corporation, agreed to provide $150 million over the following three years. Rong said the new corporation had received more than 100 proposals for projects and had signed letters of intent with three other foreign organisations covering joint ventures worth in total $30 million.

The infusion of figures into the Peking leadership in 1979-80 who supported decentralisation (notably Chen Yun and Zhao Ziyang) played a part in inducing the delegation of a previously unheard-of power to provincial authorities to make agreements with foreigners. The two most obvious regions to benefit from this policy were Guangdong and Fujian, both of which were given authority to plan their own development and negotiate their own foreign deals. Both were expected to open their own offices in Hongkong.[19] In July 1980 Guangdong pulled off an enormous coup when it negotiated a reported £255 million barter deal (getting trucks in exchange for machine tools) with the Swedish firm Volvo.

Production-sharing was yet another innovation of 1979. The supreme example of this was in the oil industry, where in the course of the year China took on a number of foreign companies to conduct offshore geophysical surveys. By June 1980 the French and Japanese had already signed shared-risk agreements on exploration for the Bohai Gulf and north Yellow Sea, and more were expected to follow. Unlike the Gang, the new leadership recognised the near-priceless value of their oil resources (the cost of their oil to the Japanese rose from $13.20 a barrel at the end of 1978 to an expected $34.625 in mid-1980) and were determined to exploit it in the only way they could — with foreign help — since they lacked the necessary technology themselves. China's own domestic oil needs were increasing, and as its biggest single export it was required to earn foreign exchange. It was determined not to be exploited by foreign companies, however, and the terms on which it allowed participation were tough.

From buying technical expertise it was only a small step to buying advice on marketing and market research. A delegation from the Foreign Trade Ministry came to London at the end of 1979 to seek advice on marketing, and were expected to expand their commercial representation abroad substantially. In July 1980 the Foreign Trade Ministry made its first agreement ever with a foreign market research company to exchange market information on China for research on markets overseas.

Despite — indeed, partly because of — the new policies, China's economy faced fresh difficulties at the end of 1980. Peking was having severe problems in controlling expenditure in the provinces. Excessive capital investment was causing inflation. Heavy industry had not been sufficiently cut back as prescribed in the original "readjustment" policy. Local spending had been increased by decentralisation, which gave provinces new planning and construction rights.

To overcome the problems Peking ordered new reductions, not just domestic building programmes but in imported plant. It first postponed, and then cancelled, the second stage of the Baoshan steel project. It dropped other Japanese plants which had already been contracted for, cut a number of US projects and delayed others. As it wrestled with unfamiliar difficulties, further cancellations seemed possible.

Conclusion

The post-Third Plenum leadership brought a completely new look to China's trading policy. This leadership was disillusioned by the failure of pre-1976 Mao-style socialism to improve the lot of the Chinese. It seemingly believed that not even the more flexible practices of the 1950s, as revived in 1977-78, would be enough to solve these serious problems of stagnation and fast-growing population. Hence it introduced bold new policies in the domestic economy to stimulate competition, harder work and independence in individual enterprises and provinces. It switched investment from heavy industry to light industry and agriculture. In foreign trade it dropped plans for large scale imports of technology in favour of new techniques such as compensation trade and joint ventures, and with its new light industry products it stepped up exports.

The leadership realised that to absorb imports usefully, China needed first to improve its educational and managerial levels, power and raw materials supply and infrastructure. It needed to establish priorities carefully to avoid waste and duplication. It had to evolve new methods to eke out and increase foreign exchange supplies. Hence in 1979 it abandoned numerous half-negotiated import contracts with western traders and began to implement plants for borrowing, securing aid, establishing assorted co-operative ventures with foreigners, the sale abroad of Chinese labour, and the promotion of exports. At the end of 1980 it began to cut its import programme further.

Four years of work since Mao's death on trade and trade practices brought substantial increases in the volume of exchanges. Total trade in 1980 was 2.7 times the 1976 figure. Exports had more than doubled. Imports had tripled. The big import growth came in 1979, despite "readjustment", as a result of contracts signed in 1978. In 1980, the import rise slowed, bringing trade almost into balance.

In the anxiety in China over economic problems in 1980, the success of exports was encouraging. The rise was partly due to the greater emphasis the Chinese themselves were placing on investing in light industry for export, but clearly also to greater willingness to meet the customer's needs. Foreign design, packaging and delivery requirements were being given greater attention.

It also became clear that the Chinese had in 1979 chosen the right import policy. The more they revealed and the more foreign visitors observed during 1979-80 of existing industries, the more obvious it was that rationalisation and improvement were needed before heavy investment of precious foreign exchange in modern equipment would be worth while. More experience in planning was clearly also essential.

By the end of 1980 it was still too soon to tell how successful the more complex long-term compensation and joint venture schemes would be. Poor quality in output and inefficient labour were bedevilling some. However, they appeared to be considered an important means of importing technology.

The stability of the new trading policies depended on the skill with which they were implemented, and therefore on how successfully the Chinese could streamline their bureaucracy. Ultimately, of course, they depended on the stability of the leadership as a whole. This was likely to rest on the success of the domestic policies to stimulate the economy, which at the end of 1980 appeared to be in difficulties.

However, the trial and condemnation of the Gang of Four and the disappearance of Chairman Hua in early 1981 indicated that Deng still commanded a majority in the leadership in favour of the new policies. The speed with which Peking had been able to introduce extensive changes suggested that disillusion with the old system and support for the new one was strong. But the new policies brought new problems and it was by no means clear that Deng and his men knew how to solve them.

III RURAL DEVELOPMENT

8

THE DISTRIBUTIVE IMPLICATIONS OF CHINA'S NEW AGRICULTURAL POLICIES

Peter Nolan

Jesus College, Cambridge

Gordon White

*Institute of Development Studies,
University of Sussex, Brighton*

Introduction: The Maoist Legacy

In this paper we examine the changes in CCP policies concerning rural distribution since the death of Mao with particular attention to the relationship between the pursuit of egalitarian socialist goals and of economic growth objectives in the context of a specific case of state socialist development. A serious consideration of the new strategy must first give some account of policies implemented during and after the Cultural Revolution and their impact on farm output and rural inequality. Only then can we gain a clear idea of the degree to which policies have in fact changed and the relationship of these changes to problems experienced during the Cultural Revolution decade of 1966-76.

Current Chinese publications portray a uniformly bleak picture of the rural situation in this "disastrous decade". They argue that ultra-egalitarian policies were widely practised with little regard to their detrimental consequences for peasant production incentives. We have argued elsewhere that the reality of rural distribution policies during this period was more complex than this retrospective condemnation would allow.[1] Correspondingly, we feel that present rural policies do not constitute such a radical break with preceding policies as is frequently suggested, either in their conception or still less in their impact on the grass roots. This is not surprising; since the disastrous experiments of the Great Leap Forward (1958-59) and the subsequent collapse of farm output,[2] all sides of the Chinese political debate have been more circumspect in their approach to agriculture than to other sectors. Agriculture still produces the lion's share of China's wage goods and export earnings. Consequently, radical organisational changes which might have adverse effects on farm output have been viewed with suspicion. In contrast to the enormous institutional changes that occurred from 1949 to 1958, the whole period since the early 1960s appears as a time of relative stability in the rural organisational structure.

Was the performance of farm output during the Cultural Revolution decade as poor as is now being suggested in the Chinese press? It appears true that by the late 1970s farm output per capita had risen little compared to the 1950s (see Table 1) and in certain sectors (for example, cotton and oilseeds) was lower than 1957.

Table 1. Per capita output of major farm products in China: 1952, 1957, 1978

Item	Unit	1952	1957	1978
Grain (incl. soya beans)[1]	kg	285	304	318
Cotton[1]	kg	2.3	2.5	2.3
Sugar cane[1]	kg	12.4	16.2	22.0
Edible oilseeds[1]	kg	6.4	5.9	4.8
Pigs (in the pen)[1]	no.	0.16	0.22	0.31
Aquatic products[2]	kg	2.9	-	4.8
Fruit[2]	kg	4.3	-	6.9

Source: [1] W. Klatt, "China's New Economic Policy: A Statistical Appraisal", *China Quarterly*, No.80, December 1979
[2] Shi Shan, "Where is the breakthrough point to rapid agricultural growth in our country?", *Nongye Jingji Wenti* (Problems of Agricultural Economics), (hereafter NYJJWT), 1980, No.2

The main advances have come in pork and sugar-cane output. With the exception of grain, average consumption levels of the main farm products are still very low[3] and it is unlikely that this has altered significantly since the 1950s. Moreover, Chinese farmers seem to have been working harder to produce a roughly constant annual output per worker; earnings per labour-day are reported to have fallen by one-third between 1957 and 1977.[4]

However, some important qualifications need to be made to this negative assessment. First, China's population growth continued at a rapid pace until the mid-1970s. On the most optimistic assumption, it was not until the early 1970s that the natural rate of population increase (apart from the exceptional interlude of the early 1960s) fell below 2 per cent per annum, and it has only fallen significantly below this in the latter part of the decade.[5] Success in reducing the pace of population growth is a valuable legacy bequeathed to the post-Mao regime. Simply to keep up with a population growth of 2 per cent or more is a major achievement for the farm sector of any country. Provided China could have maintained a growth of farm output at somewhat above 2 per cent per annum (as she had done since the mid-1950s) a declining rate of population growth would have permitted a steady rise in per capita output. There is no reason to think this would not have been possible under the policies of the Cultural Revolution decade.

A second qualification is a more careful consideration of the criteria by which the growth in farm output should be judged. The CCP inherited an agricultural sector whose growth potential was limited by the fact that the possibilities for raising output under "traditional" techniques had already been extensively exploited. Opportunities for extending cultivable land (without enormous expense) were also very limited and, since the 1950s, the total cultivated area has hardly altered. Consequently, the main route to increased farm output has been through increased yields per unit of farmland, that is by increasing the number of crops per acre per year and raising yield per crop. The multiple cropping index (sown area divided by arable area) was already high in South China in the 1950s: in Guangdong, for example, it stood at 186 (see Table 2). Further north, climate has always been a fundamental constraint on multiple cropping and, in general, labour shortages at peak times in the farm cycle have limited the degree of increase in cropping intensity. Consequently, the main channel for raising farm output has had to be increased yield per crop. Here China has been fairly successful. In Guangdong, for example, though grain yields were already relatively high by the mid-1960s for such a large, heterogeneous area, yields were pushed up significantly during the Cultural Revolution decade (see Table 2). In Hebei province in north China, annual grain yields (tonnes per hectare) rose in the following fashion: 1965 = 1.8, 1970 = 2.3, 1973 = 2.6, 1978 = 3.3.[6]

What is perhaps most striking about China's performance of farm output from the early 1960s to the late 1970s was its similarity with

Table 2. Agricultural Production in Guangdong Province 1952-1977

Item	Unit	1952	1957	1966	1977
Arable area	m.ha.	3.31	3.46	3.16	3.24
Sown area	m.ha.	6.17	7.08	6.93	7.39
of which grain	multiple cropping index	186	205	219	228
	m.ha.	5.47	6.07	5.14	5.77
% total		88.7	85.7	74.2	78.1
Yields					
grain	tonnes per sown ha	1.56	1.79	2.58	3.02
sugarcane	tonnes per sown ha	43.5	42.8	33.2	41.5
peanuts	tonnes per sown ha	1.0	0.8	0.9	1.6

Growth rate of output (physical):		1952-57	1957-66	1966-77
grain	% p.a.	4.9	2.2	2.5
sugarcane	% p.a.	10.7	2.5	3.9
peanuts	% p.a.	5.4	5.6	1.3
pigs (in the pen)	% p.a.	2.1	5.3	3.4

Source: From written data given to Queen Elizabeth House, Oxford, China Study Group, June 1979

other Asian countries. Under the initial impact of a rapid rise in the application of new farm inputs, the growth of farm output accelerated ahead of population growth in the middle and late 1960s. From 1964 to 1970 China's grain output grew at around 3.8 per cent per annum.[7] By comparison, food grain output in India grew by almost 5 per cent per annum in the late 1960s. However, in the 1970s the early hopes of an Asian "Green Revolution" were widely disappointed and the long-term growth of farm output returned to around 2 per cent per annum.[8] In China, as in other Asian countries, technological factors prevented a long-term acceleration of the growth of farm output. The early increase in the application of modern inputs yielded relatively high returns but diminishing returns set in quite quickly. The regions which have received a relatively large share of modern inputs produced since the early 1960s (the so-called "high and stable yield areas") have been those with specially favoured water supply, which tend to be the more fertile areas near large cities. Yields are now very high in these areas. In Guangdong, for example, the Pearl River Delta has been the major recipient of new inputs. In the most fertile parts of the delta (e.g. Nanhai county) rice yields are close to the highest in the world and the margin for further increase must be rather limited.

The important lessons learned by all sections of the Chinese leadership from the utopian experiments of the Great Leap Forward has also influenced official policies on rural distributive issues. No systematic attempt has been made to revive the radical egalitarian measures of the Leap; though it is true that at certain times and in certain areas the Party did attempt to introduce more radical policies on income distribution. For most of the period since the Leap, leftist leaders had to accept that it was quite unrealistic to try to eliminate rural inequality and that the most they could hope to do was to "restrict" such inequality.[9] Specific policies aside, however, ever since the establishment of collectives and the abandonment of predominantly private ownership of the means of agricultural production in the mid-1950s, there have been important institutional factors helping to constrain intra-village differentials in income and standard of living. Income distribution by the collective to its members has been primarily based on the number of "labour days" (or work-points) earned per worker. As labour productivity alters, so the value of the "labour day" alters for all members alike — in the Chinese phrase, "the boat rises (or falls) with the water level". Moreover, a portion of grain consumption has been distributed "according to need" on a per capita basis usually differentiated by age.[10] It was quite common during the Cultural Revolution decade for poor households to consume more grain than they had earned in workpoints, though the extent and terms of such "overdrawing" (*chaozhi*) was a contentious issue.

However, in spite of such constraints on differentiation within the village, important inequalities persisted, even within the smallest unit, the production team (the average size of the team in a 1979 survey was 193 people and 41 households — see Note 10). While the private sector was subject to periodic attacks, it remained throughout the Cultural Revolution decade. For example, Jiading county (in Shanghai municipality) was a focus of radical activity in the late 1960s and early 1970s, yet the free market in its main town was closed only for 2-3 weeks at the beginning of the Cultural Revolution in 1966. Since then various restrictions had limited the volume of transactions, but the market was by no means eliminated. The private sector also constituted an important, if fluctuating, share of peasant income during this period. A 1979 survey of 339 brigades, for example, showed that the private sector (still in the early stage of expansion under the new policies) already contributed 25-30 per cent of total household income.[11] Our study of the 1970s suggests that those households with more labour power or greater skills were better placed to benefit from private economic activity than their weaker neighbours[12] — this suggests a hypothesis that greater scope for private economy widens inter-household inequalities.

Except for cases where the value of grain distribution "according to need" exceeded a household's collective earnings, all collective income has been distributed according to workpoints throughout the 1960s and 1970s. During the Cultural Revolution important changes in an egalitarian direction occurred in the method of workpoint allocation. There was a pronounced tendency toward the Dazhai method, i.e. workpoints allocated to the person and recorded on a time-rate basis, rather than allocated according to task and recorded on a piece-rate basis. However it should be noted that even during the Cultural Revolution it was quite common to combine these two methods, using each for different tasks. Under the time-rate system, the gaps between workers seem generally to have been quite narrow; most adult male workers probably fell within a span of 8-10 workpoints per day's labour.

While the span of collective earnings between individual farm workers may have been narrow, the differentials in average per capita incomes between households within a given team were still substantial. The production team shown in Table 3 had changed its method of workpoint allocation little from that used before 1976. The critical factor in household income differentials was obviously the worker-dependent ratio. The degree of fluctuation in relative incomes under such a system is large as households move into different phases in the family cycle. However at any point in time differentials in per capita collective incomes are large even with relatively small differences in earnings per worker.

Let us turn now to differentials between teams or brigades within communes. During the Great Leap Forward, the formation of large communes amalgamating many collectives led to drastic diminution in inter-collective income differentials as the average value of the labour day was equalised between units under centralised commune-level accounting. The dissatisfaction expressed by better-off collectives was enormous. The early 1960s saw a reversal first to brigade and then to team level accounting and income distribution — each unit was to retain the extra income or "differential rent" accruing from favoured location as an incentive to production. In essence, this policy contrived to govern the official approach to inter-unit differentials throughout the 1960s and 1970s.

Were there any special factors that tended to constrain local

Table 3. Distribution of collective income available for consumption in No.7 production team, Xintang Brigade, Tangtang commune, Fogang county Guangdong province, 1978

Range of income (yuan p.c.)	No. of households	No. of people	No. of labour powers	Mean household size (persons)	Mean no. of labour powers per household	Mean ratio of labour powers to household size
31-50 (lowest = 36)	3	16	4	5.3	1.3	1:4.0
51-70	14	79	29	5.6	2.1	1:2.7
71-90	6	24	13	4.0	2.2	1:1.8
91-110	2	7	5	3.5	2.5	1:1.4
>110 (highest = 162)	3	5	5	1.7	1.7	1:1.0

Source: Shi Shan, *op. cit.,* (see Table 1)

(i.e. intra-county, intra-commune) differentials during 1966-76? In theory all economic relations between local units throughout this period were to be on the basis of "equivalent exchange" and generally it appears that this was how exchanges were handled. Simply on account of the similarity of local geographical and economic conditions, it might be expected that there would be certain limits to local inter-unit income differences. Moreover, poorer units in fast growing areas have probably benefitted from the spin-off effects of brigade and commune-level activities, notably in the supply of welfare facilities but also in the provision of relatively highly-paid non-farm employment. However, even at the local level income differences could widen cumulatively on the basis of differential rents. There was radical pressure during the Cultural Revolution decade — for example, through enforced amalgamation of units of different income levels or direct redistribution of the resources of richer units to their poorer neighbours. These pressures are now condemned, but, as we shall argue later in more detail, they were intermittent and limited in their impact — adjuncts to a basic set of policies which did not strongly interfere with local differentials, rather than a dominating feature of rural policy during 1966-76.

Data are meagre but they suggest the following picture of local spatial differentials within a given county. The dimension of inequality between average income levels of communes seems to be quite small. For example, in 1978 the average per capita distributed income (APCDI) in Jiading county (Shanghai) was 244 yuan. The county contained 19 communes of which the APCDI in the highest was only 121 per cent and that of the lowest 88 per cent of the average for the whole county. Fourteen of the 19 were in the range of 230-260 yuan (Trip Notes). A similar picture emerged from data on Fogang country, Guangdong, in 1978. Each commune encompasses a range of conditions, so that the range of income between the constituent units could be quite large, even at the end of the Cultural Revolution decade. For example, in 1975 in Chengdong commune in Jiading county, out of a total of 157 teams, the lowest had an APCDI of 98 yuan and the highest 219 yuan. However, 83 per cent of the teams fell between the relatively narrow range of 120-179 yuan (Trip Notes). In Chengdong commune the range between teams within brigades generally was not large. In 1978 there were 16 brigades with an average of 9.8 teams in each. In the brigade with the largest range (83 yuan) in 1978, the APCDI in the highest team stood at 185 per cent of the lowest. In only one other brigade did the income of the highest team exceed that of the lowest by more than 54 per cent. Data on local differentials, however, are extremely fragmentary and should be interpreted with much greater caution than data on broad regional differentials.

Turning to the latter, at the broad regional level, there is little doubt that differentials in gross income per farmer widened between the more and the less well placed areas in the 1960s and 1970s, as a relatively large share of new farm inputs were purchased by units in areas which were already rich. For incentive reasons, the government avoided use of the agricultural tax to siphon off rising surpluses from the richer areas. The main constraints were twofold: first, pressure to grow more grain than they wished and, second, to control consumption growth and maximise investment growth. The latter policy further exacerbated gross income differentials. Certainly, by the end of the Gang of Four, there were large regional differentials even within a single province. For example, in Guangdong in 1975, 34 per cent of teams had an average income of less than 50 yuan, 54 per cent had 51-100 yuan, and 12 per cent more than 100 yuan (2.4 per cent had more than 150 yuan) (Trip Notes). Across the whole of China in 1978 (i.e. before the new policies had begun to bite), there were 377 counties (16.3 per cent) with an APCDI of 50 yuan or less, 1387 (60 per cent) between 51 and 100 yuan and 548 (23.7 per cent) with more than 100 yuan. In Shanghai and Beijing, 100 per cent of counties had more than 100 yuan APCDI, in Heilongjiang 77 per cent, Tianjin 73 per cent, Jilin 67 per cent and Zhejiang 44 per cent. There were eleven provinces/regions with over 20 per cent of their counties with an APCDI of less than 50 yuan: Guizhou, Yunnan, Fujian, Gansu, Shaanxi, Ningxia, Inner Mongolia, Shanxi Shandong, Henan and Anhui.[13]

To summarise this section on the background to the new policies on rural distribution, it is wise to regard current accounts of the previous situation in the Chinese media with some caution. Their picture of the past is overly negative; this is unsurprising given the fact that such descriptions are provided to buttress the case for policy change. On the growth side, the picture of frustratingly slow growth and stagnation in certain areas is correct — these problems were serious enough to warrant a new approach to rural policy which will bring about a more rapid improvement in rural living standards and the general pace and volume of economic activity in the countryside. But this limited growth was in itself quite an achievement given population pressure and technical constraints, and broad sections of the rural population did gain substantially in welfare terms between the 1950s and 1970s. To the extent that these positive judgements are true, they suggest that growth and welfare objectives and Maoist "egalitarianism" were not as incompatible as current accounts would argue. In fact, many accounts published in the late 1970s tend to overplay the significance and impact of "ultra-leftism" and "egalitarianism" and to underplay basic ecological, technical and institutional factors. To this extent, the problem was not growth vs. distributive policy, but growth vs. underlying contraints. However, to the extent that radical egalitarian policies were forced upon inappropriate realities and unwilling farmers during 1966 and 1976, they did have an adverse impact on popular motivations and growth in rural living standards. At the same time, policies such as restrictions on private economy and the free market, overly high rates of accumulation and excessive redistribution were not so much a direct reflection of "leftism" emanating from Beijing or Shanghai but of *local* institutions and "local policies", (*difang zhengce*) i.e. cadres at brigade and commune levels exercising what they considered their responsibilities for accumulation and redistribution. To this extent, though there was a real clash between growth and distributive (or rather redistributive) priorities, the causes should be sought at the structural as well as policy levels. This fact is recognised by more recent Chinese critiques of previous rural strategy, in which the anti-Gang of Four litany is increasingly marginal — in fact, some of these critiques trace problems back to the mid-1950s.

At the death of Mao in 1976, moreover, the Chinese countryside contained substantial inequalities, notwithstanding a decade of

Maoist "egalitarianism". Indeed, Maoist policies sometimes reinforced or exacerbated inequalities, notably the implications of the principle of "self-reliance" for local and regional disparities. Although there was a great deal of leftist huffing and puffing about rural-urban inequalities, their impact on key indices of inequality, notably the share of state investment devoted to agriculture, and price ratios between agricultural and industrial goods, was disappointing or non-existent. Where radical measures did operate to restrain intra-rural differentials — for example, popularisation of the time-rate method of income distribution — it was in an arena (intra-village) where differentials were the least pronounced. In general, however, the most powerful restraints seem to have stemmed less from specific policies and more from the basic structure of rural organisation — the commune system — which organised production collectively and allowed for redistribution within and between units at different levels. These factors should be borne in mind in assessing the impact (or lack of impact) of the new course in rural policy in the late 1970s.

The New Course in Agricultural Policy

The basic source of the new rural economic strategy which emerged between 1977-79 was a realignment of political leadership at the summit of the CCP — the gradual consolidation of a leadership group led by Deng Xiaoping, who lay behind the anti-radical coup of late 1976 and who gradually asserted their political dominance over remnant "centre-leftist" leaders. The redistribution of power among the top leadership produced a clear switch from "left" to "right" at both ideological and policy levels — a switch so dramatic and comprehensive that it gave credence to earlier Maoist portrayals of the "two-line struggle". The key dimensions of ideological differentiation are clear: the enthronement of modernisation as the central concern of socialist development and a consequent indifference or hostility towards many of the policy initiatives previously pursued under the banner of "Mao Zedong Thought", most notably Maoist approaches to questions of equality, democratisation of state institutions, class formation, reforms in the labour process and the developmental role of politico-ideological consciousness.

In the sphere of rural policy, after an initial spurt of breakneck modernisation-mania during 1977 and 1978, under the banner of a new Great Leap Forward, the Dengist leadership ushered in a more restrained and systematic process of "readjustment, restructuring, consolidation and improvement", decided at the Third Plenum of the Party Central Committee in December 1978 and publically ratified at a meeting of the National People's Congress in June 1979.[14] We shall focus primarily on this latter phase of policy and its implementation in 1979-80, with the qualification that some of its general themes and specific policies were already current before the Third Plenum and thus form part of our data base. Indeed, much of the "new" policy direction is a return to the cautious prescriptions embodied in the "60 articles" of 1962 and to the policies and practices current in the era of advanced agricultural producer cooperatives in 1956-57. For the present leadership, these were both periods when "rationality" ruled rural economic policy. It is not our intention to provide an overview of changes in agricultural policy,[15] but to focus on those elements of the new policies which impinge upon the relationship between distribution and development. Pervading the new strategy for rural development, one can discern two major streams of ideas — rationalisation and material incentives — which have particular bearing on this problem.

Rationalisation

Current Chinese political propaganda and economic theory stress the need to rationalise the rural economy in several basic ways. First, they call on policy makers and cadres at all levels to "obey objective economic laws" through a *diversification* of the agricultural production structure — at national, regional, local and basic levels — to match specific variations in ecological conditions. Leftist leaders, it is argued, were blind to the diversity of ecological potential, imposing a policy of "grain as the key link" and pressurising collectives to grow grain where natural conditions were unfavourable, resulting in low yields and high opportunity costs.[16] Second, rationalisation of the production structure embodies the principle of *concentration*. Given the fact that the demand for modern inputs generally exceeds supply, rational allocation demands that the State's fiscal and other financial resources should be concentrated on certain key areas with proven or potential comparative advantage in the production of particular commodities, whether they be "marketable grain bases", bases for specific industrial crops, or special "export bases". The same principle is applied to the programme of agricultural mechanisation. The grandiose plans for rapid comprehensive mechanisation sponsored by Hua Guofeng in the mid 1970s have been shelved in favour of a policy which concentrates machines on a few chosen areas.[17] Third, the principle of rationalisation has involved a wide-ranging effort to improve factor productivity through more skilled and systematic management and cost accounting practices at the level of collectives and collective enterprises and in state enterprises providing goods and services for agriculture; to institute tighter financial disciplines to make more effective use of development funds and to cut down the number of "unproductive" workers — notably administrative cadres, health, culture and education personnel — at each level of the commune structure.[18]

Material incentives

Agricultural policy over the past two years has been increasingly dominated by the idea that the crucial determinants of increased agricultural output — in the short run at least — are individual and collective material incentives which are to be strengthened by suitable distributive policies and institutions. This has been accompanied by increasing scepticism about the rapid, across-the-board plans for technical transformation current in the mid 1970s. Agricultural experts have argued that the emphasis on large-scale mechanisation and chemicalisation of farming dating from the early 1960s has had disappointing economic results. For example, Zhan Wu, President of the Institute of Agricultural Economics in the Chinese Academy of Social Sciences, has pointed out that while there was an increase of 830 per cent in farm machinery and 260 per cent in chemical fertilisers during 1965-77, total production only rose by 80 per cent and agricultural expenses rose by 130 per cent.[19] The same logic leads to a re-evaluation of the balance between accumulation and consumption: excessive attention to the former decreases production in the short and medium term by reducing work motivation and reduces outlets for other processes of accumulation based on the peasants' ability to purchase industrial consumer goods. The problem was exacerbated, it is claimed with considerable justification, because high rates of accumulation were often translated into wasteful and unproductive investment.

According to the new position, the character of economic incentives and distribution policy have a major influence on production: distribution policy is described as "the core of rural economic policies". "When pulling an ox", argued one authoritative article, "pull it by the nose" — distribution policy is the "nose".[20] This is the view of Wang Gengjin, vice-director of the Institute of Agricultural Economics in the Chinese Academy of Social Sciences, expressed in two collaborative articles in the journal *Jingji Yanjiu*,

(Economic Research). At the current stage of agricultural development, he argues, stimulation of peasant "enthusiasm" is the crucial mechanism for increasing output:

> In developing the rural productive forces, we must of course make use of modernised means of production and advanced skills to arm agriculture. But modernised means of production and skills must be created and utilised by people. If their use is managed properly, the role of advanced skills in spurring agricultural growth may be fully manifest; if management is inappropriate, the role of advanced techniques cannot be developed adequately. The basic expression is a fast rise in agricultural labour productivity . . . The raising of agricultural labour productivity depends partly on the level at which advanced scientific methods are utilised and the social links of the productive process etc, but first it includes adequate development of people's enthusiasm. Our country's agricultural production is currently still based on manual labour. From the national perspective, agricultural mechanisation and modernisation are still only in their initial stages and in some areas have not even begun. The modernisation of agriculture is not the work of a day and a night; it requires a process of gradual development. At present, in conditions of manual labour and backward means of production, in order to develop agricultural production we must still rely directly on the experience and labour capacity of the labourers. In a certain sense, this still plays the decisive role. Once we adequately stimulate the socialist enthusiasm of the broad peasant masses, then we can fully develop their labour ability and intelligence and can speed up the development of agricultural production.[21]

The "socialist enthusiasm" of peasants must be aroused by appealing to their "material interest" (*wuzhi liyi*).

The new course requires recognition of the necessity of differentials (*chengren chabie*) between regions, collective units and households. Wang Gengjin *et al.* argue the case as follows:

> Because the countryside at present still implements collective ownership on the principle of "three-level ownership with the team as the basis", there are still very big differences between the level of economic development between regions and between collectives. As a result, after each production team carries out distribution according to labour, the level of payment will differ from team to team. These differences are inevitable under conditions where the production team is the basic unit of account. Recognition of this differential is beneficial for encouraging each production team to strive to develop production and increase income so as to be able to raise the level of labour remuneration. Inside a production team, there are differences between the individual labour of the members. A recognition of these differences in labour contributes to the encouragement of each member's labour effort, to raising their labour capacity and technical level as a means to increase labour remuneration. The rationale is identical.[22]

Other accounts have gone further by arguing that differentials should be encouraged as a spur to production. Material inequalities were officially granted economic value and social virtue through the slogan "getting rich first" (*xian fuqilai*). It was argued that "it is glorious to receive more pay for more work and become richer"; richer areas, collectives and individuals would act as "a great demonstration force to influence their neighbours". "Getting rich first", it was claimed, was in fact egalitarian since greater inequality would eventually lead to less inequality as the poorer units and individuals emulated the rich ones. Richer teams would "serve as examples to lead the poorer teams forward, encourage them and make them see that there is hope ahead". On the "bright road to socialism", concluded a *Glorious Daily* article, "people advance in a column, and not 'together' in a straight line".[23]

The obverse of this argument has been a campaign against the evils of "egalitarianism" (*pingjunzhuyi*), portrayed as a mode of economic sabotage used by the former leftist leadership. The critique of "egalitarianism" is overdrawn and polemical, but rests on the following central tenets: (1) previous "egalitarian" measures (for example, the compression of individual workpoint differentials within collectives or the restriction of income variations between collectives) demaged productivity by failing to make clear distinctions in material remuneration between better or worse, more or less work.

> Egalitarianism is a product of petty production and is not compatible with the socialist principle of distribution according to work. The "Gang of Four" produced a situation in which there was no difference between working and not working, doing more and doing less, doing good and bad work. This attacked diligent people and encouraged lazy people and caused great harm to the development of production.[24]

(2) The leftist leadership erroneously defined "egalitarian" principles and practices as "socialist" or "communist" with the result that "some people still look upon egalitarianism as something 'socialist' or 'communist' to worship and adore". They have also been castigated, somewhat unfairly, for equating poverty with revolution and prosperity with revisionism. Because they felt that greater poverty meant greater revolutionary fervour, runs the argument, the Gang of Four were in favour of keeping people poor.[25]
(3) Egalitarianism encouraged the idea that socialism provided an "unbreakable rice bowl" and the practice of "eating from the common pot". As a result, "Liberation has become a symbol of the work of those people who shirk responsibility, are completely

inattentive, relax vigilance and maintain neutrality" — in other words it encouraged "free-loading" and unproductive dependence on the collective.[26] This critique of "egalitarianism" leads to a thorough reorientation of theory and practice. First, "egalitarian" ideas must be uprooted and replaced by three "correct" principles of distribution, viz. "distribution according to work" (*an lao fenpei*), "more work, more pay" (*duo lao duo de*) and "do not work, do not eat". Second, payment systems must be designed to match as precisely as possible the quantity and quality of individual effort with material return.

These general priorities and caveats have been embodied in the official policies which emerged after the Third Plenum. In spite of the requisite lip-service paid to the primacy of "spiritual motivation", the new strategy has hinged on appeals to peasants' immediate material interests, notably at the individual, household or small collective levels. This has resulted in a reorientation of macro-economic policies to raise rural living standards generally through changes in investment, financial, procurement and taxation policies. For example, grain procurement prices, which rose by 69 per cent between 1949 and 1978, were increased by 20 per cent in 1979, with a 50 per cent premium for a set amount of surplus grain and 100 per cent premium for any amount beyond this. Agricultural officials have been instructed not to raise procurement quotas on the "ratchet" principle but stabilise them over several years to allow increases in production to increase peasant incomes directly. There has been an effort to increase the ratio of agricultural investment in the state budget (this rose to 12.8 per cent of total investment in 1979 and 16 per cent in 1980). The new strategy also involved policies to allow greater freedom for individuals and collectives to dispose of surplus produce, to stimulate individual labour initiative through more highly differentiated payment systems: a reduced emphasis on models (such as Dazhai brigade) which rely heavily on non-material incentives; positive encouragement of the household sector, provision for more autonomy for small workgroups below the production team level and a defence of the production team against allegedly widespread depredations from higher units and threats of transition to larger units of account. Many of those policy changes have implications for rural inequality and we shall discuss them in more detail in the next section.

The Distributive Implications of the New Agricultural Strategy

The impact of rationalisation policies

The third area of rationalisation — in the management and accounting systems — is hardly new, being a frequent theme in rural policy propaganda throughout the 1970s. The explicit and systematic formulation of the principles of diversification and concentration, on the other hand, does mark a change of emphasis, though not a basic change in policy. Their implications for rational resource use and rural welfare are compelling, but we should bear in mind certain important qualifications. First, to a considerable extent, the principle of regional concentration is the ratification and intensification of a pattern of uneven development already evident in the preceding decade. As we argued earlier, there was a tendency during this period to concentrate a relatively large amount of modern inputs in a relatively small part of China's total farm area, leading to the emergence of a number of "high and stable yield areas" which have helped to stabilise China's agricultural performance in the face of fluctuating climatic conditions. The principle of regional concentration was accepted as economically necessary since the application of new technology — a process which gathered pace from the early 1960s on — required a strategy of integrated application (water control, new seed strains, chemical fertilisers, etc). This has resulted in considerable disparities in the regional allocation of modern inputs. In Guangdong (Kwangtung) province, for example, one of the authors was informed that, as of mid-1979, the counties of the fertile Pearl River Delta use 80-100 *jin* of chemical fertilisers per *mu*, compared to only 20-30 *jin* per *mu* in areas outside the Delta. This pattern was replicated in many other provinces and was evident to even the most casual visitor during the 1970s. Judging from detailed discussions of this issue with local cadres, the areas in Guangdong marked out as "bases" during 1978-1979 were none other than those which *already* had a high level of application of modern inputs. The 27 counties of the Delta have been chosen out of the province's 107 counties as the priority zone for investment.

Second, in regard to the charge that the Gang of Four forced peasants to grow grain at the expense of other crops, there was in fact a heavy emphasis on grain production in the 1960s and 1970s, but the links between this policy and the Gang of Four are tenuous. This policy was forcefully pursued since the early 1960s and was a rational response to the following considerations: the relatively rapid rate of population increase, the desire to maintain regional self-sufficiency in food-grain production, partly for security reasons, and the attempt to ensure that the basic food needs of the whole population can be met, Hence the priority on "grain as the key link" in agricultural production. Since the rate of population growth had slowed by the late 1970s, it was possible to diversify the structure of production while meeting basic food needs. The change to a more differentiated production structure can be seen, therefore, as a response to a new *stage* in rural development, made possible by the success of previous policies which emphasised food grain.[27]

Third, the principle of concentration on "key areas" does not necessarily make economic sense in terms of maximising output, particularly in the medium or long term, since they are in most cases already high-yield areas and may respond less favourably to increased agricultural inputs than 'backward" areas where present yields are low, potential returns greater, and investment requirements substantial. Yet the success of the "marketable grain bases" is central to the success of the new agricultural strategy as a whole. If collectives throughout the country are to be allowed to diversify into more profitable crops and reduce their grain acreage accordingly, then the shortfall must be borne by the bases or increased imports. Indeed, the decision to increase the procurement and above-procurement prices of grain reflected concern about a possible rush out of grain, legitimised by the principle of diversification and aided by the principle of team autonomy. The strategy worked well in 1979 when total grain production reached 332.12 million tonnes, the highest since liberation and 27.37 million tonnes up on 1978. In 1980, however, signs of problems appeared. Total production dropped from the 1979 level by about 10-15 million tonnes, but was still the second highest since 1949. But diversification into more profitable crops had brought about a decrease of 5.3 million hectares in the total area sown to grains — this led to a policy shift in early 1981 towards renewed emphasis on grain. In 1981, priority was attached to "a good grain harvest" and a halt was called to the diminution of grain acreage.[28] There have been proposals to cushion grain shortfalls by increased imports, to be paid for (on favourable terms of exchange) by increased exports of economic crops produced by agricultural diversification. But restraints on external markets and competing import claims make this a problematic solution.

Fourth, in addition to these economic question-marks, the principles of diversification and concentration will probably reinforce an already present pattern of uneven development at the regional and local levels. For example, a revised programme was announced in early 1979 to coordinate the allocation of inputs for agricultural mechanisation with the construction of "modern production bases" in crop farming, forestry, animal husbandry and fisheries. The distributive implications were clearly spelled out:

> We need to change our past practice of spreading factories everywhere, as if we were adding pepper to food. We must make it possible, in a planned and systematic way, for some key areas to advance ahead of others in promoting agricultural modernisation and raising the people's living standards. This will play a significant, exemplary and encouraging role throughout the country by making use of the good experience of one area to lead other areas.[29]

Statements such as this are very hard-headed when defending the virtues of concentration and its concomitant inequalities, but are somewhat vague when it comes to defining the specific mechanisms whereby the benefits of the base-areas can be spread to the peripheries. Again, the logic of concentrating State funds in these islands of modernisation, already well supplied with the financial wherewithal for expanded reproduction, and virtually ignoring the sea of "non-major areas" may be questioned. Would not a programme of providing modern inputs and infrastructure across a much wider spread, a more egalitarian approach which fuelled local initiative and encouraged the capitalisation of low yield areas, provide a sturdier basis for increased output in the long run, as long as the current caveats about the need for standardisation, locational planning and rational division of labour were observed?

At local levels, the principle of diversification according to natural conditions may make economic sense but its implementation may prove highly problematic. Who is to decide what is "in accordance with local natural conditions"? What is to stop production teams from rushing into more profitable and ignoring less profitable, but macro-economically crucial, areas of production. The State plan should, of course, resolve these problems but the new course emphasises the right of production teams to ignore "blind" orders from above — again, who decides what is "blind"? These problems aside, moreover, the principle of diversification is likely to increase differentials between collective units. If production teams are allowed to exploit their differing factor endowments to the full, without significant restraint on decisions about the structure of production from above, then the gap between ecologically favourable and unfavourable collectives is likely to increase unless determined counter-measures are taken. Communes with favoured access to lines of communications and proximate markets, notably those in the suburbs of large and medium-sized cities, will prosper compared to their less well-situated counterparts.

In short, the principles of diversification and concentration, as presently stated, are problematic in conception, implementation and likely results and it is far from clear that the benefits arising from their contribution to economic growth will adequately compensate for their costs in terms of unequal development. Indeed, the current Chinese literature on agricultural economics acknowledges some of these problems and measures have been introduced to deal with them (for example, by redistributive subsidies to or financial support for profitable diversification in poorer regions and collectives).

The impact of policies to stimulate material incentives

Redistribution of institutional power: the self-determination of the production team The ideas of policy makers and advisors during 1978-80 about the economic role of the production team in the rural institutional system bear comparison with current views of the role of the enterprise in the state political economy. The production team is likened to a firm, an economic actor with its own juridical identity, administrative autonomy and scope for economic initiative, under the guidance but not direct control of higher collectives and state organs. For some higher level cadres, it is alleged, "the production team had actually become a purely administrative unit appended to the responsible administrative organ and they consider it to be a bead on an abacus that can only move when manipulated from above.[30] In many areas, peasants were quoted as follows: "We have only one production team in the whole county and only one person who knows farming i.e. the first secretary of the county Party committee".[31] As an autonomous firm, the team is capable of collective entrepreneurship to maximise its members' income through good management and "business sense". To this end, the decision power of the team is being expanded to cover methods of labour organisation, system of job responsibility, the right to determine accumulation ratios and payment systems, to dispose of surplus produce after fulfilling state assignments, to define planting plans, and defy "coercion, commandism and arbitrary orders" from above. The agricultural planning process is to be more indicative, with fewer obligatory targets and more flexible, decentralised implementation, eventually moving from a system of compulsory assignments to one of negotiated contracts.

Whereas in the earlier years of the decade, leftist propaganda had warned of the political and social implications of "collective capitalism", the new leadership selected exemplary cases of entrepreneurial teams for public emulation. For example, a production team in Sanshui county, Guangdong province, which achieved an astonishing per-capita income of 755 yuan in 1978 from agriculture and a lime plant, was praised for having "gone to rich from poor because it has grasped both grain in one hand and money in the other". Such success could not merely be attributed to good business sense, however, since ecological conditions were particularly favourable — plentiful limestone and firewood in the vicinity and easy access to transport facilities.[32]

This kind of initiative and its egregious economic results were no doubt atypical, but they reflected the CCP leadership's highest expectations about the material fruits of greater team autonomy. The team is a suitable unit for collective action because it is small enough to engage individual material aspirations directly in its operations and because it fits better into a rural scene characterised by considerable inequalities. Wang Gengjin *et al.* recognise the latter fact when they argue, from the results of a detailed research programme in Anhui province, that one of the advantages of the team as the basic accounting unit lies in the fact that "it can relatively thoroughly overcome egalitarianism *among* production teams".[33]

Given the hypothesised link between inter-team differentials and increased agricultural output, the new policies demand that the team be protected against inappropriate and arbitrary intervention from superior collective levels on the grounds that such interventions are irrationally egalitarian and therefore harmful to the crucial "socialist enthusiasm" of team members. As a result, current analysts attack three types of practice which were allegedly widespread throughout the preceding decade under "pressure" (*yali*) exerted by the Gang of Four.

(1) Restrictions on income levels Previous attempts by local officials in some areas, motivated by a "leftist" fear of "polarisation", to establish an arbitrary limit on the per-capita incomes of the collective units under their jurisdiction have been condemned as irrational "egalitarianism". In Laixi county in Shandong (Shantung) province, for example, the Party leadership had been alarmed by a pattern of uneven annual per-capita income distribution ranging from 150 yuan in the rich brigades to 60 yuan in the poor. They therefore set an upper limit of 150 *yuan* and ordered that the residuum be channelled into public accumulation. A similar system was apparently established in Peking's suburban communes viz. a limit of 150 *yuan* per capita in grain-growing collectives and 180 *yuan* in those growing vegetables.[34]

The new leadership has argued that limits of this kind restrain the initiative of peasants in richer collectives while doing little to encourage higher income in poorer units: They maintain that "the only way to narrow the gap between rich and poor production brigades is to aid the poor production brigades".[35] This reasoning is sound but we should be aware of certain qualifications: (a) it is not clear that the practice of arbitrary income limitations was widespread throughout the nation and there is little evidence that it was "official" policy emanating from Peking. It is more likely to have been a "local policy" adopted by officials in certain areas in response to intermittent egalitarian ideological cues from Peking. (b) The practice seems to have been counter-productive in any case since the residual income of the rich brigades was not confiscated, but fed into their public accumulation funds. If these funds were well invested and managed, they would in fact lay the basis for even higher future incomes, thus *increasing* the gap between rich and poor units. At present there is no intention to tax away any of the increments to gross income resulting from current policies, thus it is likely that areas with higher per capita gross incomes will be allowed to realise" their incomes in increased consumption to a greater degree than in the past. (c) The new policies may seem reasonable, but their distributive impact depends on *how much* aid is to be directed to poorer units, (particularly if this form of redistribution is opposed by richer and more powerful areas and units), what redistributive mechanisms are to be used and on what terms is to be offered.

(2) Transition in poverty (qiong guodu) According to current analysis, leftist leaders had pressured production teams to move up to brigade level accounting where material conditions were not yet ripe.[36] Though it is certainly correct that radical spokesmen in the 1970s did stress the importance of transition and encouraged it where possible, the current picture of across-the-board forced transitions, based on the idea that "insufficient (economic) conditions should not preclude transition", is clearly overdrawn.[37] There is some evidence of over-hasty transition in the mid-1970s in certain areas, presumably connected with the Dictatorship of the Proletariat Campaign in 1975. For example, it is reported that 223 production brigades in Tianmen county Hubei province became accounting units prematurely and were disbanded in 1978.[38] Even in this case, however, a considerable percentage of the mid-1970s transitions (58.5 per cent) were apparently *confirmed* by the post-Mao leadership. On the other hand, in Jiading county — in the radical base of Shanghai municipality — at the height of the Gang of Four's influence, only 25 out of a total of 243 brigades practised

brigade-level accounting and 18 of these were still doing so in June 1979 (Trip Notes).

There is evidence, moreover, of speeded transition *after* the removal of the Gang of Four. In Fuping county in Shaanxi province, for instance, a "wind of transition in a state of poverty" began in the spring of 1978 and was not reversed until January 1979 by a resolution from the provincial Party committee.[39] The problems identified with this particular "wind of transition" illustrate well the costs perceived by the Dengist leadership: (a) Rich teams did nothing while poor ones "awaited the 'coming of communism' ". In one production team, for example, the value of a labour day (*laodongri*) in No.2 team was less than half that of No.3. When the announcement of transition to brigade accounting was made, some members of No.2 team allegedly said that "things are done well in No.3 team, so let us 'enter communism' ". (b) After brigade-level accounting was established, heavier production quotas were imposed on the richer teams with the result that higher output did not result in higher income for their members. For example, in the summer harvest distribution of 1978, No.3 team's quota was 20,000 *jin* (about 40 per cent of the brigade's total) while No.2's was only 9,000 *jin* in consequence, the per-capita grain rations in team 3 were only slightly larger than in team 2. (c) The transition caused a drop in the amount of draft animals and farm tools — some of these were sold off on the sly when news of the impending transition spread; after transition, the draft animals became "orphans" with nobody to care for them properly and their health suffered accordingly. (d) The brigade leadership was not up to the new burdens of management and inefficiency increased at both brigade and team levels.

The change in policy emphasis between 1977 and 1979 reflects disagreement within the post-Mao leadership, at both national and provincial levels, about the priority of transition to higher collectives. The spirit of the "learn from Dazhai" and the "Dazhai county" movement of the mid-1970s, sponsored by Hua Guofeng and Chen Yonggui, took a more positive view of transition comparable to the Gang of Four's now vilified "transition relying on the spirit of poverty" and apparently took steps to encourage it in certain areas. With the rise of Dengist influence, however, upward transition was subjected to more criticism and policy documents have advised caution and, at least for the foreseeable future, stabilisation of the status quo. According to this position, transition must not be used to reduce inter-team inequalities; later transition is better than sooner; "transition in poverty" must be supplanted by "transition in wealth", and the leftist leadership's previous emphasis on the spiritual conditions for transition is dismissed as unMarxist. The necessary conditions for transition are "socialised means of production" which produce "socialised production":

> The course of transition should be one of agricultural mechanisation, factory production and automation . . . The transition from small collective ownership to large collective ownership can only be carried out when the large collective has acquired a fairly large amount of accumulation and become relatively rich and when the economies of the various small collectives are fairly developed and the gap between them has been narrowed.[40]

However, this theory is incompatible to some degree with the priority of stabilisation. Particularly in more prosperous areas, there are clear economic and social advantages to be reaped from transition to higher level units of account — economies of scale, greater capacity to help poorer units within the larger collectives, opportunities for more rational allocation of labour and other factors of production, more comprehensive and better quality welfare services. Indeed, in an interview conducted in June 1979 (Trip notes), the Vice-Chairman of the Peking suburban commune of Lukouqiao, where brigade accounting is the norm, defended it as "superior" since it enabled brigades to help backward teams to catch up with the advanced. It seems reasonable, therefore, that where conditions are favourable — notably a relatively homogeneous sociological and ecological context, the absence of wide disparities between teams and good management and accounting capacity at the brigade (or even commune) level — transition should be encouraged.

The new agricultural course is ambiguous on the issue. Certain policies put a damper on transition — the insistence on team autonomy, encouragement of inter-team differentials, a generally critical stance towards "blind" directives from superior collective levels and an emphasis on "stabilisation" of the rural institutional system. On the other hand, as the new policies began to take effect during 1979-80, a three-tiered policy on ownership emerged (implicitly i.e. in "advanced" areas, higher forms of ownership (including state farms) were deemed appropriate and it was possible to move to higher levels of account within the commune structure; in the majority of "average" areas, the principle of team ownership was to be stabilised; in "backward" areas, on the other hand, there have been moves towards "transition downwards", not de iure but de facto, through contracting production to households or individuals.

(3) Equalisation and transfer Consistent with the greater stress on production team autonomy, there has been severe criticism of allegedly widespread depredations visited on production teams, notably by brigades and communes but also by State organs at the county level. This has involved a general condemnation of interference, "blind commands" and intolerably heavy demands on the labour and funds of teams. The tendency for "over-concentration" i.e. the practice whereby higher collectives derived part of their accumulation from unrequited or only partially recompensed levies on teams has also been condemned.[41] More specifically, higher collective levels have been accused of "equalisation and transfer" (*yi ping er diao*) which involves the requisitioning of team resources without proper compensation according to the principle of "voluntary mutual benefit and equivalent exchange" (*ziyuan huli, dengjia jiaohuan*) and the use of higher-level projects as a redistributive device to even out differentials between teams or brigades.

Data from the late 1960s and early to mid-1970s suggests that brigades and communes did increase pressure on teams as part of a general strategy of encouraging industries and welfare facilities at higher levels, and as a reflection of the importance attached to large scale farmland capital construction projects, particularly in the area of water-control, based on the mobilisation of idle labour in the quiet seasons — the process of "labour accumulation". The number of such projects undertaken by the brigade level and above increased rapidly during the 1970s. According to Nickum's study of "labour accumulation" in the 1960s and 1970s, the principles for large-scale projects involving more than one level had been laid down in the "Sixty Articles" of 1962 and retained their normative power: voluntary participation, mutual benefit for all participants and equivalent exchange (i.e. fair compensation for transferred resources). Given the frequent financial weakness of the brigades and communes, however, there was considerable pressure to violate the principle of equivalent exchange and to use "equalisation and transfer", in Nickum's words, "a 'leftist' error involving the unrequited transfer of resources from the haves to the have-nots".[42]

To summarise, given the present emphasis on redressing the balance between accumulation and consumption and increasing production incentives, measures to protect the autonomy of the team and develop its initiative make developmental sense. The small unit allows a closer link between collective and household or individual incentives, more flexible accomodation to variations in agricultural conditions and complexities of work organisation and greater scope for basic-level democracy. At the same time, however, the new policies may bring practical problems. First, there has been a tendency to "absolutise" the principle of team autonomy: for example, in an authoritative statement by the Guangdong provincial newspaper:

> [Leading] organs may give the production teams some suggestions on their production plans . . . [The] production teams may completely accept a suggestion concerning production or management from higher authorities, they may consider the actual situation and accept it partially and they may refuse to accept it if it is wrong.[43]

This type of policy, if implemented, creates many headaches for brigade and commune leaderships. First, it becomes more difficult to enforce the implementation of state agricultural plans (e.g. by determining the basic product mix of each team); second, a strict observance of the principle of equivalent exchange results in a shortage of funds at the brigade and commune levels, a consequent diminution of their capacity to act as a redistributive, equalising force over teams or brigades and to launch relatively large-scale capital construction projects without resort to external funding. Problems of economic accumulation and distribution aside, moreover, the swing towards team autonomy has important political implications. It is likely to weaken the influence of the Party whose lowest rung of organisation is at the production *brigade* level. It also implies a significant redistribution of decisional power within the commune structure, after a long period during which higher levels, notably the brigade, seem to have been increasing their power *vis-à-vis* the team. These political constraints make it unlikely that the move towards team autonomy will be implemented in any thoroughgoing way. Indeed, complaints from brigade and commune cadres were already visible in the media during 1978-80: for instance, cadres in Liaoning province were reported as complaining that "the power of (the team's) decision is being overemphasised" and "those at lower levels are disobeying orders and everything is in a mess"; elsewhere, there were complaints that the new policies were weakening Party leadership in the countryside, or that commune cadres were having difficulties with recalcitrant teams which were only considering their own interests by choosing crops to sell at a high price and reducing their grain acreage excessively.[44] Given current policy directions, such "selfish" behaviour is hardly surprising; nor is the exasperation of supra-team cadres who are charged with the implementation of state plans and the construction of local capital projects but are being drained of the political authority and financial strength necessary to carry out these tasks. At the ideological level, these complaints and opposition were couched in terms of "progress" and "retrogression" i.e. the new policies were encouraging or allowing a "departure from socialism" by under-mining collective economy and dividing people into competing groups.[45] Such concerns are probably shared by members of the central leadership and they provide an important political base for future policy changes.

Individual and collective: the encouragement of private economy
During 1977 and 1978, a great deal of official attention was devoted to trimming down rural collectives which, it was argued, had become over-blown during previous years. It is true that there was considerable emphasis during the previous decade on increasing the rate of collective accumulation and the range of collective facilities — notably at brigade and commune levels — though this appeared to command wider support among the central leadership than the anti-Gang of Four litany would suggest. The Gang have of course been blamed for the problems which arose when rural collectives tried to expand too fast: overspending, wasteful or unprofitable investments, proliferation of cadres and other "unproductive" personnel (such as welfare or cultural workers) and a tendency for poor units to emulate the services offered by their rich counterparts, thus overstretching their resources, harming agricultural production and retarding income growth. A common official criticism in 1977-78 was that collectives had syphoned off too large a share of gross output and income for their own accumulation, with the result that they "squeezed the state above and the commune members below".[46] The new emphasis, in the words of the resurgent Zhao Ziyang, was on "pressing the centre (the collective) and guaranteeing the two ends" (the household and the state).[47] Quotas were established in the provinces to define permissible rates of public accumulation (for example, in Jilin it was fixed at a maximum of 10 per cent)[48] and the principle of increasing *personal* incomes along with increasing collective output was firmly reiterated. The policy current earlier in the decade whereby collectives with higher rates of growth were expected to raise their level of accumulation accordingly was now condemned for lowering peasant incentives through limits on personal income growth and hampering rural development by stunting the initiative of more dynamic units.

Restrictions on collective "over-accumulation" have been accompanied by policies designed to encourage production and exchange in the *private* or household sector. During the previous decade, policies towards the private sector had been ambiguous: on the one hand, it was recognised as a necessary adjunct to the collective economy; on the other hand, it was regarded with suspicion as a relic of "petty production" a potential threat to the collective economy, a cause of increased inequality between households and as a seedbed for "capitalist" activities and attitudes. Official policy thus combined retention with restriction. In practice, many local cadres found the balance hard to strike and often "deviated" in one direction or the other. Given the leftist atmosphere of these years, there was a tendency to "prefer left to right" (*ning zuo wu you*) and play safe by severely restricting or even abolishing private production and exchange.

As Elizabeth Croll's contribution to this volume demonstrates in detail, current policies have been far more favourable to private economy, reaffirming its legitimacy and taking concrete measures to promote its expansion. Private possession of livestock and sideline production have been encouraged by higher procurement prices "soft" loans and greater provision of fodder-land. The household's right to hold and manage private plots independently has also been reaffirmed and the scope of rural "fairs" expanded to foster rural commerce. Available data suggests that such measures have been effective in invigorating the rural economy and raising household incomes in the short run, though they have run into problems of implementation and local resistance. In some areas, for example, they have led to a wholesale privatisation of livestock rearing and the dissolution of collective livestock farms, even where the latter were economically viable. Moreover, the liberalisation of rural commerce has encountered resistance from commune cadres who continue to regard local fairs as "hotbeds of capitalism and impediments to agricultural production". Such fairs, they claim, encourage an over-expansion of the private sector, tempt peasants to "leave agriculture for trade" and divert agricultural and sideline produce from the state procurement net. The present leadership has proven sensitive to these and other problems, and has attempted to institute certain restriction: limitations on the size of private plots; minimum quotas (measured in workdays) for collective work by team members: proscription of private hiring of labour and increased incentives for peasants to sell their sideline produce and livestock to the state (through restrictive regulations and higher prices). Practical enforcement of these measures is another matter, however, made difficult by the provisions for team autonomy, propaganda paeans to enterprising households and individuals and a diminution of the power of higher levels to interfere effectively if things get out of hand in ways which recall the chaotic days of the early 1960s. While the present political situation is not identical with that of the early

1960s, it should be remembered that the private sector then rapidly expanded beyond the letter of the law. It is not inconceivable that the same thing could happen again if local political controls are insufficiently tight.

Preliminary figures suggest that the private sector increased its share of total household incomes between 1978-80. Moreover, the official statistics on the net income of a national sample of peasants in 1979 reported a 19.9 per cent increase over 1978; collective income increased by 14.6 per cent but income from "household side-line occupations" increased by 25.3 per cent over 1978 to 27.5 per cent of total net income.[49] Earlier experience (notably in 1957 and 1960-62) suggests that, when private sector activity increases rapidly and stronger households divert labour power from the collective to more lucrative private production and exchange, intra-village differentials increase. There is no systematic data as yet to test such a hypothesis, but scattered examples would seem to support it. For example, in Heze prefecture in Shandong, an export base for grey goat and angora rabbit products, where 95 per cent of goats and rabbits are raised by individual families, each family gained an average of 35 yuan from such activities, but some families made several hundred and even 1000 yuan.[50] Only further research can document whether this represents a general trend or an atypical case.

Intra-collective differentials: changes in payment systems During the decade preceding the death of Mao, the leftist leadership at all levels fostered a move from a task-based to a time-based system of labour remuneration. The model mode of payment was embodied in the Dazhai (Tachai) system which assigned a work-point grade to each worker on an annual basis after extensive discussion. Time-rate systems, whether close to the Dazhai model or not, were favoured for their relative simplicity (and consequent lack of divisiveness — in theory at least) and relative equality (since they compressed differentials between different qualities of labour-power). In many areas and units the time-rate system made little headway; in others it was tried for a while, then dropped; in others, it was combined with piece-rate systems of various kinds.[51] Where it did make headway, it probably contributed to a narrowing of collective income differentials within the team or brigade. Time-rates or not, however, the payment system in most collectives was egalitarian in the sense of providing a guaranteed floor under individual incomes through a system of "basic rations" (*jiben kou liang*), which combined the "communist" principle of distribution according to need with the socialist principle of distribution according to work, i.e. the rations still had to be earned through workpoints. If an individual or household earned insufficient workpoints, they still received the ration but owed the shortfall to the collective.

The Dengist leadership has attempted to stem any tendency towards egalitarian payment systems, arguing that poorer households benefit from a general rise in agricultural production not from specifically egalitarian policies. One delegate to a Henan (Honan) conference argued the point as follows: "Practising egalitarianism is not a solution to the households beset with difficulties .... Only when the collective economy has become large can the incomes of members go up. As the water swells, the boat rises".[52] Thus the new leadership have attempted to move rural collectives towards systems of piece-rates comparable to those current in the early 1960s. Official spokesmen have favoured one type of payment system in particular — a form of "collective piece-rates" based on the ideas of "fixed quotas on the basis of work-groups and work evaluation on the basis of individuals". This has several components: (1) the accounting unit sets fixed quotas for different agricultural tasks, the system of "fixed quota management" (*dinge guanli*), (2) responsibilities for fulfilling quotas are assigned to work-groups — the system of "guaranteeing work to the work-group" (*baogong dao zuoyezu*). The work-group is assigned responsibility for a fixed plot of land throughout the farming cycle and is rewarded with a fixed amount of workpoints for completion of the quota, and bonuses or penalties for over or under-fulfilment. Thus, if a work group in the Evergreen commune in suburban Peking in mid-1979 overfulfilled its quotas, it received a bonus of 55 per cent of the over-fulfilled amount; in the case of shortfalls, it suffered a penalty of 30 per cent of the unfulfilled amount (Trip notes). The work-groups are not temporary, ad hoc forms of labour organisation but take on a more permanent identity, taking over some of the team's original functions. (3) The distribution of workpoints to individuals is to be on a piece-rate basis as far as possible and is handled primarily within each work-group through a precise personal responsibility system. In some cases, work-norms within the work group are established by the group leader whose performance in any particular task becomes the norm (*zuzhang daitou gan*).[53]

This type of system is viewed as optimal for a number of reasons: it encourages initiative and thus productivity by matching reward more precisely with effort or skill; it improves the organisation of production and labour by subdividing management responsibilities and encouraging a disciplined sense of responsibility among members of each work-group. It was introduced in 1978 and clearly made slow initial headway in many areas. For example, in Fogang county in Guangdong province in June 1979, under one-fifth of production teams were using work-groups in their fully-fledged form; time-rate systems were still in widespread use, especially during the slack seasons. But official policy has tried to encourage adoption by urging flexibility, i.e. allowing experimentation with different forms and combinations of payment systems along certain basic lines and advising teams to adopt the specific form which suits their conditions. But by April 1980 only about one-quarter of the nation's production teams had adopted the basic system.[54] One can identify certain constraints which will continue to impede its implementation. First, experience from the 1960s shows that, given the complex nature of agricultural work, a sophisticated piece-rate system which can accurately measure and remunerate different levels of quantity, quality, intensity or skill is very difficult both to design and manage. For example, the Party committee of Deyang county in Sichuan estimated in mid-1980 that there were 834 agricultural work processes in the county — labour norms were established for each. The problem of setting appropriate norms and quotas is not merely a technical headache for unit cadres, it is also a political headache since complex piece-rate systems of this nature tend to be divisive and "troublesome" (*mafan*). Judging from the amount of official concern during 1979-80 about poor team management and the need to train team cadres, implementation of the new systems was proving troublesome. Second, though the devolution of management responsibilities to work-groups may cushion some of these problems, the introduction of semi-permanent work-groups must be seen as a mode of "decollectivisation", a devolution of former team functions to a unit situated between team and household. This encourages a tendency towards the development of a "small collective" consciousness among team members which may well lead to conflicts between group and team interests and to competition with other groups for resources (such as manure, water, tools and machines) and lucrative quotas. More seriously, it has led in some areas to an informal disbanding of the team as the unit of ownership and account. As such, the work-group system may well be resisted by team cadres who fear organised "pluralism" in the team and resent their loss of power. The same problem also attends the extension of the principle of decentralised contracting to the household and the individual, a system introduced in 1980 for a minority of teams with particularly bad economic performance and weak collective economies.[55] Third, the piece-rate system is likely to increase collective income inequalities between households and individuals and the work-group system, if not handled properly, might lead to growing differentials between strong and weak groups. Policy-makers are aware of this latter danger and controls have been instituted to balance the allocation of resources evenly between the groups, to set production contracts in a fair way and to reshuffle assets every year. However, the question again arises of whether in practice such controls will prove effective in the long run.

The egalitarian system of "basic rations" has not been altered fundamentally, but the leadership has attempted to introduce two marginal changes: first, by decreasing the ratio of ration grain to "work-point grain" (*gongfenliang*) — for example, from 8:2 to 7:3 or 6:4 — a change regarded as necessary not merely to stimulate incentive but to restrain population growth; second, by adopting a tougher line on unpaid "overdrafts" (for example, by charging interest on them).[56] The latter may prove difficult to enforce since, as one report on Guangdong pointed out, it is nearly always cadres or people with close connections with cadres who have the biggest overdrafts and take the longest to repay them.[57] These changes may increase inter-household differentials to some limited degree but, as long as the rationing system remains in force, it has an egalitarian effect on intra-collective differentials by providing a floor under household incomes (notably for "difficulty homes", *kunnanhu*).

In sum, it is likely that, for the foreseeable future, basic-level payment systems will vary widely from unit to unit, area to area — as indeed they did in the preceding decade in spite of leftist pressure in favour of time-rate systems in general and the Dazhai system in particular. It is likely, moreover, that the inegalitarian tendencies inherent in a move towards piece-rates will be restrained by several factors: first, the retention of the ration system; second, the presence of ideologically motivated leadership cadres at team and brigade levels who view wide gaps in income as "unsocialist"; and, third, mechanisms of community solidarity — both socialist and pre-socialist — at both the team and brigade levels which will impose informal group constraints on the widening of inter-household differentials.

Conclusions

It is as yet too early to make a definite assessment of the new policies — these conclusions will be preliminary judgements. It is important to avoid a black and white view of the pre- and post-Mao stage. This may lead one, on the one hand, to overestimate the amount of leftist influence over rural policy before 1976 and exaggerate the levelling effect of egalitarian policies in this period and, on the other hand, to overestimate the amount of change embodied in the new policies and particularly their actual impact on the grassroots. Many of the new policies are mere changes of emphasis or ratifications of pre-existing policy or reality rather than massive swings in orientation — the basic commitment to collectivised agriculture appears to be unimpaired.

We must analyse the new strategy as a serious effort to tackle long-standing problems and to raise rural output and living standards. In certain key aspects, it represents an attempt to further Maoist goals through non-Maoist means. There is a basic commitment to raising rural living standards, increasing state investment in agriculture, encouraging basic-level democracy and mobilising the "enthusiasm" of the peasantry — these were central elements of the Maoist credo. But these are now being pursued by methods which Mao rejected, distrusted or only grudgingly accepted: stimulation of individual material incentives, expansion of free markets, a weakening of the collectives, and encouragement of inequalities.

At this early stage in the new strategy, its impact on rural economic growth and peasant living standards appears to have been very favourable on most indices: gross output of key commodities, average rural incomes (rising from 117 yuan per capita in 1977 to 160 in 1979 and 170 in 1980), volume of rural market activity and growth in rural savings. Yet it is wise to be cautious in interpreting these statistics. In the early years of new policy strategies, statistics tend to be favourable for political reasons and problem areas tend to be downplayed or ignored. Some of the "new" statistics, moreover, may reflect either an increase in the state's capacity to collect information or the inclusion of data (for example, on household economy or free markets) which was previously embarrassing or tabu. There is also a basic question about the extent to which the dramatic improvements of 1979 and, to a lesser extent, 1980 are evidence of a long-run upward trend or a "once-for-all" surge which will soon peter out, leaving the new leadership faced by the basic constraints which confounded their predecessors, notably inadequate investment, ecological and technical limitations and population pressure. The attempt to bring more rapid increments in rural living standards have also contributed to the state's financial problems which became critical at the end of 1980. Although the rise in procurement prices pumped more money into the countryside (estimated as an extra 8,000m yuan in 1979 and even more in 1980), it contributed to a spiralling budget deficit in 1980 and fuelled inflationary pressures in the economy as a whole, eroding some of the nominal gains in rural incomes. This financial crisis reveals the difficult predicament in which the new leadership finds itself, caught in a vice between three sets of priorities and political forces: the big spending organs of the state, both civilian and military; the urban population clamouring for long denied wage increases and a rise in general welfare standards; and the peasantry. These fix the parameters of what is financially possible. Thus it was extremely difficult to compensate for a dramatic increase in rural expenditure through substantial savings elsewhere (for example, decreasing urban food subsidies or slashing ministerial budgets) and the leadership finally resorted to printing more money with consequences which had become alarming by early 1981, precipitating an intensification of the process of macro-economic "readjustment".

Though there appears to have been a substantial improvement in aggregate rural growth indices between 1978 and 1981, the fruits of increasing prosperity have been shared unequally. In other words, the new rural strategy has intensified an already existing pattern of inequalities at regional, local and intra-unit levels. Does this mean that these policies, pursued consistently and effectively, will produce the "polarisation" about which the previous leftist leadership had cautioned? There are certain influential countervailing factors which may well keep increases in rural inequality within reasonable bounds. At the *policy* level, questions of equality have not been completely abandoned — they have been put on the back burner. There are officials and experts at all levels concerned about the economic, social and political consequences if present policies are taken too far. For example, measures have been taken to curb excessive private economic activity, dramatic declines in accumulation ratios at the team level, the tendency to break up teams into small units and divide land and means of production amongst them, and unwise forms of diversification. There is concern, moreover, about differentials between poor and rich units in specific localities. Present policy dictates, that, though richer units should not be impeded from increasing their wealth and realising it in higher personal incomes, provision must also be made to help poor units caught in a vicious cycle of backwardness — for example, exemptions from agricultural tax or industrial and commercial taxes on collective enterprises, state development grants and low-interest loans particularly for infrastructural projects such as roads in hilly regions. But this redistributive thrust is not substantial as yet. In the late 1970s, direct aid in the form of constructions and rural relief funds was running at 1.5 billion yuan per year, (8.6 per cent of total state aid to agriculture), a relatively small amount given the fact that ¼ of all teams are defined as "poor". In early 1980, moreover, notice was given that the level of funds from the state could not increase for the forseeable future.[58] Perhaps it is unrealistic to expect these forms of redistribution to increase given competing claims on resources at the national levels and the capacity of richer, more powerful units and localities to torpedo redistributive programmes at the local level. The relative autonomy of local party networks from vested interests is a crucial factor in tackling this problem. At the intra-unit level, as we have seen, the system of "basic rations" has been retained with marginal changes, and the new regulations governing the expansion of private production and exchange contain provisions to keep the private sector within bounds. By contrast, there seems much less official sensitivity to the impact of present policies on regional inequality and the principle of concentration will almost certainly reinforce the already existing pattern of uneven development. In short, problems of increasing inequality grow more serious as we move up from the unit to the regional levels.

Policies are little more than statements of intent, however, and it is at the level of practical implementation that issues of equality and inequality will be worked out. Here, the question of *political control* is central and one might hypothesise that, from the point of view of Peking at least, this becomes more problematic the lower the level in the chain of command. The new agricultural strategy contains certain elements — notably the encouragement of private economy, the reallocation of power within the teams and the communes — which threaten to get out of control and lead to rapidly widening inter-household and inter-collective disparities and incipient forms of informal exploitation. This same strategy, moreover — through its attempt to promote a "hands off the team" approach and to stimulate a kind of cellular market economy with the team as the basic unit — has weakened the ability of the state in general and the Party apparatus in particular to correct "deviations" at the basic level. Evidence of "deviations" has been plentiful during the latter part of 1979 and early 1980 — notably the move in some areas towards an informal partition of the production teams — and these tendencies may well produce policy backpedalling in the direction of recollectivisation, notably a restoration of political and economic power of brigades and communes. This recollectivisation may prove economically necessary, moreover, since changes in the basic, underlying determinants of agricultural growth — farmland capital construction and technological change — requires a strengthening of the authority and economic power of the higher collectives.

Policy changes may also result from political opposition to the new course. Constant references in the official press to opposition, disagreement and "ideological confusion" suggest strongly that the more egalitarian conception of socialist development which dominated public propaganda and shaped rural distribution policies during the decade before Mao's death and which was clearly associated with the personal beliefs of Mao himself, penetrated the consciousness of people at all levels of society. To such people, the present "developmentalist" conception of socialist development is unacceptable. They appear to retain considerable power at all levels, from Politburo to production team, and may be expected to intervene to curb those elements of the new course which threaten egalitarian and collectivist ideals. Far from being a strategy which will regulate the course of Chinese development well into the 1980's, therefore, the new course may well be just another curve on the undulating graph of Chinese rural development.

9

RURAL ENTERPRISE IN CHINA, 1977-79

Jack Gray

Institute of Development Studies,
University of Sussex, Brighton

Introduction

The purpose of this paper[1] is a simple one: to look at the state of rural enterprise in China since the death of Mao Zedong and to attempt to answer four questions:
1. Has rural industry continued to grow?
2. Does the new regime continue to attach importance to its growth?
3. If so, has there been any significant change of purpose in relation to local enterprise?
4. Have there been changes in control?

An answer to these simple and straightforward questions may assist us in finding the answer to the bigger question concerning the post-Mao regime: have there been changes in economic and social strategy of such a kind and in such a degree as to constitute a breach with Mao Tse-tung's own strategy of growth and change?

First of all one historical point perhaps ought to be made. Most of us have accepted that there was a profound difference of view between Mao and Liu on the subject of local industry.[2] I believed this myself. Now I am inclined to think that there was a good deal less divergence than we supposed. I am inclined to agree with Carl

Riskin's point that the closing down of so many of the new local enterprises at the end of the Great Leap Forward was the result of the extreme scarcity of resources rather than of ideological differences, although there remains no doubt that Liu Shaoqi, even if it was only a matter of individual temperament, took a considerably less optimistic view than Mao of the potentialities of rural bootstrap operations. We have now accumulated enough information about the early history of China's rural industrial enterprises[3] to suggest that there was a good deal more continuity of policy than has hitherto been supposed. That the period of retrenchment in the difficult years was so short is perhaps more surprising than the fact that retrenchment took place. Put in another way, that Chinese rural industry made such a hopeful second start so soon is more surprising than the fact that the first over-enthusiastic efforts of 1958 were a disaster.

The Rationale of Local Industry

Economic arguments

The economic arguments put forward in favour of development of local industry before 1977 were as follows:
(a) Local industry could make use of scattered raw materials which it would be difficult for modern large-scale industry to mobilise.
(b) It could make use of the surplus of labour in the countryside in more or less labour-intensive development, and so diminish unemployment.
(c) It could serve to mobilise rural savings and even, by stimulating new demands, call forth savings which otherwise would not exist.
(d) It could provide locally a flow of consumer goods which could be made available without long gestation periods in order to off-set the tendency to inflation which occurs, OTRE, when massive resources are being invested in long-gestation projects in the producer goods sector.
(e) This flow of consumer goods could also assist in maintaining incentives among the peasants.
(f) The profits of local industry which were expected, as a result of wartime experience with INDUSCO, to be high could be invested for further growth of the rural economy, with priority given to investment, direct and indirect, in agriculture. In this respect, local industry cannot be considered in isolation from agricultural development; in particular, it cannot be isolated from the labour-intensive farmland capital construction projects which were its complement.

(g) As the modern industrial sector rose to a higher technological level, and in so doing became more dependent on long mass-production runs, there was a growing need for small factories with the flexibility for short-run production of spare parts, accessories, and goods suitable for local conditions.

The ideological arguments

(a) Local industry, by maximising participation in co-operative enterprises, provided, Mao believed, the quickest route to socialism and the creation of new socialist man. An economic process which began with short-gestation or nil-gestation projects, and used the profits of these for longer-gestation development, would, by putting short-term interests at the service of long-term interests, provide a concrete education in socialist organisation. The high degree of popular participation involved would prevent the process from running into a bureaucratic cul-de-sac. The measure of success in this transition to socialism would be the free acceptance by the members of the production teams of the raising of the level of basic ownership from team to brigade and brigade to commune, as income from commune and brigade industry began to overtake income from the team's agriculture.

(b) The industrialisation of the rural areas would gradually eliminate the distinctions between industry and agriculture, mental and manual labour, and city and countryside. This would take place as the result of the involvement of an increasing number of peasants in industry, of the use of progressively higher technology demanding higher levels of education among workers and peasants, and of the extension to the countryside of amenities traditionally associated with the towns.

(c) Mao believed that the problem of bureaucracy in socialism was not a mere matter of political style, but a fundamental question of class power. The development of the local communities via self-reliant industrialisation, and the transformation of agriculture which this industrialisation would make possible, would both minimise the need for bureaucracy and at the same time create a countervailing power. It expresses in a new form a very old Chinese idea, one which was particularly associated with the seventeenth-century thinkers who had such a profound influence on Mao's generation, and one which determined the interpretation which that generation gave to the socialist ideas then being introduced to China.

Has the new regime in China betrayed this vision? The development of rural industry in China was so central to the whole Maoist strategy of economic development and social change that if his successors maintain that development in the same fashion and with the same aims, then I for one would be reluctant to conclude that China has repudiated Maoism.

The Growth of Local Industry in the Late 1970s

Local industry in China is difficult to define for the purpose of measurement. The relationships among the different levels of organisation, and the division of labour among these levels, are highly flexible. For the purpose of this paper I will confine myself as far as possible to those enterprises which are collectively owned and not state owned; ie., to industry at commune and brigade level. In 1977 there were in China a total of 1 million such enterprises. In 1978 this rose to 1,390,000. By July 1979 this had risen to 1,500,000.[4] This latest figure represents an average of two enterprises per brigade. In September 1979, Peking Review reported that the total output value of rural industry (presumably including county as well as commune and brigade industry) in 1978 was Y99,000 million. On 21 February 1979, Hung Ch'i reported that since 1970 the output of commune and brigade industry had grown at an average of 30 per cent per annum. Some qualification of this figure may be necessary. This 30 per cent may not entirely represent new capacity. Some of it may be accounted for by the substitution of factory production for production by individual artisans or small co-operative groups, and some of it by the transfer of certain lines of production down from the state to the collective sector. So much of it, however, is accounted for by the increasing manufacture of new products (e.g., chemical fertilisers, hydro-electric power, farm machinery) that these qualifications can hardly alter the conclusion that the rural industry sector in China has been, and continues to be under the new regime, the fastest growing sector of the Chinese economy.

The greatest leap came in 1977, when total output value of commune and brigade industry increased by 43.7 per cent. Most of this increase must have been the result of plans put into operation under the Gang of Four, but the further growth of 25 per cent in 1978 and a further 14.3 per cent in the first half of 1979[5] indicates that the new regime has continued the policies of the old. The rate of increase in 1978 and 1979 has been of the same order as the annual rate of increase since 1970 if the exceptionally high growth of 1977 is excluded. There is no doubt from these figures that the development of local industry is still being pursued with vigour.

Commune and brigade enterprise, which employed 17 million

people in 1977, in 1979 employs 28 million[6] The contribution of these enterprises to the total output value of local industry had risen to about 50 per cent in 1978.[7]

If one looks at the contribution of local industry as a whole to the economy, one finds that (a) by 1977 small collieries distributed around 1,168 xian produced 45 per cent of China's total coal output, and by late 1978 commune and brigade owned mines were producing 15 per cent of national output; (b) commune and brigade enterprises were producing 80 per cent of China's building materials; (c) such enterprises also produced high proportions of China's non-ferrous ores; (d) communes and brigades ran a large majority of China's small hydro-electric plants, which numbered 90,000 in 1979 and were distributed around 1,500 xian.

Sixty per cent of nitrate fertilisers in China come from small plants, mostly operated at county level; in the most developed counties this proportion can be as high as 80 per cent. These are distributed around roughly 1,400 xian. Since the end of 1977, virtually all counties have had plants able to repair and manufacture farm machinery.

In 1977 commune and brigade industry provided on average 23.1 per cent of total commune income (i.e., income at commune, brigade and team level),[8] By 1979 this had risen to 30 per cent.

Finally, in 1978 30 per cent of the iron and steel used in local industry in its widest sense — from prefecture level down — was locally manufactured.[9]

When one looks at local industry in terms of achievement province by province, the picture is more confused. I have only been able to find provincial figures for the number of existing commune and brigade enterprises between 1977 and 1979 for seven provinces, figures for total output value or revenue for only five, and figures for the proportion of commune income derived from commune and brigade industry for only five. It might be supposed that this large majority of provinces which did not apparently give a public account of their achievements failed to do so because they had nothing much to boast about. Arguments from silence, however, are very dangerous in Chinese affairs. Only two provinces confessed to backwardness in the development of local industry. In August 1979 a conference on commune and brigade enterprise in Yunnan reported that these were "still in a backward state".[10] In early 1978, Wang Enmao, First Secretary of Jilin party, complained that the province had not yet succeeded in creating an agriculture-oriented industrial system; production of chemical fertiliser was said to be well below the national average; the development of local industry as a whole had been slow and there had been little development at commune and brigade level.[11] Consequently, Wang Enmao stated, the province had been unable to develop agricultural production.

Although it is possible, therefore, that the majority of Chinese provinces have not done so well in the development of local industry that they are ready to make public the results, there is no sign of the sort of provincial foot-dragging which in China has so often accompanied deep divisions over policy at the centre. Virtually every province has its xian or commune models of industrial development, and the details given of these can be assumed to have the usual prescriptive force.

It may be noted, however, from the list of the provinces which did actually report (Liaoning, Heilongjiang, Guangdong, Shandong, Hunan, Shansi, Sichuan, Jiangsu, Zhejiang) that, with the exception of Shansi and Sichuan, they are all either coastal provinces or provinces with highly developed modern industries. Sichuan is neither, but rich in resources. Shansi is the only poor province to report. It is already apparent on other evidence that, as common sense would suggest, the most prosperous, the most industrialised, and the most accessible provinces of China enjoy an advantage in the development of local industry, and so it may be that the silence of most of the hinterland provinces is significant. It may also be significant that in the case of the four provinces which reported the percentage of total commune-brigade-team revenue produced by commune and brigade industry, the proportion was well above the national average of 23.1 per cent: Guandong 1978, 34.8 per cent; Shandong 1977, 41 per cent; Hunan Jan-Oct 1978, 43.3 per cent; Shansi 1977, 35 per cent.[12] No firm conclusion, however, is possible without further research.

The pace-making province at present is Jiangsu; the most successful area in Jiangsu is Suzhou Prefecture; and the model for the whole country is Wuxi xian in that Prefecture. Wuxi lies, of course, at the very heart of the area of China which even in the eighteenth century was the most sophisticated, the most educated and the most industrialised, and whether Wuxi provides for the whole of China a model of development more relevant than Dazhai is a good question. Wuxi's achievements, however, are very impressive. They are well-known, but for the sake of the argument I will recapitulate them here.

Wuxi xian has 35 communes. It has a labour force of half a million, 20 per cent of which works in commune and brigade enterprises. It is claimed that between 1971 and 1977 on average agricultural production rose by 5.4 per cent per annum. In one brigade Y5 million was invested over these years in farmland capital construction, entirely financed by 16 commune and 62 brigade factories, the total profits of which last year alone were Y5,500,000. Of this, Y2,640,000 went into farmland capital construction, agricultural machines and scientific experiment. Total output value of commune and brigade industry in 1977 was Y360,000,000 and from county factories Y220,000,000. Taken together, local industry as a whole provided 74.2 per cent of the xian's total output by value. Forty per cent of net annual industrial income went into agriculture, 10 per cent on increased peasant incomes, individual and collective. The other 50 per cent was ploughed back into the factories. About a quarter of commune and brigade enterprises serve agriculture, and have contributed to making possible treble cropping — wheat, rice, rice — on 40 per cent of the land.

These economic achievements have made it possible to create new welfare services. In one commune medical services are provided for 80 cents a year. The more prosperous brigades cover all educational expenses up to senior middle school. In 1977 when there was a poor wheat harvest, Y10 million was drawn to maintain peasant incomes.

Wuxi has also been able out of these resources to secure some redistribution of income in favour of poorer units. In 1970, for example, a brigade on waterlogged land was given pumping stations and the right to run the commune's phosphate fertiliser plant, part of the profits of which were ploughed back into soil improvement. In 1977, this formerly poor brigade was itself able to give interest-free loans to three of its poorer teams to build pig farms, and to plough and irrigate free for all its teams.

There is no pretence that these achievements are anything but exceptional, made possible by rich soil and adequate rainfall, a long tradition of highly productive agriculture, and an equally long tradition of highly-skilled craftsmanship in textiles which for a century and a half gave Suzhou's silks and Nanjing's cottons an unrivalled place in the world's markets. Its pre-eminence in the development of local industry is not surprising. What is particularly interesting here is the pattern of use to which the profits of local industry are put when this level of development is reached: massive direct and indirect investment in agriculture; rapid further development of industry; increase of peasants' personal incomes; the establishment of welfare services; and the levelling up of resources between team and team and between brigade and brigade. It is also to be noted that while the 20 per cent of the population in the employment of local industry produce almost 75 per cent of the wealth, their wages are only 5-15 per cent higher than average peasant income in the locality. The industrial enterprise pays the teams for the labour they supply, these payments are added to the rest of the team's income, and the industrial workers are paid work-points valued on the basis of the team's total income, but with each work-point earning 5-15 per cent extra.

This vivid example is important not only as evidence of the continued interest of the new regime in the development of local industry, but also as evidence that the aims and expectations formerly entertained with regard to local industry have not changed. Statements of policy from the centre and from the provinces constantly reiterate these.

On 4 April, 1978, People's Daily published an article, "We Must Greatly Develop Enterprises Run by Communes and Production Brigades". The article begins by quoting Mao's statement in 1958: "At present, things directly owned by the people's commune, such as commune-run enterprises and undertakings, and public accumulation and welfare funds, are scanty. Nevertheless, it is here that our great, bright and splendid hope lies." Chairman Hua Guofeng is then associated with these sentiments; he is in particular quoted on the importance of the development of commune and brigade enterprises for "the strengthening and expansion of the collective economy of the people's communes, agricultural mechanisation and the elimination of three great differences".

The importance of local industry as a source of investment funds for agriculture is then stressed. "Agriculture requires substantial capital. Where is this to come from? Since agriculture's financial accumulation is very low, the problem must be solved by relying mainly on . . . . the financial accumulation of commune and brigade enterprises."

Mao's policy on agricultural mechanisation is re-stated, though without mention of Mao: agricultural machines should be mainly manufactured in the localities and should be mostly medium and small machines and should be purchased mainly by the collectives themselves. It is then stressed that this policy demands strong commune and brigade enterprises. The Wuxi case is then referred to and its main points enumerated.

The editorial then turns to the ideological aspects and quotes the Resolution of the 6th Plenum of the 8th Central Committee on Some Questions Concerning People's Communes, on simultaneous development of agriculture and industry in the communes, and on the importance of this for the elimination of the three great differences. The Resolution, of course, explicitly indicated commune and brigade enterprises as the instrument to achieve this.

The editorial ends by condemning the view still held among "some comrades" that "the development of industry will oust agriculture". A year and a half later, on 10 September, 1979, *People's Daily* again reasserted the importance of commune and brigade industry, and returned to the attack on those who sought to limit its growth.

Meanwhile *Hong Qi,* on 1 November, 1978, in an article entitled "Vigorously Run Commune and Brigade Industry" (again quoting Mao's Resolution on Some Questions Concerning People's Communes) made, among other points we have already seen from elsewhere, the point that commune and brigade enterprise could serve both to achieve the mechanisation of agriculture and to employ the increasing number of peasants which the process of mechanisation would release from agricultural labour.

In the Decisions on Agricultural Development adopted by the 4th Plenum of the 11th Central Committee on 28 September, 1979, the importance for grass-roots accumulation of the processing of farm crops was re-asserted. The importance of local industrial development for the prospects of raising the level of ownership from team to brigade has been constantly re-asserted.

Finally, the role of local industry, and in particular of commune and brigade industry supplemented by the products of side-line occupations, in helping to provide an adequate flow of consumer goods has again been increasingly stressed. After a short-lived move to re-emphasise the importance of the development of heavy industry — this time largely by importing foreign high technology — the new regime returned to the emphasis on light industry and agriculture which Mao first advocated in the Ten Great Relationships. The Minister for the Metallurgical Industries (speaking in Tokyo), stated that China was reviewing the target of producing 60 million tons of crude steel by 1985 (twice as much as present production). "China," he said, "must first develop its agriculture and light industries."[13] Soon after, *Hunan Daily*,[14] in words which recall the ideas of Shanin, stated, "Light and textile industries are characterised by requiring little investment, achieving quick results, making high profits, and having a high rate of foreign remittance earnings."

In the allocation of investment from the profits of local industry, and in particular of commune and brigade industry, the highest priority has continued to be given to investment in agriculture. On 10 December, 1977, Zhong-guo Xin-wen (Hong Kong) in a review of local industrial policy in China, gave figures for 14 provinces, stating that one-third of all funds accumulated by xian, communes and brigades in 1976 were invested in agriculture. These funds paid, among other things, for almost the whole of the water conservancy programme and farmland capital construction generally. The major part of agricultural mechanisation so far has also been paid for from the profits of local industry. By the end of 1977 China had on average 0.7 h.p. per 10 mow available in machines — equal, said a Chinese commentator,[15] to the USA in the mid-40s (in Chinese conditions, however, the bulk of this power has to go into irrigation rather than mechanisation proper).

Price policies and taxation policies continue to favour grass-roots accumulation. The price of fertiliser and of other farm inputs have been substantially reduced over the years. Taxation has remained constant while rural production, both agricultural and industrial, has risen, so that total taxes (agricultural, commercial and industrial) are said now to represent only 3.35 per cent of output value, probably one-fifth to one-quarter of the percentage taken in the early 1950s. In the summer of 1979, new regulations increased the period of exemption from taxes of new commune and brigade enterprises, and increased 5-fold the income which such enterprises are permitted to earn tax-free.[16]

A new feature of policy, new at least in its vigorous and systematic application, is the attempt further to increase grass-roots accumulation by devolving from city to county, and from county to commune and brigade, the simpler forms of production. This was anticipated by Mao Zedong in 1958, although at that time he did not expect it to occur until a much later stage of local industrial development. It began to become important after the Cultural Revolution. At that time, however, it seems to have been confined mainly to the sub-contracting of the simpler ancillary manufacturing processes. Now whole lines of production are being shed by the modern sector, and with the aid of technical assistance and training, credit and equipment from urban industry, local industry is taking over tasks which have hitherto been regarded as the prerogative of the modern sector — not without resistance by urban factory managers and fears that the process might lead to the "regressive" handing over of assets owned by the whole people to mere collectives. Mao, in his comments on Stalin's comments on the proposals of comrades Sanina and Venzher, had denied that such transfers were necessarily regressive; and the present regime has been at pains to insist that collective enterprises are as socialist as state enterprises.

A number of reasons are given for the new policy. First, it will free the modern sector for more sophisticated operations. Second, it is said that industrialisation in Peking and in other major Chinese cities has "reached saturation point", with serious pollution and the crowding out by industry of essential services. The third argument, however, is the one on which most stress is laid, that this policy will increase accumulation at the grass roots. Counties also have, for that reason, been urged to hand over to commune and brigade management as many as possible of those of their enterprises lying beyond the confines of the county town. There could be no more conclusive evidence of the continued devotion of China's present leaders to Mao's economic strategy than this positive driving of the sources of accumulation back to the grass roots.

We may end this section on general policy towards local industry with another interesting piece of evidence that China's new "pragmatists" have not thrown "Mao's ideology" out of the window, as both right and left in Europe would have us believe. The destruction of the three great differences is no longer entirely in China a utopian ideal. The 4th Plenum of the 11th Central Committee decided that as a consequence of the rapid development of commune and brigade industry, many of China's villages were turning into small industrial towns, and that they must now be given the right to create the amenities of towns.

The Limits of Local Industry

The main limiting factor in the further development of local industry is the scarcity of fuel and power. The acute shortage of electricity has been recently dramatised in a rather humiliating way by the inability of the new, ultramodern Wuhan steel complex to work at more than half capacity for lack of electricity. In the North, state industry has been for the present at least given priority in electricity supplies, and the construction of small iron and steel works, which are extravagant users of power, suspended. There are complaints elsewhere that peasant communities act as if they think they can plug into the grid and draw power *ad lib*, that their lines dissipate 20 per cent of power in transmission, and that the inefficiency of so many small nitrate plants is a chronic drain on power supplies. The reaction, however, has been far from negative; it has included a tremendous drive to exploit hydro-electric power and to open or extend local coal mines.

Power is the first essential. According to a broadcast from Shenyang, "the power industry has become a strikingly weak link in the economy".[17] Given power, industry can be created. The case of one xian in Guangdong is quoted as an illustration of this. The xian built 170 small hydro-electric stations, averaging just over

70 kW capacity each. It was then able to build a nitrate plant, a phosphate plant and a cement factory, and make a start on industrialisation.

In an article on 3 May, 1978, *Guangming Daily* backed the hydro-electricity campaign with an analysis of the possibilities which China's topography and her 50,000 rivers offered, calculating that at only 40 per cent exploitation of the theoretical possibilities, power equivalent to that provided by 500 million tons of coke could be won.

More recently, a campaign to develop methane production has got under way. A Chinese scientist reported, in support of this campaign, that the crop residue of 1 ton of grain could provide energy equivalent to almost 1 ton of coke.[18] The use of methane could be of more than marginal importance in an intensively cultivated country. Crop residues can feed livestock; the dung can produce methane by a very simple technology; and the residue has then lost virtually none of its value as fertiliser.

Local coal production has expanded rapidly, especially in the formerly coal-starved south, and has made possible, for example in Guangdong, an impressive recent growth of local industry.

Local industry may provide much of its own power, but it is unlikely to pass much on to other sectors, apart from its own local agriculture which probably consumes about 12-20 per cent of locally available electricity. In some other branches of heavy industry, however, the counties, communes and brigades may have a wider role. On 4 August, 1979, Guangming Daily listed as the weak links in the national economy "coal, petroleum, power, communications and building materials". To several of these, local industry can make a more or less substantial contribution. We have seen that one-third of China's coal, and substantially more than half of the total production of the southern provinces, comes from county level and below. The manufacture of building materials is overwhelmingly in the hand of commune and brigade enterprise. The creation of a local road network has now reached the point where over 90 per cent of communes are linked by road, and where over 90 per cent of them have found it possible to create their own system of local road transport; most of this has been done with local labour and out of local funds. Indeed it is perhaps the very success of the counties and communes in developing this network of local roads which accounts for the great strain now felt on the national network of trunk communications.

If power is the main limiting factor in the process of rural industrialisation, the next is steel. Here, too, competition between state sector and collective sector is sharp, and the localities must as far as possible develop their own resources. Yu Chiu-li in early 1978, discussing agricultural mechanisation, stated that in order to achieve the targets set, local steel, which now provides for 30 per cent of the consumption of rural steel-making industries, must in future raise 40 per cent of local needs. There has been a substantial development over the years, primarily (for reasons of economy of scale) at the prefectural level but by no means wholly so. A recent invention which makes economic steelmaking on a very small scale may soon bring steel-making right down to the machine-shop and foundry of commune and brigade.[19] It would perhaps be frivolous to say that this belatedly vindicates the backyard-blast-furnace campaign of 1958; it would not be so frivolous, however, to find in this innovation evidence that the Chinese, passionate about grass-roots self-reliance, have never quite given up on their 1958 hopes.

The insatiable local demand for power, steel, cement and chemical fertilisers has biassed local development towards heavy industry, and reporters on local development are always ready with figures for production in these sectors, while consumer goods industries are usually dismissed with a string of miscellaneous products to which few or no figures are attached. At first sight it might seem that the important role once intended for light industry and consumer-goods production generally, in reducing tendencies to inflation, providing incentive goods, and making quick profits for investment, has fallen into the background. This is not so. As we have seen, the importance of light industry — especially as a means of raising profits rapidly — has recently been stressed once more, and the role of commune and brigade industry in this sector emphasised. In some of the least well-endowed parts of China, the development of light industries has recently been recommended as the best starting point for the linked process of rural industrialisation and agricultural mechanisation. And it is still an established part of policy that each province and municipality should seek to achieve "basic self-sufficiency" in providing for the daily needs of its citizens.

The market certainly exists. In September 1979, NCNA reported that peasant purchasing power was expected to increase in 1979 by Y10,000,000,000, and that in the first part of the year purchases of consumer goods by peasants had increased by 13.8 per cent.[20] Scarcities of goods — bicycles, sewing machines, vacuum flasks — were reported from various areas. Curiously, there were signs of demand changing, as peasant incomes rose, to include not only such factory products as those above, but also silks, satins and woollens — a new demand which commune and brigade enterprise could very easily meet with local resources and simple equipment.

It is of course obvious that, whatever the rate of saving and investment in China may be, and however much of production is ploughed back into the producer goods industries, the market for consumer goods of all kinds, from processed food, tobacco and alcohol to wristwatches and transistor radios, is enormous, and is probably still the largest source of grass-roots capital accumulation. In spite of the lack of figures on the subject, it is still the rule of thumb in local industry that it is the profits of the light consumer goods factories which provide the capital for local heavy industry as well as for the modernisation of agriculture. The figures, if they were available, might well vindicate Mao's belief that the surest source of funds for the development of industry lies in the increase of peasant purchasing power. It certainly seems probable from the information available that those xian with the strongest grasp on consumer goods production, such as Wuxi in Jiangsu and Shaodong in Hunan, have done best in local industrial development.

Local Industry and Income Distribution

One of the questions raised by the development of local industry in China is that of the effects on the distribution of incomes. The regional disparities of income in a country as varied as China are immense. The disparities of income in any one locality, especially where population pressure in the last two or three centuries has forced a substantial part of the farming population on to marginal land, are equally serious; but they are also potentially more divisive; this is especially so where the marginal land is occupied by descendants of migrants from elsewhere, or by a minority clan — common situations in which communal loyalty and inter-group hostility sharpen the envy on one side, and contempt on the other, of two groups, one poor and the other by comparison rich. Differences in resources and consequent differences in income have in the past proved to be an intractable problem for the CPC. In 1956, in the wake of collectivisation, a campaign was launched to secure the equalisation of resources between the constituent teams of the APCs by transfers of land, tools and animals. The campaign was a bruising failure; Party cadres in the richer teams resisted as vehemently as the peasants any attempts at such transfers. In 1958, the communes, in their first form, involved the bringing together, into one unit of ownership, of poor and prosperous villages, and this (as could be seen at the time, and as Mao, we now know, soon perceived) was the main reason why the original unitary commune could not be sustained. Now, however, although there has been an end to premature attempts to raise the level of ownership from team to brigade, and so eliminate the differences between teams, the profits of local industry can be used for the development of the poorer teams. We have seen the example of Wuxi xian. Zhoukoudian (home of Peking man) outside Peking could be quoted as another; in this case the reduction of differences between teams has been so successfully achieved that of 17 brigades making up the commune, seven have become the basic unit of ownership.[21] It is noteworthy, however, that Zhoukoudian commune, like Wuxi xian, is a unit in which income from industry already far exceeds income from agriculture.

The main means of the levelling up of teams and brigades, however, is farmland capital construction, especially the extension of irrigation and drainage which is most often the form that such construction takes. In this, it is generally the poorer teams and brigades which gain most; they are usually poor because their land is unirrigated or ill-drained. Thus in the biggest operation typically undertaken out of the profits of local industry, a significant degree of equalisation is the result.

The county can to some extent bend the location of new commune and brigade enterprise to favour the poorer localities, but there is little evidence of this. There is even less evidence that the province can do much; Jiangsu found means to assist the province's poorer communes, but this is the only case I have found.[22]

In general, above the commune level relatively little can be done to transfer resources sufficient to make much difference to disparities of income in different regions, except when the state has new major industries to locate, or large water conservancy schemes in hand. Given this limitation, the policy of self-reliant development at the commune and county level is more likely to increase regional disparities than to reduce them: rich places tend to get richer faster than poor places, in China just as in the world as a whole. In the long term, the theoretical solution is that when collective ownership has given way to state ownership everywhere, it will be possible to even up incomes over the whole of China, But this is a long way off.

Meanwhile, however, a special effort is made to assist the national minorities. Development in their autonomous units is very heavily subsidised.

The Control of Local Industry

Our final question is that of the control of commune and brigade industry. In Mao's own conception, local economic development was the central and the supreme application of the mass line. Participation was to be voluntary on the part of the collectives concerned. Control was to be in their hands. In his marginal comments on the Soviet Textbook of Political Economy, Mao shows himself utterly opposed to the Soviet dictum that local industries should always be under the supervision of the representatives of the central ministry concerned.

In fact there was from time to time, and in Mao's own lifetime, considerable use of coercion in the development of the local economies. Of coercion in the Great Leap of 1958, we need say no more; after the Cultural Revolution, however, similar things happened. Labour, land and resources were commandeered without payment, teams in fact forced to support local industrialisation. We need not ascribe these evils to the Gang of Four as their successors do; there were other and more extreme left-wing groups at work in China in these years, and some of them were less committed than Zhang Chunqiao and Yao Wenyuan to the ideal of a participating democracy. The descriptions now given of these abuses are usually followed by a list of detailed rules designed to prevent their recurrence, however, and this suggests that such abuses were actually widespread and serious, as well as indicating that the new regime intends to eliminate them.

The ability of commune or brigade enterprises to make their own decisions is circumscribed, in the first place, by the conditions of their access to resources. A brigade or commune may have its own supplies of raw material, and in fact the existence of a surplus may be the starting point of the idea. It may be able to raise its own initial capital, but it is probable that at some fairly early point in its history it will have to seek finance from outside. It will almost certainly be dependent on "the higher levels" for certain key inputs — access to electric power, machinery, steel, technical assistance — and it is almost bound to be in keen competition these days with other groups for a share in such scarce resources. The authorities are in a seller's market. As far as administrative questions are concerned, it will have to seek formal permission from the commune or the county before beginning operations; and it will have to apply in any case for tax relief. It will have to buy and sell mainly through the supply and marketing co-operative.

It seems clear, indeed, that the initiative in founding a new enterprise usually comes from above rather than from below. I have found no record from 1977 to 1979 of any enterprise explicitly said to have been founded on the initiative of the brigade or commune itself. The supply and marketing co-operatives seem to play the main role in discovering unused resources and unfulfilled markets. County Party committees perform the same entrepreneurial function. Urban industry has lately also taken a hand, and the newest entrepreneur in the Chinese countryside is the representative of one of the foreign trade departments. It is of course possible that there is a good deal of mass initiative involved, but that this is taken for granted. Only closer acquaintance with local industry could answer the question. Meanwhile, it seems safer to assume that the higher levels usually take the initiative; that having done so they will provide the means; and that these means being very scarce, the opportunities for unofficial entrepreneurship must be pretty limited. The commune or brigade enterprise is thus likely to start work in conditions laid down by the state authorities, to be dependent on state sources of credit and of key inputs, and to sell primarily in the form of fulfilling a contract or meeting a quota stipulated by or on behalf of the supply and marketing co-operative. The phrase "freedom of decision-making" in these circumstances must be pretty narrowly interpreted.

This is not meant as a criticism, or as somehow reflecting what the commune members involved in the enterprise are bound to feel. They are perhaps more likely to welcome their new opportunities than to resent the limitations on their freedom, provided the withdrawal of labour from agriculture does not reduce income from farming, and provided there is some assurance that the new enterprise will be profitable to them, directly or indirectly, individually or collectively.

The state, in its attitude to this circumscribed freedom, is at present somewhat ambiguous. On the one hand, it seeks to widen this freedom. First, by ensuring that the brigade or the commune does not force the teams, as in the past, to provide labour or resources. Second, by enlarging the freedom of decision of enterprises in order to encourage them to use initiative. Regulations to protect the teams' interests have been published. Experiments have taken place in allowing enterprises to sell any surplus over their contracted amount or quota, to increase their production and seek further markets, to process the raw materials of other units, and even to sign contracts with foreign firms. *Guangming Daily,* in an October 1978 article, Promote Economic Democracy, criticised "Soviet over-concentration of authority", quoted the Ten Great Relationships on the need for decentralisation and local initiative, and called for autonomy for all enterprises, right down to the production teams: "at present," stated Guangming, "the masses of workers and commune members have very little say . . ."

Arguments for autonomy are that the power to make their own decisions will encourage initiative, prevent corruption, and create responsible attitudes in the use of resources. A wider argument, however, was given in *People's Daily* by a Vice-chairman of the Revolutionary Committee of Wuxian (in Suzhou Prefecture, adjacent to Wuxi xian): "The state should not regard the countryside as a kind of colony for the industrial sector, which takes away all raw materials and monopolises industry and commerce." This is the basic point, and a very Maoist one.

Yet while the new regime has shown, both in theory and in concrete regulations, a keen acknowledgement of Mao's insistence that "local industry should be controlled by local people", at the same time there are pressures which work against this. The local industry sector is now spending vast sums of collective and public funds; its operations must be subjected to some kind of supervision. The sector is now so large that it competes with the state sector for vital resources, such as electricity and steel; it must be brought, at least in general terms, into the planning system. Instructions have gone out on both points.

If we look at the situation from the wider perspective of the general policies and attitudes of the new regime, however, and if we look at it in terms of the new post-Cultural-Revolution power relations, the future of self-reliant self-managed commune and brigade industry may be less secure. In spite of criticisms of the efficiency of some specific parts of the local system — especially of the small-scale nitrate plants — no-one now seems to dispute the importance of commune and brigade industry; even the science and technology establishment has lent its authority to the idea. The economic logic of local industry is accepted; but with the Party back in untrammelled control, keenly supporting the technocrats, and denying that bureaucracy is a problem of class, the logic of power rather than the logic of economics may prevail, and collective grass-roots industry may well end up as the bottom end — and very likely the underprivileged end — of the official industrial establishment.

Epilogue

In 1980, in the year since this paper was first drafted, the encouragement of local industry has continued unabated. No overall figure for development during 1980 is as yet available, but interim statements by provincial authorities suggest that the pace of development has not slackened.

NCNA, reported on the 19th of September 1980 that for the

first six months of the year, the output value of commune and brigade enterprises throughout the country was 20 per cent over the figure for the same period of 1979. They employed almost 10 per cent of the rural labour force, and provided one third of the total income of the three commune levels. NCNA also noted — and this is significant of the new stress on the team — that team enterprises "are even greater in number" than the 1.48 million firms owned by communes and brigades. In the pace of continual development, Jiangxi (58 per cent) and Zhejiang (35 per cent) led.

By 1980, the spread of local enterprise was almost complete, with 90 per cent of communes and 80 per cent of brigades operating such enterprises.

It is to be noted however, that although output value had continued to rise substantially, the total number of enterprises has not risen; this is certainly because new ventures were off-set by closures and mergers in the course of general economic rationalisation.

This continued growth is all the more significant because there is no longer, as there was before the fall of the radicals in late 1976 (and even for some time after), the suspicion that the pace was being forced, and commune and brigade industries created by the coercive requisition of labour and resources from the production team. How common such coercion was it is impossible to determine, but the seriousness with which the new leadership now regards such practices lends some colour to their assertion that they were widespread during the Cultural Revolution years.

Local industry as a whole has not escaped entirely from the rationalisation measures which are being applied to the whole economy though affected only to a lesser extent. It can certainly be said that, while there has been no slackening of encouragement for or growth of local enterprise, the framework within which it operates has changed.

The new regime is critical of the indifference both to costs and to market possibilities shown by Chinese industry at all levels, and points to many cases of gross misinvestment and of massive stockpiling of unsaleable goods. These faults were possibly at their worst the lower one moved down within the state system, to levels at which minimum control coincided with minimal managerial ability. At the lowest level of all, however, below the state sector and among the collective enterprises of the communes and brigades, there already existed a certain market discipline, in so far as these enterprises, being outside the planning system, did not receive systematic allocations of state funds and resources. It is true that during the Cultural Revolution, they were not operated entirely on the basis of the profit and loss of individual units as may be the intention now; it was then deliberate policy to use the relatively high profits of consumer-goods producers to subsidise, in the initial stages at least, local primary production. However, it seems obvious that there were limits to the free reallocation of resources among collectively owned firms as well as limits to state subventions, so that to a considerable extent these enterprises could survive only if they were commercially viable. Their continued growth in numbers, production and total profits even after the left-wing pressures of the early seventies were removed suggests that they do not require much subsidisation, and may well represent — in their simple way — the most cost effective sector of the Chinese economy. They are now, in common with most firms in the state sector expected to be responsible for their own profit and loss as individual enterprises. The leadership is confident that the rapid increase in the market for consumers' goods, along with the flexibility and versatility of such small firms, will enable them to be commercially viable, provided caution is used and efficiency improved in enterprise in local producers' goods industries.

Two types of local producers' goods industry have nevertheless been under attack: local iron and steel plants and local fertiliser factories. Relatively few of these are owned by communes or brigades. Typically, the local steel plant is run by the prefecture, and the fertiliser factory (or at any rate the nitrate factory) is run by the county. An attack on these does not much affect rural collective, as opposed to prefectural and county, enterprises.

These two industries have one relevant common factor: they use large quantities of energy and, at such a small scale of operation, use it very inefficiently. The growing pressure on them has built up parallel with China's growing concern at the scarcity of energy, which causes a substantial part of state industry to run at well below capacity. The scarcity is not, of course, due to a paucity of natural energy resources in China. Far from it. The problem is that for the authorities at all levels the most attractive investment in the past has been in manufacturing industry, and so the development of energy resources has been allowed to lag. One must also bear in mind that the obsession with steel production, which Mao condemned in 1956 (and then himself succumbed to in 1958) has played a major part in the proliferation of small plants in this field, which may well represent the most typical and the most wasteful example of the uncontrolled and ill-considered local investment in construction which the new leadership sees as having been the chief fault of the pre-1977 economy.

The small fertiliser plants were more positively encouraged by the central leadership, and have played a vital role in agriculture, providing about two-thirds of available nitrates. Yet the process of small-scale nitrate manufacture is very inefficient and the product is of variable quality and uncertain durability. Unlike other local industries, it cannot be expected to have a secure long-term future. It is a stop gap until China can provide adequate fertilisers by normal methods of production. It has the further disadvantage that as the whole process depends on the use of coal, it is not economic if coal is unavailable locally: the cost of transporting the coal offsets the main advantage of local fertiliser production, which is the saving on transport of fertilisers from distant modern plants. Hitherto, the vast majority of small-scale nitrate plants have been heavily subsidised, as a contribution to agricultural efficiency. Now the leadership is determined that they should pay their way. The preferred solution, however, is not to close down the less efficient, but to assist them to improve; and success in this is now being reported.

These are therefore, on economic grounds, the two most vulnerable of local industries. Some plants have now been closed down or turned to other uses. Yet while the arguments in support of these closures in the Chinese media sound very ruthless, the number of closures has not been great, and the bulk of the plants remain in operation.

More generally, there has been some pressure on the lowest levels of local enterprise, the commune and below, to avoid the hazards of investment in heavy industries and to concentrate on those lines which will bring the quickest returns for the least investment. The stress is now, as it was in Mao's original conception of the policy, on the processing of local crops, the manufacture of farm tools and simple machines and the production of consumer goods. The Governor of Liaoning Chen Puru, at a provincial conference on commune and brigade enterprises, called for support for local processing of marketable grain and other farm products, and stated that from now on all processing of farm, forestry and other local products should as far as possible be returned to the villages, that no new grain processing plants would be built in the towns, that state-owned plants situated in the communes should be put under commune control.[23] Again, Mao's "great and bright prospects" comment is quoted. Added to this, increasingly, is processing for factories in the modern sector.

The other dimension of local industry still strongly encouraged is mining. China is now, as Europe was until the seventeeth century, an area in which scattered and easily worked mineral deposits often still exist. They are of great value to the local economy. At the same time, worry is now being expressed at the uncontrolled expansion of local extractive activities. Small coal mines in some areas have been worked in such numbers and in such a way as seriously to damage the environment. This is part of the larger threat of uncontrolled industrial expansion which has polluted cities and towns and eaten drastically into China's arable. Efforts to apply some restriction cannot be seen as an attack on local enterprise as such, but merely as part of an attempt to correct a general lack of effective environmental control. This lack is another consequence of Peking's inability hitherto to exert its authority over investment; even Peking city itself has defied the attempts of the national government to call a halt to the pollution of the capital by the indiscriminate expansion of industry.

The present encouragement of local economic initiative has added to the problems. In Honan, a rash of miniscule oil refineries has appeared at commune and brigade level in response to the acute shortage of fuel; their products are said to be of dangerously poor quality, and they have had to be ordered to compensate their irate customers. It is reported that in one Honan brigade, every household was individually engaged in refining oil, with consequences that may be readily imagined.[24]

In Shandong a more encouraging development has taken place. Here, there is a veritable peasant gold rush; in some villages, 40 per cent of income is earned from small-scale gold mining,[25] to which the government attaches great importance as an earner of foreign exchange.

Perhaps the most significant intervention in the operation of local industry has been concerned with textile manufacture. Entry into simple cotton and silk weaving is relatively cheap, and high levels of skill are not necessary. In cotton growing or mulberry growing areas, it is thus an obvious line of development. The problem is that the local small plant competes with the modern large-scale state factory for the raw materials, which are very scarce. The modern filatures and weaving mills stand idle while the local workshops boom. Worse, the peasants keep the pick of the silk cocoons and sell the trash to the state, but what they produce even from the superior raw material is not good enough for world markets. Yet even here the policy has not been one of systematic closures. Instead, the local authorities are urged to assist these small enterprises to find alternative sources of supply by entering into contracts with neighbouring collectives.

There have been some highly important organisational changes in local industry. The first of these has arisen from the new emphasis on the autonomy and independence of the production team — which in the end is the gainer or the loser, as it is the teams' members who supply the labour and in the last analysis much of the savings which are needed. With this rule established, it is logical that the team rather than the brigade or commune should directly undertake such development with the consequence (as we have seen) that *team* enterprises now outnumber commune and brigade enterprises. Clearly, what the individual team can do is very limited; but with the authority of Zhao Ziyang teams are now being encouraged to co-operate with each other in launching new enterprises, even across brigade and commune boundaries, rather than resort to the brigade level. This particular kind of flexibility is only one of the new forms of co-operation, which include sub-contracting, compensation trading, and joint ownership. In this last case, the team, brigade, or commune provides land, labour and sometimes buildings, while the higher level provides technology, training and equipment. Joint ownership takes the form of the ownership of shares on which a dividend is paid.

Finally, there is more stress than ever on the permanence and stability of local collective enterprises. Ren Zhongyi has strongly emphasised that they are not, for the foreseeable future, to be regarded as transitional, on the way to becoming state enterprises, and it is forbidden to turn them into state owned firms — as often happened to the more successful ventures in the past.

On the whole, then, with all the qualifications made, local enterprise, and especially owned by the collectives, still flourishes and grows, and still represents a vital part of China's development strategy. And it remains, as it was to Mao, the main potential source of funds for investment in agriculture, and therefore a major means of equalisation of resources among the villages within the commune and within the county.

10

THE PROMOTION OF DOMESTIC SIDELINE
PRODUCTION IN RURAL CHINA 1978-79

Elisabeth J. Croll

*Contemporary China Centre,
Queen Elizabeth House, Oxford University, U.K.*

A marked characteristic of rural economic policies in the late 1970s has been the legitimation and promotion of household or domestic sideline production. Domestic sideline production is an umbrella term which refers to: the cultivation of private plots of land allocated on a per capita basis by the commune and the cultivation of unused hillsides or mountain slopes or reclaimed portions of waste land; collecting firewood or grass for fuel; raising domestic animals and fowls such as pigs, sheep, rabbits, chickens, ducks and geese; engaging in handicraft production such as braiding, weaving, sewing and embroidery; and the undertaking of subsidiary activities such as collecting medicinal herbs, fishing, hunting, raising silkworms or bees and growing fruit, trees, bamboos and other plants alongside the house.[1] At the time of the establishment of communes and the socialisation of the means of production, government policy continued to allow for the operation of small domestic sidelines by peasant households. In 1958 the Resolution on Some Questions Concerning People's Communes and the Revised Regulations on the Work of People's Communes of 1962 both clearly stipulated that members of communes might cultivate a private plot, retain small numbers of trees by the side of their houses, small farm tools, small work tools, small quantities of livestock and poultry, and that they might continue to engage in certain small family subsidiary occupations.[2] Since the establishment of communes, peasant households have come to depend on the operation of domestic sidelines to generate the majority of their non-staple food supplies of vegetables and meat and a substantial portion of their cash income. However, despite the importance of domestic sidelines to the domestic and national economy, their very existence has constituted a source of tension and debate, and domestic sidelines have been the subject of policy changes. Indeed in the past twenty-five years, government policy towards domestic sideline production has been marked by several attempts to either eliminate it or impose limits, but on each occasion these attempts have been followed by a restoration of domestic sidelines as legitimate occupations.[3] The present policies of legitimisation are also seen very much as procedures designed to restore domestic sideline production following a period of disruption and suppression by the previous government. Since 1977, domestic sidelines have been promoted as an important means to increase rapidly both the supply of non-staple foods and small goods and the material standards and morale of peasant households, all deemed to be prerequisites to the general achievement of the "Four Modernisations" programme. This government's concern for peasant welfare and prosperity is constantly contrasted with the neglect of its predecessor.

This paper examines the period immediately preceding the recent change in policy emphasis, the form that policies legitimising domestic sideline production have taken, and their promotion during the years 1978 and 1979. It asks if the policies of these two years follow past cyclical patterns or whether the present process of promotion is qualitatively different from former periods of legitimation. Finally the paper suggests what might be the likely effects of these recent policies on the structure of peasant households and the sexual division of labour.

The Period Preceding Promotion

The recent reaffirmation of domestic sideline production is viewed by the present government as a necessary step to restore it to its rightful place as a supplementary but important component of the rural economy following a period when domestic sidelines were apparently disrupted and their very existence threatened by the policies of the previous government under the leadership of the Gang of Four. How far this distinction can be held to be an accurate reflection of the differing governments' policies is a difficult question to analyse even in its crudest form. It does appear from media reports in 1978-79 that in some localities in the mid-1970s, domestic sidelines may have been curtailed or restricted, sometimes severely, and occasionally suppressed altogether. The very existence of domestic sidelines and the exchange of sideline products at rural fairs tended to be associated by the previous government with the individual pursuit of personal wealth and capitalist phenomena.[4] Domestic sidelines and rural fairs were described as "hot beds breeding capitalism" or "the soil that generates capitalism" and were both accused of encouraging a drift towards capitalist activities and nurturing the traditional small-producer mentality of peasants.[5] Local authorities, subscribing to the banner of criticising capitalism and restricting bourgeois rights, are reported to have formulated a number of policies, frequently labelled the "Ten Prohibitions", which were designed to cut off such "capitalist tails". In some areas affected by these policies, it seems that local authorities set limits to the acceptable levels of cash income from domestic sources or determined the amount and kind of land, the types and quantities of livestock, and the amount and types of products which might be derived from sidelines. For instance only certain crops could be grown on private plots, specified numbers of livestock or fruit trees allowed and only certain kinds and amounts of goods exchanged at rural fairs. For example in Guangxi, commune members were prohibited from marketing products from their private plots, fruit from their own trees and products made from their own bamboo, timber or charcoal, and any violators were to be criticised for pursuing capitalist activities and "severely handled".[6] In other areas it was not just the exchange of products deriving from domestic sidelines, but their production itself which was also limited or prohibited. Quite a few localities prohibited commune members from collecting wild plants on waste land and hillsides, from selling privately-woven or knitted items, raising sows, planting ginger, medicinal herbs and other industrial crops on private plots or the cultivation of fruit trees in the courtyards of their houses.[7] On the outskirts of Beijing it was reported that fines were imposed on those who picked almonds, workpoints deducted from households which kept sheep, and commune members were prohibited from engaging in the "minor autumn crop harvest" or the collection of fodder grasses from hillsides.[8] In other areas there were reports that under the previous government poultry rearing was limited to one chicken or one duck per household and any reared above this quota were confiscated. In Gansu province, a quarter of the production brigades in one county deprived peasants of their entire plots for private use and of their privately owned trees and sheep.[9] One of the more extreme cases of "blocking the capitalist road" concerned a production team in Liaoning province where any sign of household production was reported to constitute evidence of small-scale production on the rise. Any household manure or enriched top soil applied to the private plot was removed, and peppers, onion and garlic grown on private plots and climbing pumpkin vines on house walls were also apparently destroyed. This report from the same production team also speaks of the slaughtering of chickens, lambs, of how vegetables and melons were pulled up, fruit trees felled and tools for bamboo and rattan weaving confiscated. There are also reports from a number of areas that village fairs were banned.[10] As a result of local suppressive policies, peasants in Shaanxi were reported to have had a hard time without food and cash income supplements from private plots and from handicraft production.[11] A letter to *Renmin Ribao* from Hebei similarly reported that rations there had been insufficient, and that the people had suffered considerably by not having access to private plots to augment their food supplies.[12] There were also reports of shortages of fodder and insufficient supplies of non-staple foods such as meat products, vegetables, eggs and fruit reaching the cities to meet consumption requirements of urban residents as a result of these policies.

It is difficult to ascertain how far the accounts of these incidents, which are almost all retrospectively reported, are the result of hindsight or serve to legitimise current policies; and if they are accurate, how far they are representative. This is not the first time that our knowledge of a prior period has been increased by the revelations of subsequent years, but it seems probable that the reports of limitation or suppression in the media were not as representative or widespread as subsequently estimated by the Chinese media or by informants within China. For example, there is little evidence to support the general conclusion of an article in *Liaoning Ribao* that it was the ultra-left policy forbidding peasants to engage in domestic sideline production in their spare time that brought the economy to the verge of general collapse.[13] There is also little evidence for the impression given to a Delegation of the American Association of Advancement of Science that the decline of domestic sideline production and consequent fall in living standards were so great as to give rise to a considerable discontent and the eventual fall of the Gang of Four.[14] These general observations, which draw a distinction between a current government aiming to foster domestic production, peasant morale and raise rural incomes and a previous government which ignored and obstructed these goals, are somewhat overdrawn, and both ignore the complexities of the issues involved and exaggerate the impact of the Gang of Four on rural policies and especially on the domestic economy. However, statistics on rural production do not seem to support the view that the rural economy was on the verge of "imminent collapse". However, there are enough reports from a number of differing localities to suggest that some direction probably emanated from the central government and that the repercussions for morale, livelihood and supply of goods may have been significant in some areas. Just why some particular localities should have been subject to these policies of disruption rather than others will have to await further investigation, but what is clear is that the government is now drawing on some past discontent to attract support for making the present sustained attempt to raise the morale of commune members, better their livelihood and increase the supplies of foods and goods available to rural and urban consumers.

The Promotion of Domestic Sideline Production

Government directives promoting domestic sidelines are based on the assumption that there had been a deviation by the Gang of Four from the correct principles and policies originally formulated by Mao Zedong and the central government, which had always allowed for domestic sidelines to continue within the communes. It is thus merely a case of present policies reaffirming commune members' rights to engage in domestic sideline production most recently outlined in the Sixty Articles of 1962. To further legitimise and give emphasis to these rights, they have also been written into the constitution adopted by the Fifth National People's Congress. Thus Article Seven stipulated that:

> provided that the absolute predominance of the collective economy of the people's commune is assured, commune members may farm small plots of land for personal needs, engage in limited domestic sideline production, and in pastoral areas they may also keep a limited number of livestock for personal needs. In order to implement this policy firmly it is imperative to eradicate the pernicious influence of the Gang of Four, eliminate the chaos they created and establish order and distinguish right from wrong in theory and policy[15]

Taking their cue from the central government, many provinces, counties and municipalities published circulars in 1978 and 1979 which abolished "indigenous policies" prohibiting domestic sideline production within the areas under their jurisdiction and reaffirmed the right of commune members to engage in "legitimate" and "proper" domestic sidelines and to exchange sideline products at rural trade fairs. The national model, Dazhai, was also criticised for having taken excessive measures forbidding peasants to farm their private plots and attend village fairs. *Guangming Daily* suggested that, although it was not necessary to dismiss Dazhai as a model in its entirety,

> we should under no circumstances learn from Dazhai's so-called experience in "blocking the capitalist road". Shanxi's and the whole country's experience proves that if we copy this experience we will prohibit sideline production, run counter to the principle of "to each according to his work", seize private plots and put an end to village fair trade, thus disturbing the rural economy and creating tremendous difficulties in developing collective production and improving the commune members' livelihood[16]

The publication of a set of ideological prescriptions defining domestic sideline production signified another attempt of the government to clarify the relationship between the collective sectors of the economy and domestic sidelines. The association of domestic sideline production with small-scale capitalist production has been the source of much intellectual tension and debate during the last twenty years and especially in the early 1960s when domestic sidelines had been similarly legitimated and promoted on a large scale following a period of greater discouragement. In 1961 though there was still much debate surrounding the nature of domestic sideline production and whether or not it was an appropriate occupation in a socialist society. Then it was argued, to various levels of sophistication, that domestic sideline production, based as it was on the individual rights or use of the means of production, rights of business management, the ownership of tools for production and the individual control of the products themselves, was fundamentally capitalist in nature. Others, however, maintained that the establishment of collectives, the proportion of labour time, the ratio of income and the restraints provided by the collective economy on domestic sidelines all demonstrated the socialist character of domestic sideline production. Some pragmatists took an intermediate position and argued that, although domestic sideline production was primarily socialist in character, it also contained vestiges of the capitalist system of private ownership and could thus only legitimately operate in a socialist society within certain limits and under certain restricted conditions. In 1978-79 there have been no such debates or arguments conducted in the media, rather the re-affirmation of the legitimacy of domestic sideline production has taken the form of the publication of a brief set of ideological prescriptions defining "proper" and "appropriate" sideline occupations.

Legitimation and clarification of the position of domestic sidelines in a developing socialist economy has taken the form of a short summary of the main factors differentiating domestic sideline production and capitalist small-scale commodity production. The two are admitted to be similar to the extent that the unit of management is the individual household, the material bases are commonly individual labour and individual ownership of certain small production tools and that surplus products from both are sold in rural markets. However, ideological prescriptions identify four points which distinguish domestic sideline production from capitalist small-scale commodity production and legitimate domestic sidelines within present day socialist China. First, domestic sidelines are not based on private ownership of the means of production, but are individual undertakings based on public ownership of the means of production. That is, the plots of land for personal cultivation are allocated to commune members by the collective, and the commune members only have the right to use, but not own them and they are not permitted to transfer, lease or sell them. Secondly, commune members engaged in household production are not small private owners as in the past, but peasants of a collective who have joined the people's communes. They thus devote most of their labour to collective production and engage in household production only during spare time and holidays. Third, commune members' incomes derive mainly from their collective undertakings, their livelihood depends minimally on the collective economy and their domestic sideline production is only a means to supplement any shortages in the collective economy. Fourthly, the success of commune members' domestic sideline production is dependent on assistance from the socialist economy and their production, procurement and marketing are run in close coordination with state-managed commerce and the operation of supply and marketing co-operatives. These listed factors not only differentiate "legitimate" domestic sidelines from capitalist small-scale commodity producers, but also relegate domestic sidelines to a subordinate and supplementary position *within* the socialist economy.

What this means in current practice is that it is the relation of domestic sideline to collective production which ultimately determines its legitimacy rather than the scale of the operations themselves. If domestic sidelines only take up spare-time, holiday and chiefly auxiliary labour, involve no speculation or profiteering and do not infringe upon the resources of the collective or State, then they are deemed to be in the public interest. As one policy document points out, it might look as if a household of seven persons, which kept two hogs and one sow which bred 21 piglets and raised 15 chickens, 16 ducks, 10 geese and four rabbits, was indulging in capitalist activities. In fact the activities of the family were beyond criticism for at the same time it had three able-bodied labourers, who in the 1977 Autumn distribution were given a total of 1,163 work days, averaging 388 work days each, all of which was greatly in excess of their work quotas. The family also turned in farmyard manure equivalent to 7,274 work points, which was more than double their quota.[17] It was these latter factors which in this case legitimised the scale of the household's domestic sidelines. According to this criterion, several families who were previously criticised for conducting their domestic sidelines on an inflated scale have recently been rehabilitated. One family formerly discredited for earning Y500 through raising 6 pigs, 80 ducks and four hives of bees, and another for simultaneously raising 6 pigs, 50 rabbits and some poultry, were both rehabilitated once their fellow-villagers took their contribution to collective labour into account.[18]

Families operating multifarious and lucrative sideline occupations were selected as models for emulation in 1978-79. One example which caught the eye of the Western press came from Guangdong province where a family of eight persons, with three able-bodied members, were congratulated in the media on fulfilling their collective work quotas and at the same time raising numbers of pigs, poultry, vegetables and mushrooms which were responsible for an astonishing 60 to 70 per cent of their annual income: 5,900 yuan in 1978. Apparently the family had been forced to keep its sideline income to a maximum of Y2,000 in previous years for fear of being attacked as a "spontaneous capitalist force".[19] Now, due to hard work and efficiency, the family could achieve, and very importantly, be seen to achieve maximum prosperity. What is interesting about this and similar models is that examples of individual peasant enrichment or differentials between households no longer constitute a source of embarrassment to local cadres and the national government, but are now seen as a testimony to the efficacy of the principle: "the more work, the greater the rewards". The government has been at pains to point out that if some commune members work longer hours, make greater efforts, earn more work points, run their private plots well, raise more pigs, chickens, geese or ducks, then they will not only benefit themselves, but also encourage others to do likewise and add to the general prosperity. The government has argued that since legitimate domestic sidelines production contains its own ceilings or limits, its promotion will not lead to large differentials in incomes deriving from this source. The ultra-left policy of "absolute egalitarianism" drawing everyone towards "a deadend of common poverty" is contrasted with the present promotion of pace-setters which will encourage emulation and raise national material standards.[20]

Current policies are not only couched in terms of ideological prescription and approbation, for collectives have also been urged to actively aid the growth of domestic sideline production by implementing a series of practical measures. Funds are to be set aside and loans made accessible to enable peasants to purchase animals, seedlings, fodder and tools and veterinary services from the collectives.[21] Local leaders are urged to ensure that work schedules and quotas are such that commune members have sufficient spare time and holidays to attend to domestic sidelines. They are to offer material incentives to peasants to sell their produce to the State. For example, in one area for every kilogram of eggs sold to the State, peasants receive a bonus of coupons for 1 kilo of rice and four ounces of sugar. The bonus for each pig sold to the State consisted of coupons for 25 kilo of rice and two feet of cloth. To provide an outlet for surplus sideline products and to encourage peasant households to produce goods over and above those necessary for family subsistence, the government has legitimised and promoted rural fairs or markets where goods can be exchanged between one producer and another at a negotiated and agreed price according to the supply and demand for the produce.[22] The purpose of the rural market is to provide an outlet for surplus sideline products and to directly meet an increasing consumer demand for foodstuffs and small goods. The products which enter the rural markets for exchange are largely made up of perishable products from private plots and livestock, surplus agriculture and animal husbandry products and handicrafts. They do not usually include products subject to State purchase and marketing, and the purchase of goods for resale in order to make a profit is prohibited. Current policies simply state that at present the State-owned commercial channels and supply and marketing co-operatives are neither developed enough to supply all that commune members need nor are they able to purchase all the non-staple foodstuffs, small handicrafts and implements which peasants wish to sell. At China's present stage of development, rural fairs like domestic sidelines are thus seen as a necessary and legitimate form of activity.

Domestic Sidelines and the Economy

There is no doubt that the legitimisation and promotion of domestic sideline production at this particular conjuncture is a direct result of the current search for every available means to expand the economy. It is clear that domestic sideline production is one of the most immediately expandable areas of production which offers quick returns and an immediate expansion in the supply of foods, consumer goods and raw materials for industry. Moreover, the recent suppression of domestic sideline production without establishing substitutes had illustrated that cutting off this present and potential source of supply had important repercussions for the national, collective and domestic economies.

> If the commune members are not allowed to engage in household sideline production, they will experience difficulties in their livelihood and there will be a shortage of agriculture and sideline products on the market. Judging from actual conditions, commune members' household sideline production is indispensable to the State, the collective and the individual.[23]

As government policy continues to point out, the production of individual households may be scattered and the output small, but the products from and the productive potentialities of the side occupations of 100,000,000 households of members of rural people's communes are very significant in any development plans. The development of domestic sidelines has the advantage that it need not detract from the resources of the collective, for it mainly utilises the resources of the household such as its auxiliary labour force, which is rarely fully employed by the collective, and otherwise idle corners of land and household courtyards. There is little capital investment required of the collective. For instance to mobilise peasant households to raise chickens it is not necessary to invest large sums of money to procure labour, equipment, tools and raw materials. However, if the same chickens were raised by the collective, it would involve assignment of personnel, the erection of sheds and procurement of fuel, equipment and food. Domestic sideline production thus has the advantage that the labour and resources are chiefly provided by the individual household and it is this private and domestic source that is primarily being tapped by the present promotion of domestic sidelines.

Present policies are equally a response to the pressures to increase the material standards of the peasants and the government's means of offering them an immediate incentive to expand production and support the "Four Modernisations" programme. Any expansion in domestic sidelines increases the supply of non-staple foods for the peasant household's own subsistence and most estimates of the average proportion of peasant income furnished by domestic sidelines have ranged between 10 and 25 per cent.[24] The raising of two pigs per household alone can add 100 yuan to the family budget. In early 1979 it was calculated that the per capita income of peasants in Jiangsu province had risen by as much as twenty per cent as a result of the recent policies encouraging private undertakings.[25] Domestic sideline production also supplies a substantial portion of non-staple foods and other goods required by non-peasant households. In 1978 it was estimated that one quarter of the agricultural and sideline products purchased by the commercial departments throughout the country were domestic in origin, and the proportions of some products such as pigs, poultry and eggs are much larger.[26] Thus any expansion in domestic sideline production immediately affects the diets and cash incomes of peasant households and the supplies of foodstuffs for city residents.

The importance of domestic sideline production for maintaining the non-staple subsistence sector and generating wealth and materials for both the individual household and the State generally seems to be recognised by both the government and commune members. Nevertheless it may be that the new policies have not been uniformly welcomed, and in some areas there may even have been some reluctance to promote the new policies. It could be that in some localities current policies are seen to potentially disturb the working balance that has been evolved between the collective and domestic economies which is an acceptable ideological and practical compromise and establishes a balance which is seen to serve the interests of both the collective and individual peasant households. In practice, the most obvious tensions surrounding the coexistence of the two sectors of the economy, the competition for labour and fertiliser, have been resolved in many areas by allocating prior labour and fertiliser quotas to the collective sector. Thus a minimal quota of collective labour days and fertiliser is required of most commune members before they can attend to, or allocate resources to, their domestic sidelines. There may have been little debate or opposition expressed to the new policies in ideological terms, but the fact that certain local cadres have been criticised by the central government for not giving sufficient encouragement, or even continuing to suppress domestic sidelines, may suggest some degree of opposition to the new policies at the practical and local level.[27] Local cadres with long experience and memories, and the responsibility for fulfilling State quotas, may well be aware of the potentially dangerous consequences of policies which call for the rapid expansion of the household economy. One or two reports in the media also speak of the "lingering presence of a morbid fear of making right deviations", and several comment on the discomfort or insecurity bred by the "recent turn about" in policy.[28] However, it would not do to give undue emphasis or exaggerate the degree of opposition to present policies, for the overwhelming impression given by the media is of peasant households welcoming the new directives and taking advantage of the new opportunities to expand their domestic sidelines. During 1979 reports of a positive peasant response to these policies, and even some abuses of these policies, increasingly began to outweigh any examples of resistance cited in the media.

The Collective and Domestic Tightrope

As in the period of domestic sideline expansion in the early 1960s, commune members have once again been accused of taking more care of their own domestic sidelines at the expense of collective property, occupations and prosperity. In some areas, production teams have taken a further step and begun to dismantle the collective economy by formulating output quotas based on small work groups of close kinsmen or neighbours or even individual households. In a manner reminiscent of the *sanzi yibao* policies in the early 1960s, some teams have apparently fixed contracts with these work groups and households who now organise and manage their own production and in some cases their own land which has been redistributed to them by the team.[29] The commercial and marketing transactions of the rural fairs provide as many, if not more, opportunities for abuse, and some peasants are reported to have taken advantage of the revived rural fairs to engage in some speculation and profiteering.[30] A few persons are reported to have given up agriculture for commerce, but more common are the reports of reselling special products from distant places or the selling without discount of defective or substandard commodities by warehouses, stores or factories. For example, one report speaks of the sale of filter cigarettes or thermos flasks acquired from shops by improper means and sold at village fairs well above the purchase price. In another case, sunflower seeds were purchased at 50 to 60 fen a catty from markets in neighbouring provinces and sold elsewhere at Y1.3 per catty at local fairs.[31] There have also been complaints about the sales of substandard meat and the absence of effective measures of food inspection. All of these malpractices have been denounced in no uncertain terms in the media, and the government has frequently called for more effective regulations to deal with these abuses. What policy documents and media reports alike insist, however, is that evidence of malpractice should on no account be used as a pretext by local cadres to interfere in, or restrict, the implementation of current rural policies promoting domestic sidelines and rural markets.[32]

In responding to these policy abuses, the government has shown itself to be sensitive to the dangers of unlimited expansion, and it clearly perceives its role as legitimising, promoting and encouraging domestic sidelines but within certain well-defined limits. Limits that are to do with the size of private plot, prohibitions against the hiring of labour, sources of fodder and the prior demands of collective work and manure quotas which have not changed over the years, and limits which result from the ideological education and the raised political consciousness of peasants. The question is how sure can the present leadership be of maintaining these limits? Could it rely on a new political campaign to act as an ideological brake should events get out of hand? Though there are rarely any references to the consequences of similar policies in the early 1960s, the likely parallels and potential dangers must be apparent. Then a new socialist educational movement to raise the consciousness of peasants was required to act as an ideological brake on the expansion of the domestic economy. A close reading of the recent media in China would suggest that, although the current promotion of domestic sideline production may be interpreted as yet another swing in the alternating policies towards domestic sidelines of the past twenty years, the mandate and resources of the central government to limit the swing of the pendulum or determine and alter the direction of the pendulum in the future may have been irretrievably weakened.

The resources at the command of the central government or local cadres to impose limits may well constitute a major difference between present and past policy fluctuations. Certainly many commune members have taken advantage of a period of "liberalisation" and the government's explicit concern and attention given to their material benefits and their livelihood to complain about the constant political campaigns of the past, both their effects and the assumptions on which they operate. A number of reports suggest that some peasants do feel themselves to have been somewhat duped by the counterposing of material interests against levels of political consciousness or the equation of riches with "revisionism", and perceive themselves to have gained but a negligible increase in the standards of living or in many cases have experienced an absolute decline in their material well-being. Political campaigns are described as showpieces held for the benefit of outside observers but often at the expense of the participants themselves. A letter to a newspaper in Hebei province described the fickleness of past policies in which private plots had been continuously taken away, handed back and taken away.[33] The result was that peasants were no longer taken in by the conflicting goals of sequential campaigns and they were increasingly unhappy and disgruntled about losing their sources of supplementary income and food. In Gansu province, peasants described the effects of the inconsistencies and rapid changes of policy over the years on their own lives. "Beginning in 1959," they said,

> one political movement was launched right after another in our villages. With each, the peasants' life became a little more intolerable. Things were especially bad during the Cultural Revolution, the largest movement of all. During the ten years of great upheaval, there were many smaller movements . . . . [Lastly] the peasants had their private plots confiscated, allegedly to help them get rid of their traditional money-making mentality. The peasants demand that the Communist Party and the government carry out correct, consistent policies for the rural areas. The policies have changed too quickly over the years. For example, they had been allowed to plant fruit trees around their houses, raise a few sheep and grow vegetables in their private plots, but just when they were about to benefit from their sidelines, trees were felled and sheep and plots confiscated.[34]

They ended their complaints, as have others, with the hope that the Party and government would never again go back on their word and would guarantee the future of domestic sidelines. The government on its part has responded to these requests and has guaranteed that "nobody again will be allowed to recklessly interfere in these activities".[35]

In general what these reports suggest is that the government may well have forfeited its ability to use political campaigns again as a mechanism for the adjustment of policies, especially policies which like domestic sideline production directly affect material standards. At the present time, however, the immediate advantages of expansion are seen to outweigh the potential dangers, and this situation leaves us with the intriguing question of what considerations will primarily and finally determine the response of peasant households and production teams to these central directives. At what point might local cadres and peasant households deem it profitable to alter the previous balance evolved between collective and domestic production, how will collectives accommodate an expanded domestic sector and what would be the repercussions of such a move for the collective sector of the economy? Could the collectives continue to structure the priorities of the rural economy or might they themselves become appendages to a much expanded domestic sector and even eventually disappear? What will be the effects of this expansion of the domestic economy on the peasant household itself? The last section of the paper focuses briefly on some of the likely repercussions of any expansion of domestic production for individual peasant households which may determine its response to present policies.

Domestic Sidelines and the Household

What has received little attention in the media is the repercussions of the current policies for the household itself, both for its structure, function and intra-familial relations. Indeed the implications of rural economic policies for the peasant household have not been widely discussed by any government since the time of the Great Leap Forward. Following collectivisation in the 1950s, the presence of domestic sidelines has contributed to the maintenance of the household as a unit of production. During the mid-1950s a number of policies collectivising the means of production removed the property basis of the household and reduced the socio-economic functions of the family. The subsequent definition of the domestic group as "mainly a unit of life in which the husband and wife share their married life together, rear and educate their children and care for their elder near relatives together" thus omitted any reference to a property base or the functions of production and consumption.[36] However, the economic organisation of rural China has continuously demanded that a peasant household continue to meet a number of organisational demands, namely its contribution to the collective sector, undertaking domestic sideline production and the transformation of materials for consumption. On this basis the household is still a unit of production albeit reduced in scope, for outside its grain needs, it continues to produce foods and goods both for its own subsistence and for exchange in return for other necessities. To meet these needs, a peasant household has to mobilise its material and labour resources and any promotion of domestic sideline production is likely to increase these demands on the resources of the individual household.

Before 1949, anthropologists had noted a definite correlation between the complexity of the *jia* estate (defined as that body of holdings such as lands, residences, household effects, farm tools and livestock to which the process of family division is applicable) and the size of the domestic group. They argued that the key factor in the maintenance of a complex or joint family among certain socio-economic groups in the past was the existence of an estate sufficient in size to meet the claims of its members, but that the payment of individual wages, the collectivisation of land and the collectivised organisation and management of production in the 1950s were all responsible for destroying the *jia* estate or economic basis of the complex or joint family in contemporary China.[37] In fact the operation of domestic sidelines has required the existence of a residual estate which includes certain household effects, tools, small numbers of livestock, plants and access to, although not ownership of, lands for individual cultivation. Any increase in domestic sidelines then might require of, and furnish the household with, increased material resources or an expanded *jia* estate. More importantly, however, the maintenance of flourishing domestic sidelines requires the household to maintain its labour resources and distribute them efficiently between the collective and domestic sectors. In the collective sphere of the economy, the income and staple food supply is very much dependent on the ratio of wage-earners to dependents within the household. Domestic sidelines and the processing of sidelines products for consumption and exchange furnishes an important food resource and cash contribution to the household economy and also relies on access to labour and especially the "auxiliary" labour of women and the older generation. The plight of households composed of the very old, sick or disabled, or of bachelors and the widowed, who are without sufficient labour to maintain even the most minimal of sideline activities, have been well documented.

The continuing demands of domestic sidelines on the household's material and labour resources have had repercussions for the structure of the peasant household and any future expansion of domestic sideline production may well encourage certain trends particular to rural areas. It can be argued that, despite policies to reduce the function of the peasant household, it may now be more complex or elaborate in form, at least for part of its developmental cycle, than at any other time in the recent past. Although at first sight it appears that the average number of persons constituting a peasant household has remained at between four and six persons,[38] similarities in average size may mask the range in size of households present at any one point in time, the variations within any one individual household at different points in its developmental cycle and the substantial differences between rural and urban household structures. In rural areas, post-marital residence is still generally patrilocal. Thus the marriage of sons immediately occasions the expansion of the domestic group and the establishment of stem and joint families, although it eventually also. precipitates fission, *fenjia,* and its concomitant economic partition. Normally, however, the latter takes place some time after the marriage of the second or third son or the birth of several grandchildren. As I have noted from my own field work, at any one time in the village, there may be households which are of the conjugal, stem or joint form depending on their stage in the developmental cycle.[39]

Several demographic and economic factors, including the demands of domestic sidelines, have encouraged the expansion in numbers, a new vertical and horizontal proliferation of the generations within the same household and the elaboration of peasant household forms at least for certain periods of the developmental cycle.[40] General improvements in diet, welfare services and in health have increased the number of surviving sons and lengthened the life-span of individuals. The increase in employment opportunities not tied to the narrow property base of the individual family and the obstacles to migration to the cities have also contributed to an increase in numbers of family members in close proximity to one another, if not within the same household. The economic organisation of rural China demands that the household maximise its labour resources, for the larger the household, the greater the rewards from the collective economy, the greater the number of domestic sideline occupations that can be undertaken and the greater the total material benefits to the family. The employment of auxiliary labour, especially in domestic sidelines and household servicing, has strengthened the economic interdependence of the generations. Indeed the joint phase of the developmental cycle following the marriage of a son or sons may serve as a unique opportunity for the household to make maximum use of the labour resources of different generations to specialise or diversify the economy of the domestic group and accumulate wealth immediately prior to division. If the sector of the economy most amenable to expansion and quick returns for the household is domestic sidelines, then the promotion of this sector may well benefit larger households and in turn contribute to an expansion in household size. Already there are signs that any promotion of domestic sidelines may encourage households to reallocate their labour resources at the expense of the collective, and this can only affirm the continuing interdependence of family members, counter *fenjia* or partition and further elaborate peasant household forms.

If access to labour forms one of the major resources of the household and control over labour becomes a major source of differentiation, then the recruitment and reproduction of labour by the household is constantly in demand. In rural China this very significant factor has had repercussions for the intensity of female labour, controls over the exchange of women in marriage and the sexual division of labour. Sideline occupations such as tending household livestock, making handicrafts and tending vegetables have traditionally been allocated to the women of the family. In March 1962 an editorial in *Zhongguo Funu* (Women of China) observed that the raising of animals and fowls and the cultivation of plots of private land were mostly in the charge of women. It appears that the combined demands of domestic sidelines and domestic labour have frequently kept women out of waged employment on a full-time basis and they are thus more likely to be part-time or seasonal in employment especially at particular periods of their life-cycle.[41] It is a common sequence of events for a woman of the older generation to leave the collective labour force and allocate her time to domestic sideline production and domestic labour on the recruitment of a new daughter-in-law to the household who takes the place of the older woman in the collective labour force. Any promotion of domestic sidelines is likely to intensify the already-large demands on peasant women's labour, and, in turn, this may affect the scale of her individual remuneration and the degree of women's participation in collective political decision-making. Distributing her labour primarily to domestic sidelines will not necessarily affect a woman's bargaining power and position within the household as the sidelines do furnish an important contribution to the budget in cash and kind. However, the income generated by the domestic sidelines does not necessarily affect the relations of exchange within the household and participation in the collective labour force at least allowed for her direct involvement in waged labour and the visibility and remuneration of women as individual producers.[42] If the considerable portion of her time and energy is devoted to sidelines and activities frequently indistinguishable from domestic labour, it is also less likely that women will have access to local collective decision-making arenas given that political and productive units overlap. This may be particularly so at a later stage in a woman's life cycle when other factors are less likely to penalise her in regard to political participation. A woman of the older generation may no longer be a "temporary" or "outsider" member of the village, she is more likely to have become familiar with the political arena and to have built up her own networks of support and influence, but she may well have withdrawn from the collective productive arena.[43] Any promotion of domestic sideline production is therefore more likely to both intensify the demands on women's labour and make any redefinition of the sexual division of labour more difficult.

In the absence of private hiring of agricultural or domestic labour, which is prohibited by law, marriage has become one of the major, if not the only means of recruitment and reproduction of labour. One of the most common explanations or rationalisations given by parents in rural areas for maintaining their control and arranging the exchange of women in marriage was that cited in terms of the recruitment of additional labour, usually a woman's, to maintain the household as an economic unit. One of the most common explanations given for the persistence of the betrothal gift in rural areas was that it took the form of compensation for the expenses of a daughter's upbringing and the subsequent loss of her labour on marriage. It is clear that to make the most of the opportunities offered by the negotiation of marriage to maximise the socio-economic resources of the household, the older generation felt that they had to encourage the members of their household to marry at or as near to the legal age as possible and encourage the rapid birth of grandchildren who would be able to replace the grandparents on their retirement from the labour force.[44] Moreover, domestic sideline production adds to the resources of the domestic group, and the control of these resources has in the past placed certain sanctions at the disposal of the older generation and enabled them to maintain their authority and controls over the younger generation. The private ownership of housing and the organisation of the household economy into one joint budget meant that, although they contributed to the common fund, the young were ultimately dependent on the household to meet the expenses of marriage and to provide housing. The importance of this source of support for the younger generation is confirmed by the difficulties which *xiaxiang* boys who are without the support and resources of a household experience in negotiating a marriage. Indeed the demands on the labour resources of the peasant household have been an important factor instituting early and semi-arranged forms of marriage and the tardy implementation of birth control policies in rural areas.

What emerges in a study of both rural and urban China is a direct correlation between the composition of the household, the economic interdependence of the members of a household and the demands made on the household such as those generated by domestic sidelines and the processing of domestic products for consumption or exchange. The demands of the collective labour force are of course common to both urban and rural households, but in urban areas where there is minimal if non-existent private and domestic sector of the economy, and where there are institutional State and community and retail provisions to service and share in the maintenance of the household, the functionality of the household lessens. It is less a unit of production and consumption and the residential patterns tend towards those of the nuclear or conjugal type at the time of marriage. In rural areas demographic factors and economic policies have already contributed to the establishment of elaborated peasant households and it seems probable that the promotion of domestic sideline production will further maximise the demands on the labour resources of the rural household with concomitant repercussions for its structure and composition. Indeed the contrasting socio-economic functions of the household in rural and urban areas can be said to have already contributed to the rise of a new dual familial form in contemporary China for the main differences in familial structure are no longer primarily those between social classes as formerly, but between urban and rural China. Given that the structure of the household and intra-familial relations in each can be correlated directly with the socio-economic functions of the households, of which domestic sideline production is a distinguishing component, any promotion of domestic sidelines may well exacerbate these present trends.

11

THE IMPACT OF CHINA'S NEW ECONOMIC POLICIES IN THE RURAL SECTOR

Neville Maxwell

Institute of Commonwealth Studies, Oxford

The impact of the policies put into effect in China since 1976 has been least marked in the rural areas, probably because it is necessarily more diffused and will therefore take years to make itself felt. Paradoxically, the impact upon production, upon which the whole strategy is promulgated and by which it must be justified, will remain difficult to discern. Agricultural production had been increasing at an average annual rate of about 3 per cent since the mid-1960s and continuation of the policies associated with the Cultural Revolution appeared — to the Chinese until 1977 and to outsiders — to promise at least an extension of that achievement. There were broader grounds, furthermore, for expecting some acceleration. The achievements in agriculture since Liberation reflected essentially the intensification and improvement of traditional agricultural techniques, together with the unquantifiable contribution of the changed institutional framework. There has been a gradual addition of modern production factors but those are still far from dominant in the total structure of inputs. But the continuing technical transformation of Chinese agriculture, with chemical fertiliser becoming more widely and copiously available and mechanisation spreading, should have brought about in the 1980s the pay-off from decades of investment, expressed in acceleration in the rate of increase in production. Presumably it was that expectation which led the planners in Beijing to propose and the leadership to accept a grain target of output of 400 million tons in 1985. This suggests that just as the charges that "Lin Biao and the Gang of Four" occasioned agricultural stagnation in the 1970s look insubstantial when set against the figures of production achieved in the context of natural conditions, so claims of credit for acceleration achieved will have to be at least partially discounted. The output figures for 1978 (305m tons) and 1979 (estimated at over 317m tons) are not discordant with the rate of increase achieved over the earlier 1970s.

The new policies express a fundamental reversal of the basic strategy for rural development. The previous strategy looked to a steady but accelerating advance over the whole agricultural front, entailing a process of equalisation through the support given to areas and units that although backward had become dynamic, while expecting advanced areas to rely primarily on their own efforts and achieved momentum to sustain their progress. This had appeared to be creating a durable productive base with a steady, secular pattern of increased productivity, together with a wide-spread generation of demand. The new strategy, clearly kindred to that of the "green revolution", looks to concentration of resources in those advantaged and already high-yield areas where the pay-off can be expected to be most immediate and rewarding. In such circumstantially favoured areas "production bases" are being formed from state farms or from combinations of communes. According to a recent formulation of this approach, "agriculture will be modernised area by area, through concentrated use of farm machinery, first in areas where conditions are superior. In the first few years, efforts will be concentrated in areas with 5 per cent of the rural population".[1] Units outside these production bases will be encouraged to pursue modernisation "according to local conditions and in the spirit of self-reliance".

The development of these production bases is part of a generalised emphasis on specialisation in agriculture which again runs counter to the previous, Maoist strategy. Another aspect of this shift lies in the down-grading of the policy of making "grain the key link". This looked to the attainment of local food self-sufficiency on a priority basis, and was linked to the injunction to "store grain everywhere" — a practice which, though valuable in seasons of deficiency and especially in events of natural calamities or war, must also have worked against the state's need to maximise the quantity of grain marketed. It applied a levelling effect, in that a unit in a high-yield, advanced area which could use its arable land to much greater profit by putting it to cash crops, would be expected to keep a signficant portion under grain for its own members' consumption. The green light now given to specialisation in cropping will accentuate the effect of the production base approach in sharply widening regional income disparities.

That the present leadership has no misgivings about the widening of income differentials in the society which its policies must entail found confirmation in observations by Vice-Premier Deng Xiaoping, interviewed in Peking in June 1979. He brushed aside questions suggesting that such widening disparities could be divisive and in the long run politically dangerous to socialism. The demonstration of achieved prosperity, even if by only a few, he argued, must have the effect of spurring the rest to greater efforts. As for the possibility of re-emergent class stratification, there was no such danger because in China there was the system of "ownership by the people".

On the macro-level, the peasantry has been offered the comprehensive inducement of higher grain prices, going into effect with the 1979 autumn harvest. The basic procurement price for grain sold to meet the state's planning quotas has been increased by 20 per cent. The price for grain sold to the state in excess of the quota — but under the annually-adjusted state plan — has been increased by 50 per cent and any units whose production is such as to enable them to sell an extra quantity may be offered an even higher price, at the decision of the local county, to a limit of double the base procurement price. Complementarily, there have been tax concessions to the peasants. The agricultural tax is to be waived in backward areas where the per-capita availability of grain is below minimum standards; and the level of profit at which industrial and commercial undertakings in the communes are subject to taxation is being raised sharply, from Y600 to Y3000.[2]

Thus increasing the savings potential in the rural areas may be supportive of the drive to mechanise agriculture. However, a shift in policy on mechanisation, again amounting to reversion to pre-Cultural Revolution practice, makes that outcome uncertain.

China was already launched on a mass campaign to push forward the modernisation of agriculture, and specifically to achieve the "basic mechanisation" of agriculture, before that was subsumed in the drive for "four modernisations". That campaign was closely linked with the broader campaign for the self-reliant intensification of collective farming whose slogan was "Learn from Dazhai". With much else, a change in policy on mechanisation appears to be signalled in the discarding of the Dazhai model.

Conflict over policy on agricultural mechanisation was prime among the sharp differences which led to the great split temporarily resolved in the Cultural Revolution.³ From the beginning Mao had insisted that while the fundamental way ahead for agricultural lay in mechanisation, advance on the social/political front should not await mechanisation, but rather prepare for it. The essence of Mao's approach was to encourage and assist the collective units (i.e. the communes, production brigades and production teams) to invest in agricultural machinery and ultimately tractors as their savings and/or the availability of state assistance permitted. The machinery would thus be owned, managed, manned and used either by the same unit as owned the land serviced (in most instances the production team) or by the brigade or commune of which the team was a member. The operators and technicians would be members of those collectives and their income, like that of their fellow-members, would be a share in the team's production distributed according to labour performed. That income, plus the skills of operation, maintenance and accountancy which the use of the farm machinery demands, would remain within the collective system.

Mao and his supporters opposed the system of agricultural machinery stations (AMS) which had been established in the 1950s on the model of the Soviet machine tractor stations, seeing them as contributing to the strengthening of the state bureaucracy, with attendant openings for elitism and corruption, while denying the peasant the experience which would help make him into the worker-peasant whose creation is among the basic aims of Marxism. In the course of the Cultural Revolution the AMS were dissolved and their equipment distributed to the communes. Now they are to be set up again.

"Tractor stations will be set up by the state to serve the communes and brigades in return for reasonable expense fees", it was announced in early 1979.⁴ Communes and brigades are to be allowed to retain the tractors and other machinery they already own; but the re-establishment of the AMS must result in the level of mechanisation with the communes being held down, at the least. That was an essential part of a fundamental change in policy on agricultural mechanisation, away from the advance on a broad front, with particular emphasis on "levelling up" backward units with assistance from higher units or the state (which Mao had advocated and, in the Dazhai campaign, seen implemented) and in favour of concentrating mechanisation, with other modern productive inputs, in selected areas where the pay-off can be expected to be biggest and fastest. These "production bases" are being formed from new or enlarged state farms or from combinations of communes situated in circumstantially favoured areas; for example, in

Kwangtung 27 of the province's 100-odd counties are being thus singled out, all of them in the rich Pearl River delta. Units outside these "production bases" will be allowed to pursue mechanisation "according to local conditions and in the spirit of self-reliance".

So far as CCP policy on *distribution of income* in the communes was concerned, the signals appear to have been reversed early in 1978. Until that time the approved model was Dazhai's method of work-point distribution, with its emphasis on attitudinal ("political") factors being taken into consideration along with the obvious ones of strength and skill, and its attenuation of the links between specific work performance and rewards, expressed, for example, in the infrequency of assessment meetings. Beginning in the summer of 1978 and, it appears, under instructions passed down to the communes from the Party, there was a wholesale turning away from the Dazhai model in favour of the piece-work system practised before the Cultural Revolution. Under this system, every job in the farming almanac — or as nearly as practicable — is given its fixed quotient of work-points. Typically, the scheduling of those quotients is done at brigade level, and codified in booklets which are distributed to the production teams. One such booklet produced by a brigade in Jiangsu specified over 200 jobs, under categories mostly associated with crops. A selection from the category "Wheat" is shown in Table 1.

Table 1

Job	Unit	Workpoints	Requirements
Carrying pig manure	50kg	0.5	200m as standard distance
Spreading pig manure	50kg	0.1	Spread evenly
Digging ditch	100m	10	Straight; depth 1.5m
Harvesting	1 mou	10	Clean, short strokes
Trussing	1 mou	3	Neat

This method of relating work performed to income-entitlement had been rejected during the Cultural Revolution as being cumbersome and time-wasting, tending to separate cadres from members (because of the need for close supervision of the quality of work) and to widen income differentials between families within a production team. But cadres of production teams which had reverted to this method, interviewed in June 1978 (Chang Ching People's Commune, under Suzhou Municipality), stated that the piece-work system was much more popular with members, worked to the benefit of women, and had stimulated production. A small minority of units, here and in other parts of China visited in 1979, are reported to have persisted with the Dazhai method — which commune members generally describe as desirable once political consciousness is sufficiently developed.

Partly, it appears, as a consequence of the piece-work system, work-groups (or job-groups) have been reinstituted as an organisational device within the production teams. While these may be either temporary or permanent, typically they appear to be semi-permanent, set up for a period of a year and subject to reorganisation by the team leadership annually. Again, these work-groups are said by the cadres of production teams which have organised them to have been beneficial in increasing production, and it is claimed that their membership is closely vetted to prevent their taking on kinship contours and balanced by exchanging members so as to attain approximate equality of strength and skill. Some team leaderships stated that they rotated work-groups so that they would not have responsibility for the same portion of the team's land for more than one year. While this revived deployment of a team's work-force into groups has the active encouragement of the national authorities (it is advocated in the "Sixty Regulations" as "a good policy which is of benefit in accelerating the development of collective production and is welcomed by the masses"), there have been frequent reports of teams pushing the work-group system too far, and dividing up among those groups not only a team's land but also tools and funds — in other words, breaking the production team down into sub-units which replace the team as units of account. For example, a Guangdong newspaper reported in February 1979 that "the production teams in some places have decided to divide themselves up into small units, and also to divide up the common property of the production teams".[5] While reported from many parts of China, this appears to have affected only a very small proportion of production teams: an investigation mounted by a prefecture in Sichuan showed that less than one per cent of the production teams there had made work-groups into units of account.[6] Nevertheless, it is clear that the work-group system has its critics in China, who deny that it is merely a form of labour management and see in it a "right deviationist retrogression" which undermines the solidarity of the production team and thus weakens the commune structure at its foundation. Such critics are described as being "deeply poisoned by Lin Biao and the Gang of Four" and as "abstractly hold[ing] that the higher the degree of public ownership, the more revolutionary the policy".[7] The comment may suggest that some who criticise the work-group system also oppose another expression of the new policy line, the retarding of the process of raising the level of account within the communes.

It is one of the most tangible charges against the "Gang" that they pushed this policy, encouraging "the transition in poverty": that is, inducing, sometimes forcing, units to raise their level of account before their circumstances justified such a change. This charge is at least much exaggerated, and may be false. Commune cadres interviewed about this process on various visits in rural China during the 1970s invariably emphasised the pre-conditions that had to be fulfilled before the level of account could be raised; and pointed out that such changes were allowed only after investigation and ratification by Party levels above the commune. That the Gang shared the view that changes in the level of ownership in the communes must be approached very cautiously is indicated by the textbook on political economy produced under their auspices in Shanghai, which stipulated explicitly that the current system, with the production team as the basic accounting unit, was superior and "must be maintained stable and unchanged for a quite long period of time".[8] Furthermore, it appears that only a very small proportion of units which raised their accounting level under "Gang"-pressure have since reverted — for example, only three out of 27 brigades in a county near Shanghai. But the conscious aim of raising the level of account, from team to brigade and thence to commune, which was usually met in rural units before 1977, is now very rarely voiced; and some commune cadres state that such changes will not be considered in the foreseeable future. On the other hand, there is some evidence that prosperous and confident units are allowed to be judges of their own best interests in this regard, and to raise their accounting levels — for example, the big Evergreen People's Commune, on the outskirts of Beijing and known to many foreign visitors, raised its accounting level to commune in 1978.

The emphasis placed on material incentives, most clamant in the industrial sector, also effects the countryside. It is the rationale of the change in the work-point system, and the associated framework of bonuses and fines which some units have established. Just as the emphasis on production and rewards has greatly heightened expectations in the cities, so in the countryside the emphasis on the need to improve the living standards of the peasantry has been noted and applied: "After a bumper harvest is reaped", said *People's Daily* in June 1979, "communes and production teams in some localities insist on distributing and consuming more grain on the pretext of improving their living conditions . . . The cadres and

and masses should be educated to promote the fine tradition of hard work and thrift and consume less grain and use it in a planned way".[9] With the peasantry's greatly increased purchasing power, consequent upon the increases introduced in autumn 1979 in the procurement prices of grain and other produce, this phenomenon of increased consumption is only to be expected.

So far as political relations in the countryside are concerned, one marked change consequent on the new policies is the effective disappearance of that small minority of commune members who until the late 1970s had still been "capped" or "five elements". Random sampling at all rural units visited through the 1970s, had indicated that a remarkably consistent one per cent of a unit's population was still classified as "five elements". Over the years, the great majority of such people had been "de-capped", and the one per cent appeared to be a residual group, seen by their fellow commune-members as inveterate recalcitrants. Again on orders from above, beginning in 1978 rural units submitted their remaining "elements" to a re-screening which resulted in a vast decrease in their numbers. This instance appears typical: one commune had 74 members registered as various types of bad "element"; upon screening, five of those were found to have been incorrectly classified; the "hats" were removed from 65, and only four were judged to be unreformed. Since the impulse for this move came from above, it is not surprising that "some comrades have some misgivings" about it.[10]

The emphasis the new policies give to the role of experts and intellectuals also has an impact on the countryside, notably in changes affecting the relationship of the "educated youngsters" from the cities with the rural masses. Rather than being distributed in the communes, with some attached to peasant households, others living in their own "households" at production team level, and all generally in close working proximity to commune members (the better to "learn from the poor and lower-middle peasants"), beginning in 1978 the educated youngsters began to be separated out from lower level units. They were first concentrated at brigade level, in specially built — and state-funded — dormitories, there to work in separate enterprises; but those small enterprises were run by their adoptive brigades. Under the new policy, these youngsters will no longer be assigned to production brigades and teams but will from the beginning of their — now finite — spells in the countryside be attached to their own separate units. Thus, rather than working with the peasants, they will be working among the peasants in their own light-industrial or service undertakings. Since they have "attained certain educational levels" (i.e. levels higher than the peasants') and have "also gained some practical experience" the Central Committee has now ruled that "they should be admitted to agricultural colleges, agro-technical secondary schools or training classes" so that they can be made into a "backbone force" for modernising agriculture.[11] Inevitably this will mean more limited entry for peasant youngsters into agricultural colleges and related institutions, and the consequent entrenching and widening of the educational disadvantages they already suffer *vis-à-vis* urban youth. Since the schools in the rural areas are mostly practising a nine-year system — at the most — and only ten-year schooling can prepare students for university entrance, in the words of Hubert Brown, "the vast majority of students from rural areas will not be able to sit for university enrolment examinations, at least not for the foreseeable future". Of that disability, Brown comments that "there is no other single deliberate change of policy that so completely reverses the social and political priorities of the Educational Revolution, which sought, above all else, at least in theory, to bring poorer peasants into the mainstream of education".[12] In this crucial regard, the new policies can be said to have accepted as necessary a widening and consolidation of the "great gap" between city and countryside.

The new Dengist policies now in application are, of course, only a re-imposition of the line which was followed in the early 1960s — conservative economists in the West are hailing it as "neo-Liuist" — and which was vigorously, often violently repudiated in the Cultural Revolution. That this reversal is resented, in the rural areas by some cadres and commune members, and will be opposed when opportunity offers, is indicated by the frequency of allusions in the Chinese media to the continuing "pernicious influence of the ultra-leftist line of Lin Biao and the Gang of Four, [which] runs very deep and has not yet been completely eliminated".[13] The position of such opponents of the new policies was recently summed up — without condemnation — by the first Party secretary of Jiangxi province. As he put it, opponents argue that the concentration on production, with political factors relegated, is responsible for the appearance of social problems; that the "reversal of verdict on some [former] bad elements" is related to the reinstatement of formerly disgraced cadres; that the opening of village fairs and the "*enrichissez-vous*" policy have released spontaneous capitalist tendencies among the peasantry; that the emphasis on the rights of the production teams to autonomy has led to difficulties for the communes; and that the restoring of traditional dramas has encouraged the reappearance of "feudal and superstitious" activities.

That has the echo of a comprehensive indictment of the new policies, and it appears likely that as their effect in the countryside deepens, so will such criticism build up.

Postscript – 1980

The impact of the set of policies previously signposted in China as "the capitalist road" may have been slower to make itself felt in the rural areas, but by mid-1980 it had become clearly apparent, at least in one revisited commune known to the writer through repeated visits during the 1970s (Chang Ching, near Suzhou). The most profound or at least most pervasive change lay in the marked shift of expressed concern of the cadres and commune members, away from the structure and directions of their community and towards an occupation with production and its obverse, consumption, for its own sake. With the new maxim, "Politics serves economics", confidently voiced by central government cadres, has come a depoliticisation of the commune membership, most audibly expressed in the new selection of tunes played over the loudspeakers – instead of the bouncy blare of revolutionary music, sentimental themes from Indian films or even the alien twangs of "I'm Bound for Alabama".

Within the production team, whose autonomy *vis-à-vis* the higher levels of brigade and commune is so much a concern of the Dengist leadership, there are marked changes in structure and practice. The work-group, urged by the Party almost to the point of being made mandatory, is used as an organisational sub-unit of the team practically throughout the commune, and is claimed by the commune leadership to have led to greater labour efficiency and increased production. The experience of one team investigated had been that, introduced in 1978, the work-group system had by the end of 1979 all but split the team into two, so sharp had the competition between the two work-groups become for the property and services remaining at the disposal of the team itself. Atypically, this team had drawn back from what its leadership and membership saw as regression, abolished the work-groups and reverted to organising its labour as a single unit.

So far as income distribution is concerned, the job-specific or piece-work system of work-point allocation is general, and its practitioners as committed in commendation of its virtues as they were when speaking, in the mid-1970s, of the contrary, Dazhai-type approach. A new development is a change in the remuneration system for commune members working in factories run by the commune. Previously such members continued on the work-point system, drawing their income as a share of their team's, in accordance with their accumulation of work-points, and with the commune enterprise paying their wage into the coffer of the team. The result of that system was that inequalities of income appeared between workers in the factory, with those from richer teams receiving higher income than those from poorer teams. The system now spreading is that members working in commune factories are paid salaries direct; in consequence income disparities will appear between those team members who continue in agricultural work and those assigned to factory work in the commune. Taken with the effect of the stress now laid on the obligation of every family to work hard to enrich itself directly, rather than through the raising of the income level of the team as a whole, this policy change promises to work against the social solidarity of the production team.

A more immediate effect on the balance between the collective and what was the residual private sector of the economy at the team level is likely to result from the closing down of the small pig-farms previously run by the teams. Established over 1977 and 1978, as a rule, these piggeries were seen at that time as a means of strengthening the collective economy at team level as well as maximising pork and fertiliser production. They were not seen as in any way competitive with the rearing of pigs by individual families, indeed they served a complementary role in that a team piggery would often sell piglets to families for fattening and re-sale to the state marketing organisation. But some time in late 1979 the instruction came down from higher levels that these piggeries were to be closed. The pigs were sold off to families, the quite newly built styes put to any available use — which usually meant as inefficient store-huts. Pork quotas are now set directly for families. The explanation for this change is given in exclusively economic terms: the team piggeries were expensive in labour requirement, pig-rearing is a skill at which the team's organisation often showed itself deficient, with consequent waste and losses. The change has led to a marked increase in the amount of pork sold to the state in this commune.

The organisational structure at brigade and commune level has not so far been changed and the commune's management committee is essentially the former revolutionary committee renamed. But reports that the Central Committee of the Party is considering a fundamental change in commune organisation were readily confirmed by central cadres, who emphasised however that no decisions had yet been reached in this matter — and that meanwhile it was not a matter for discussion with the mass of the commune members. This change looks to the separation of the function of state administration from the commune, in effect the re-establishment of the township level of administration which was absorbed by the communes on their formation in 1958. If that change is implemented, the effect would be to leave the commune as an organisation concerned only with development, narrowly defined, and production — rather like the "blocks" in the Indian community development programme. The consequence would be to increase the gap between the administrators and the administered, and to cut the democratic linkages which the commune's electoral processes provide between the rural masses and the level of the state with which they come most closely into contact.

Such a change would further the obliteration of the Maoist reliance on mass initiative and support which the Dengist leadership is carrying out. An early expression of the under-lying sense that people can be relied upon only when they are disciplined, and discipline is a function of reward and coercion, not commitment, may be seen in the methods used to drive home the party's decision that the "four modernisations" require a severe and immediate reduction in the birth-rate. Whereas previously the motto was, in effect, "two children good, one child better", now it is "only one child allowed". The commune has instituted a severe, even punitive array of what are in effect fines against such couples as intend, or slip, into adding a second child. There is no suggestion that this new approach has the expressed approval of the commune membership, far less that it is an expression of lower-level initiative: the policy has been handed down from the top, and the rigour of its implementation is suggestive rather of the lack of enthusiasm for it in the commune than the opposite.

Through most of the 1970s the exemplar of Dazhai had appeared a live factor in the development strategy of Chang Ching commune. Not only was the Dazhai method of work-point allocation in general use among the production teams, but the commune as a unit and separate brigades within it would engage themselves in construction or land-reclamation projects in the name of "Learning from Dazhai", linked in a comprehensive ten-year development plan worked out at commune level, in consultation with the brigades and with the cooperation of administrative levels above the commune. As the sense of what this impoverished and famine-prone area outside Suzhou had been before Liberation faded, the sense of what it was to become took on tangibility. Plans had been made for construction of new housing centres at brigade level, and for raising the level of account to brigade, unit by unit and gradually, over a fairly prolonged period. With the steady and accelerating expansion of the industrial sector at commune-level generating an ever-increasing proportion of commune income, the prospect of ultimately making the commune as a whole the unit of account, though still very distant — perhaps a generation away — was more than theoretical. That whole movement has now been annulled, and the sense of direction and momentum it gave has been dissipated. Commune members' expressed sense of the future has become one-dimensional, visualised in terms only of cash income and consumer commodities.

Citation of findings in a single commune appear to take to the extreme the foreign observer's practice of generalising from a very narrow base. But experience of Chang Ching People's Commune through the 1970s indicated that as an organisation it was closely and quickly responsive to shifts in the line of the CCP, and the marked and striking changes evident there by mid-1980 are all in keeping with the changes in rural policy made explicit in the Chinese press.

Central to the change of line has been the handling of the Dazhai model, for so long the emblem and prime exemplar of the Maoist approach to development. Immediately after the Praetorian coup d'état which followed Mao's death, the Dazhai leadership associated itself with the attacks on the "Gang of Four", and made their own contributions to the official anthology of horror stories about Chiang Ching. That "me too-ism", and no doubt more significantly the fact that Hua Guofeng, before he turned his coat, was personally linked to the "learn from Dazhai" campaign in its enlarged last phase, may have served to protect the Dazhai brigade and its leadership for some time — Chen Yongkuei outlasted others identified as "whateverists" (Maoists) among vice-premiers. But the Dazhai model, which had originally been singled out precisely to stand as the politico-economic antithesis of the Liuist or capitalist-road policy line for which Deng Xiaoping stood and — "unrepentant" — stands, could not be left intact as an implicit alternative to the party's reversal. At first, Dazhai was simply left unmentioned, and alternative models advanced — for example, the brigade of a state farm in Heilongjiang which was given, so to speak, a credit card with which lavishly to equip itself with the latest heavy farm machinery from John Deere Ltd, USA, thus to demonstrate the truism that mechanisation increases productivity *per capita*. Canards about Chen Yongkuei himself surfaced in Hongkong journals with links to the Beijing leadership: it was reported that far from being an illiterate poor peasant in origin he was in fact a repressive landlord, who had passed himself off as a poor peasant and over time wormed his way into the leadership. The next step was foreseeable, because unoriginal. The charges of falsification of production data, levelled against Dazhai brigade in the early 1960s, were refurbished and brought again. In the 1960s they had been shown to be framed charges, serving political necessity: the necessity is the same now, and there seems no reason to doubt that the charges are as false now as they were shown to be then. It would take another, and inevitably convulsive, change of line in China for the charges against Dazhai to be examined there, meanwhile they stand as in effect sentences, and are accepted in even specialist circles in the West as "disclosures" rather than being seen as allegations.

The change of line in China demanded the repudiation of the Dazhai model, and tactical considerations required that this be achieved via gradual relegation. Dazhai was always a political model, and the campaign in its name expressed in essence the heart of Mao's development strategy, with its crucial emphasis upon human consciousness. Mao's approach premised the need to increase, and continue to increase, production and to use a part of that increase immediately and tangibly to improve living standards; but it made the end and purpose of the process not only production/ consumption, not industrialisation or modernisation, but the fulfilment of social needs and the consolidation of socialism, perceived as a new social order, just, equal and humanly creative. "Politics in command" was the slogan to express that order of priorities, and its operative clause lay in Mao's injunction, "Never forget class struggle" – and the sense of a reversal in China reaching beyond policy to ideology finds perhaps its most clamant expression to date in the Dengists' call for an armistice in the "class struggle".

The concept of "class struggle" can be seen to have grown through changes of emphasis and direction of thrust throughout the post-Liberation period. It began as the watchword for vigilance against the powerful residuum of classes dominant in the old order, which revolution had dispossessed of property and power; it developed into campaigns against the patterns of thought and social attitudes which the old order had bequeathed to the new; and it became in addition, in the Cultural Revolution, an identification of and challenge to those bureaucratic elements in the new society, with potential allies in the intelligentsia, whose demand for privilege and status would, if not curbed, transform them into a stratum and ultimately, especially through their monopolisation of higher education, into a class – a "new bourgeoisie". "Class struggle" in those different senses was implicit in the Dazhai model, making up a key element of its ideological burden.

To call off class struggle in every sense, the Dengist leadership has declared that its time is past. The historical period of great and turbulent class struggle is over; while the concept should not be wholly forgotten, there are dangers in "over-estimating the gravity of the class-struggle in the socialist period" and "we should not go in artificially for class struggle".[15] The purport of such admonitions can only be to soothe disquiet and tranquillise resentment aroused by the reemergence of privilege and status, not now as socially disapproved aberrations but as a necessary and accepted toll for the "four modernisations". *Animal Farm* makes now an inescapable reference in China; it is as if the Chinese had written an additional penultimate chapter, beginning in revolutionary triumph with the Cultural Revolution, concluding with the second restoration of Deng Xiaoping — and leaving the book's ending, at least for the present, sadly unchanged. And the incident in which the pigs, *Animal Farm's* new bourgeoisie, added the nullifying clause (". . . but some are more equal than others") to their revolutionary maxims finds an evocative parallel in this qualifying-out of Mao's "Never forget class struggle" with: "But don't remember it either".

IV EDUCATION

12

NEW DIRECTIONS IN EDUCATIONAL POLICY

John Gardner

*Department of Politics,
University of Manchester, Manchester*

Introduction

On 1 December 1980, *People's Daily* published a major editorial entitled "The Whole Party and Nation should attach great importance to education".[1] In vigorously affirming the key role that education must play in promoting "socialist democracy" it had an uncompromisingly contemporary ring to it. In asserting that "a developed educational front has a tremendous impact on production" it echoed a belief held by Chinese reformers from the middle of the nineteenth century onwards. And in insisting that education was essential for "a high degree of civilisation" it linked itself to the ancient Confucian Tradition.

Given the central role accorded to education throughout most of China's recorded history it is scarcely surprising that the educational arena should have been a major battleground (arguably *the* major battleground) in the Cultural Revolution. Insofar as that movement arose out of bitter disagreements over development strategy, education was commonly regarded as a key issue. Many of those involved in the battle, from commanders-in-chief to "poor bloody infantry", had educational connections. If one dares reduce the struggle to a simple "Left-Right" dichotomy, it may be noted that middle school or university students provided the backbone of the Red Guards, and that they were led and encouraged by Leftist *literati*. Similarly, their opponents were often members of the academic and cultural "Establishment".

In the Cultural Revolution decade (1966-76) the radicals were generally in the ascendant. In 1972 and again in 1975 more conservative leaders, headed by Zhou Enlai, did seek at least a partial return to the policies prevailing up to 1966. But these attempts were beaten back and, on the whole, a "Revolution in Education" was implemented.

In evaluating this one must, as usual, distinguish between aspiration and reality, between propaganda and fact. The published statements of the radicals were by no means ignoble, even to those who would reject them. *Inter alia* they claimed to be distributing educational resources more equitably, both on a geographical and class basis, by providing elementary education for the many rather than advanced education for the fortunate few. They emphasised vocational training and "learning by doing" and advocated flexibility by establishing educational institutions of many different forms. They proposed more democratic management of schools and universities by the involvement of laymen. Even their insistence on a high degree of politicisation in a society which had always stressed the importance of "correct" thinking, made a certain amount of sense when presented in terms of inculcating a spirit of selflessness along the lines of Mao's celebrated injunction "Serve the People". Many foreign visitors had little difficulty in finding Western parallels such as "sandwich courses", "positive discrimination", "community power" and "education for life".

The problem was, as subsequent official admissions made clear (and *émigré* testimony has confirmed), that high ideals were all too rarely implemented. The desire to educate and elevate "the masses" frequently degenerated into the crudest forms of anti-intellectualism and "levelling down". The acquisition of a high degree of skill was regarded as a contemptible ambition and those who had it were branded as "stinking intellectuals". Practical work sometimes became a substitute for formal instruction instead of a complement to it. "Democratisation" often simply replaced the authoritarianism of experts with the despotism of the ignorant, the tyranny of the teacher with mob rule in the classroom. Politicisation stifled intellectual creativity and led to widespread intimidation and demoralisation. According to the official indictment of the "Gang of Four" no less than 142,000 cadres and teachers under the Ministry of Education were falsely accused and persecuted during these years.²

Before Mao's death a number of educators were arguing that the "Revolution in Education" had gone badly awry and was causing enormous damage. In particular this message was spelled out on a number of occasions in 1975 by Zhou Rongxin who, as China's first Minister of Education since the Cultural Revolution, was in a position to know.³ But the radicals prevailed for the simple reason that they could claim Mao's support. It is undoubtedly true that the "Revolution in Education" had been engendered by a number of iconoclastic utterances made by Mao from 1964 onwards.⁴ His position on educational matters in the 1970s and his relations with the radicals in the last years of his life remains open to debate. It may be, as his successors have claimed, that the Gang of Four had crudely distorted his instructions on education as on other matters and that the Chairman had criticised them for this on a number of occasions. If so, it is unfortunate that his views were not more widely circulated at the time. Until September 1976 the Gang continued to speak in his name and those who challenged them received short shrift.

"Reversing Verdicts"

The fundamental fragility of the radicals' position was revealed within a month of Mao's death. At the time of the Gang of Four's arrest, steps were taken to remove from office (and often to arrest) their most prominent supporters in the field of education. Chi Qun, who was the Gang's *de facto* Minister of Education, was an early victim of the new regime. A soldier of limited education, Chi had entered academic life by way of a propaganda team sent into Tsinghua University in 1968. There he subsequently became a Vice-Chairman of the university's revolutionary committee and the key figure behind a "mass criticism group" established jointly by Tsinghua and Beida which served as a principal propaganda vehicle of the Gang. In November 1975 he had masterminded a campaign of vilification against Zhou Rongxin, accusing him of fanning a "Right Deviationist Wind" in education circles. Chi's harrassment of Zhou allegedly caused the latter's untimely death of a heart attack in April 1976.⁵

Xie Jingyi, a Vice-Chairman of both Tsinghua and Beida revolutionary committees, a close confidante of Chi, and the radicals' most senior "female follower" in educational circles, was also arrested. In Liaoning, Mao Yuanxin also disappeared from view. As Mao Zedong's nephew, Yuanxin had been the recipient of several of his uncle's statements on education and, having risen to prominence in the Cultural Revolution, had been a principal advocate of the "Revolution in Education" in North-East China.[6] The purge of the Gang's followers in Shanghai also removed a number of people who had been active in educational work.

The removal of Leftist educational leaders was accompanied and followed by a plethora of attacks on their policies. By the end of November 1976 a "Mass Criticism Group" under the Ministry of Education was active.[7] Thereafter articles began to appear under the pen-name of "Yuan Ding". A homonym for "Gardener", this was chosen in honour of a Hunanese opera, "The Song of the Gardeners". First produced in 1972, this dealt with the attempts of two teachers to persuade a naughty pupil to study hard. One had used coercive methods, but the second had used persuasion and tact and had been successful. Jiang Qing had suppressed the opera on the grounds that the second teacher was just as bad as the first, but was more subtle in cultivating a revisionist seedling. Now, "Yuan Ding" signalled, the gardeners would be out in force.[8]

A popular target of the critics were the "models", both human and institutional, so beloved of the Gang of Four. Of these the most famous was Zhang Tiesheng. In 1973 Zhang had attempted to enter college to study veterinary science. As the story was originally told, Zhang was infuriated to find that he was expected to take a difficult academic entrance examination for which he was unprepared as he had devoted five years since leaving school to agricultural work. He duly used his answer book to write a spirited letter to the authorities, arguing that his commitment to production and his political purity made him better qualified than the "college fanatics" who had neglected their duties to prepare for the examination. Zhang's case was taken up by the radicals who praised him as a "hero in going against the tide". He was admitted to college and offered to the nation's youth as a model for emulation, and subsequently enjoyed a brief spell as a spokesman for young people.

In December 1976, however, Zhang was branded as a "new-born counter-revolutionary clown" by no less a critic than Hua Guofeng. Thereafter a revised version of his examination "answer" was published. According to this Zhang had, in fact, attempted the examination but, having done abysmally, resorted to his unprincipled appeal. Further attacks chronicled his alleged incompetence as a veterinary student, carrying the implied message that nothing else could be expected when academic criteria were ignored.[9]

Another "model" to come under fire was Huang Shuai. As a primary school pupil in Peking in 1973, Huang had been inspired by

Zhang and other "rebels" and had provided her teacher with a comprehensive list of his shortcomings. In response the teacher subjected her to "persecution" whereupon she took her case to the newspapers and, in turn, was espoused by the radicals for her shining example in courageously fighting against authoritarian attitudes in the classroom. Because of her extreme youth she was not, of course, held to be responsible for her actions but was merely presented as a "dupe" of Xie Jingyi and Chi Qun who had cynically used her to undermine "revolutionary discipline" in the schools.[10]

The "Mazhenfu Commune Middle School Incident" was also subjected to a drastic reinterpretation. This concerned the tragic death of a young girl in 1973. Chi Qun, who investigated the incident, had in 1974 propagated a version of events by means of tape recordings played to educational gatherings. According to these the girl had been savagely criticised by her teachers because of her inability to learn English and had been driven to suicide. This harrowing tale was used by the radicals as an effective means of resisting attempts to restore a measure of authority to the teaching profession.

By late 1977, however, another version of the tale was being told. This presented the girl as a victim of the Gang of Four under whose pernicious influence she had come to believe that "study is useless". She flunked most of her examinations and, on an English test paper, wrote: "I am Chinese. Why should I study a foreign language? Without learning A B C D I can still be a [revolutionary] successor". She was criticised for her attitude and drowned herself. According to this version, the teachers concerned had "failed to handle adequately a student with shortcomings and mistaken ideas" but their mistakes were merely "in the methods of work and style of work". The radicals had been completely unjustified in having them arrested and in using the case to promote "anarchism".[11]

Of the institutional models attacked, the best known was the Chaoyang Agricultural College in Liaoning. Created in the Cultural Revolution in response to Mao's call that agricultural colleges should be based in the countryside, Chaoyang concentrated on providing short-term, low-level courses for students of little academic background, who subsequently returned to their production units to apply their new-found skills.

What aroused the ire of many Chinese educators was not so much what Chaoyang was doing, as the insistence that it be emulated by all and sundry. For in late 1974, Mao Yuanxin and Chi Qun held a conference on "Learning from Chaoyang" at which it was launched as a national model.

This was resented for two reasons. First, there were other institutions which had been established much longer and were believed to be better: in particular, there was the Kiangsi Communist Labour University set up in 1958. The "Chaoyang experience" was regarded as an attempt by the radicals to "up stage" a superior model for which they could not claim the credit. Second, it was held to be of little relevance to the major universities which were, nevertheless, required to send delegations on pilgrimage to Chaoyang in order to learn from its example. Consequently, in 1977, the college's deficiencies were discussed in exquisite detail in the press and university journals.[12]

In some instances institutions which had been praised in the Cultural Revolution were themselves active in denouncing their role in it. The famed "July 21st University" of the Shanghai Machine Tools Plant, for example, complained of "sabotage" by the Gang of Four. Tongji University, which had been much lauded for combining formal teaching with practical work, similarly claimed that there the Gang had "peddled Dewey's trashy doctrine of pragmatic education, undermined the unity of theory and practice and negated the practice of systematically learning theories".[13]

Although the major attacks on Leftist models came in 1977, the post-Mao leadership continued to seek out new "negative examples" whenever it deemed it appropriate. Thus, as recently as November 1980, the "educational experience" of Dazhai was refuted. In its schools Dazhai had proclaimed a policy of encouraging "good thought" rather than academic achievement, teaching pupils to be assertive rather than "little lambs", and insisting that peasants rather than "bourgeois intellectuals" be in control. However, it was claimed, the slogan "In Education, Learn From Dazhai" did enormous harm. It caused the cultural and scientific knowledge of the younger generation to decline to a "shocking extent" and "large numbers of illiterate thugs emerged".[14]

Critics of the "Revolution in Education" initially faced great difficulties in attacking it without being too disparaging of Mao and the Cultural Revolution in general. One popular stratagem was to select from his pre-Cultural Revolution writings those "balanced" passages in which the Chairman had praised intellectuals, called for the setting up of high academic and scientific standards, and urged that "book knowledge" had an honourable place. Another was to quote from previously unpublished material relating to the 1970s. Thus it was claimed that Mao had seen "The Song of the Gardeners" and had approved of it. More importantly, it was said that he had taken exception to the "two evaluations". This referred to the

National Educational Work Conference held in the spring of 1971 with minimal publicity. At the conference Chi Qun had advanced the theses that in the seventeen years before 1966 Mao's educational line was not implemented and that most of the students graduating in that period had become underminers of socialism. In 1977, however, it was claimed that Mao had angrily "refuted" the "two evaluations". Moreover, it was added, he had generally approved of the "Sixty Regulations on Higher Education". These had been drawn up in the early Sixties, supposedly under the direction of Liu Shaoqi, and were designed to impose rigorous academic standards in the tertiary sector. In the early years of the Cultural Revolution they had been attacked by the radicals as the quintessence of elitism.[15]

Attempts were also made to reinterpret Mao's more extreme Cultural Revolution utterances. A notable case here concerned his "May 7 Directive" of 1966 to Lin Piao in which he had railed against "bourgeois intellectuals' domination" in the schools. In 1977 it was explained that Mao had, of course, only been referring to a small minority of institutions.[16]

A further development came in November 1979, when the Ministry of Education convened a conference to discuss Mao's educational thought. This not only presented his views in a moderate light but also diminished his part in formulating them. His educational thought, it was said, "did not fall from the sky". Rather "it was the crystallisation of the hard work of our educational workers".[17]

Ultimately, the problem was subsumed under more general political changes. The steadily growing power of Deng Xiaoping and the corresponding decline in the fortunes of Hua Guofeng was accompanied, from 1978 onwards, by an increasing willingness to criticise the Cultural Revolution and Mao himself. By the beginning of 1979 Chinese educators openly referred to the "Revolution in Education" as "ten wasted years". In December 1980, Hu Yaobang, Party General Secretary, stated that "It is the unanimous view of our Party that the decade between 1966 and 1976 . . . was a period of catastrophe. Nothing was correct or positive . . . The whole thing was negative."[18] Education was among the disaster areas he specified.

And finally hard facts were paraded to show the damage that had been done. The press was filled with sad articles rehabilitating, often posthumously, distinguished intellectuals and educational administrators who had suffered in the Cultural Revolution. Scholars and scientists published bitter diatribes detailing the wholesale closure of research institutes and the destruction of research programmes. Statistics were also utilised. These showed that as a result of the Cultural Revolution China had "lost" over a million university and college graduates. More damning, in view of the radicals' supposed commitment to basic education for all, was the admission in December 1979 that there were still over 120 million illiterates under the age of forty-five.[19] By 1980, therefore, the "Revolution in Education" had been thoroughly condemned. We can now turn our attention to what has replaced it.

Education in the Post-Mao Era

The purge of the Gang's supporters was accompanied by a series of new appointments at all levels of educational work, and a shift in power in favour of the professionally qualified. The post of Minister of Education, vacant since the death of Zhou Rongxin in April 1976, was filled by Liu Xiyao at an unspecified date towards the end of the year. A member of the Central Committee, Liu had held a series of senior appointments in scientific, educational and economic work before the Cultural Revolution. Unusually, for a cadre of his background, he appears to have gone through the upheavals of the late Sixties relatively unscathed and, from 1972 to 1975, was leader of the "Science and Education Group under the State Council". His ability to survive the policy switches of the period suggests that he was not only a skilled politician but that he was perhaps regarded more as an efficient administrator than as a formulator of policy. This is further borne out by the fact that he made only one ministerial speech of significance. This was a report to the National Conference on Educational Work held in April 1978,[20] by which time it had become clear that the driving force behind educational changes was Deng Xiaoping.

As early as March 1977, Deng's 1977 report on the Academy of Sciences (which had criticised the Gang's science policy in terms analogous to Zhou Rongxin's strictures on education) had been transformed from a "poisonous weed" into a "fragrant flower".[21] Although not formally rehabilitated until July 1977, there is reason to believe that Deng had assumed special responsibilities for scientific and educational work somewhat earlier. In July he addressed a forum of intellectuals and, one Western visitor was reliably informed, this was a turning point in persuading the academic community that it was safe to reject completely radicalism in educational affairs. Thereafter, Deng's increasing challenge to Hua was based partly on his appeals to the scientific and academic "constituency". When a gigantic National Science Conference was held in March 1978, it was Deng's speech which drew the greatest applause and not Hua Guofeng's, despite earlier attempts by the latter to claim that he had been the moving spirit behind the proposed reforms of 1975. In April, Deng's address to the Education Conference was published immediately. The press did not find space for Liu Xiyao's until almost two months later.

In February 1979, Liu was replaced as Minister by Jiang Nanxiang. This was in no sense a demotion for Liu, who was given another senior post. But Jiang's elevation indicated vividly that Deng was achieving success in restoring to office the cadres who had directed education before 1966. Jiang had been a long-serving principal of the celebrated Tsinghua University, and had also held the post of Minister of Higher Education. At the start of the Cultural Revolution he was seen by the Red Guards as the epitome of a "capitalist roader" in the educational field, and he was reviled for his commitment to maintain Tsinghua as a centre of excellence and to keep Higher Education as the preserve of "intellectual aristocrats". Unchastened by his experiences and unimpressed by the "Revolution in Education", in the mid-Seventies he had spoken out with a frankness worthy of Deng. Referring to the tertiary sector he scathingly observed on one occasion, "it may say 'university' on the signboard, but it is only teaching a middle school curriculum to students of primary school level".

His ministerial appointment was followed later in 1979 by his election to the Central Committee. By that time a proliferation of appointments at deputy minister level had restored to office many of those dismissed in the Cultural Revolution including some like Li Qi, who had spent much of that period under various forms of imprisonment. At university level many of the Party secretaries, principals and deputy principals of 1966 reappeared either in their old jobs or, like Lu Ping of Beida (who had had the dubious distinction of being the target of the first major wallposter of the Cultural Revolution) in roughly comparable positions.

This trend percolated through the educational hierarchy. In the universities revolutionary committees were disbanded and the "propaganda teams" of soldiers and workers, sent into the campuses in the Cultural Revolution, were sent on their way with the message that their "historic task" had been accomplished. Authority was restored to the "professionals" for, although the Party remained firmly in control, it chose to remain in the background and give intellectuals considerable leeway in restoring standards.

It should be noted that this restoration of professional control (which was also evident in the Academy of Sciences) could frequently be equated with giving power to people who were relatively old. By 1979 it was quite common for foreign visitors to meet Chinese scholars of advanced years who would cheerfully admit to ill-health and infirmity, but who had been urged to stay at their posts, (and in some cases had been ordered to come out of retirement), until the damage caused by the "Revolution in Education" had been put right and a new generation of scholars trained. Younger people, appointed and advanced in the Cultural Revolution, were not necessarily dismissed. They were, however, widely regarded by their superiors as being academically incompetent, were often deprived of the right to teach, and were expected to undergo lengthy training to raise their academic level.

A similar pattern emerged in the schools. Education Bureaux below the Ministry regained the powers they had exercised before the Cultural Revolution, particularly with reference to determining the curriculum and the right to hire and fire teachers. Teachers who had become "detached" from their schools, either by having been sent to the "production front" or by having fled their classrooms for more congenial work, were ordered back to their desks. Laymen were moved out of the schools as were some "unqualified" teachers. The need for adequate teacher-training and in-service training was again stressed. As in the early 1960s, campaigns were mounted to raise the status of teachers among the general population as well as among pupils. Even the message of childrens' comics changed in this respect. In place of the rebellious Huang Shuais of the mid-1970s, cartoon strips showed naughty children becoming models of good behaviour under the patient ministrations of wise and kindly teachers. The most famous model soldier of the 1960s reappeared as "Uncle" Lei Feng, a hard-working pupil who did as he was told.[22]

In institutional terms the post-Mao leadership sought rigorously to rebuild and expand at the higher levels. A principal beneficiary of the new policy was academic research which, on the Soviet model, was largely confined to specialised institutes separate from the universities. Thus the Academy of Sciences was restored to its former eminence. In 1973 it had been reduced to a body controlling only fifty-three research institutes with 13,000 scientific and technological workers. After the convening of the National Science Conference in March 1978, however, it was encouraged to develop at a remarkable rate. By 1980 it possessed 113 research institutes with over 36,000 scientific and technical workers. It ran four universities and had reintroduced postgraduate training programmes. In

1977 the Academy had also spawned a separate Academy of Social Sciences to cater for the whole range of the Humanities. By 1979 twenty-one institutes were active, of which several dealing with different branches of economics were the most pre-eminent.[23]

The university and college sector also grew remarkably as a number of institutions closed down in the Cultural Revolution were reopened and new ones were established. In 1976 there were approximately 400 colleges and universities; by 1979 there were 598. Student numbers increased at an even faster rate, from "about" 500,000 in 1976 to 850,000 in 1979.[24]

At lower levels, however, the situation was rather different. Secondary school provision had increased dramatically from just over 14,400,000 enrolments in 1965 to 46,000,000 in 1976. A further increase took enrolments to nearly 69,000,000 in 1978. But after that the press began to publish articles claiming that attempts to provide *general* secondary schooling on a massive scale had been wasteful of scarce resources and that they should stop. At primary level enrolments actually declined from a peak of 150,000,000 in 1977 to 140,000,000 in 1979.[25]

Various factors were responsible for the slowing down or cessation of growth of the school population. One was demographic in that birth control campaigns were having some success in reducing the primary school age population of some urban areas.[26] Others arose from the new emphasis on quality rather than quantity. This resulted in four developments which, although obviously not designed to weaken general educational provision, clearly did affect it. One was the tendency, especially in the rural areas, to dismiss those teachers whose qualifications were poor or non-existent, even though there was no possibility of replacing them with people of greater skills. A second was that, particularly from 1979 onwards, official encouragement was given to the further development of *technical* middle schools which would provide specialised vocational training for the few at the expense of general schooling for the many. Thirdly, the "streamlining" approach of the Cultural Revolution was rejected in favour of a return to lengthening the period of schooling at all levels from primary upwards. More years in school meant fewer could be accommodated. And fourthly, the "keypoint" concept was revived.[27]

"Keypoint" schools were set up at all levels. Their purpose was to train the most able pupils to a very high standard as speedily as possible, although this pure elitism was presented in terms of these institutions serving as models for emulation by demonstrating what could be achieved. The "keypoints" naturally received a disproportionate share of resources, weakening somewhat the facilities available elsewhere.

The keypoints also illustrated another feature of the new policies: the strong emphasis on competition. Rigorous university entrance examinations were reintroduced in 1977 and were conducted on a unified basis across the nation from the following year onwards.[28] Initially the net was cast widely with the regulations permitting secondary school graduates of the mid-1960s to compete. Very quickly, however, the system reverted to one in which the normal pattern was to progress directly from senior middle school to university. In some instances pupils of outstanding academic ability were allowed into university without having completed the full middle school course, often on the basis of having achieved success in national "talent competitions". Such gifted pupils, and teachers who had obtained good sets of examination results, were officially publicised and praised. Examination and regular testing speedily spread throughout the system, and streaming by ability became standard practice in many schools. In some cases examinations were introduced to determine entry to primary schools.

Curricular reform was another development. Apart from the lengthening of courses mentioned above, the balance of time allotted to different subjects was altered. A major sufferer was political education. It did not disappear entirely and, indeed, lip-service continues to be paid to its importance. (It remains, for example, a compulsory subject in the university entrance examination.) But it was downgraded and ceased to permeate the curriculum. Moreover, its content changed so that it became a means of inculcating attitudes supportive of the "Four Modernisations" rather than "class struggle" and the like. Productive labour also lost its appeal. Although stipulated in various regulations foreign visitors have rarely seen students engaged in it and it seems that the term is now used to cover "project work" which may be a far remove from manual labour. Time devoted to basic subjects, and particularly science, has increased correspondingly.

Curricular reform also involved an attempt to upgrade and standardise teaching materials. In the Cultural Revolution there had been much emphasis on producing materials related to local needs and these were frequently rewritten to take account of changes of line. From 1977 onwards the Ministry of Education began to compile series of textbooks for general use.[29]

In compiling new textbooks China was reported to have shown a keen interest in what was on offer elsewhere in the world, and to have bought copies of foreign science books, particularly from Japan.

Whereas virtually all other educational changes since Mao's death can be seen as a return to, or exaggeration of, policies which were practised in the early 1960s, this is illustrative of a trend which is quite new. For in recent years there has been a willingness to look to the West in a way which has not been seen since the Republican period. Seminars were held on Western educational system and Western specialists were invited to China to "share their experience" with Chinese colleagues.

Most notably, from 1978 onwards there was a dramatic increase in the number of Chinese sent to study in the West and Japan. In November 1980 it was reported that 5,100 students had been sent to forty-five countries over the previous two years. Of these 3,900 were "visiting scholars" undertaking research, 560 were "post-graduate students" and 660 "college students". More than 4,600 of them were studying the natural sciences, while 110 were social scientists and 380 were specialists in foreign languages. Fang Yi, the vice premier with general responsibility for science and education, affirmed the value of "learning from the strong points of other countries" and confirmed that this policy would continue. Interestingly, the official desire for foreign skills was by this time so great that, in addition to those financed by the government, encouragement was also given to privately-financed students. In practice this means that students with wealthy relations in the overseas Chinese community or those whose parents had worked abroad in the past, and established close friendships with foreigners, are now free to call on such resources.[30]

Some Major Problems

The educational changes of the past four years have been welcomed by the Chinese intelligentsia. Teachers at all levels have been given improved status (including, in the tertiary sector, the restoration of academic titles); they have been given more authority; they have also been promised higher salaries and better material conditions.[31] They now operate in an intellectual atmosphere which is far freer than at any time since 1949. They can read foreign books, discuss professional matters at meetings of numerous associations which have sprung up in recent years and, if they are very senior, they can hope for an opportunity to travel abroad. They can expect that their own children will be particularly well-placed to climb the academic ladder by means of a competitive system which, some cynics would suggest, is beginning to resemble the "examination hell" of Imperial China.

It is significant that the "Democracy Wall" phenomenon of 1978-80 was essentially a movement of "little people": no Chinese Sakharov or Solzhenitsyn appeared, and this suggests that the intellectuals are reasonably content because of changes which, five years ago, would have been beyond their wildest dreams. Their satisfaction is no doubt shared by all those who suffered in the Cultural Revolution and who see a technocratic development strategy as the key to prosperity.

Nevertheless, there are groups who do not necessarily share this contentment. These include many young people who received education under the criteria prevailing in the Cultural Revolution and also are now widely regarded as "ignoramuses". A vivid example of a conflict which must run throughout society may be seen in the friction at Beida in 1977-78 between "worker-peasant-soldier" students admitted in the Gang of Four days and the first year admitted under the new entrance examinations, who constituted the intellectual cream of China.[32]

Another reservoir of discontent must be those who aspire to higher education but who are unable to gain admission. For the new system not only benefits the academically gifted, it favours the urban areas where schooling is best and particularly it benefits the children of intellectuals and people of similar "middle class" background. As early as the end of 1978 it was officially recognised that discontent existed. *Red Flag* admitted that "rather more" students were coming from intellectuals' families. It justified this on the grounds that China needed a scientific and technological elite in order to modernise and, therefore, had to admit to university the best qualified. Often these tended to be children from intellectuals' families. This, it was explained, was entirely the fault of the Gang of Four who had reduced the schools to such a shambles that they could not provide decent education. Intellectuals, however, were able to compensate by providing instruction at home and hence their children did well when examinations were brought back.[33]

It is difficult to know how effective such arguments are, especially in view of the policies discussed above which are likely to widen the urban-rural gap and, related to it, the differential distribution of educational facilities among different social classes. In Peking, Shanghai and other major cities children are virtually guaranteed primary education, are almost certain to go on to secondary school and have a reasonable chance of progressing further.[34] By contrast it was reported in 1980 that of the more than 90 per cent of school-age children who attend primary schools, only 60 per cent complete their five-year courses and only 30 per cent of them are able to pass the graduation examinations.[35] Most of these "failures" are obviously peasant children.

The root of such problems is, of course, money. A refreshing development in 1980 was that China began to discuss the financing of education and revealed that, overall, educational expenditure had been extremely low regardless of the educational strategy being pursued at a particular time. The deficiency common to both educational strategies was a tendency to juggle with existing resources rather than increasing the funding.

One newspaper revealed that in 1975 per capita educational expenditure was only US$2.70 in China. This was not only insignificant in terms of spending in the developed countries (US$471.40 in the United States, US$247.70 in Japan) but even lagged behind India (US$3.90).[36] After a visit to several European countries in the autumn of 1979, Jiang Nanxiang reported that the total educational funds in China for that year amounted to 7,011,000,000 *yuan*, while the total number of students was 213,000,000.[37] Hence only 32.80 *yuan* was spent for each student. Educational journals published articles on the consequences of such parsimony. One of these revealed that in Shandong some primary school pupils were not even provided with wooden desks and benches, but had to use desks improvised from mud with stone slabs as seats. These were relatively fortunate in comparison with other pupils in Kiangsu who either had to carry benches with them to school or squat on the floor.[38]

By the end of 1980 the need for increased spending was officially recognised. To conclude with the *People's Daily* editorial with which we began. This attacked those who felt that China was too poor to spend more on education at present. It pointed out that the "Four Modernisations" would be successful only if the importance of "educational construction" were recognised. It blamed the "stupid mistakes" in economic work in the late 1970s on the lack of skilled manpower and the inability to use effectively what was available. It called for an end to wasteful expenditure on grandiose capital construction projects and the diversion of the funds realised to the educational sector. It remains to be seen if the call will be heeded.

13

CONCLUSION

Jack Gray

*Institute of Development Studies,
University of Sussex, Brighton*

New Directions

At the end of 1979, about one thousand Chinese state enterprises were chosen to take part in an experiment in autonomous self-management. By the spring of 1980, the number had trebled. At this point, the State Council called a halt: no more firms should be brought into the experimental programme until more experience had been gained. Yet three months later the number had risen to 6,600, representing 60 per cent of the total output by value of the state-owned manufacturing sector, and 70 per cent of its profits. This demonstrates the momentum which has developed behind the new-course policies.

At the same time as these policies are being rapidly extended to the country as a whole, they are moving further away from both of the twin, rival models of the past — the centralised command economy of the First Five Year Plan, and the mass-mobilisation economy of the Great Leap Forward of 1958 and the Cultural Revolution. In Sichuan, where factory autonomy and the retention of a portion of profits by the enterprise first began, a group of firms has recently been chosen for the further experiment of leaving all profits in the hands of the enterprise, subject to a roughly graduated enterprise "income tax".

At the same time, the transformation of the "companies" (administrative units mediating between ministry and enterprise) into trusts, responsible for their own profits and losses and responding to the market, is proceeding space; and this is accompanied by a defence of Liu Shaoqi's similar policy in 1961.

The new regime's determination to add a market dimension to the economy is nowhere more clearly shown than in the fact that already in two provinces (Guangdong and Henan) the County Economic Commissions, which had only recently replaced the county-level bureaux of the ministries, have now been transformed into enterprises, retaining part of their profits and responsible for their own profits and losses — trusts again in fact, but responsible for the co-ordination not of the production of a particular range of commodities or the supply of a particular range of materials, but of the whole industrial economy of the county community.

The commune itself, operated since 1958 as both an economic unit and an organ of state, is now to have its political powers abolished, and is to become simply an economic enterprise with a trust-like role comparable, though at a lower level, with that of the county economic commission.

The general (though not universal) assumption from now on is to be that enterprises which show a loss will close, or will be merged with more profitable rivals. Firms will compete. The vertical links of central and provincial planning will be reduced in importance, to be partly replaced by horizontal links in the form of freely negotiated inter-enterprise contracts. The powers which the autonomous firms will enjoy include the right to hire and fire; to determine the uses to which retained profits are put; in most instances to fix the selling price of whatever is produced surplus to the requirements of the state plan, the prices being either within a range laid down by the government or freely negotiated with customers; and to retain part of any foreign exchange earned as a result of participation in international trade.

Some quite startling indications of the new commercial atmosphere have been publicised. We find firms which have recruited their managers through open advertisement; "broker" firms which bring together buyers and sellers and offer transport and warehouse facilities — legitimised *blat;* even a construction company set up by former capitalists on funds privately subscribed. In agriculture, the pace of change is comparable. 1980 has seen not only continued and increased encouragement for the rural private sector comprising private plots, privately reclaimed land, and independent handicrafts, along with extended opportunities for private trading in rural fairs. It has also seen the confirmation of the right of the production team to take its own decisions, guided by economic indicators rather than dictated to by administrative cadres. Change, however, has now gone much further. After a variety of local experiments, the organisation of production within the team has been generally changed to a system in which the team leadership ceases to manage farming directly, but instead contracts with team members, as individuals or groups, for the performance of farming tasks.

At first sight there is little in China's new course which is entirely novel. Hungary and Yugoslavia provide the obvious analogies with, if not the actual origins of, many of the new policies. Yet it would be a mistake to suppose that China is merely imitating either or both. So superficial a view of what is happening would neglect the fact that in China the background is quite different. The memories are not the same. The expectations — both hopes and fears — diverge.

There are other obvious differences. The first is the size of China, the variety of local conditions, the unprecedented nature of the self-imposed task of the CCP in attempting not only to rule but to revolutionise a thousand million people. Sheer scale makes almost insoluble (as it has throughout China's history) the problem of maintaining both central control and local initiative.

Second is China's independence of the Soviet Union, which means that Chinese reforms need not move cautiously along the brink of Russian tolerance, but can be as boldly pursued as her leadership may propose and her people may accept.

Third is that the nature of the Chinese economy, and its low levels even now, have been such as to make manifestly irrelevant those two great obsessions of Lenin which compelled him to create a system of centralised authoritarian socialism, in tragic contradiction to his personal commitment to a socialism of democratic communes — namely, his misunderstanding of the economics of American prairie agriculture, and his exaggeration of the economies of scale in European capitalist industry.

Fourth, and most important of all, China's "liberal" reforms do not represent as similar measures have represented elsewhere a simple and direct relaxation of the orthodox planning system. They have come out of a long and bitter struggle between two contrasted alternatives to that orthodox system. These alternatives were referred to in China as "the two roads" — the socialist road and the capitalist road. Some students of China have been sceptical as to their existence, perhaps because the alternatives were so often represented by ideologues both in the west and in China, and both of the right and of the left, as a struggle between good and evil. Scholars are right to regard such demonology with a proper degree of cynicism; but in this case in doing so perhaps they were led to underestimate the degree of polarisation potentially involved. There were indeed two roads, but they were not the narrow road and the primrose path. They were two honest, rationally defensible but apparently irreconcilable views of how to give Chinese socialism a more human face. In the process of struggle, and in the alternative policies each side sought to apply when dominant, China gained a unique breadth of experience. If we remember this, and work on the hypothesis that the new regime is likely to have learned positive as well as negative lessons from former opponents, we will not misjudge what is happening now, and conclude that China has simply copied familiar East European methods. Nor will we conclude that socialist China has simply thrown away her entire past.

At first sight it might seem to be so: Chinese spokesmen sometimes speak as if it were. The time when China's new course could be seen merely as a reaction against the Cultural Revolution is gone. The policies of the Great Leap of 1958-59 were next condemned; and the clean sweep of the past has not stopped even there, but now extends to take in even the years of the First Five Year Plan, that is, to embrace the whole history of Chinese socialist planning, with the partial exception only of a few months in 1956-57 and a few more in 1961-62.

This comprehensive repudiation of the past seems at first a signal sort of perversity on the part of leaders who continue to boast (with not too much exaggeration) that China has enjoyed the highest rate of economic growth in the world. One might think that this was success; but the new leaders point to the fact that the standard of living of the Chinese people has not risen at anything like the same speed. Per capita grain consumption was actually a little less in 1977 than in 1957. In the world league-table of per capita incomes, China is well down, in the hundredth place. In one county in six, agricultural production is said scarcely to have risen at all since 1949, although the population has doubled. The gap between the average income of the urban minority and that of the rural majority is still such as would be considered a scandal in any country, far less in one committed for thirty years to socialism. This, at least, is how the members of the new administration see their situation.

Deng Xiaoping has emphatically stated that the problem is not merely one of management methods or of planning techniques; it is not the economic ministries which have been to blame, said Deng, but the Party centre itself. It is strategy which has been wrong, not tactics.

The Re-Appraisal of the Past

The point in the past to which — as far as the problem is seen in terms of the past — the Party now seeks to return is the occasion of the 8th Congress in 1956, which took place after three months of intensive discussion in the Central Committee of Khrushchev's condemnation of Stalin and — in relation to this — of the strengths and weaknesses of the Russian-type strategy which the Chinese had employed in their first five-year plan. The decisions then taken expressed a firm consensus but it was the last occasion on which the Party spoke with a single voice, for these decisions proved to be open to two very different interpretations. They could be taken to justify a mere relaxation of the existing order; or they could provide the basis of a positive and radical alternative. Briefly, what was decided was to decentralise, to cut down the high investment priority hitherto given to heavy industry, to lower the rate of central accumulation of capital, and to offer more opportunity within and beyond the Party for free criticism and discussion.

Mao Zedong, in the course of the debates of this time, was summing up his own sense of Stalin's errors, China's situation, and the deliberations of the Congress. In two major documents, his speech *On the Correct Handling of Contradictions Among the People,* and his marginal notes to Stalin's *Economic Problems of Socialism in the USSR,* he produced a number of propositions which were soon to form the basis of the left-wing policies of the Great Leap Forward and of the Cultural Revolution. These policies are now condemned; but the propositions themselves are still accepted as valid theory, and we will not understand the new course unless we appreciate that this is so.

The first proposition was that the Russians had maintained too high a rate of accumulation — they "drained the pond to catch the fish".

The second was that Stalin's order of sectoral priorities was the reverse of the proper order. Stalin sacrificed investment in light industry and in agriculture to heavy industry and so, by leaving the population — especially the rural population — with incomes little above subsistence, and very little in the way of consumer goods on which they might spend what they had, actually prejudiced the growth of heavy industry itself. Mao called for a new order of priorities: agriculture first, then light industry, and heavy industry last. "If you really want heavy industry to develop, you should concentrate your resources on agriculture and light industry."

The third was that the primary motive force of development in a poor country is not capital accumulation, but the increase of mass purchasing power. Of all Mao's contributions to the theory and practice of Marxist socialism, this denial of the central role of accumulation, this insistence on the primary importance of stimulating demand, is the most radical. It strikes at the roots of Preobrazhensky's monstrous advocacy of "objective feudalism" on which Stalin's strategy was based. It restores the common-sense view that the best way to make people better off is to make them better off, not to make them worse off.

The fourth was that Stalin had neglected individual incentives and over-emphasised collective incentives, failing to appreciate the necessity of careful handling of the conflicts between the individual's interest as a consumer, as a member of a collectivity, and as a citizen of the state.

The fifth was that Stalin had carried out the revolution from the top and by coercion. He did not allow the masses to participate in development, and so failed to engage the most powerful force for change — the energies of a committed people.

The sixth was that Stalin was mistaken in asserting that socialist society is harmonious; on the contrary, argued Mao, differences of experience, viewpoint, and interests continue to exist, and therefore conflict among the people is inevitable. By the same token, there will inevitably be conflict between the people and the socialist state. Moreover, such conflict is healthy; it is the drive to resolve such conflicts that impels the revolution forward.

The seventh was that at China's economic levels, which were even lower than those of Russia in 1917, the market must play a greater part in socialist development than in the Soviet Union; more precisely, many producers' goods as well as consumers' goods must be bought and sold rather than allocated.

The Great Leap Forward was meant to express Mao's alternative strategy based on these propositions. Limits were set to capital accumulation at the Centre, and instead the villages were encouraged, by holding out to them the prospect of rapid, democratic self-development, to accumulate and invest for themselves. They could establish their own simple appropriate-technology industries, and use the profits to revolutionise agriculture. The consequent improvement of agriculture would rapidly increase the purchasing power of the peasants, and feed an accelerating process of economic growth. Creating new resources for and through agricultural and industrial change, the peasants would directly and indirectly create a market for producers' goods; they would buy for themselves (as collectives) new means of production, and in doing so they would drive heavy industry forward. The democratic organisation of grass-roots development would maximise participation; and it would by the same token reveal to the people the true relationships of individual, collective and state interests.

The Great Leap was for the most part a dismal and demoralising failure. There were many specific reasons, but they can be subsumed under two. Politically, it was impossible to maintain the necessary democratic basis when the only instrument of leadership available was a party whose power was subject to no check: who troubles to persuade when he can command? Economically, the new concept of planning, by which the provincial and central authorities would simply respond to the needs generated by grass-roots initiative, was overwhelmed by the force of existing habits: what happened instead was that central, authoritarian, material-balance planning was driven right down into the grass roots, and resources recklessly re-allocated among individuals and collectives as if these resources were the property of the state.

Mao was the first, as Deng Xiaoping has himself stressed, to see what had gone wrong. He roundly condemned it as "banditry", and defended the right of the peasants to resist. At the same time, however, he insisted that the Great Leap should not be abandoned. And it was at this point that the Party split. It has remained split ever since. There are those whose image of the Leap is of the first great inspiring wave of mass enthusiasm, and those who remember only the desperate and often brutal efforts used to continue it in the face of chaos, hunger, defeat and demoralisation; and the latter are in the great majority.

Thus Mao's plan for a non-bureaucratic socialist alternative failed and could not easily be revived in the face of the bitter hostility which the disasters of the Leap had generated at every level of society. Mao soon began to see, in the restoration of elite control which followed, the Party-state bureaucracy itself as the main obstacle to his own sort of popular revolution. In 1965 he launched the Cultural Revolution to re-open the way to democratic socialism as he conceived it. However, insofar as the Cultural Revolution resurrected the strategy of 1958, it also re-enacted some of its excesses, and added to them the experience of ten years of factional strife. To the tragic irony of one great movement whose aims were democratic but which ended in tyranny was added another of the same.

Yet those experiences are not regarded in China as having been wholly without value. Polemics against the Gang of Four are one thing; sober consideration of all possible alternatives within socialism is another, and in this latter context spokesmen of the regime emphasise in discussing "China's own experience" the value of a good deal which is actually drawn from the years of left-wing dominance.

Broadly speaking, there are three forms of organisation which are possible. The first is orthodox, central, near-total material-balance planning. This has been rejected by all parties since 1956. China is too large and too varied and her transport and communications system too undeveloped while her economy — low as its levels still remain — is already sophisticated enough to be producing twenty to thirty million different commodities. No conceivable system of central planning could cope with such a task.

The second alternative — the Great Leap alternative — is to decentralise to enterprises and communities, but to keep the system of non-market allocation, with the various levels accumulating funds locally and investing them autonomously. In theory, the process was subject to direct or nearly direct popular control, which should have prevented both authoritarian abuses and the wasteful use of resources. In practice, it prevented neither. The gross imbalances and the gross waste of investment funds made the system economically unsustainable, while the dictatorial mode of management was in the long run politically intolerable.

The third possibility is to maintain decentralisation to the enterprises and the communities, but while giving them freedom to make their own decisions, at the same time imposing on them — through the new market dimension of the economy — the responsibility for economic success or failure.

The Gang of Four chose to revive the Great-Leap model of localised allocation, but to try to make good in practice the democratic assumptions on which it was theoretically based, by subjecting local Party leaders to popular control through the Revolutionary Committees. This was an attractive solution but the radicals were defeated and their solution discredited. Yet a considerable element of it remains in use, as we shall see, in the new-course policies.

New Policies on Old Premises

Before attempting to characterise this new course, one should recall Deng Xiaoping's insistence that past mistakes have been a question of wrong strategy rather than wrong tactics — a failure on the part of the Party centre to enforce the proper priorities, rather than a mere failure of managerial implementation. This theory, however, is not altogether valid. The strategy had been changed by 1956, yet the dismaying fact is that almost nothing of what was advocated by Mao, agreed at the 8th Congress in 1956, and not disputed thereafter, was ever honoured in policy-making. The priorities in practice did not change. The rate of accumulation did not fall; on the contrary, it rose to 36.6 per cent – a very large burden for a people the majority of whom are still little above subsistence level. Agriculture was at no time given its promised priority. The proportion of investment going into light industry actually decreased over the successive five-year plans, while heavy industry still received the bulk of investment. Worse, a substantial part of the product of heavy industry was devoted to the further development of heavy industry itself; and even in the light industry sector, about 40 per cent of output consisted of new means of production rather than of consumers' goods.

It is now clear that nothing else could have happened, given a system of decentralised but still authoritarian allocation of resources, which was operated by cadres who had internalised Stalinist assumptions. Through these they could rationalise the enhancement of their own power and status by expanding their control over means of production, and so the situation was predictable. The Party had built a sprawling, localised apparatus of accumulation which was largely out of control. If one considers the system in terms of the possible creation of a new, post-revolutionary ruling class, one must give weight not only to the central bureaucratic and technocratic apparatus favoured by the "right", but also to the uncontrolled decentralisation of authority to local cadres which was perpetrated (though in spite of, rather than in pursuance of, their theoretical aims) by the "left". We are back, ironically, to a very old Chinese political issue: which is more liable to abuse authority, the class of great national officials, or the class of local power-holders? Gu Yanwu would be quite at home with the problem.

It is not enough, however, to discuss the new policies as separate alternative strategies, for there are substantial overlaps. In terms of Mao's 1956-58 theories, there is quite clearly considerable continuity. If we refer back to the seven points in which we have summarised Mao's strategy, this is clear. The rate of accumulation is to be cut from its recent peak of 36.6 per cent to about 25 per cent. Agriculture is at last to be given real priority. The idea of development driven by increased purchasing power rather than by capital accumulation – Mao's most significant break with socialist orthodoxy — has now been taken up with vigour and conviction. The cultural-revolution denial of the need for material incentives — the most obvious of the left's deviations from Mao's own ideas — has been reversed, as indeed it must be if consumption is to be the motor of economic growth. Producers' goods are now to be largely treated as commodities. The new guarantee of the rights of the local communities to make their own economic decisions without bureaucratic or Party interference, the continued encouragement of commune and brigade enterprise, and the mounting campaign to make a reality of workers' control and the election of managers, are good earnest that however strongly the new regime insists on the need for professional management, it regards the maximisation of participation as fundamental. It has repeatedly gone on record with the view that autonomy of the enterprise is inseparable from and unacceptable without workers' control. The features which are most characteristic of Chinese socialist theory — many of which are now for the first time being put into effective practice — are still mostly Maoist.

This raises the interesting question, whether there can be such a thing as "market Maoism". Mao certainly believed that the market would have to play a greater role in China than in the Soviet Union; the argument which underlay this assertion was that China would be obliged to develop commodity production to a far higher level before full socialism (defined as full public ownership of the major means of production) could be contemplated. At no time did Mao ever condemn the continuation of a private sector of agriculture; indeed he once stated, in the jocular style with which he sometimes emphasised serious points: "What's wrong with a little capitalism? Life would be pretty dull without it! I'm prepared to grab a rifle and go out and fight for their right to indulge in a little capitalism!" However, the issue of "market socialism" of the kind which China has now to a significant extent adopted did not seriously arise in Mao's lifetime, and his attitude was thus never tested. We do not know what his reply would have been had a Yugoslav, such as Vanek, put to him the idea that there can be no true self-management without the market because in its absence the theoretically self-managed firm is merely obeying the orders of the bureaucratic planner — or, as at times in China's case, of the Party mass-mobiliser. It is probable that such an argument would be readily entertained by many leaders in Peking today. Although the point has not been explicitly made, it has been stated repeatedly that democracy and the command economy are incompatible, and that China's failure in the past to guarantee democratic rights has been due primarily to the authoritarian and monopolistic nature of her economic system. Proof that these statements are to be taken seriously is to be found in the present campaign, begun at the 5th National People's Congress, to secure the creation of a body of economic law which will guarantee economic rights and protect economic contracts as an essential part of the building of democracy.

One must not exaggerate the changes which have occurred. First, the centre's material-balance plan is still the backbone of the economy; the eight targets for industrial production still stand, and no enterprise, no matter how profitable its total operations may be, can retain any of its profits if it has not first reached these targets. Second, some measures which seem to increase the autonomy of firms, such as the replacement for many purposes of state allocation of funds by loans negotiated with the banks, are actually, in the context of the extreme looseness of past control of investment, a measure of tighter (though it is hoped more discriminating) control. Third, in agriculture although the team now contracts with rather than directly manages the work force, it retains its investment and welfare functions, and it shares very substantially in the profits of the ancillary, quasi-private enterprises of its members, as the state does in the profits of autonomous factories. Fourth, while firms retain a substantial part of profits, on the evidence so far only a very small proportion of these is distributed as personal income in the form of bonuses; by far the greater part is ploughed back in development and expansion, so that in one sense it is only robbing Peter to pay Paul – retained profits replace the state's former allocations of capital – and the new system does not so much reward the successful as penalise the unsuccessful, which is what it is meant to do. Finally, as far as industry is concerned, the state has not committed itself to irreversible change; it has full power to increase or reduce targets, to vary the level of retained profits or of enterprise taxes where these apply, to allocate more raw materials or less, and to expand or contract, merge or abolish enterprises. It has full power to fix prices. In such circumstances, the questions of autonomy, of retention of part of profits, of responsibility for profit and loss, would seem to have little ideological significance; the socialist government can make as much or as little of these new aspects of industrial organisation as it chooses. One should not speak of China as a "market economy". It is a planned and regulated economy in which market relations among collective enterprises are encouraged, but only within the framework of government control, for limited purposes and for pragmatic reasons – the provision of a measure of incentives, some guarantee of the responsible use of resources, and a greater responsiveness to demand.

Politics and Economics

The political implications of the new course, as the present leadership sees them, are inseparable from the economic. They might be summed up by saying that the new economic system will make a greater degree of democracy both possible and necessary. There will be less need for *dictat* from higher levels, and so more possibility of popular decision-making. There will be a greater need, as control from above is relaxed, for democratic control from below.

The economy, in fact, is to be operated under three types of restraint: the plan, the market and the workforce. These are regarded as the necessary framework of a decentralised economy.

It has been strongly emphasised that the new economic course, based on autonomous enterprises and working communities, makes sense only if the working members of every production association control the conditions of production. The workers' congress is not regarded as something marginal to the new policies, but as something central.

Decentralisation to working communities, however, implies a wider form of democracy than the industrial workers' congress alone can supply. The population must be in a position to supervise and criticise not only their immediate managers, but also the political leaders, the representatives of the state and the Party who determine and administer national policy and apply it locally. In this respect, the national leadership rightly regards the county (*xian*) level as critical; it is the point at which state and society meet; and it is more critical than ever now that the commune is to be deprived of its status as a unit of political administration. Hence, the first step to a new election system has been to provide direct elections at county level, by secret ballot and with more candidates than posts, and therefore some political competition.

China (it is said) is not yet ready for direct elections at provincial and national levels. County issues are directly relevant to the lives of the people and they have the knowledge to cope with them; this is not yet so, it is argued, at higher levels. Nevertheless, strong action has been taken to ensure more democratic proceedings there also. The 5th National People's Congress was prepared with "great fanfare", in the Chinese phrase. The message was that the NPC was constitutionally the highest authority in the country; that the Party should not pre-empt this authority; and that NPC members would be expected to debate and disagree, and criticise the administration.

In the event, there was a rather impressive amount of criticism and debate at the NPC, fully reported in the media.

The leadership has demanded that the Press should be more critical. There has been a campaign in the last weeks of 1980 to induce newspapers to pay more attention to readers' letters (which now pour into the People's Daily office alone at the rate of 2,000 a day), follow up their complaints, and expose those in authority who fail to deal with them. There is much more debate in the press now, and reporting is far more frank and open than in the past. Yet we still have a Chinese journalist demanding why, at press conferences at which both foreign and Chinese journalists are present, it is the foreigners who ask the questions while the Chinese sit silent. His colleagues replied that they kept quiet so as not to lose their jobs. However, perhaps the significant point is that this journalist's protest was published.

The arts and literature now also enjoy far greater freedom than during the Cultural Revolution when the Gang of Four, believing that officially-sponsored art and literature simply supported the new elite, persecuted many writers and artists vigorously while failing, as far as can be seen, to produce a viable and more democratic alternative literature and art. Yet one must ask whether or not, in spite of the new freedom, the left can now publish any more freely than the right could in the early seventies.

In matters of law, it is now said that it was wrong from the beginning to assert that the ideas of equality before the law, the independence of the judiciary and the procuratorate, and the right to a defence lawyer were bourgeois ideas. On the contrary, they are to be regarded as the bastions of socialist legality. Yet the trial of the Gang of Four does not give one confidence that due process of law will in future always take precedence over political prosecution.

What are the limits? Perhaps they are best analysed by beginning from the motivation of the movement. But first it is important to stress the considerable support which has existed in the CCP leadership for a measure of formal democracy since the early fifties. Mao had little to say on this: his democracy was one of consciousness, of participation; he attached little importance to institutions. This was perhaps the most serious limitation of his view of politics; his early experience with China's first discreditable experiments with western-type democratic institutions led to failure to realise the importance of legal and institutional guarantees of the democratic process. This failure was undoubtedly part of the reason (perhaps the chief reason) for the eventual defeat of the Great Proletarian Cultural Revolution.

Other CCP leaders were less hostile to the institutionalisation of democracy. Peng Zhen, Liu Shaoqi and others took the 1954 constitution literally. In 1962 they very promptly accepted Khrushchev's idea of a party and state of the whole people, and linked this with human rights. So there is some historic support within the Party for at least a degree of democratisation, in terms of acknowledging the power of the NPC, the rights of the press and of writers and artists generally, and the importance of the rule of law.

Experience since 1965 seems to have confirmed and strengthened this support. In the lawless chaos to which the Cultural Revolution led, it was the dang-quan-pai — the members of the establishment, now restored — who suffered most. Their conversion to a belief in the rule of law has thus a pointed sincerity to it.

The other side of the Cultural Revolution inheritance, however, is the belief that repression of criticism must in the end lead to an explosion. For seventeen years little criticism or protest was allowed. Then came Mao's dictum, "to rebel is justified", and for ten years the Chinese people were free to protest, to organise, and to put people out of power. The habits have not been lost. The Party destroyed much of its own moral authority in the Cultural Revolution, and it is no longer always obeyed. The young who took to the streets and led the rebellion feel they were betrayed, and they are disillusioned. Many of them, it is clear, have repudiated Marxism; some have swung to cynical self-interest, but others are demanding democracy in the full western sense of a pluralistic political system operating in conditions of adequate freedom. This "human rights" movement, however, is complicated, and to some extent discredited, because the protests are inextricable from the grievances of those who suffered in the Cultural Revolution and have not been (and cannot be) compensated; from the disillusionment of poor peasants where collective agriculture has failed ("No more hunger, no more persecution."); and from the appalling problem of youth unemployment in the cities ("We want to survive, we want to eat, we want to work."). In these circumstances fair criticism, slanderous anonymous posters, violent demonstration and outright rebellion, form a continuum not easy to divide into the tolerable and the unacceptable. And behind all this is a force of cadres over 50 per cent of whom were installed as Cultural Revolution supporters. They are still in power; they feel personally threatened; and they could easily provide the nucleus of an organised opposition.

In these circumstances, it is no great paradox that while the new regime is being widely praised for its liberalism and tolerance, we have cases like those of Wei Jingsheng and the human rights leaders who are now in detention without trial for having protested at his conviction. We have, too, a report from Amnesty International which finds the new regime scarcely less guilty of imprisonment and execution than its predecessors.

It is nevertheless to the credit of the new leaders that the serious problems of public order and social discipline which threaten China today have not plunged them into policies of wholesale repression. In 1957, when Mao had launched his first popular anti-bureaucratic campaign, the Party reacted very strongly indeed to the threats to public order which resulted, threats which were insignificant compared with present dangers. They overruled Mao's pleas for continued freedom, and launched the "anti-rightist" campaign to suppress criticism and dissent. That campaign was run by Deng Xiaoping. Now, Deng is the foremost champion of moderate democratisation. It is ironical that he in 1980, like Mao in 1957, has found himself overruled by his fellow leaders, in this case in his wish to permit continued tolerance of Democracy Wall. The campaign against the Wall was, in fact, run on very similar lines to that which was used to launch the anti-rightist movement.

The debate on the limits of freedom continues. This is plain in the opposing lines taken by *Workers' Daily* and *Enlightenment Daily* over the issue of the Wall and the wall newspapers. *Workers' Daily* takes a hard line: "is nothing to be considered counter-revolutionary except arson and murder?" it asks incredulously. (The irony here is that it was Mao himself who demanded during the Cultural Revolution – in vain as it proved – that no-one should be arrested as a counter-revolutionary *except* for arson or murder.) A compromise was attempted by which Democracy Wall was moved to a remoter part of the city (as if Hyde Park Corner's rostrum had been moved to Wandsworth Common), with a rule that while the authorities would not demand that posters be inspected before being put up, the authors should be obliged to identify themselves; but the new Wall did not flourish, and the right to put up wall newspapers in public places, as opposed to within one's own unit, was struck out of the constitution. The main argument against them was that they could be exploited by class enemies. There is another irony here, for Mao had defended the *dazibao* precisely because they were "classless" – anyone, no matter how poor, could find paper and ink enough to make his protest.

At the theoretical level, the repressive aspects of policy towards dissent have been justified by the usual stale and boring arguments about the difference between "bourgeois" and "socialist" democracy. Six months ago, the evolution of "bourgeois" democracy was being described as a "great leap forward in human history", and comment suggested that Chinese opinion was edging close to the idea that the machinery of freedom and representation is as neutral as mathematics, and as applicable in socialist society as in any other. But there has been some reaction since.

At the same time, in dealing with dissent, the authorities are making a valiant effort to distinguish between counter-revolutionary ideas on the one hand, and on the other the propagation of such ideas in a manner to incite to breaches of the peace or cause danger to the state. Only incitement is illegal; but this principle of not "opening windows into men's souls" is then promptly compromised by the further argument that it is the motive, not the action, which determines guilt or innocence — the rock on which Wei Jingsheng perished.

In observing the scope and the limits of China's democratisation, one is reminded of the British Army's oldest Catch 22: if one man complains, that's a complaint; but if two men complain, it's mutiny. Freedom of organisation is not one of the freedoms which Deng's regime offers. In imperial China, the individual official who remonstrated with the Emperor was a hero, but the official who sought support among his fellows for his remonstrations was a traitor. The sentiment lives on. In China now (and it is understandable enough) factionalism is the great fear. While the mass organisations and the united front associations have been revived, and are being encouraged actively to represent the interests of their members, a strenuous effort has been made to restore the Party fractions within them, in order to re-assert control. Recent demands in China for free trade unions, the result no doubt of events in Poland, have been uncompromisingly condemned.

Growth Versus Distribution

The most conspicuous change in China since 1976 has been the suspension of those measures during the Cultural Revolution which aimed at creating greater equality. The change, however, may be more apparent than real.

There were several separate issues involved in the egalitarian policies. First was the attempt to arrest what was regarded as the development of a new ruling class: the question of equality — or at least of less inequality — between the mass of the working population on the one hand, and the political leaders, administrators, technicians and intellectuals on the other. There is no doubt that to bring this class under control, partly by means of new forms of democratic political organisation and partly by curbing their earnings and perquisites, was the chief immediate aim of the Cultural Revolution radicals.

Quite separate were the other issues, which were concerned primarily with income differentials within the mass of ordinary people. Five such issues have been recognised in China as matters of political concern. There is gross inequality between average urban and average rural incomes. There are very large inequalities between one region and another. There are differences in income among adjacent villages, differences not on the whole large, but made significant by the fact that the incomes concerned are at best little above subsistence level and at worst below it. There are differences among individual peasants in the same production team, and these again can vary round subsistence level. Finally, in the industrial sector there is a sharp (and very unsocialist) difference between the pay and perquisites of the permanent, pensioned workers (usually skilled) and the casual labourers, who on the eve of the Cultural Revolution are said to have numbered about twelve million.

To these different issues, the cultural-revolution radicals took different attitudes. They showed concern over urban-rural differences, but apparently could not decide what to do. They do not seem to have had any particular policy on the problem of regional disparities; on the one hand, their overstrained devotion to the idea of local self-reliance (in itself excellent) may well have tended to confirm and increase regional differences, while on the other hand their reluctance to encourage regional specialisation of cropping may have had some equalising effect, in a negative way, by depriving of higher incomes areas with a potential for specialised growing of cotton, beet and other non-grain crops.

The question of differences of resources, and hence of incomes, among adjacent rural communities is one which has caused considerable strife in China. In 1956-57 in the wake of collectivisation an attempt was made to re-allocate resources among the production brigades. The attempt broke down. In 1958, on an even larger scale, a similar policy was attempted; in fact a major reason for the creation of the commune was to try to equalise resources by bringing a number of villages, rich and poor, into one unit of account. This proved to be one of the principal causes of the collapse of the commune system in its first large-scale, unitary form, as Mao himself readily admitted in 1959. The small team then became the unit of work, ownership and distribution, and the redistributive purpose of the original commune system was abandoned. During the Cultural Revolution, a further effort was made from time to time and from place to place to raise the level of ownership from team to brigade. The Gang of Four did not encourage this, indeed Zhang Chunqiao condemned it, but left-wing elements in the countryside persisted. The evidence suggests that this was highly unpopular and counterproductive; and looking back at the history of the various efforts made to equalise the resources of adjacent villages, one is forced to conclude that there is no way in which, at present, the more prosperous villages in China can be induced to make sacrifices for the less prosperous.

The differences between the incomes of one peasant and another within the collective are not, to any degree, differences of class. To some extent former rich peasants may have superior experience and so be able to make more profitable use of their private plots and of the opportunities for individual handicrafts. For the rest, differences in prosperity seem to reflect differences in health and strength or in skill, and — perhaps most important — the influence of the life-cycle: small children or other dependents drag down the family's per capita income, grown-up sons and daughters increase it. By 1958 many of the poor-peasant beneficiaries of land reform had married and had small children, so that their former poverty was in a sense prolonged. It was partly for this reason that the new communes instituted a free-supply element into the remuneration of members, along with simple welfare measures, and these elements still remain, though now much reduced below the 1958 levels, which were almost universally condemned as too destructive of incentive. During the Cultural Revolution there does not seem to have been one consistent radical policy on the question, but the attack on "bourgeois right" — directed primarily at the political and economic establishment rather than at any section of the working masses — led local cadres to play safe by cutting down or cutting out private plots, limiting trade at rural fairs, and generally discouraging attempts to earn by individual enterprise. In the same way, attempts were made to do away with piecework and contract work in farming, in favour of time rates.

There was little sign of consistent and explicit support from Peking for these changes. On the whole, the Gang of Four had not much interest in these questions. To them, Dazhai's egalitarian system of remuneration was more of a moral stick with which to beat privileged cadres.

On the issue of contract workers, the Cultural Revolution leadership simply brought them out on the streets, and then denied them a better deal.

The egalitarianism of the Cultural Revolution, therefore, is to some extent illusory. The leaders had no answer to city-rural or regional differences, or to the problem of the underprivileged contract workers. They opposed the raising of the level of ownership within the commune. Only with respect to differences of income among individual commune members does there seem to have been anything approaching widespread change, but this is perhaps the least significant inequality in China — certainly the least amenable to analysis in class terms — and the policy was (and was already known to be) strongly disincentive; it could be expected to have the minimum effect on China's inequalities, and the maximum effect on productivity, a levelling down of the kind which Mao had so often himself condemned .

The most significant and positive redistributive policy of the radical leadership was the encouragement of commune and brigade enterprise, the profits of which could be accumulated for redistributive investment in the locality. This was Mao's most practical contribution to the solution of the agonising contradiction in poor countries between growth and redistribution.

When one compares the policies relevant to redistribution of the new regime with those of the old, there are two obvious differences and one obvious similarity. First, the differences: the new leadership has repudiated the idea that China's officials and intellectuals are "a class whose interests are antagonistic to those of the workers and peasants", although this theoretical difference has not prevented strenuous new attempts to subject those in authority to democratic control. They have also repudiated the suppression of private plots and the rural private sector generally, and on the contrary are encouraging the peasants to show the utmost initiative both within and without the collective system. The similarity is the continued encouragement of commune and brigade industry, and the use of revenues from it for redistributive purposes.

For the rest, they have boldly grasped the nettle of growth versus redistribution, and decided that growth must come first, for without it there will be very little to distribute. Many Chinese no doubt oppose this, and many foreign observers deplore it. Perhaps it is wrong, but at least it is in the logic of the strategy which Mao bequeathed to them — that increasing peasant purchasing power is the key to development. In practical terms, this means allowing those peasants who can quickly become prosperous to do so, so that part of their surplus can, through taxes on and profits from their consumption, be invested redistributively, as in the Wuxi County example. This is a main function of the commune, and of the County Economic Commission, and of the provincial administration.

There is undoubtedly a danger that the new course, if uncontrolled, could undermine such equality as exists, as Peter Nolan and Gordon White have argued; yet to deplore this *"enrichissez-vous"* policy as one which leaves redistribution to mere casual trickle-down would be mistaken. The administration, at all levels from the centre down to the brigade, has the power to redistribute systematically. What is scarce is the means; and a freer economic system, a partially market system, will they hope and expect supply the means more rapidly. It is unlikely that major regional income differences or the gulf between city and country, can be eliminated quickly in China by present policies, or by any other policies tried in the past or imagined for the immediate future. Whether the new policy is right or wrong, however, there is no need to doubt China's continuing commitment to the limitation of income differentials. There has been no observable change at the macro- *or* the micro-level in the general pattern of aid and loans or in welfare provision, while steps more positive than any during the Cultural Revolution have already been taken to increase rural incomes in comparison with urban incomes. Nor is there any doubt that, if the state and Party choose, they have the authority, the machinery and the experience, to use for redistributive purposes a substantial part of the increased wealth which they expect the new economic system to produce. China is still in this respect of interest to the developing world.

Aspiration and Reality

The final question concerns the extent to which the new system, especially on its economic side, has so far been successfully implemented. Experience has shown that the gap between intention and performance in China can be a wide one; this is another way of saying that control neither from above nor from below has ensured that Peking's will is always carried out. The new policies face both resistance to implementation and inherent difficulties in the course of implementation. Comments from the provincial level show that the new policies are not equally popular with all authorities, though the opposition seems to have been worn down. There is also evidence of considerable perturbation in the PLA; there has been a prolonged and steadily intensified campaign to convince its members, who have been encouraged for twenty years to believe that their way of life offers the best model of socialist organisation, that the new policies are as socialist as the old. Similar evidence shows that many middle-level cadres (prefecture, municipality and county cadres, as well as those directly supervising large enterprises), for whom control of the means of production is the main source of personal power, and most of whom were promoted to their present positions during the Cultural Revolution, are showing great reluctance to make the recommended changes. Questions of power and prestige apart, it can readily be imagined that they must be dismayed by the imposition of a new system which will involve them in a drastic change of working methods, modes of analysis, criteria of success, and lines of responsibility. Mao had urged them for years to act as socialist entrepreneurs rather than as bureaucrats. Now under his successors, and in a rather different form, the moment of truth has arrived, and time alone will tell if the cadres are both willing and able to respond.

The main criticism made in the Chinese media is that cadres show great reluctance to accept the implications of autonomy for enterprises and working communities. This autonomy, it is said, is still in many places no more than a formality. On the other hand, the retention of a part of profits is predictably less unpopular. The result, however, can be that while the firms' managers will now be judged in economic terms of profit and loss, the Party supervisors do not always leave them free to make the decisions which will determine profit or loss. The battle for enterprise autonomy is as yet far from won.

The changes in agriculture do not seem to have met the same resistance, although on grounds both of ideology and of power one would expect rural cadres to oppose them. In the case of farming, however, the peasants are much more directly affected by the new policies, while they have a power of passive resistance which factory workers cannot so easily enjoy; and on the whole it seems that this power has been used to support rather than to oppose the new course. While in 1979 there was much discussion of resistance by commune and brigade cadres reluctant to see their ability to control the collective so sharply curtailed, in 1980 the major problem seems to have been that the relaxation of farm policy might encourage peasants to undermine the collective system entirely.

On the whole, however, it seems certain that if the new regime are prepared to persist, the policies will be fully implemented. Only a change of heart at the top could prevent this, and such a change is not at present in question. Deng Xiaoping, Zhao Ziyang, Hu Yaobang and Ren Zhongyi make up a pretty formidable combination.

The threat to the new course come less from opposition to it than from the practical problems involved. The inexperience of the cadres in economic as opposed to bureaucratic management has already been touched on. More important perhaps is the fact that the partial replacement of planned allocation by a regulated market may simply create a new set of distortions as intractable as the old. There are already reports of factories resorting to manipulations of the planning indicators in order to maximise retainable profits. The simplest means to increase profits is also the most dangerous and potentially destabilising — raising prices to the consumer, a practice which is made very easy by the monopolistic nature of the whole organisation of industry in a perpetual sellers' market, and which has already contributed to an inflation of some 5 per cent in 1980. The leadership's answer is competition. Once this has been established and has eroded away the existing monopoly positions, prices will be stabilised, and sharp practices eliminated. So they believe. It is an interesting perspective for a socialist country.

NOTES AND REFERENCES

Chapter 1

1. See Michael Sullivan: "The politics of conflict and compromise", in B. Brugger (ed): *China Since the "Gang of Four"* (London: Croom Helm, 1980), pp. 20-50.
2. See Charles Bettelheim: "The Great Leap Backward", in Neil G. Burton and Charles Bettelheim (eds): *China Since Mao* (New York: Monthly Review Press, 1978). For a more orthodox analysis, see *The Capitalist Roaders are still on the Capitalist Road: The Two Line Struggle and the Revisionist Seizure of Power in China* (Denver: China Study Group, 1977).
3. R. H. Tawney, *Land and Labour in China* (London: Allen and Unwin, 1932), p. 161.
4. See Mark Selden: "China's Uninterrupted Revolution", *Monthly Review*, 31:5 (October 1979), pp. 24-36; Gregor Benton, "The Factional Struggle in the Chinese Communist Party", *Critique*, 8 (Summer 1977), pp. 100-123; Harry Harding, Jr., "China After Mao", *Problems of Communism*, XXVI:2 (March-April 1977), pp. 1-18.
5. See Rudi Volti: "The Absorption and Assimilation of Acquired Technology", in R. Baum (ed): *China's Four Modernizations* (Boulder: Westview Press, 1980), pp. 179-201.
6. Suzanne Pepper: "Chinese Education After Mao: Two Steps Forward, Two Steps Back and Begin Again", *China Quarterly*, 81 (March 1980), p. 1.
7. See Jan S. Prybyla: "Changes in the Chinese Economy: An Interpretation", *Asian Survey*, XIX:5 (May 1979), pp. 409-35.
8. See Qian Xuesen: "From Social Science to Social Technology", *Wen Hui Bao*, 29 October 1980, p. 3.
9. This argument is developed more fully in my paper "The Post-Revolutionary Chinese State: Dictatorship, Democracy and the

Distribution of Power", in Victor Nee and Edward Friedman (eds): *State and Society in Contemporary China* (Ithaca: Cornel. University Press, forthcoming).
10. Edward Friedman, "On Maoist Conceptualization of the Capitalist World System", *China Quarterly*, 80 (December 1979), pp. 806-837.
11. See Graham Young: "Non-revolutionary Vanguard: Transformation of the CCP", in Brugger (ed): *op. cit.*, pp. 51-87.
12. For information on continuing factional struggle, see Frank Ching: "The Current Political Scene in China", *China Quarterly*, 80 (December 1979), pp. 691-715.

Chapter 2

1. Hua Guofeng: "Report on the Work of the Government", *Main Documents of the Second Session of the Fifth National People's Congress* Beijing: Foreign Languages Press, 1979) p. 24.
2. Hua Guofeng: "Political Report to the Eleventh National Congress of the Chinese Communist Party", *The Eleventh National Congress of the Chinese Communist Party* (Documents) (Beijing: Foreign Languages Press, 1977), p. 53.
3. "Unite and Strive to Build a Modern Powerful Socialist Country", *Documents of the First Session of the Fifth National People's Congress* (Beijing: Foreign Languages Press, 1978), pp. 35ff.
4. See *Renmin Ribao* (*RMRB*) (People's Daily), December 24 1978.
5. *Peking Review* (*PR*), no. 52, 1978, pp. 13-14.
6. *Ibid.*, p. 15.
7. See for example: *Neimenggu Ribao* (Inner Mongolia Daily), 8 March 1979.
8. *Jiefang Ribao* (Liberation Daily), 12 February 1979.
9. See Ye Jianying's speech on the thirtieth anniversary of the founding of the PRC in *Beijing Review* (*BR*), no. 40, 1979.
10. The Fifth Plenum decided that the labels of "scab, renegade and traitor" be removed from Liu Shaoqi. The accusations against him were described as the "biggest frame-up our Party has ever known". This rehabilitation of Liu was accompanied by the republication and discussion of his writings which obviously gave more strength to those leaders who favoured the re-introduction of policies associated with Liu.
11. BBC: *Summary of World Broadcasts: The Far East* (*SWB:FE*), no. 6518.
12. "Refuting Lin Biao's Claim: Every Sentence is Truth", *PR*, no. 30, 1978.
13. *SWB:FE* 6497.
14. "Communique of the Third Plenum of the Eleventh Central Committee", *PR*, no. 52, 1978, p. 15.
15. "Correctly Understand the Role of Individual in History", *RMRB*, 4 July 1980.
16. *Ibid.* This point had been made by Ye Jianying in his speech on the thirtieth anniversary of the founding of the PRC when he stated: "Of course Mao Zedong Thought is not the product of Mao Zedong's personal

wisdom alone; it is also the product of his comrades-in-arms, the Party and the revolutionary people and, as he once pointed out, it emerged from the 'collective struggles of the Party and the people' ". *BR*, no. 40, 1979, p. 8.
17. "A Fundamental Principle of Marxism", *PR*, no. 28, 1978, p. 6.
18. "Notice from the First Plenary Session of the Central Commission for Inspecting Discipline Under the Party Central Committee", in *Guangming Ribao* (*GMRB*) (Glorious Daily), 25 March 1979.
19. Compare "Fundamental Change in China's Class Situation", *BR*, no. 47, 1979, p. 15.
20. Mao Zedong: "On the Correct Handling of Contradictions Among the People", in *Selected Works* (Beijing: Foreign Languages Press, 1977), vol. 5, p. 397.
21. *BR*, no. 47, 1979, p. 16.
22. *Ibid.*, p. 17.
23. "Improving the Party's Style of Work", *BR*, no. 30, 1979, p. 5.
24. "NPC: Lively Political Atmosphere", *BR*, no. 28, 1979, p. 20.
25. Chen Zihua (Minister of Civil Affairs): "On China's Electoral Law", *BR*, no. 37, 1979, p. 18.
26. *RMRB*, 15 August 1979.
27. Chen Zihua, *op. cit.*, p. 15.
28. *GMRB*, 11 March 1979. This article was attributed to a "special commentator", but was in fact written by Li Honglin.
29. *RMRB*, 1 February 1979.
30. *Ibid.*
31. Article 55 of the Constitution of the People's Republic of China (1978), *Documents of the First Session of the Fifth National People's Congress of the PRC* (Peking: Foreign Languages in Press, 1978), p. 170.
32. "Ensuring Full Democracy Inside the Party", *RMRB*, 11 January 1979.
33. Huang Kecheng in *SWB:FE* 6333.
34. *RMRB*, 1 February 1979.
35. *SWB:FE* 6375.
36. *Ibid.* The principles are: adhere to the Party's ideological and political line; uphold collective leadership and oppose arbitrary decision-making by a single person; safeguard the Party's centralised leadership and strictly observe discipline; uphold Party spirit and root out factionalism; speak the truth and match words with deeds; promote inner-Party democracy and take a correct attitude to conflicting views; protect the rights of Party members against any encroachment; elections should fully express the wishes of the electorate; struggle against erroneous tendencies, bad people and bad actions; treat comrades who have made mistakes correctly; accept supervision by the Party and the masses; and study hard and strive to be red and expert.
37. *RMRB*, 11 January 1980.
38. *GMRB*, 21 November 1978.
39. Notice of the Beijing Municipality Revolutionary Committee, *Beijing Daily*, 31 March 1979.
40. *SWB:FE* 6511.

41. See, for example Li Honglin: *Dushu*, no. 1, April 1979, p. 3.
42. *Shiyue*, no. 1, August 1978.
43. *GMRB*, 4 November 1979.
44. For a writer's view, see Liu Binyan: "Literature and Art as a Mirror of Life", *BR*, no. 52, 1979, p. 13.
45. *SWB:FE* 6361.
46. Hua Guofeng: "Report on the Work of the Government", *Documents of the First Session of the Fifth National People's Congress* (Beijing: Foreign Languages Press, 1978), p. 86.
47. *PR*, no. 42, 1978.
48. *BR*, no. 45, 1979, p. 7.
49. *BR*, no. 2, 1979.
50. *PR*, no. 49, 1978, p. 9.
51. *BR*, no. 45, 1979, pp. 6-7.
52. In 1979 the Shanghai Film Factory held three such congresses: *BR*, no. 2, 1980, p. 6. The workers' congress of the Tianjin Clock and Watch Factory was attended by 246 representatives (8.6 per cent of those on the payroll). Of these 66 per cent were workers, 26 per cent were cadres and 8 per cent technicians (*PR*, no. 49, 1978).
53. Chen Zihua: *BR*, no. 37, 1979, p. 18.
54. This was first suggested by Zhou Enlai in his "Report on the Work of the Government" in 1957.
55. See Peng Zhen's speech to the Third Session of the Fifth NPC, in *SWB:FE* 6515.
56. *RMRB*, 10 August 1980. All these provinces had previously carried out pilot projects. The 13 are: Heilongjiang, Jilin, Liaoning, Inner Mongolia, Shandong, Jiangsu, Zhejiang, Fujian, Henan, Hubei, Hunan, Guangxi and Yunnan.
57. "Effectively Safeguard the People's Democratic Rights", *Hong Qi* (Red Flag), no. 17, 1980.
58. *SWB:FE* 3400.
59. Hua Guofeng: *Report on the Work of the Government in Documents of the First Session of the Fifth National People's Congress* (Beijing: Foreign Languages Press, 1978) pp. 85-86.
60. *Ibid.*, p. 86.
61. Peng Zhen: *Explanation of the Seven Draft Laws in Main Documents of the Second Session of the Fifth National People's Congress* (Beijing: Foreign Languages Press, 1979) p. 219.
62. *SWB:FE* 6518.
63. *Ibid.*
64. *Ibid.*
65. *The Times*, 28 July 1980.
66. The five were Deng Xiaoping, Li Xiannian, Chen Yun, Xu Xiangqian and Wang Zhen. In addition the session also accepted Wang Renzhong's resignation following his assumption of "an important Party post". Chen Yonggui's "request" to be relieved of his post as Vice-Premier was also approved. *SWB:FE* 6521.

67. Article 41 of the State Constitution (1978).
68. Peng Zhen: *op. cit.*, p. 219.
69. *Ibid.*, p. 201.

Chapter 3

1. Ross Terrill: *800,000,000 The Real China*, (London: Penguin, 1975) p. 235.
2. See for example discussion "Round Table", *Far Eastern Affairs* (Moscow), no. 3, 1978, pp. 14-22.
3. See my *China's Role in World Affairs* (London: Croom Helm, 1978), chapter 10.
4. For an analysis of the conflict on foreign trade see Anne Fenwick: China's Foreign Trade Policy and the Campaign Against Deng Xiaoping", in Thomas Fingar (ed), *China's Quest for Independence: Policy Evolution in the 1970s* (Colorado: Westview, 1980).
5. See "Report on Financial Work" delivered by Wang Bingqian, Minister of Finance at Third Session of Fifth National People's Congress on 30 August 1980, *Beijing Review* (*BR*), no. 39, 29 September 1980.
6. Alexander Eckstein: *China's Economic Revolution* (Cambridge: Cambridge University Press, 1977), pp. 253-277.
7. See "Foreign Relations" section of "Chronicle & Documentation", *China Quarterly*, nos. 78 and 80 under "Japan".
8. The value of foreign trade (export and imports) in 1979 was 45 billion Yuan which the per capita GNP was officially calculated at 253 Yuan, which suggests a total GNP of 250 billion Yuan. See *BR*, no. 43.
9. See, for example, Hua Guofeng's speeches to the various sessions of the NPC in *Peking Review*, no. 10, 1978; no. 27, 1979; and no. 38, 1980.
10. For similar statements in the 1980s, see the Political Report of the CPC Eighth Congress of 27 September 1956 and a Zhou Enlai Report to the NPC on 28 June 1956. *People's China*, supplements no. 22, p. 7 and no. 14, pp. 5-6, respectively.
11. See the speech of U.S. Secretary of the Treasury, W. M. Blumenthal, cited in Daniel Tretiak, "China's Vietnam War and its Consequences", *The China Quarterly*, no. 80, (December 1979), p. 760.
12. See *Xinhua News Agency*, 26 October 1980 account of Hu Yaobang (General Secretary of the Central Committee of the CPC) conversation with the visiting Spanish CP leader Carrillo.
13. This is the view of Nayan Chanda: *Far Eastern Economic Review*, 6 April 1979.
14. See *Pravda* Commentary of 5 March cited in *International Herald Tribune*, 6 March 1979.
15. *Financial Times*, 7 August and 25 September 1979.
16. See *Zheng Feng*, May 1979.
17. See, for example, Hua Guofeng's Report to the First Session of the NPC on the reasons for China's new modernization plans *PR*, no. 10, 1978.

18. See Daniel Tretiak, *op. cit.*, p. 752.
19. See Report on the final state accounts for 1978 and the draft state budget for 1979, *PR*, no. 27, 1979.
20. *Time*, 29 December 1978.
21. See account of and comment on Hua's press conference in Bonn of 24 October 1979 in BBC: *Summary of World Broadcasts: The Far East*, no. 6255.
22. *Xinhua News Agency*, 6 September 1979.
23. See "Foreign Relations" section of "Quarterly Chronicle and Documentation", *China Quarterly*, no. 80 (December 1979), pp. 895-6.
24. *PR*, no. 51, 1978.

Chapter 4

1. For example, see *Beijing Review*, XXIII:32 (11 August 1980), p. 5.
2. See Marc Blecher and Mitch Meisner: "Economic Growth and Equality in Rural China: Xiyang County as Development Experience and Model", *Comparative Political Studies*, January 1981.
3. M. Selden: *The Yenan Way in Revolutionary China*. (Cambridge: Harvard University Press, 1971).
4. F. Schurmann: *Ideology and Organization in Communist China*. (Berkeley: University of California Press, 1968).
5. There were about 2,200 counties in China in 1971. (Donald P. Whitaker and Rinn-Sup Shinn: *Area Handbook for the People's Republic of China* (Washington: Department of the Army, U.S. GPO, 1972), p. 25.) In 1967, Barnett estimated the average county population to be 300,000. (A. Doak Barnett: *Cadres, Bureaucracy, and Political Power in China* (New York: Columbia University Press, 1967) p. 119.) Today the average county population is undoubtedly at least 400,000.
6. B. Stavis: *People's Communes and Rural Development in China* (Ithaca: Cornell University, 1974), p. 42.
7. In this section we are indebted to the comparative study of Theda Skocpol who examines the relationship between social structure and political power. "France, Russia, and China: A Structural Analysis of Social Revolutions", *Comparative Studies in Society and History*, 18 (April 1976) pp. 175-210, especially pp. 198-201.
8. Mao Zedong: *Selected Works* (Beijing: Foreign Languages Press, 1967), vol. 1, pp. 23-59.
9. See Tang Tsou, Marc Blecher, and Mitch Meisner: "Organization, Growth, and Equality in Xiyang County: A Survey of Fourteen Brigades in Seven Communes, (Part I)" *Modern China*, 5:1 (January 1979) pp. 3-39.
10. Jack Gray has reminded us of one outlandish idea, current around 1958 in some parts of China, for a "county-wide commune". Personal communication.
11. Skinner, *op. cit.*, p. 397.
12. An interesting example of the "mixed" character of the commune level in relation to State policies comes from an interview with a former county

(technical) cadre in Guangdong province. Commenting on the role of county agencies in carrying out policies to cut off "labour outflow" from the agricultural economy to other areas of employment, he states that:

> . . . the communes also took a part in controlling this. You need papers from the commune to get outside work, and these have to be renewed every month by the commune at the time when you remit part of your salary to your team. At these times of control of labour outflow, the communes would refuse to reissue papers to these people. But after a short time, the communes — particularly the poorer ones with excess labour power and population, where the outflow problem was most serious — would permit them to go again, since the outflow has advantages for the communes, which receive their sideline fee.

When individual peasants contracted to work outside the collective, they were required to remit a set amount of money to the production team. Interview, 6 July 1978, YFMIA/7-8 (Blecher).
13. A. D. Barnett: *op. cit.*, p. 142.
14. In his analysis of the county as a strategic unit for administering agricultural modernization, Butler sees one of the two key functions of the county as being a distribution point for sophisticated inputs produced elsewhere. S. Butler: *Agricultural Mechanisation in China,* (New York: Columbia University Press, 1978).
15. Interview, 6 July 1978, YFMIA/2 (Blecher).
16. V. Falkenheim: *China Quarterly,* no. 59, (1974), pp. 518-543.
17. Our major informant on recent county government informs us that "Of course, one factor motivating the expansion of agricultural mechanization was the needs of the county itself. But more important was the demands of the higher levels. But the higher levels also supported this county-level undertaking, with bank loans and materials distributed." Also, "If other kinds of machinery production lost money, they [the county] got criticised; but not agricultural machinery factories. Yes, I think this has to do with the movement to learn from Dazhai." 6 July 1978, YFMIA/5 (Blecher).
18. Interview, 6 July 1978, YFMIA/4 (Blecher).
19. B. Y. Ahn: *Chinese Politics and the Cultural Revolution.* (Seattle: University of Washington Press, 1976), p. 118.
20. "Forum on Building a Socialist New Countryside Through Revolutionizing the Leadership of CCP Hsien Committees", *Renmin Ribao (RMRB)*, beginning 12 October 1965, in *Current Background,* no. 779 (17 January 1966), p. 28.
21. A. Donnithorne:*China Quarterly,* no. 52, (1972), pp. 605-619.
22. Interviews, Shulu County, 1979.
23. Interviews, Shulu County and Changzhou City, 1979.
24. Interviews, Shulu County, 1979.
25. Hua Guofeng: *RMRB,* 31 October 1975.
26. See Mitch Meisner's dissertation: "In Agriculture Learn from Dazhai: Theory and Practice in Chinese Rural Development", University of

Chicago, 1977, pp. 384-412; see also Tsou, Blecher, and Meisner, *op. cit.*, and Part II of the same article in *Modern China*, 5:2 (April, 1979); Thierry Pairault: *Dazhai recupéré: La politique economique rurale au début des années 1970* (Paris: Publications Orientalists de France, 1977); Pairault: "Etude de Tachai et développement économique en Chine: la conférence nationale de l'automne 1975", *Mondes Asiatiques*, no. 8 (Winter 1976-1977), pp. 467-498; Neville Maxwell: "The Fourth Mobilization: New Phase of the Tachai Movement", *World Development*, 6 (1978), pp. 499-518.

27. For a discussion of Dazhai's leadership, see Meisner, *op. cit.*
28. "Comrade Ch'en Yung-kuei's (Chen Yonggui's) Report at the Reporting Meeting held Jointly by the Ministry of Agriculture and Forestry and the Chinese Communist Party Peking Municipal Committee", *Union Research Service*, 74:14 and 15 (15 and 19 February 1974) pp. 187-188. In his talk, Chen spoke of one brigade that had changed its leaders every month for a year. Dazhai's neighbouring Wujiaping brigade, whose Party secretary Li Xi Shen was a close ally of Chen's and is now vice-secretary of the Xiyang County Party Committee, is reported to have had eight brigade leaderships and 24 production team leaderships between 1958 and 1965. (Wilfred Burchett and Rewi Alley: *China The Quality of Life* (London: Penguin, 1976), p. 128.) In Guangdong around the time of the Cultural Revolution, a lot of county secretaries were transferred from one county to the next to help shield them from more criticism, "since in the new county their background would not be known so well". (Interview, 6 July 1978, YFMIA/2 (Blecher).)
29. Pairault makes the point particularly strongly when he connects emphasis on revolutionization of county cadres to the programme of the linking of Dazhai-type agricultural development to the establishment of an industrial base at the county level. (*Mondes Asiatiques*, pp. 489-491).
30. Guo Fenglian: "Jianchi da pi zibenzhuyi, jianchi da gan shehuizhuyi", *RMRB*, 25 September 1975. Guo is the present secretary of the Dazhai brigade Party branch. She was a protege of Chen's and succeeded him.
31. Interview, Hebei Province (Shijiazhuang), 1979.
32. Tsou, Blecher, and Meisner, *op. cit.*, pp. 3-39 and 139-185.
33. Pairault believes (and with good sense, we think) that the kind of leader desired in the development strategy implied by the Dazhai-county programme is not above all a technician, but rather, "a leader of men, a guide . . . red more than expert, more a Schumpeterian entrepreneur than a Burnhamian manager".
34. N. Lardy: "Economic Reform in China: Retrospect and Prospect." Unpublished paper (1980).
35. See Pairault: *Mondes Asiatiques*, pp. 495-498, for a good statement analysing the primacy of farm capital (or infrastructural) construction for rural development. See also Chin Chi-chu: "All-Out Effort to Develop Agriculture", *Peking Review*, no. 26 (30 June 1978).
36. T. Pairault: *Mondes Asiatiques*, pp. 467-498.
37. Interview, Chinese Academy of Social Sciences, June 1979.

38. For example, in Xitang Brigade, Qianzhou Commune, Wuxi County, visited in 1979, under brigade supervision complex measures have been taken to amalgamate the economies of the production teams into several sub-brigade units to provide a transitional form to facilitate a move underway toward brigade-level accounting.
39. Maxwell (*op. cit.*, p. 513) has the following to say about the attitudes, relatively speaking, of county and commune cadres about taking measures (here a relatively radical one) to promote equalization:

> The writer's discussions with cadres of the Chinese administration have shown a divergence of attitude . . . at county level, for example, cadres are more likely to stress the raising of the unit of account to brigade level as a necessary consequence of the Tachai campaign; while down at commune level cadres are much more cautious and tentative.

In Yunfu County, "In the peasants' eyes, the commune and county represent the state, and the team and brigade represent them." Interview, 20 July 1978, YFMIA/43.
40. For comments on this point see: *Rural Small-Scale Industry Delegation*, (Berkeley: University of California, 1977), p. 152; also, Pairault, *Mondes Asiatiques*, pp. 482-494.
41. Pairault, *Mondes Asiatiques*, p. 189.
42. For example, Chen Yonggui reported in 1973 that when the past year's drought conditions had caused what appeared to be a likely failure of the harvest in six communes, there was considerable unrest.

The response of the county Party committee was to announce that they would guarantee the receipt of 460 *jin* (506 pounds) of grain whatever the outcome of the harvest. "Comrade Ch'en Yung-kuei's Report," *op. cit.*, p. 185.
43. Marianne Bastide, in "Authority, Participation and Cultural Change in China", ed. F. S. Schram. Cambridge University Press, 1973, p. 181.
44. In applying here the familiar terminology describing a shift from the "political" to the "economic" in determining various investment and production decisions, we refer to the weakening of direct decision-making powers of party and government officials and instead allowing more leeway to directors of production units to shift for themselves in a world in which the gates are guarded in the first instance by economic sentries such as profits, prices, competitive contract criteria, etc. In this shift, undoubtedly, real power has passed into different sets of hands.
45. See for example: "Treating the Concrete Experience of Dazhai as a Law is Undemocratic", *Nanfang Ribao*, 14 March 1979, p. 2; "It is Necessary to Take Off the 'Anti-Dazhai' Evil Spell", *Jiefang Ribao*, 7 March 1979, p. 3; "At Enlarged Meetings of the Xiyang County Party Committee and Party Standing Committee, Comrade Li Xishen, on Behalf of the County Party Committee, Examined Seven Problem-areas", *Wenhui Bao*, 8 March 1979.
46. Interview, Jiangsu Province (Nanjing), 1979.
47. "The Correct Direction for Hastening Agricultural Mechanization",

RMRB, 6 February 1979.
48. An interesting question arises here: Will this compete or conflict with measures taken to decrease urban unemployment, especially among youth?
49. Our thanks to Ben Stavis for this point.
50. Robert F. Dernberger and David Fasenfest: "China's Post-Mao Economic Future," *Chinese Economy Post-Mao, Volume I, Policy and Performance*, (Washington: U.S. Congress Joint Economic Committee, 1978), pp. 24-26. The authors argue that the efficient use in boosting productive output in agriculture by even the technical-capital improvement package alone may be limited effectively to better endowed regions with more access to water, transport, urban markets, and good communications.
51. See Deng's interview with Oriana Fallaci, *Washington Post*, 31 August 1980.
52. During a year-long interview project in Hong Kong in 1974-75, Blecher was surprised to find repeatedly that old class distinctions fixed 25 years or more in the past still seemed to be discernibly related to the distribution of entrepreneurial skills and economic acumen (but not wealth or income). Interviews, XHMI, ZCMI, *passim* (Blecher).
53. See note 50.
54. We are grateful to Jack Gray for suggesting this point.

Chapter 5

1. *Renmin Ribao (RMRB)*, 4 July 1978, p. 1. Full text is in *Zhonggong Yanjiu*, XII:10, (October 1978), pp. 122-134.
2. A. Watson (1978a): "Worker Self-management and Political Participation in China" in M. Sawer (ed): *Socialism and Participation* (Australian Political Science Association Monograph, no. 24), pp. 19-25 and A. Watson (1980): "Industrial Development and the Four Modernizations", in B. Brugger (ed): *China Since the Gang of Four* (London: Croom Helm, 1980) pp. 90-95, on which the following argument is based.
3. For a succinct outline of these points see "Do not allow Socialist Enterprises to be Drawn onto the Rotten Path of Capitalism", Hongqi (*HQ*), no. 13, 1967, pp. 39-42.
4. Meng Kui and Xiao Lin: "A Critique of Sun Yefang's Reactionary Political Standpoint and Economic Programme", *HQ*, no. 10, 1966, pp. 26-37.
5. Xiang Jiwei: "The Cultural Revolution and Industrial Development", *HQ*, no. 6, 1976, pp. 52-55.
6. B. Brugger: *Contemporary China*, (London: Croom Helm, 1980), vol. 2, chapter VII.
7. B. Brugger: *Peking Review (PR)*, no. 14, 4 April 1975, pp. 5-11.
8. *Ibid.*, p. 7.
9. Yuan Qing: "A Major Issue in the Relations of Production" *HQ*, no. 5, 1975.
10. Deng Xiaoping (1975a): "On the General Principles for the Work of the

Party and the Country", 7 October 1975, in *Zhonggong Nianbao*, 1977, section r, p. 62.
11. *Ibid.*, p. 65.
12. Deng Xiaoping (1975b): "Several Questions Concerning the Acceleration of Industrial Development", 2 September 1975, in *Zhonggong Nianbao*, 1977, section 5, pp. 67-76.
13. See the argument in Watson (1980), *op. cit.*, pp. 92-95.
14. *RMRB*, 17 February 1977, p. 1.
15. CCP.CC *Zhongfa*, 37 (1977); *Issues and Studies*, XIV:11 (November 1978), p. 103; Hua Guofeng: *PR*, no. 10, 10 March 1978, p. 12; "The Exhibition on Waste Illustrates the Importance of Strengthening Management", *Jingli Guanli*, no. 1, 1979, pp. 10-13.
16. Compare, for example, the discussion of the law of value in those journals in 1978 and 1979 with the discussion by many of the same authors during 1961 and 1962 as outlined in G. W. Lee: "Current Debate on Profits and Value in Mainland China", *Australian Economic Papers*, IV:1/2 (June-Dec. 1965), pp. 72-78.
17. *HQ*, no. 1, 1977, pp. 3-24 and pp. 70-73.
18. Deng (1975b), *op. cit.*
19. Watson (1980), *op. cit.*, pp. 101-103.
20. *PR*, no. 39, 23 September 1977, p. 11.
21. See the discussion in A. Watson (1978b): "Industrial Management — Experiments in Mass Participation" in B. Brugger (ed): *China: The Impact of the Cultural Revolution* (London: Croom Helm, 1978), pp. 180-182, and Watson (1980), *op. cit.*, pp. 95-97.
22. Jiao Jili (1978): "On the Question of Improving Our System of Economic Administration", *Jingji Yanjiu*, no. 12, 1978, pp. 26-31, argues that despite efforts since 1954 to change Soviet methods of economic administration "up to the present we still basically do things in that way".
23. Jiao Jili (1979): "Observe Objective Economic Laws, Use Economic Methods to Manage the Economy", *Jingji Guanli*, no. 2, 1979, pp. 9-11; *Guangming Ribao (GMRB)*, 18 November 1978, p. 3; *GMRB*, 13 January 1979, p. 4; *blat* in the Soviet Union is examined by J. Berliner: *Factory and Manager in the USSR* (Cambridge: Harvard University Press, 1957), pp. 182-199.
24. Jiao Jili: *PR*, no. 10, 10 March 1978.
25. *RMRB*, 20 October 1979, translated in *Summary of World Broadcasts: The Far East (SWB:FE)*/ 6270/C/1-7.
26. *Ibid.; New China News Agency (NCNA)*, 26 November 1979, in *SWB:FE*/ 6288/C/1-6.
27. *PR*, no. 10, 10 March 1978, p. 25.
28. See M. Sullivan: "The Politics of Conflict and Compromise", in B. Brugger (ed): *China since the Gang of Four* (London: Croom Helm, 1980), pp. 20-50, for an analysis of this debate, especially pp. 36-45.
29. *PR*, no. 52, 29 December 1978, pp. 6-16.
30. *Beijing Review (BR)*, no. 10, 10 March 1980, pp. 7-10.
31. The following discussion is based on the version in *Zhonggong Yanjiu*,

XII:10 (October 1978), pp. 122-134.
32. *PR*, no. 28, 14 July 1978, p. 3.
33. *HQ*, no. 8, 1978, pp. 24-41 and *PR*, no. 30, 28 July 1978, pp. 6-17.
34. *PR*, no. 30, 28 July 1978, p. 8.
35. *Ibid.*, p. 11.
36. *Ibid.*, p. 17.
37. See, for example, *NCNA*, 5 July 1978, in *SWB:FE*/5863/B11/11-13; *GMRB*, 11 July 1978, p. 4, 26 August 1978, p. 4; Sun Yefang: "Justly Grasp Socialist Profit", *Jingji Yanjiu*, no. 7, 1979, pp. 47-58. Liang Wensen and Tian Jianghai: "A Trial Discussion of Assessment by Efficient Use of Capital", *Jingji Yanjiu*, no. 9, 1978, pp. 26-31. Jiao, *op. cit.*; Liu Guangdi: "A Trial Discussion of the New Role of Banks in the New Period", *Jingji Yanjiu*, no. 1, 1979, pp. 29-35; Tian Chunsheng: "On the Economic Nature of the Depreciation Fund for Fixed Capital", *Jingji Guanli*, no. 2, 1979, pp. 48-51.
38. *RMRB*, 6 October 1978. Translated in *PR*, no. 45, 10 November 1978, pp. 7-11, no. 46, 17 November 1978, pp. 15-23 and 24 November 1978, pp. 13-21.
39. *PR*, no. 45, 10 November 1978, p. 7.
40. *HQ*, no. 8, 1978, p. 35.
41. Jiao (*op. cit.*); Liang and Tian (*op. cit.*).
42. *PR*, no. 46, 17 November 1978, p. 21.
43. *PR*, no. 52, 29 December 1978, pp. 6-16.
44. *BR*, no. 37, 15 September 1980, pp. 3-9. Zhao acknowledged the special status of Sichuan in a speech in March 1980, see *NCNA*, 20 April 1980, in *SWB:FE*/6403/B11/1-6.
45. *SWB:FE*/6041/B11/9-11.
46. *SWB:FE*/6038/B11/1-2; *SWB:FE*/6067/B11/6-7; *SWB:FE*/6081/B11/6-7. The enterprise figure was quoted in *Jingji Yanjiu*, no. 1, 1979, p. 54.
47. *GMRB*, 17 March 1979, p. 4.
48. *NCNA*, 8 March 1979, in *SWB:FE*/6065/B11/8 and *NCNA*, 13 March 1979, in *SWB:FE*/6068/B11/11.
49. *SWB:FE*/6071/B11/10.
50. *GMRB*, 13 January 1979, p. 4 and *BR*, no. 2, 12 January 1979, p. 10.
51. A useful summary of these arguments is Shi Zhengwen: "Readjusting the National Economy: Why and How?", *BR*, no. 26, 29 June 1979, pp. 13-23.
52. *BR*, no. 27, 6 July 1979, pp. 5-51 and *BR*, no. 29, 20 July 1979, pp. 7-16.
53. *BR*, no. 29, 20 July 1979, pp. 13-14.
54. *BR*, no. 30, 27 July 1979, pp. 9-11.
55. *GMRB*, 11 July 1978, 12 August 1978, 26 August 1978, 23 September 1978, 21 October 1978, 2 December 1978, 27 January 1979, 10 February 1979 and 10 March 1979.
56. *Jingji Guanli*, no. 3 1979, pp. 39-41.
57. Luo Yuanzheng, Beijing, November 1979.
58. See Yu Guangyuan: "On the 'Theory of Socialist Economic Targets' ", *Jingji Yanjiu*, no. 11, 1979, pp. 2-7, the report on an October 1979 forum

on this question in *Jingji Yanjiu*, no. 12, 1979, pp. 23-41 and *BR*, no. 51, 21 December 1979, pp. 9-13.
59. On the laws see Tong Zhimin: "On the Question of Establishing Laws for the Economy", *Jingji Yanjiu*, no. 2, 1979, pp. 58-62. The re-establishment of the Insurance Company is reported in *RMRB*, 2 December 1979.
60. The impact of the increase in food prices is reflected in *NCNA* and provincial reports of October and November 1979 in *SWB:FE*/6264/C/1-14.
61. *NCNA*, 7 February 1980, in *SWB:FE*/6345/B11/8-11.
62. *NCNA*, 26 March 1980, in *SWB:FE*/6386/B11/2.
63. *NCNA*, 25 April 1980, in *SWB:FE*/6408/C/1-3.
64. See the editorials of 5 and 23 November 1979 in *SWB:FE*/6270/C/9-11 and *SWB:FE*/6288/C/2-6.
65. *SWB:FE*/6403/B11/1-6.
66. See the reports by Hua Guofeng and Yao Yilin in *BR*, no. 38, 22 September 1980, pp. 12-43, especially p. 13 and pp. 30-32.
67. *BR*, no. 39, 29 September 1980, p. 17.
68. *Ibid.*, p. 21.
69. *NCNA*, 17 September 1980, in *SWB:FE*/6529/B11/1.
70. *NCNA*, 2 December 1980, in *SWB:FE*/6594/C/1-2.
71. *NCNA*, 27 November 1980, in *SWB:FE*/6594/C/2.
72. For an analysis of this discussion see Watson (1980), *op. cit.*, pp. 112-112. Typical articles are Jiao (1978) *op. cit.*; Jiao (1979), *op. cit.*; Luo Jingfen: "The Planned Economy Can Use Flexible Plans", *Jingji Guanli*, no. 2, 1979, pp. 12-14; Li Chengrui and Zhang Zhuoyuan: "Some Questions Concerning Carrying Out Modern Socialist Construction at High Speed", *Jingji Yanjiu*, no. 2, 1979, pp. 2-11.
73. Sun, *op. cit.*; He Jianzhang, Kuang Rian and Zhang Zhuoyuan: "On the Question of Profit Rate of Capital and Production Prices in a Socialist Economy", *Jingji Yanjiu*, no. 1, 1979, pp. 47-59.
74. Huang Fanzhang: "Tentative Thoughts on 'Consumer Power' ", *Jingji Guanli*, no. 2, 1979, pp. 25-27.
75. Luo *op. cit.*, p. 14.
76. Liu Guoguang and Zhao Renwei: "On the Relationship Between the Plan and the Market in a Socialist Economy", *Jingji Yanjiu*, no. 5, 1979, pp. 46-55 (an abridged version of this article was published in *BR*, no. 31, 3 August 1979, pp. 8-12) provide a concise summary of the main areas of discussion. See also Sun Shangqing, Chen Jiyuan and Zhang Er: "Some Theoretical Considerations on Combining Planning and Marketing in a Socialist Economy", *Jingji Yanjiu*, no. 5, 1979, pp. 56-67; Liu Chengrui, Hu Naiwu and Yu Guanghua: "Combining the Plan and the Market is a Basic Means of Reforming China's Economic Management", *Jingji Yanjiu*, no. 7, 1979, pp. 37-46; Tang Zongkun: "The Law of Value, the Market Mechanism and the Socialist Planned Economy", *Jingji Yanjiu*, no. 7, 1979, pp. 47-58; Jiang Xuemo: "On Co-ordinating Plan and Market Adjustment", *Jingji Yanjiu*, no. 8, 1979, pp. 52-57; Xue Muqiao (1979): "A Study in the Planned Management of the Socialist Economy", *BR*, no. 43, 26 October 1979, pp. 14-20; *RMRB*, 7 February and 8 February

1980 translated in *SWB:FE*/6358/B11/11-13 and *SWB:FE*/6364/B11/7-11; He Jianzhang, Wang Zhiye and Wu Kaifai: "On the Problem of Coordinating Planned Readjustment and Market Regulation", *Jingji Yanjiu*, no. 5, 1980, pp. 19-25; Xue Muqiao (1980): "A Tentative Study of the Reform of the Economic System", *Jingji Yanjiu*, no. 6, 1980, pp. 3-11. Another version of these arguments by Xue appeared in *RMRB*, 10 June 1980, p. 5.
77. Liu and Zhao, *op. cit.*
78. *Ibid.*, p. 48.
79. *Ibid.*, pp. 49-51.
80. *Ibid.*, p. 51.
81. Jiang *op. cit.*, p. 52.
82. Sun Xiaoliang, "Competition under Socialist Conditions", *RMRB*, 23 June 1980, p. 5.
83. The proposed role for the plan is neatly summed up in He Jianzhang: "Problems in the Management of a Planned Economy Under the System of Ownership by the Whole People and the Orientation of Reform", *Jingji Yanjiu*, no. 5, 1979, pp. 44-45.
84. *BR*, no. 49, 7 December 1979, pp. 4-5.
85. *SWB:FE*/6409/B11/8-10.
86. *SWB:FE*/6408/C/6-7.
87. *NCNA*, 12 August 1980, in *SWB:FE*/6498/B11/7-9.
88. *RMRB*, 19 August 1980 in *SWB:FE*/6504/B11/4-7.
89. He, Wang and Wu, *op. cit.*, p. 19.
90. *Ibid.*, pp. 23-25.
91. Xue (1980), *op. cit.*, p. 6.
92. *SWB:FE*/6403/B11/1-6.
93. *Ibid.*, p. 2.
94. *NCNA*, 19 August 1980, in *SWB:FE*/6504/B11/8.
95. *BR*, no. 45, 10 November 1980, p. 20.
96. See, for example, Rong Wenzuo: "Actively Develop Collectively Owned Industry", *Jingji Guanli*, no. 8, 1979, pp. 9-12; Hong Yuanpeng and Weng Qiquan: "On Collectively Owned Industries in Urban Areas", *Jingji Yanjiu*, no. 1, 1980, pp. 62-67; Zhuang Qidong, Shen Jiyan and Wu Yan: "The Urban Collectively Owned Economy Must be Greatly Developed", *Jingji Yanjiu*, no, 4, 1980, pp. 10-16.
97. Rong, *op. cit.*, p. 9.
98. *Ibid.*, pp. 9-10.
99. Hong and Weng, (*op. cit.*), pp. 62-63.
100. *Ibid.*, pp. 63-64.
101. *Ibid.*, p. 65.
102. Zhuang, Shen and Wu, *op. cit.*, p. 13.
103. For an analysis of this model see Watson (1980), *op. cit.*, pp. 119-122. The most comprehensive description of this model is Wu Jiapei and Li Wenrui: *Changzhou Gongye Fazhan de Daolu (Changzhou: the Path for Industrial Development)* (Beijing: Renmin Chubanshe, 1979).
104. Hong and Weng, *op. cit.*, p. 62.

105. *Ibid.*, p. 65.
106. *RMRB*, 7 July 1980, p. 5. An abbreviated translation can be found in *SWB:FE*/6471/C/1-2.
107. *Ibid.*
108. "How to View the Nature of the Urban Individual Economy", *RMRB*, 10 July 1980.
109. *NCNA*, 19 August 1980, in *SWB:FE*/6504/B11/7-9.
110. See, for example, Xue Muqiao: *BR*, no. 36, 8 September 1980, pp. 18-23.
111. F. Schurmann: *Ideology and Organization in Communist China* (Berkeley: University of California, 1966), pp. 175-178 and 196-199.
112. Audrey Donnithorne: Public Seminar, University of Adelaide, September 1980. See also the report by Xue Muqiao: *BR*, no. 14, 7 April 1980, pp. 20-26.
113. Watson (1980) *op. cit.*, pp. 115-117.
114. Yang Peixin: "Lenin's Thinking on Socialist Banks Lights the Way Forward for the Work of China's Banks", *Jingji Yanjiu*, no. 3, 1979, pp. 45-54.
115. Liu Shibai: "A Trial Discussion of Economic Reform and the Improvement of the Socialist System of Public Ownership", *Jingji Yanjiu*, no. 2, 1979, p. 31.
116. *Ibid.*, pp. 31-35. See also Ye Xiangzhi: "A Proposal to Implement Loans for Basic Construction and to Set Up an Investment Bank", *Jingji Guanli*, no. 2, 1979, pp. 17-18; Liang and Tian, *op. cit.*
117. *NCNA*, 16 November 1979, in *SWB:FE*/6279/C1/1-2; *NCNA*, 26 November 1979, in *SWB:FE*/6288/C/1-2.
118. *NCNA*, 17 September 1980, in *SWB:FE*/6529/B11/1.
119. People's Bank of China, Chongqing Branch: "The Work of the Bank in the Enterprises Where Enlarged Autonomy is Being Tried Out", *Jingji Guanli*, no. 6, 1980, pp. 17-21.
120. Watson (1980), *op. cit.*, pp. 118-122.
121. See, for example, *BR*, no. 14, 7 April 1980, pp. 26-27.
122. Gui Shiyong: "It is Necessary to Establish an All-round Responsibility System in Industry", *Jingji Yanjiu*, no. 6, 1978, p. 22.
123. *Jingji Guanli*, no. 4, 1979, pp. 52-53.
124. Zhu Fulin and Xiang Huaicheng: "Some Problems Concerning the Expansion of Enterprise Financial Authority", *Jingji Guanli*, no. 6, 1979, pp. 14-17; Liu Shibai, (*op. Cit.*); He, (*op. cit.*).
125. He, *op. cit.*, pp. 42-43.
126. *BR*, no. 12, 24 March 1980, pp. 25-26.
127. Beijing radio, 14 January 1980, in *SWB:FE*/6322/B11/5-7 and *NCNA*, 19 February 1980, in *SWB:FE*/6352/B11/1.
128. Zhang Shuguang: "A Tentative Discussion of Responsibility for One's Own Profits and Losses", *Jingji Yanjiu*, no. 8, 1979, pp. 70-75.
129. *RMRB*, 20 August 1980, p. 1, translated in *SWB:FE*/6505/B11/6-8.
130. *RMRB*, 7 July 1980, p. 5.
131. Mao Zedong: "Report to the Second Session of the Seventh Central Committee of the Communist Party of China", 5 March 1949, *Selected*

Works, (Beijing: Foreign Languages Press, 1961), vol. 4, pp. 367-369.

Chapter 6

1. *Zhonggong jimi wenjian huibian* (Collection of secret documents of the CCP) (Taipei: Institute of International Relations, 1978), pp. 443-445.
2. *Ibid.*, pp. 154-155.
3. On events in Hangzhou, see *People's Daily* (*PD*) 28 July 1975, p. 1; 15 August 1975, p. 1; 11 September 1975, p. 1.
4. The target for 1980 had been fixed by Zhou Enlai at the 1st session of the 3rd NPC in December 1964. This target remained the same in his report of January 1975.
5. This study, dated 22 August 1975, was published in a Hong Kong journal *Zhan Wang* (Perspectives), no. 372, 1 August 1977, pp. 31-36. The text has never been published officially, but the mainland press has referred to it many times and quoted extracts from it during the criticism of Deng Xiaoping.
6. This decision dates back in fact to April 1978.
7. There is a summary of the "70 Points" in *Documents of the CCP Central Committee,* (Hong Kong: Union Research Institute, 1981), September 1956-April 1969, vol. 1, pp. 689-693; see also Kenneth Lieberthal: *A Research Guide to Central Party and Government Meetings in China, 1949-1975,* (New York: IASP, 1976), pp. 177-178. The exact date of the promulgation of the "70 Points" was 16 September 1961, according to *PD,* 6 October 1978, p. 3, n. 25.
8. Text of the "30 Points" in *Zhonggong Yanjiu* (Research on the CCP), no. 142, October 1978, pp. 120-134.
9. Created by a decision of the 8th Congress of the Central Committee in 1961, with the aim of organising economic development, the regions were dissolved during the Cultural Revolution.
10. For radical criticism of the "20 Points", see *Xuexi yu Pipan* (Study and Criticism) (*S&C*), no. 4, 1976, pp. 28-35.
11. 20/14 numbers the three sectors in this order only to affirm the necessity of maintaining a *balance* among them.
12. *PD,* 12 September 1977, p. 1.
13. *S&C,* p. 32.
14. *S&C,* pp. 30-32. The definition of the three words *guan, qia, ya* given by Zhou Enlai at the 10th Congress of the CCP in 1973 can be summarised as follows: *guan,* management of enterprises by regulations; *qia,* to stop forbidden practices by regulations; *ya,* to suppress illegal trading. The radicals gave a different definition in their criticism: *guan,* uniform management by regulations; *qia,* uniform stifling of the workers' enthusiasm; *ya,* oppression and slavery of the workers.
15. *PD,* 6 October 1978, pp. 1-3.
16. 20/16, 20/17, 20/18; 30/23, 30/24, 30/25, 30/26, 30/27.
17. Compare 20/18 and 30/23. For criticism by the radicals see *S&C,* p. 34.
18. *S&C,* pp. 29-30.

19. See Hu Qiaomu: "Respect Economic Laws and Speed Up Modernisations", *PD*, 6 October 1978, pp. 1-3.
20. See the editorial, "Implement the Programme to Lead the Country and Promote a New Leap Forward", *PD*, 19 April 1977; also the article by Hua Guofeng, dated 2 April 1963, praising the merits of the Great Leap Forward, *PD*, 24 April 1977. In fact, the "new leap forward" began, as is clear from listening to local radio stations, from the start of the 1st quarter of 1975, just after Zhou Enlai's speech on the four modernisations at the 4th NPC. The 10-Year Plan was never more than the quantified expression of that "new leap forward".
21. For example, Anhui Radio, 18 January 1979, which reported the conclusions of a meeting of Anhui provincial committee on agricultural problems, held after the 3rd plenum.
22. See, for example, *PD*, 2 April 1979, p. 1; 3 April 1979, p. 3; 6 April 1979, p. 3; 8 April 1979, p. 1; 10 April 1979, p. 3.
23. *PD*, 25 May 1979, p. 3.
24. *Hongqi* (Red Flag) (*RF*) no. 2, 1971, p. 47.
25. *PD*, 24 February 1979, p. 1; 6 April 1979, p. 3.
26. *PD*, 17 April 1979, p. 3.
27. *PD*, 30 May 1979, p. 3; 25 May 1979, p. 3.
28. *PD*, 25 May 1979, p. 3.
29. *Ibid*.
30. *Jingji Yanjiu* (Economic Research) (*ER*), no. 5, 1979, p. 52.
31. There was a decision, taken in May 1979, to speed up the development of light industry, cf. *PD*, 30 May 1979, p. 1.
32. *PD*, 10 April 1979, p. 3; 13 April 1979, p. 3; 15 June 1979, p. 3.
33. See, for example, *New China News Agency* (*NCNA*), 15 June 1978.
34. Director of the Institute of Economic Research of the State Planning Commission, advisor on planning, in *PD*, 15 June 1979, p. 3. This draft is reminiscent of another put forward by the same author in 1957 in *Jihua Jingji* (Planned Economy), no. 9, 1957, pp. 20-24.
35. *ER*, no. 5, 1979, p. 44.
36. *PD*, 15 June 1979, p. 3.
37. *RF*, no. 6, 1979, pp. 30-31; the author of this article is the distinguished economist Sun Yefang — called the Chinese "Libermann" during the Cultural Revolution, against which he defended himself — whose position in the Academy of Social Sciences is not known exactly.
38. *PD*, 28 June 1979, p. 2; this saying alludes to the fact that formerly, and even today in some overseas-Chinese communities, very poor Chinese get badly into debt to buy in their lifetime their ideal coffin.
39. *PD*, 24 March 1979, p. 1; 28 March 1979, p. 2; 10 April 1979, p. 3.
40. *Zhengming* (Forum), no. 5, 1979, p. 9.
41. The lack of investigation before opening industrial premises was denounced by *PD* which reported the opening of a coal mine, the workings of which endangered a school and a central electricity station (16 April 1979, p. 2).
42. *RF*, no. 6, 1979, p. 25.

43. *Ibid.*
44. *ER*, no. 9, 1978, p. 46.
45. *Ibid; PD*, 27 August 1977, p. 1; 15 November 1977, p. 1.
46. *ER*, no. 5, 1979, pp. 35-36.
47. The author does not mention explicitly the "30 Points", but refers to the eight criteria proposed in them.
48. He Hianzhang is even more explicit than Sun Yefang concerning the management of the depreciation funds of the Anshan steel works: the depreciation rate (2.92 per cent) has to allow for renewal of capital every 34 years; but as 50 per cent of these funds are returned to the State, its is necessary to double the amortisation period and amortise in 68 years. Of the remainder, 60 per cent must go towards innovation and 20-40 per cent to anti-pollution measures, so there is nothing left, so to speak, for renewal of working capital.
49. Cf. *ER*, no. 4, 1979, pp. 52-80; no. 5, pp. 35-80 (particularly pp. 35-67); no. 6, pp. 43-74.
50. Wan Dianwu: "Proposal to Replace Turnover by Added Value as the Main Economic Indicator", *ER*, no. 4, 1979, pp. 50-51.
51. *PD*, 9 March 1979, p. 3; 18 March 1979, p. 1; 24 March 1979, p. 1; 28 March 1979, p. 2.
52. Hu Qiaomu, *op. cit.*
53. *PD*, 29 June 1979, pp. 1 and 3; 30 June 1979, pp. 1,3 and 4.
54. For opposition to the policy of readjustment, cf. *PD*, 17 July 1979, p. 1.
55. An economist like Xue Muqiao justifies the order of priority "agriculture, light industry, heavy industry" by the actual need for readjustment of the economy, but only after having reaffirmed that the rate of modernisation in China depends on priority for the development of heavy industry (*ER*, no. 6, 1979, p. 8).
56. Cf. *PD*, 19 June 1979, p. 3; 12 July 1979, p. 1; 14 July 1979, p. 1; 16 July 1979, p. 1; cf. also *SWB:FE* /W/1041/A/1-2, *SWB:FE* /1043/A/1-4, *SWB:FE* /6183/B11/11.
57. *PD*, 7 June 1979, p. 2; 17 June 1979, p. 1.
58. *PD*, 3 July 1979, p. 4.
59. *NCNA*, 14 June 1979.
60. Cf. interview with Xue Muqiao in *Beijing Ribao* (Peking Daily), 18 July 1979, p. 1.
61. *PD*, 8 May 1979, p. 1; *Gongren Ribao* (Workers' Daily), 23 May 1979, p. 1 (speech by Ni Zhifu); 26 May 1979, p. 2.
62. *PD*, 9 September 1979, p. 1.
63. Amount paid in 1979 for these imports: Y4730 million, or an increase of 220 per cent compared with 1978; whence the 1978 total: Y1480 million; whence the absolute increase for 1979: Y3250 million; whence the proportion of that Y3250 million in the 1979 deficit, evaluated at Y5600 million: 60 per cent.
64. Cf. the article by Xue Muqiao in *RF*, no. 8, 1979, p. 24.

Chapter 7

1. *Chinese Economy Post-Mao: A Compendium of Papers submitted to the Joint Economic Committee, Congress of the U.S.* (Washington: JEC, 1978), p. 710.
2. *U.S. China Business Review,* January-February 1975.
3. For an excellent discussion of the radicals' effect on trade policy, see Ann Fenwick: "Chinese Foreign Trade Policy and the Campaign Against Deng Xiaoping", in Thomas Fingar (ed): *China's Quest for Independence: Policy Evolution in the 1970s* (Colorado: Westview, 1980).
4. BBC: *Summary of World Broadcasts: The Far East, (SWB:FE)*, 18 October 1976.
5. *SWB:FE,* 25 November 1976.
6. *SWB:FE,* 29 December 1976.
7. *JETRO China Newsletter,* Japan External Trade Organisation, October 1977.
8. *Xinhua News Agency* (Xinhua), 24 June 1977.
9. *SWB:FE,* 13 September 1977.
10. *Financial Times,* 3 November 1977.
11. *FT,* 31 October 1977.
12. Yu Qiuli: "Report to the National People's Congress", *Xinhua,* 29 June 1979.
13. *SWB:FE,* 3 October 1978.
14. *Reuter East-West Trade News (REWTN),* 19 July 1978.
15. *FT,* 10 June 1978.
16. *SWB:FE,* 28 February 1979.
17. *Xinhua,* 8 July 1979.
18. *REWTN,* 27 June 1979.
19. *Sino-British Trade Bulletin,* August-September 1979.

Chapter 8

1. Peter Nolan and Gordon White: "Socialist Development and Rural Inequality: the Chinese Countryside in the 1970's", *Journal of Peasant Studies,* 7:1 (October 1979), pp. 3-48.
2. In Guangdong province, for example, the index of output (physical) (1957=100) stood as follows in 1960: grain=80, sugarcane=75, peanuts= 55, pigs=59, draught animals=84. (Written data given to the Queen Elizabeth House, Oxford, China Study Group, June 1979 (hereafter Trip Notes).)
3. The average p.c. daily intake of calories in the mid-1970s was estimated to be only about 2100, of which over 80 per cent came from grain. (H. J. Groen and J. A. Kilpatrick: "Chinese Agricultural Policy", in Joint Economic Committee, U.S. Congress, *Chinese Economy Post-Mao* (Washington: U.S. Government Printing Office, 1978), p. 645.) The average p.c. daily calorie intake in 38 low-income countries in 1977 was estimated to be 2052 (*World Bank, World Development Report 1980*

(New York: Oxford University Press, 1980), p. 152).
4. Zhang Liuzheng: "Developing Agricultural Production; Transforming the Peasants' Living Standard", *NYJJWT*, no. 1, 1980.
5. J. S. Aird: "Population Growth in the People's Republic of China", in U.S. Congress, *Chinese Economy Post-Mao*, (Washington: U.S. Government Printing Office, 1978), p. 467.
6. Trip notes, June 1979.
7. Groen and Kilpatrick, *op. cit.*, p. 649.
8. World Bank, *op. cit.*, pp. 112-113.
9. For a discussion of policies on rural distribution before the death of Mao, see Nolan and White, *op. cit.*
10. A national survey of 339 production brigades in 1979 found that in 1978 76.5 per cent of the members' grain ration was "according to need". In 1979, the figure had declined to 70 per cent (People's Communes' Management Section of the Department of Agriculture: "A Survey of Income Distribution in 339 Brigades in the People's Communes in 1979", *NYJJWT*, no. 9, 1980, p. 29)
11. *Ibid.*
12. Nolan and White, *op. cit.*, pp. 25-6.
13. Shi Shan: "Where is the Breakthrough Point to Rapid Agricultural Development?", *NYJJWT*, no. 2, 1980.
14. See "An Important Policy Decision on Accelerating Agricultural Development", *Renmin Ribao* (People's Daily) (*RMRB*), editorial, 22 January 1979, translated in Foreign Broadcast Information Service, *Daily Report: People's Republic of China* (*FBIS*), 23 January, 1979, pp. E2-E6. Compare "Premier Hua Guofeng's Report on the Work of the Government" (delivered at the second session of the Fifth National People's Congress on June 18, 1979), *New China News Agency* (*NCNA*), 25 June 1979.
15. See Benedict Stavis: *Turning Point in China's Agricultural Policy*, Working Paper No. 1, MSU Rural Development Series, Department of Agricultural Economics, Michigan State University, East Lansing, Michigan, May 1979, and Bill Brugger: "Rural Policy" in B. Brugger (ed): *China Since the "Gang of Four"* (London: Croom Helm, 1980), pp. 135-173.
16. See, for example, "On so-called 'Eating the Grain of Guilt' ", *Liaoning Daily*, 3 February 1979, reported by Liaoning provincial radio, Shenyang, and translated in *FBIS*, 8 February 1979; He Dongjun and He Maoji: "Voice From the Land of Lovage", *NCNA*, Beijing, 18 March 1979, translated in *FBIS*, 21 March 1979; *NCNA* (English edition), 6 Feb 1980.
17. For example, see Tung Ta-Lin and Pao Tung: "Some Views on Agricultural Modernisation", *RMRB*, 8 December 1978, p. 3, in *FBIS*, 18 December 1978 and "A Correct Policy for Speeding Up Farm Mechanisation", *RMRB*, editorial, 6 February 1979, in *FBIS* 6 February 1979.
18. For example, see Kirin province's directive on income distribution (issued by the provincial CCP Committee on 9 November 1977), reported by Kirin Radio, 14 November 1977, in *FBIS*, 22 November 1977, sections 3 and 6; *People's Daily* editorial on improving commune management,

19. *Guangming Ribao*, 10 April, 1980, translated in *Summary of World Broadcasts: Far East (SWB:FE)*, no. 6437/B11/5.
20. "Distribution Policy" (one of an eight-lecture series), Beijing radio (domestic service), 22 April 1978, (translated in *Joint Publications Research Service (JPRS)*, 24 May 1978.
21. Wang Gengjin, Yang Zhangfu and Wang Songpei: "To Speed Up the Development of Agricultural Production Requires Adequate Concern for the Peasants' Material Interests", *Jingji Yanjiu* (Economic Research) *(JJYJ)*, no. 3, 1979, pp. 23-24.
22. *Ibid.*, p. 28.
23. "It is Glorious to Receive More Pay for More Work and to Become Richer", *Fujian Ribao* (Fujian Daily), 13 March 1979, in *FBIS*, 16 March 1979; "Let Some Peasants Become Well-off First", *Beijing Review*, 9 (2 March 1979), pp. 5-6; "We Need to Encourage a Part of Our Peasants to Become Well-to-do First", *NCNA*, Beijing, 17 February 1979; Jin Wen: " 'Getting Rich Through Labour' is in Conformity with Socialist Principle", *Guangming Ribao* (Glorious Daily) *(GMRB)*, 15 April 1979, in *FBIS*, 30 April 1979.
24. Wang, Yang and Weng, *op. cit.*, p. 28.
25. Jin Wen, *op. cit.*
26. Liang Wen: "Holding an Unbreakable Rice-bowl and Eating from the Common Pot", *Jilin Ribao* (Jilin Daily), 20 May 1979, reported by Jilin Provincial Radio, Changchun *(FBIS,* 22 May 1979).
27. For a historical review of this issue, see the article by Yu Guoyao: *Hongqi* (Red Flag), 5 March 1980.
28. For example, see the interview with the vice-minister of agriculture, Zhu Rong, in *NCNA* (English edition), 29 January 1981.
29. "Correct Policy for Accelerating Agricultural Mechanisation", *RMRB*, editorial, 6 February 1979, in *FBIS*, 9 February 1979, p. E18.
30. Lu Chen-mao: "The Production Team is also an Enterprise", *GMRB*, 18 November 1978, in *FBIS*, 5 December 1978, p. E13.
31. *GMRB*, 6 November 1979, in *FBIS*, 15 November 1979.
32. "Southern Daily Hails Enrichment of Peasants", Guangdong provincial radio, 4 March 1979, in *FBIS*, 6 March 1979.
33. Wang Gengjin and He Jianzhang: "Some Problems in Implementing Rural Economic Policies", *JJYJ*, no. 8, p. 17.
34. "Lin Hujia Visits Beijing Suburban Counties", *NCNA* Beijing (domestic service), 27 February 1979, in *FBIS*, 5 March 1979, compare "One Should not Postulate . . . ", *NCNA*, 6 June 1979, in *SWB:FE*, 9 June 1979.
35. "Shandong County Lifts Limit on Peasant Income", Shandong provincial radio, Jinan, 28 November 1978, in *FBIS*, 30 November 1978.
36. For a comprehensive analysis, see Xu Dixin: "On 'Transition in Poverty' ", *JJYJ*, no. 4, 1979, pp. 2-7.
37. For example, see Jin Wen (Chin Wen): "On 'Transition in Poverty' ", *Liberation Army Daily*, 5 December 1978, in *FBIS*, 7 December 1978.
38. Hubei provincial radio, 14 January 1979, in *FBIS*, 16 January 1979.

39. Shaanxi provincial radio, 10 January 1979, in *FBIS*, 17 January 1979.
40. Jin Wen, *op. cit.*
41. For example, "Effectively protect . . . ", *RMRB* editorial, 24 January 1979, in *FBIS*, 26 January 1979, p. 12.
42. J. E. Nickum: "Labour Accumulation in Rural China and its Role Since the Cultural Revolution", *Cambridge Journal of Economics*, no. 2, 1978, p. 284.
43. "We Should Respect the Right of a Production Team to Make its Own Decisions", *Nanfang Ribao* (Southern Daily) (*NFRB*), Canton, 28 October 1978, in *FBIS*, 9 November 1978.
44. Beijing radio (domestic service), 1 June 1979, in *SWB:FE* 6133, 5 June 1979: "Boldly Strengthen Correct Leadership of the Production Teams", *NFRB*, 26 March 1979, in *FBIS*, 27 March 1979.
45. For discussions of these problems, see the *People's Daily* article on rural cadres in *NCNA* (domestic service), 6 February 1980, and Wen Zhu: "This is Advance, not Retreat", *GMRB*, 2 February 1980.
46. *RMRB*, 15 February 1978, in *FBIS*, 17 February 1978.
47. Sichuan provincial radio, 22 December 1977, in *FBIS*, 4 January 1978.
48. For the Jilin regulations, see Jilin provincial radio, 14 November 1977, in *FBIS*, 22 November 1977.
49. *NCNA* (English edition), 2 January 1981.
50. *NCNA* (English edition), 15 May 1980.
51. For example, see Yi Xindian: "The System of Production Quotas Must be Implemented", *RMRB*, 22 April 1978, in *JPRS*, 431, 24 May 1978.
52. "Henan Conference Urges 'More Pay for More Work' ", *NCNA*, Beijing (domestic service), 21 January 1978, in *FBIS*, 24 January 1978.
53. For example, see Guo Xiusheng and Gao Xiansong: "Recording Workpoints on the Basis of Fixed Labour Quotas is a Good Way of Implementing the Policy of Pay According to Work", *RMRB*, 2 December 1978, in *JPRS*, 487, 31 January 1979; compare the article by Wu Xiang and Zhang Guangyou: *NCNA* (domestic service), 9 April 1980.
54. *RMRB*, 2 April 1980.
55. For a discussion of this innovation in Hebei, see the speech by Li Erzhong, reported by Hebei radio, 10 August 1980, in *FBIS*, 165, R2; compare Guizhou radio, 20 July 1980, in *SWB:FE* 6479.
56. For example, see Jilin radio, 11 November 1980, in *SWB:FE* 6580.
57. *NFRB*, 1 December 1979, in *SWB:FE* 6298/B11/3.
58. *RMRB*, editorial, 17 January 1980.

Chapter 9

1. The paper is based mainly on monitored Chinese broadcasts. There are two series: the United States' Foreign Broadcasts Information Service and the BBC's Summary of World Broadcasts: The Far East. The importance of these for a study of local institutions lies in the fact that they provide regular material from provincial stations. In the footnotes these series are referred to as: (i) *FBIS* number/origin/date of broadcast; (ii) *SWB:FE*

number/origin, date of broadcast. *SWB:FE* /W/ refers to the SWB Weekly Economic Supplement. It is significant that many references are to the New China News Agency's English language broadcasts (*NCNA* (E)), in itself indicating the importance which Peking attaches to local industry in general, and commune and brigade enterprise in particular.
2. On the earlier development of rural enterprise in China, see especially: D. Perkins et al.: *Rural Small Scale Industry in the People's Republic of China* (Berkeley: University of California, 1977); John Sigurdson: *Rural Industrialisation in China* (Cambridge: Harvard University Press, 1977); S. Aziz: *Rural Development: Learning from China* (New York: 1978); Carl Riskin: "Small Industry and the Chinese Model of Development", *China Quarterly,* no. 46, 1979; "China's Rural Industries", *China Quarterly,* no. 73, 1978; "Political Conflict and Rural Industrialisation in China", *World Development,* no. 6, 1978; John Sigurdson: "Rural Industry: a Traveller's View", *China Quarterly,* no. 50, 1972; "Rural Industrialisation: a Comparison of Development Planning in China and India", *World Development,* no. 6, 1978.
3. Industry is the heart of diversified development of the villages, but Chinese reports often do not distinguish between industrial and other enterprises; many lines of production which in the West would be considered a part of agriculture are regarded as non-farming enterprises, because traditionally "farming" refers only to cultivation of the arable. Animal husbandry and fruit farming, for example, are not referred to as agricultural activities.
4. *SWB:FE* /W/966/A8, *NCNA* (E), 3 January 1978; *SWB:FE* /W/104/A19, *NCNA* (E), 4 December 1978; *SWB:FE* /W/1042/A8, *NCNA* (E), 6 July 1979.
5. *Peking Review,* 39, pp. 4-5, 28 September 1979; *SWB:FE* /W/1051/A7, *NCNA* (C), 11 September 1979.
6. *SWB:FE* /W/1035/A2, *NCNA* (E), 3 January 1978.
7. *SWB:FE* /W/1042/A8, *NCNA* (E), 6 July 1979.
8. *SWB:FE* /W/1035/A2, *NCNA* (E), 3 January 1978.
9. *SWB:FE* /W/1042/A6, *NCNA* (E), 6 July 1979.
10. *SWB:FE* /W/971/A3, *NCNA* (C), 28 January 1978.
11. *SWB:FE* /6195/A8, Yuannan rado, 11 August 1979.
12. *SWB:FE* /6196/B11 16, Guangdong rado, 5 August 1979; *SWB:FE* /W995/A3, *NCNA* (C), 7 August 1978; Changsha radio, 20 September 1978; *SWB:FE* /W/967/A12, Shansi radio, 18 January 1978.
13. *SWB:FE* /W/1026/A20, Kyodo (E), 26 March 1979.
14. *SWB:FE* /W/1043/A16, 16 June 1979.
15. *NCNA* (C) 5 May 1979.
16. *SWB:FE* /W/1023/A13, Peking radio, 4 February 1979.
17. *SWB:FE* /W/1038/A15, Shenyang radio, 26 June 1979.
18. *SWB:FE* /W/1040/A9, *NCNA* (C), 13 June 1979.
19. *NCNA* (E) 18 March, 1979.
20. *NCNA* (E) 6 September 1979,
21. *SWB:FE* /W/995/A3, *NCNA* (E), 7 August 1978.
22. *SWB:FE* /W/1022/A15, *NCNA* (E) n.d.

23. *FBIS*/139/53, Liaoning radio, 15 July 1980.
24. *SWB:FE* /6574/B1114, *NCNA* (C), 7 July 1980.
25. *SWB:FE* /6640/C5, *NCNA* (C), 30 January 1981.

Chapter 10

1. Although in some localities private plots have been dispensed with altogether, this list illustrates that there may still be a substantial number of private sidelines or occupations. Within the family courtyard, for example, commune members might grow fruit trees, shrubs for making brooms and mats, sunflowers, tobacco, peppers and raise a couple of pigs, chickens, sheep, goats, or rabbits. J. Chen: *A Year in Upper Felicity* (London: Harrap, 1973), pp. 7-10.
2. "Defence of Sideline Production", *Summary of World Broadcasts: The Far East* (*SWB:FE*), 27 April 1978.
3. K. Walker: *Planning in Chinese Agriculture, Socialisation and the Private Sector, 1956-62*, (London: Cass, 1965).
4. "Abolition of the Gang's Indigenous Policies", *SWB:FE*, 10 February 1978.
5. "Gansu Cadres Criticise the Gang of Four's Agriculture by Dictatorship", *SWB:FE*, 4 February 1978.
6. "Thriving Sideline Production", *Xinhua News* (*XH*), 10 November 1978.
7. "Implementation of Rural Policies in Hunan", *SWB:FE*, 10 June 1978.
8. "Abolition of the Gang's Indigenous Policies", *SWB:FE*, 10 February 1978.
9. "Report on Gang of Four's Policies", *XH*, 15 February 1978.
10. *SWB:FE*, 27 April, 1978; "Village Fairs in Anhui Province", *Renmin Ribao* (*RMRB*), 20 June 1978.
11. "Rural Problems in Shaanxi Province", *SWB:FE*, 11 November 1978.
12. "Low Rations for Peasants in Hebei Prefecture", *SWB:FE*, 9 December 1978.
13. "Liaoning Newspaper Calls for Implementation of Rural Policies", *XH*, 8 May 1979.
14. W. Carey: "Report of Delegation of American Association for Advancement of Science", *Science*, 9 February 1979.
15. *SWB:FE*, 27 April 1978.
16. "Indigenous Policies Corrected in Guangxi", *SWB:FE*, 16 March 1978.
17. "Thriving Sideline Production", *XH*, 10 November 1978.
18. "Rehabilitation of Persecuted Peasants", *SWB:FE*, 26 January 1979.
19. "Commentary by Xinhua Correspondents", *RMRB*, 19 February 1979.
20. *Hongqi*, 1 March 1979.
21. "Peasants' Domestic Sideline Production Stimulated", *XH*, 2 May 1979.
22. "Policy on Village Trade Fairs", *SWB:FE*, 27 July 1978.
23. "Defence of Sideline Production", *SWB:FE*, 27 April 1978.
24. S. J. Burki: *A Study of Chinese Communes* (Cambridge: Harvard University Press, 1969), p. 40; W. Parish, and M. Whyte: *Village and Family in Contemporary China* (Chicago: University of Chicago Press, 1978),

p. 119.
25. "Jiangsu Peasants Increase Income", *XH*, 26 February 1979.
26. "Defence of Sideline Production", *SWB:FE*, 27 April 1978.
27. "Lecture on Sideline Production", *SWB:FE*, 17 May 1979.
28. Editorial, *RMRB*, 13 February 1979.
29. Editorial, *RMRB*, 28 March 1979.
30. "New Problems in Sichuan", *SWB:FE*, 20 April 1979.
31. "Calls to Combat Illegalities in Village Fairs", *SWB:FE*, 3 May 1979.
32. "Disastrous Years in Rural Guangdong", *SWB:FE*, 19 May 1979.
33. "Low Rations for Peasants in Hebei Prefecture", *SWB:FE*, 9 December 1978.
34. "Gansu Official on Peasant Demands", *SWB:FE*, 17 January 1979.
35. "Problems with Peasant Individualism in Fujian and Hunan", *SWB:FE*, 23 March 1979.
36. Yang Liu: "Reform of Marriage and Family Systems in China", *Peking Review*, 13 March 1964.
37. M. Cohen: *House United, House Divided, The Chinese Family in Taiwan*, (New York: University of Columbia Press, 1976), p. 231; M. Freedman: *Lineage Organisation in Southeastern China*, (London: Athlone Press, 1958), p. 30; W. Goode: *World Revolution and Family Patterns* (New York: Free Press, 1963), pp. 301-302; H. Lethbridge: "The Communes in China", in E. F. Szezepanik, (ed): *Economic and Social Problems of the Far East*, (Hong Kong: Hong Kong University Press, 1962), p. 380; C. K. Yang: *"Communist Society: The Family and the Village"* (Reading: MIT Press, 1959).
38. I. Taueber: "The Families of Chinese Farmers", in M. Freedman (ed): *Family and Kinship in Chinese Society*, (Stanford: Stanford University Press, 1970), p. 71.
39. Elisabeth Croll: "Jiang Village: A Household Survey", *China Quarterly*, no. 72, 1977.
40. Elisabeth Croll: *The Politics of Marriage in Contemporary China*, (Cambridge: Cambridge University Press, 1980).
41. Elisabeth Croll: *Women and Rural Development: The Case of the People's Republic of China*, (Geneva: International Labour Office, 1979).
42. Elisabeth Croll: "Socialist Development Experience: Women in Rural Production and Reproduction . . . ", Discussion Paper 143, Institute of Development Studies, Sussex, 1979; D. Davin: *Women-Work: Women and the Party in Revolutionary China*, (Oxford: Clarendon Press, 1976).
43. Elisabeth Croll: *Feminism and Socialism in China* (London: Routledge and Kegan Paul, 1978); N. Diamond: "Collectivisation, Kinship and the Status of Women in Rural China", *Bulletin of Concerned Asian Scholars*, Jan-March, 1979.
44. W. Parish: "Socialism and the Chinese Peasant Family", *Journal of Asian Studies*, XXIV: no. 3, 1975.

336 Notes and References

Chapter 11

1. "Decisions of the Central Committee on accelerating agricultural development", *New China News Agency* (*NCNA*), London, 5 October 1979.
2. *NCNA*, London, 10 February 1979.
3. Benedict Stavis: *The Politics of Agricultural Mechanization in China* (Ithaca: Cornell University Press, 1978).
4. *NCNA*, Peking, February 6 1979.
5. *Nanfang Ribao* (Southern Daily), Canton, in *Summary of World Broadcasts: The Far East* (*SWB:FE*), 6053/B11.
6. *NCNA*, domestic service, in *Foreign Broadcast Information Service* (*FBIS*), Daily Report, no. 139, 18 July 1979.
7. *Ibid.*
8. Cited in Bill Brugger (ed): *China Since the Gang of Four* (London: Croom Helm, 1979), p. 154.
9. *People's Daily*, 25 June 1979, in *FBIS*, CIII/79/133.
10. *FBIS*, CIII/79/145, 26 July 1979.
11. "Party Decision on Accelerating Agricultural Development", *SWB:FE* 6241/C/12.
12. Hubert O. Brown: "Education and Modernization in the PRC", in Steve S. E. Chin (ed): *Modernization in China* (Hong Kong: University of Hong Kong, 1979).
13. Wuhan radio, 11 April 1979, in *SWB:FE* 6096/B11/5-6.
14. *People's Daily*, 22 February 1979; *NCNA*, London, 9 March 1979.

Chapter 12

1. *People's Daily* (*PD*), 1 December 1980, in *Summary of World Broadcasts: The Far East* (*SWB:FE*) 6592.
2. *New China News Agency* (*NCNA*), 20 November 1980.
3. For further details of Zhou's views, see John Gardner: "Chou Jung-hsin and Chinese Education", *Current Scene*, November-December 1977.
4. For an excellent compilation which includes Mao's most radical statements, see "Mao Tse-tung on Education", *Chinese Education*, Winter 1973-74.
5. *PD*, 28 August 1977.
6. *Chinese Education*, pp. 30-31 and 34.
7. *NCNA*, 24 November 1976, in *SWB:FE* 5379.
8. Peking radio, 28 February 1977, in *SWB:FE* 5463.
9. The original story was given in *PD*, 10 August 1973; the revised version appeared in *PD*, 30 November 1976. See also, Feng Hua; "Analyse the Black Model Zhang Tiesheng", *Liaoning Daxue Xuebao* (Liaoning University Journal), no. 6, 1976, pp. 28-34.
10. The original story is in *PD*, 28 December 1973; the revised version appeared in *Guangming Daily*, 17 March 1973.
11. *NCNA*, 8 December 1977, in *SWB:FE* 5694.
12. *NCNA*, 16 May 1978, in *SWB:FE* 5817.

13. Peking radio, 9 December 1977, in *SWB:FE* 5694.
14. Shanxi radio, 6 November 1980, in *SWB:FE* 6573.
15. Ministry of Education Mass Criticism Group: "A Great Polemic on the Educational Battlefront", *Red Flag*, no. 12, 1977, pp. 3-13.
16. *Ibid.*, p. 10.
17. *Guangming Daily*, 8 November 1979, in *SWB:FE* 6279.
18. *NCNA*, 14 December 1980, in *SWB:FE* 6662.
19. *NCNA*, 12 December 1979, in *SWB:FE* 6299.
20. *NCNA*, 10 June 1978, in *SWB:FE* 5843. Since April 1978, a host of conferences to discuss different aspects of educational work have been held in China. For brief details see Wang Hsueh-wen: "Educational Reform on the Chinese Mainline; Besetting Problems", *Issues and Studies* (December 1980), pp. 39-42
21. *PD*, 9 March 1977 and 16 March 1977.
22. See, for example, *PD*, 23 February 1977 in *SWB:FE* 5453; "Who Are Masters of the School?", *Peking Review*, no. 38, 1978, pp. 18-19.
23. For a useful guide to the recent work of the Academy of Social Sciences see A. F. Thurston and J. H. Parker (eds): *Humanities and Social Science Research in China*, (New York: Social Science Research Council, 1980).
24. The figure for 1976 was given to me by a Ministry of Education official in April that year; the 1979 figure is given in *NCNA*, 23 September 1979.
25. The figure for 1976 as above; other school enrolment figures as given by Susanne Pepper: "Chinese Education After Mao: Two Steps Forward, Two Steps Back and Begin Again?", *The China Quarterly*, no. 80, p. 6. Dr Pepper's article is by far the most comprehensive study of the post-Mao changes to have so far appeared.
26. *Ibid.*, p. 7.
27. "Keypoint" schools had flourished before the Cultural Revolution and had been condemned as "training grounds for intellectual aristocrats".
28. *NCNA*, 20 October 1977, in *SWB:FE* 5648.
29. "Textbooks Revised", *Peking Review*, no. 39, 1978, p. 26.
30. *NCNA*, 8 November 1980.
31. *PD*, 1 December 1980, in *SWB:FE* 6592.
32. Robin Munro: "Settling Accounts with the Cultural Revolution at Beijing University 1977-78", *The China Quarterly*, no. 83, pp. 308-333.
33. *NCNA*, 12 May 1978, in *SWB:FE* 5813; Canton radio, 23 June 1978, in *SWB:FE* 5852.
34. Although hard information is difficult to come by, there is reason to believe that the students chosen to study abroad are overwhelmingly drawn from Peking, Shanghai and one or two other major cities.
35. *PD*, 19 April 1980, in Wang, *op. cit.*, p. 45.
36. *Guangming Daily*, 26 March 1979, in Wang, *op. cit.*, p. 49.
37. *Jiaoyu Yanjiu* (Educational Research), no. 2, 1980, p. 11, in Wang, *op. cit.*, p. 49. *Jiaoyu Janjiu* no. 3, 1980, carried further extremely detailed statistics on educational inadequacies.
38. Wang, *op. cit.*, p. 49.

INDEX

April Fifth Movement, 27, 29

Bo Yibo, 150, 162, 163
Brugger, Bill, 90
"Bureaucratism", 26

Cadres, 26, 62-3, 67-8, 72, 74, 261, 309
Changzhou model, 110, 115
Chen Duxiu, 52
Chen Xilian, 94
Chen Yongguei, 56-7, 68, 150, 196, 267
Chen Yun, 21, 36, 47, 78-9, 94, 130, 150, 163, 168
"Chinese Model", 12
Class, 59, 80
    class struggle, 24, 89, 268-9
Chi Qun, 277, 279
Collective leadership, 26, 28
Communist Party, 15, 27-9, 293
    Central Commission for inspecting discipline, 27
    Eighth Congress, 25, 27, 35
    Eleventh Congress (1977), 19, 211
    Fifth Plenum, 27, 77, 93
    Party Schools, 27
    Party – State relations, 32-4
    Third Plenum, 20, 24, 94, 98, 129, 162
Confucius, 119, 120
County, 56-84, 179, 182, 290

Cult of the individual, 22
Cultural Revolution, 20-21, 25, 36, 52, 89, 90, 92, 93, 131, 175-184, 258, 284, 295, 302, 306-7

Dazhai, 55, 57, 66-8, 73, 81, 82, 296, 202, 240, 257-60, 266-8, 278
Decentralisation, 78-81, 92, 112, 113, 134, 300
Democracy, 26-32
    democracy movement, 29
    "democracy wall", 29, 163, 286, 303
    elections, 31, 32
    intra-party, 27-9
Deng Xiaoping, 8, 24, 29, 31, 36, 46, 48, 81, 90, 92, 93, 97, 115, 120, 121, 150, 154, 162, 166, 168, 171, 184, 203, 257, 267-9, 280, 292, 303
Dernberger, Robert, 78
Domestic sideline production, 235-254
Donnithorne, Audrey, 113

Eastern Europe, 9-10, 12, 15
Eckstein, A., 39
Economic Administration, 104-109
Economic Zones, 28-9
Education, 273-87
    Chaoyang Agricultural College, 277-8
    Curriculum reform, 284

finance, 287
"keypoints", 283-4
"Sixty regulations on higher education, 279
"Egalitarianism", 188-9

Falkenheim, Victor, 63
Fasenfest, David, 78
Feudalism, 26
Finance, 112-115
Foreign finance, 39, 50
    foreign debt, 39
    foreign exchange, 99, 160, 162, 164
    investment, 38-9, 168
    loans, 50, 156, 157, 165-6
Foreign relations, 37-54
    Angola, 37
    ASEAN, 46, 51
    Chile, 37
    Europe, 47-53
    Japan, 37, 38, 41, 47-53, 136
    Kampuchea, 42
    Soviet Union, 37-47, 54
    United States, 37, 43, 44, 47-53
    Vietnam, 37-47
    Yugoslavia, 37
Foreign trade, 38, 45-6, 48-51, 146, 147, 149-171
    Britain, 49, 153, 167
    Europe, 152, 155, 159
    France, 49, 158
    Italy, 49
    Japan, 49, 152, 153, 155, 158, 159, 169
    Soviet Union, 49, 152
    United States, 152, 158-60, 169
    West Germany, 49, 159, 167
"Four bigs", 29
"Four modernisations", 10, 19, 91, 92, 94, 121, 236, 245, 287
Friedman, E., 11

"Gang of Four", 22, 25, 26, 89, 92, 93, 114, 150, 171, 190, 195, 200, 239, 261, 263, 275, 296, 301
Goodman, D.S.G., 36
Great Leap Forward, 20-1, 51, 93, 130, 294-96
Growth versus distribution, 304-8

Gu Mu, 49, 99, 154

He Jianzhang, 139
Hong Kong, 38, 39, 50
Hu Qiaomu, 96, 97, 104, 113, 126, 127-9, 140
Hu Yaobang, 94
Hua Guofeng, 19, 21, 24, 33, 34, 38, 50, 55, 66, 67-9, 82, 93, 97, 121, 131, 151, 156, 157, 158, 163, 171, 185, 196, 218, 267, 280
Huang Shuai, 276

Ideology, 20-7
Industry, 87-148
    enterprise management, 30, 95, 115
    "five fixes", 115-116, 125
    intra-regional cooperation, 122
    readjustment, 129-30, 142-8
    reform, 115-7, 129-30
    "thirty points", 95, 115, 121-9
    "twenty points", 121-9
Intellectuals, 30, 262-3, 286, 307

Jiang Qing (Chiang Ch'ing), 8

Lardy, N., 70-6
Legal system, 27, 34-5
Lenin, 24, 113, 291
Leninism, 3, 10
Li Honglin, 26
Literature, 30, 301
Li Xiannian, 96, 150, 157, 160
Lin Biao, 29, 119, 120, 263
Liu Guoguang, 132
Liu Shaoqi, 21, 211-2, 267, 279, 302
Liu Xiyao, 280-1

Macao, 38, 39, 50
Mao Yuanxin, 275-7
Mao Zedong, 6, 20, 22, 23, 37, 59, 94, 118, 120, 121, 250, 211-2, 213, 218-9, 220, 221, 224, 226, 233, 239, 258, 268, 275, 279, 293, 294, 295, 301, 307
    "Mao Zedong Thought", 22, 184, 297-8
Maoism, 6-11, 122, 184

Market, 108, 104-9, 299
Market Socialism, 2, 9, 88, 290, 298
Marxism-Leninism, 22
May Fourth Movement, 27, 52
Mixed Economy, 109-12, 115

National People's Congress,
    Fourth Congress, 120
    Fifth Congress, 19, 21, 29, 33,
        34, 239, 300-1
"New Long March", 19, 21
Nickum, J., 198

Overseas Chinese, 50-1, 53, 167

Pairault, T., 73
Peng Zhen, 33, 34, 35, 302
Pepper, S., 8
Plan, 105-9, 134, 135
    Fourth Five Year Plan, 132
    Ten Year Plan, 21, 157-8
Politics and government, 19-36
Population growth, 177

Riskin, Carl, 211-12
Rural Development, 55-84, 175, 269
    brigade, 226-7, 265
    commune, 180-2, 226-7, 265-6
    Cultural Revolution, 175-84, 258
    domestic sector, 200-5, 235-54
    enterprises and industry, 211-33
    farm output, 176-8, 183
    income distribution 179-184, 190-205, 224-5, 264-5
    Maoist legacy, 175-189
    mechanisation, 257-9
    team, 199
    work-group system, 280-4

Saich, A., 15
Selden, Mark, 58
Schurmann, Franz, 58, 65, 78-81
Sichuan, 98
Soviet Union, 10, 15, 35, 53
Stalin, 220, 293, 294
State,
    apparatus, 34-5
    constitution, 27, 33, 35
    Council, 34
Sun Yefang, 75, 89, 91, 137, 138

Taiwan, 50
Tawney, R.H., 4
Technocracy, 10
Technology, 156
"ten prohibitions", 237-8
"Two Hundreds" policy, 30

Wang Dongxing, 28, 94, 150
Wang Enmao, 215-6
Wang Gengjin, 186-7, 194
"Whateverists", 28, 94
Women, 252-3
Workers,
    congress, 31
    participation, 30
Wu De, 28
Wuxi County, 215-7, 224

Xiyang County, 56, 67, 73, 81
Xue Muqiao, 75, 91, 134, 141, 148

Yahuda, M., 9, 14
Yanan (Yenan), 27
Yao Wenyuan, 6, 24
Ye Jianying (Yeh Chian-Ying), 21, 25
Yu Guangyuan, 111, 117
Yu Qiuli, 142, 143, 145, 146, 154, 156, 157, 223

Zhang Chunqiao, 6, 23, 24, 90
Zhang Jingfu, 143, 144, 145
Zhang Tiesheng, 276
Zhao Ziyang, 34, 98, 101, 108, 150, 156, 163, 168, 200, 233
Zhou Enlai, 37, 120, 129, 274
Zhou Rongxin, 275, 280